DATE DUE

DATE DUE		
NOV 22 '89		
DEC 1 9 '90		
5/28/93		
10/18/94		
FEB 2 4 '99		
APR 01 '02		
5/14/04		
NOV 9 '05		

Sex Signals

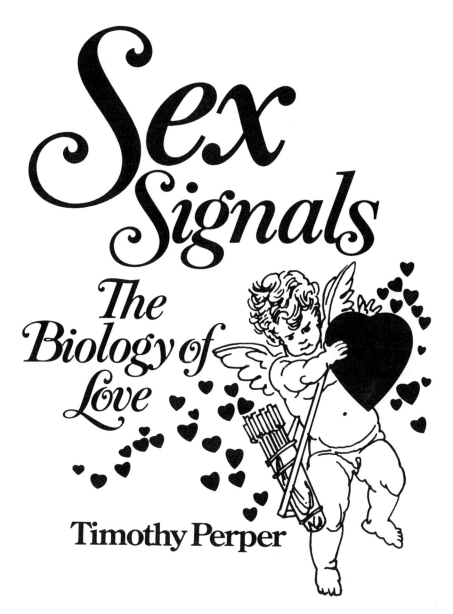

Sex Signals

The Biology of Love

Timothy Perper

iSi PRESS

Philadelphia

Published by

iSi PRESS •A Subsidiary of the
Institute for Scientifc Information®
3501 Market Street, Philadelphia, PA 19104 U.S.A.

Library of Congress Cataloging-in-Publication Data

Perper, Timothy, 1939–
  Sex signals.

  Bibliography: p.
  Includes index.
  1. Courtship. 2. Sociobiology. 3. Interpersonal
attraction. 4. Intimacy (Psychology) I. Title.
HQ801.P373 1985   306.7'34   85-14420
ISBN 0-89495-049-5
ISBN 0-89495-050-9 (pbk.)

Printed in the United States of America
92 91 90 89 88 87 86 85   8 7 6 5 4 3 2 1

To Martha, with love.

Contents

Preface

This book is woven around two themes—biology and love. It is also about how people *see* love: how the lovers see each other, and how scientists, scholars, and laypeople have seen intimacy and its relationships to our cultural, social, and biological lives. It is about *us,* here today in the United States, and about how *we* try to find another person with whom to share our lives.

Such yearnings for love and intimacy are deeply built into human biology. But times have changed since the "good old days" when love—and its seemingly necessary partner, marriage—was believed guaranteed. As people relocate as old neighborhoods and communities change, or as they follow the job market and climb various ladders of success, traditional assurances that we would marry and live happily ever after have vanished. The crux of these changes is that what originally was *socially* guaranteed—finding a mate through family, friends, school, church or temple, or community—has become almost completely a *personal* matter of luck, good chemistry, good vibes, the stars. . .

One result has been that books and magazine articles on "how-to-find-your-perfect-mate" have proliferated like mushrooms after a rain. We are still a romantic people. We *want* to believe that somewhere out there is Mr. Right or The Ideal Woman, that person from whom all happiness flows. But *Sex Signals: The Biology of Love* is not a how-to book. It tries to explain *why* our behavior is what it is and to show that, despite these changes in sexual, cultural, and marital customs, something very real remains.

That "something" is deeply built into our biological selves: the ability and desire to bond intimately with another person is the *biosocial core* of our search for love and intimacy. It exists at the center of an immense array of beliefs, feelings, symbols, and yearnings, ranging from the personal experience of love as a transcendent and beautiful emotion to the complex symbols of the wedding. As we trace outward from this core, we encounter virtually every emotion that men and women have for each other, from the lovers' belief that each is involved with a unique paragon of loveliness or excellence, to far darker angers that, sometimes, can turn to violence and rape.

My purpose is to describe *how* love, intimacy, and courtship grow from a biological core to affect our entire lives. And the warp and weft of this purpose are two themes: the courtship sequence and biosocial functionality. The courtship sequence, described in detail in Chapter 4, involves talk and body movement integrated into a single form of loving, intimate communication. Eventually, it surrounds the lovers with a world of fascinated entrancement and mutual involvement. The description is based on extensive field observations (supported by The Harry Frank Guggenheim Foundation between 1979 and 1981 but continued thereafter) of men and women in the United States and Canada. Biosocial functionality is the warp on which my descriptions are woven. It is described first in Chapter 3, where I propose that many behavior patterns, beliefs, institutions, and traditions that social scientists see as purely cultural nonetheless serve profound, if not always obvious, biological functions.

As those themes develop, a contrasting theme also develops. Few social scientists think that biology offers anything important for understanding human behavior. Yet, I argue that biology has immense value for helping us understand the human condition. Indeed, I am aware of doing social scientists a certain disservice in this book, because I am quite critical of how social scientists usually see biology. My criticisms are not of social scientists in person or in particular but of social scientific education, particularly an education that allows mythology to masquerade as biology. The social sciences *must* recognize biology as centrally important for understanding love, intimacy, courtship, and even our *symbols* of love.

A set of subsidiary themes also appear in the book: templates, ethnobiology, proceptivity, search polygamy, male oblique discourse, and the concept of the Sacred. Each arose as I confronted seeming contradictions between the field observations or interviews and what we in the United States firmly believe about male–female interactions. Templates represent people's indwelling visual images of potential sexual partners, and appear in Chapter 1, together with the opening salvo against the myth that makes us believe that Nature and Nurture are so different. Chapter 2 discusses ethnobiology, the set of myths about Nature (and genes) that laypeople *and* social scientists believe characterize the real science of biology. Of course, those myths could not be farther from the truth. Chapter 3 presents something of the biosocial approach. It stresses the falsity of myths of "biological determinism," and develops the crucial concept of *biosocial functionality*. I hope that no readers of Chapters 2 and 3 will ever again believe that biology is "reductionistic," to use a word much favored by critics of the biological approach to human behavior. Proceptivity (Chapter 5) is a term used by Frank Beach in 1976 for female initiation and maintenance of sexual or sociosexual interactions. I apply the term to human behavior, and I argue that women historically always have been proceptive—and still are. In Chapter 6, I discuss women's rejection strategies, including "incomplete rejection" or "delay," which often bewilders men. Chapter 6 also discusses search polygamy—what a moralist calls "modern sexual promiscuity"—and I suggest that some women engage in coital polygamy not for reasons of lust personified, but as part of the search for a man with whom to form a permanent mateship. Chapter 7 deals with men and their confusions about women's signals, intentions, and behavior. Male oblique discourse refers to the curiously opaque and metaphoric way men talk about women and sex. It will surprise women who believe that men "talk dirty" all the time. Chapter 7 also deals with differences in how men and women treat sexual intercourse, and with the intense loves and hatreds men feel for women. I also make some comments about rape in this chapter.

In Chapters 8 and 9, the scope widens, for by now the lovers have encountered cultural beliefs that make sexuality and love far more than merely personal matters. In Chapter 8, I discuss the Sacred—a term used by the French sociologist Émile Durkheim for analyzing non-Western beliefs about higher powers—and argue that historically we have surrounded sexuality with an immense set of symbols of purity and impurity that affect nearly *every* aspect of our lives.

But these symbols and customs have been deeply challenged in recent years by economic change, by feminism, and, above all, by a biological science that, in creating contraception and abortion, *sundered* the once inevitable connection between sexual intercourse and pregnancy. From that sundering have grown hatreds and anxieties about the place of sex, love, women, and even marriage in our culture. Yet the biosocial core has remained, and new symbols and beliefs are being re-woven about love and sexuality.

Throughout, I have tried to show that courtship in all its complexities, from individual behavior through the Sacred symbols of the wedding, is rooted in biological realities and, especially, in the absolute requirement that women and men meet, court, become sexually intimate, and have intercourse. In this warp and weft of argument, I have, above all, tried to show that the Nature/Nurture dichotomy is *false,* a myth that derives not from the facts of biology, but from our beliefs about sexuality *itself*.

I have omitted many topics, some of which are dealt with by Donald Symons in *The Evolution of Human Sexuality* (1979). I share Symons' viewpoint that both cultural and biological processes are inseparably part of human sexual behavior. I am no genetic determinist, as I hope the book makes *very* clear. Likewise, I hope my feminist biases are obvious, for my background includes three generations of feminist women, including my mother's mother, who was an activist and a suffragette in the early days of the century.

To these ends, I draw on many fields and disciplines, including my own, and have tried to make the book readable, and interesting, to many readers, including laypeople unfamiliar with biology.

Throughout, I argue that science must deal with the details of the real world rather than with *hypotheses* about the world. This position is called "realism," and I describe it in the Appendix, together with my observational methods. After the manuscript was essentially finished, I read Jerrold Aronson's *A Realist Philosophy of Science* (1984) and found, to my delight, that it contained a detailed philosophical justification for the kind of science I feel is needed for understanding how biological and cultural processes operate *together* to shape our lives. I offer the Appendix as a contribution to a currently on-going controversy in the philosophy of science.

And yet, in weaving my arguments, I have no doubt made errors. These I hope others will correct, not in a spirit of destruction, but of scientific replacement of false ideas with ideas less false. Nonetheless, I know full well that *some* readers—

including some social scientists!—will greet a book about the *biology* of love with scorn and distaste, and will make every effort to find its errors. For them, and for others, I should therefore mention briefly my bibliographic technique. No book this wide in scope can cite every important or necessary work. I have chosen works that have influenced me greatly, or represent a major statement of an idea or position, or present evidence for my assertions. I take responsibility for these choices and apologize to people whose work I have not cited. But, still, the critic of the biological approach will look for points of attack when, by accident, the need for brevity, or ignorance, I fail to cite an important piece of evidence. Likewise, that critic will search the Appendix seeking places to misunderstand or even misrepresent my comments. These critics' reactions will be inevitable, for the application of biology to social science is wildly controversial. And, though I hope to stimulate discussion of the role of biology in the social sciences, I do *not* welcome the spirit in which certain critics of the biological approach have offered their criticisms. Our subject—love, intimacy, and the yearning people have for each other—is too important, too ancient, too much a matter of poetry and profoundly held feeling, for us to discard the biological approach. Indeed, it is in the hope that this approach will help us understand our own behavior that I offer this book to the reader: not as the last word, nor as a ponderous treatise on curious animals or exotic peoples, but as an exploration of our behavior and our feelings when we meet, look, and—suddenly—find ourselves in love.

Acknowledgments

A study of this duration owes much to many people. Its beginnings and much of the most intense field work were made possible by a 2-year grant from The Harry Frank Guggenheim Foundation, and it is with deepest appreciation that I thank George Fountaine, Robin Fox, and Lionel Tiger for making the grant possible. I also want to thank the students and colleagues who spent many hours observing, with me and alone: Nancy Stone, Nancy D'Anna, Marilyn Frasier Pollock, Vivienne Matalon, and Donna Kurtz. Their first-rate observational skills contributed a great deal to the accuracy of the results. And I owe a particular debt of gratitude to Dr. V. Susan Fox, an anthropologist, who took on the job of field interviewing— and it is no easy task to interview slightly tipsy men in a singles bar!

I also want to thank the anthropologists at Rutgers University collectively and individually. As the "anthropology people," they made my biological questions welcome and introduced me to the mysteries—and powers—of anthropology. It is a pleasure to thank Jay and Darcy Callen, Jim Chisholm, Paul Heyer, Linda Marchant, George Morren, Dan and Debbie Myers, John and Marilyn Pollock, Bill and Marla Powers, Carmel Schrire and Bill Steiger, Dieter and Cathy Steklis, and Harriet Warne. Heather Remoff's continuous interest, as well as her own work in female sexual strategies, played a major role in focusing my thinking, especially when our results began to converge as strongly as they have. And so too Bob Rockwell's probing and original ideas, especially about science and myth, pointed me in directions I have continued to explore. But, above all, I owe a special debt to Robin Fox and Lionel Tiger. It was their active interest in the biological bases of human behavior that encouraged me to enter what has been, for me, the new field of human social biology.

I also owe debts of gratitude to Maggie Paley and Janet Gardner. As journalists, they helped make me aware of how important love and romance are to millions of Americans, and their articles on my work have stimulated a fair amount of interest. And I also want to thank Robert Wells, whose first-rate videocamera work produced one of the finest examples of courtship behavior I have ever seen (it is described briefly in Chapter 4).

Then too I want to thank so many people, often anonymous, who made our bar observations possible. In particular, the staff at "the Marriott"—actually, the Main

Brace Lounge at the Somerset, N.J., Marriott hotel, but no one called it that—were unfailingly pleasant, helpful, and courteous. So too was Frank Perger, of Highland Park's (N.J.) The Homestead, a great bar if ever there was one. And let me extend my thanks to people in other bars also, even if they did not know that we were quietly observing.

I also want to thank Robert Francoeur, who invited me to join The Society for the Scientific Study of Sex, at which I presented the first version of this work (in 1980). And for their interest in my work—and comments!—I thank Elizabeth Rice Allgeier, Arno Karlen, Fred Klein, Naomi McCormick, and David Weis. Dave, in particular, has been a rich source of ideas and comments. Naomi kindly provided me with unpublished data.

Special thanks go to Margot Crosbie, then at the University of Windsor, Windsor, Ontario. With her invaluable assistance, I was able to do field observations in Canada, and she provided the sample of Canadian women discussed in the text.

Many thanks also go to Maryanne Soper, my editor at ISI Press. Her tact and humor were much needed!

Above all, I want to thank Martha Cornog, my wife, for her endless interest and enthusiasm. True, Martha also typed the final versions of the manuscript (and we want very much to thank M. Lynne Neufeld, Executive Director of the National Federation of Abstracting and Information Services, Martha's employer, for permission to use their word processor), but my thanks go far, far beyond such matters. It was Martha's fascination with the subject that made this book possible. With her I have discussed essentially the whole manuscript over many hours, and her insightful and thoughtful comments and editorial assistance have been immensely valuable. Her support—emotional and concrete—never flagged. In many ways, it has become *our* book.

And so, to her, my greatest thanks—and love.

Chapter 1

That Ole Black Magic

Neal and I were sitting in my kitchen, the tape recorder microphone between us on the table. We were talking about love and a summer's evening in the Virgin Islands.

"What happened when you met her?" I asked.

So we went to this place. . . . It was really crowded. Elbow to elbow with people. And we were moving back of the bar drinking. . . . And he said, "Elaine is here. Come over and meet her." So we elbowed our way across the dance floor to get to the other side of the bar. And I couldn't see anybody— it was really crowded. I couldn't see who he meant. So finally we got to the other side and the crowd sort of parted. . . . And he said, "This is Elaine." And immediately, as soon as we saw each other, we took a step towards each other. We just knew—it was serious, like we'd always known each other. "Hi."

Some six years ago, I began this study hoping to understand what actually happens during those few seconds when two people look at each other and *know* that they are interested in each other. I asked Neal what he thought.

Elaine and I had such an obvious attraction for each other. . . . You could just cut the electricity with a knife. It was instantaneous. And I just wanted to run off and marry her.

The eyes of love—we all *see* differently when we are in love. Everyone calls it *love at first sight,* but why isn't it love at first touch, or first conversation? What is so special about *the way she looks* that men will simply freeze with fascinated attention, all other thoughts vanished, to gaze at a woman? And why do our thoughts dissolve in gentle confusion when she looks back and our eyes meet? Why are we so *sure* that some kind of electricity has flowed between us?

And so many men speak of chemistry, good vibes, electricity. Again, why? Are men so stupid that they cannot better describe a woman's attractiveness?

1

Women too speak of the magic of first meetings; are they so dense that a man's attraction cannot be expressed except through metaphors of energy? The answer is *No:* neither men nor women are stupid and dense. Yet few people can describe exactly what makes someone else so suddenly fascinating and beautiful.

We all have had such feelings. They come on us unexpectedly and at the oddest moments. Another man had been driving down Third Avenue in New York City when he saw a woman walking along the sidewalk ahead of him. He parked, he said, followed her into a restaurant, where they met—and later, they married. But all he could say was how beautifully she walked.

Over and over, I have heard men and women talk about love, attraction, and magic moments like these. Often, they mention eye contact: the glance is held ever so slightly longer than usual, and the muscles around the eyes relax. But eye contact is only a small part of it. Courtship involves a whole series of events: certain kinds of touches, certain kinds of turns, certain kinds of movements made in synchrony with the other person. But why are these looks, touches, smiles so potent?

And sometimes women find men just as fascinating. Soon, we are entranced with each other, and no one else exists except this wonderful person, so lovely to look at, to touch, to be with, to make love with.

Toward the end of Volume 4 of *Mythologiques,* the great French anthropologist Claude Lévi-Strauss (1971, pp. 559ff) speaks of how an immense number of threads unroll from a seemingly simple event in life. So it is here: the threads of feeling and behavior that unroll from a first meeting can alter one's whole life. But it is only the first event in a complex tapestry of how love develops. I should warn the reader who expects a simple discussion, like those in the pop psych and self-help books. Because the tapestry involves much more than love at first sight, it must remain incomplete: no final answers appear in this book, because, as yet, none exist. If any subject has escaped the scientist's eye, it is love and romance.

How shall we understand love? We might focus solely on the instant fascinations of love. Indeed, there is precedent for that, for the Psalmist said that one of the four mysteries is the way of a man with a maid. But here we reach a fork in the road.

The Lover's Eyes

One way leads to mysticism, to an exaltation of love that so defies rational understanding that we attribute to it supernatural powers—for that is what "good chemistry" means: that Ole Black Magic.

Totally entranced with the other person, the lover has no explanation for the power or suddenness of love except to see the supernatural at work. The lovers can easily believe that their every act together is an unprecedented miracle of intimacy that no one, anywhere, anytime, ever, experienced before.

Other people smile at the lovers and say *They have eyes only for each other.* The outsider is tolerant, remembering his or her own entrancements, or is restless, remembering disappointments. Sometimes that outsider is embarrassed, averts the eyes, and scurries away.

And why is *that*? What is so potent about the entrancements of love that other people react as if love could reach out and affect even an uninvolved passerby? We do not usually turn away if someone is tying a shoelace, nor do we smile reminiscently. We ignore it and go our way.

But not with love. Not even the cynic who says *it will pass* or *the honeymoon never lasts* can quite ignore the lovers. And again we avert our eyes, even after our first smiles. Not to do so brings down nasty names on the watcher: voyeur, pornographer, Peeping Tom. It is no explanation to say that love should be private, for that only raises another question: why do we believe that love's emotions are so powerful that we *want* to keep them private?

Mysticism provides one answer. It sees in love an electricity or a force that can flow from its source—the lovers—to other people, to change and alter everything around it. Judging from how frequently we sequester love and keep its expressions private, we must believe that it is a dangerous force indeed. Sacred, and dangerous if misused, something best kept in darkness, kept away from the innocent, such as children, lest they be permanently contaminated and fall helpless victims to a force that we deem so powerful that until recently it has been illegal to depict sexual intercourse publicly.

Is it simply prudery? Of course. But that is no answer. Why are people prudish? After all, we do not feel prudish about eating, certainly as "natural" a function as sexuality. But when it comes to the genitals—used for either of their biological functions, sexuality or excretion—a curtain is drawn, and aspects of life which every adult (and many children) knows all about suddenly vanish. A curtain of darkness, of privacy, and all too often—of profound ignorance falls to enshroud love and its magic *and* its materiality.

The Scientist's Eyes

But there is a second path, less exalted and less transcendent. I will take that path in this book, a path of science simultaneously rooted in biology, anthropology, and the social sciences. To the lovers themselves, it may seem a cold and horrible language that I will use, because I want to *study* the emotions of love and how love develops during courtship.

We cannot underestimate the horror that some people feel when they confront science. "You're talking like people were bugs or something," they say. "You're trying to dissect things that can't be dissected and shouldn't be dissected." We do not hear in these voices rational arguments against science, but an exaltation of love as transcending the commonplace.

But does love really stand outside the physical world that science studies? "Of course!" some people say. "Love is spiritual, not physical. It is a union of souls and hearts and minds, not something you can put under your microscope and understand!''

Yet it is not so. The lovers' affection is expressed physically, with their bodies, their looks, their touches, their proximity. Even if love's spirituality exists for some people, its materiality exists for *all* people.

When a man says of his woman that she is very beautiful, he does not really mean her soul. He means her living body, which he sees, touches, tastes, feels. And it is the same for her: her man is not a disembodied mind, to be admired for its Platonic purity. He is a man, whom she too sees, touches, tastes, feels.

''But it's *more* than that,'' people say. To be sure, love is much more than mere physical coupling, but even as love is *expressed* by physical and biological intimacy, so too it may have its *origins* in the physical and biological processes of our living bodies. And *that* is the second path for understanding love: to see it as arising from our living *selves.*

''It cannot be,'' people say. ''It is too simple and makes love just animalistic and just biology.'' But few people know how complex biology really is. There is nothing simple about amoebas or paramecia, nor about how a plant develops from a seedling. Anyone who has ever watched a mimosa plant curl up its leaves when the sun sets and then open them at dawn will sense just how complicated biology really is.

Some people *do* think biology is simple. For them, the body seems only a collection of wheels and gears and pumps that somehow tick and whir together. They are wrong. Not even *cells* are simple, and the human body contains hundreds of billions of them. And anyone who thinks that animal behavior, especially courtship, is ''simple'' should watch animals for a while and then explain exactly what is so simple about them.

Biology did not grow by studying courtship or other forms of human behavior. Instead, it focused on other aspects of life, such as anatomy, physiology, embryology, genetics, evolution. One consequence is that biologists sometimes think that behavior is simple—reciprocating the insult, so to speak, that social scientists hurl at biologists. ''Oh, that's just sociology, not science,'' all too many biologists say. But human behavior is far more complex than such sneering would make it. If love is not the disembodied and fleshless union of minds, neither is it the same as the copulatory behavior of rodents, primates, or fish. People create conscious meaning for their actions, share those meanings in their cultures, express them in language and symbol, act on expectations and attributions, and seek meaning beyond the purely personal for their thoughts and emotions.

But, even so, can these incredibly complex human activities be treated as if they originated from elsewhere than the physical materiality of the world? The theologian will answer *Yes,* seeing the hand of the Deity in all that occurs. Yet we live in a world of materiality—of the lover's glance, of a touch, of two people merged in intimacy in a social world that also exists in this material world. For my purposes, I will set aside questions of how and why God works, for I wish to understand not the mind of God, but how people live in *this* world, which is a world of biological and physical realities.

The way of science does not—for it cannot—seek to trace the threads of causation from the material to the immaterial. It limits itself to what we can know with certainty from facts and evidence rather than revelation, from data rather than Authority, from nature rather than holy books and canon law.

Not all people wish to take the way of science. But when one does, the first step is an assumption: that human emotions, thoughts, behavior, and culture arise from and in the living human body. Amplified through immensely complex social processes, human life, and especially love and its attendant emotions and institutions, have their ultimate roots not in Pure Mind or Thought, but in the anatomy and physiology of the human brain and the organs that support the life of the body. The only question is to explain *how* human social life emerges from human biology.

This perspective, which I will call *biosocial,* differs greatly from that of social science. For many social scientists and philosophers, human social behavior and the organization of society according to social rules simply cannot emerge from biology. These scholars are trapped in a deep dichotomy between *body* and *mind,* and can see no path between them. In this book, however, I reject that dichotomy and propose rebuilding both the biological and social sciences, an overwhelmingly huge task. But, nonetheless, this path will lead to some treasures.

For example, a man looks at a woman, and, suddenly, she is altogether the most fascinating being he has ever seen. How is it possible for him to have this reaction? That question is a bit too broad, so let us narrow it somewhat. Do men typically have such intensely fascinated reactions when they see ferns in a botanical garden, or when they watch a softball game, or when they stare at the beer in their beer glass? If a man did, he would be deeply disturbed or even psychotic. We would probably try to ignore him as potentially dangerous. So the question becomes simpler: why are such reactions in men evoked by *women,* rather than, say, by the tires of a bus as it passes by on a crowded street? And why do women focus so intently on men, rather than, say, on the shapes of seagulls or pigeons as they fly past? The same questions hold for homosexual men and women as well. Why are these sexual reactions all so incredibly specific?

Or consider marriage. I know of no society in which men marry turtles and women marry each other. Nor does any society fail to distinguish *male* and *female,* even though there are many ways to divide people into groups—e.g., into tall and short, or old and young, or even into symbolic categories which could be defined arbitrarily, like square and triangular, or are defined by custom and tradition, as in clan and moiety names among non-Western peoples. Despite the existence of categories, still there are no unisex societies.

But before I can discuss how biology shapes falling in love or even marriage, I must deal with certain commonly held opinions about the origins of categories like *man* and *woman* and about institutions such as marriage. These are the opinions of social scientists who hold biology and its insights in great suspicion, and for whom learning, socialization, and acculturation are the *only* possible ways for love and its institutions to develop. Since the failure of these opinions was, in part, the source of my choice of the biosocial perspective, I must explain a bit further.

An Infinite Regress

The province of the social sciences has been to investigate the range and variety of human behavior, and to seek explanations for human customs, beliefs, behavior, and so on. Though the social sciences have had many successes, in one domain they have not (to date) succeeded: their explanations of human behavior are too often *dis*embodied and have replaced inquiry into the biological origins of human behavior with an infinite history of learning. Let me illustrate.

"A man or woman adopts a certain gender role," the social scientist might say, "because he or she has *learned* to enact that role." As long as our focus is *solely* on an individual, such explanations are reasonable. An individual born into a given society does somehow learn how to be a man or a woman in that society. A little boy might explicitly be taught that men dress simply and austerely, while women wear finery (as in our own society). Or he might learn the opposite in another culture or another time. The little girl might learn to be shy with men, or that she must take the initiative during courtship.

But where did the child's teachers, mentors, models, and exemplars learn how to be men and women according to the standards of their culture? From the previous generation of teachers, mentors, models, and exemplars, the answer runs. And where did they learn from? From the generation before them, and before them, and before *them* . . . and soon we are confronted by an infinite regress of learning that takes us back to the dim dark past when someone thought up the whole thing. Ultimately, this is no answer, of course, because now we want to know why *that* person thought it up that way.

This "regress" exists in the theory even if the traditions passed down generation to generation changed with time for historical, economic, or social reasons. The question left unanswered is *how* a particular custom, belief, habit, or behavior pattern arose in the first place.

Fidelity of Transmission

A second, deeper question is also unanswered by assuming that people's behavior derives from an endless sequence of learning that leads back into prehistory. In fact, this problem leads to my most basic objection to the usual social scientific explanations of human behavior.

To understand this problem, imagine for a moment that learning does account for all our habits and customs. People are then like computers, who obtain their programs (their software) from other people (other computers). Hence the process is like computers that program computers that program computers, way back to the first computer. If we look at that computer—the Ur-computer, if you like—we see that it has its own program (though we cannot quite understand where it got it). But assume that it has its program, and that it transmits it to the baby computers nearby. The program is thus *installed* in the babies from the world external to them. Now the Ur-computer passes on to the Great Silicon Valley in the sky, leaving the baby computers to grow up and have their own babies. In turn, the now mature babies install their programs in their own babies and die in their turn. Generation after generation, computers install their own programs into the babies.

So far so good. If nothing causes changes in these programs, then the babies of a distant generation receive the programs of the Ur-computer. But no one argues that social custom, cultural habit, and personal behavior have remained unchanged. We live differently today than people did in 1700. They, in turn, lived differently from people in ancient Rome, and so on. Thus, in my analogy, we know that the programs transmitted from grownup computers to the babies *have* changed with time.

Yet what has kept these changes in the programs within limits? If we assume that men today do not marry turtles or women each other because (a) the Ur-people did not do so and (b) the habits of the Ur-people have been transmitted down to us, what was responsible for the fidelity of the transmission process? In particular, imagaine that culture consists of a computer program, with millions of lines, to be sure, but a program nonetheless. A baby or child ''acquires'' its culture when it acquires this program, that is, when the cultural program is copied by the baby or child. Now, anyone who has ever copied a large program or database knows that errors creep in during copying. Indeed, the larger the database, the more certainly will errors occur during copying—a letter changed here, a number there, and slowly but surely the program or database begins to differ from the original. With repeated copyings, such errors are transmitted, and new errors creep in. It follows, of course, that our ''cultural programs'' must differ from those of the Ur-people. And, if so, we cannot assume that we obtained our habits from them, for the cultural programs with which they began have changed as they were copied over and over in the intervening years. Obviously, we cannot explain our present-day habits by attributing them to our ancestors and predecessors.

Variation Within Limits

Yet we know that despite historical change, individuals within a given culture do behave in similar ways. Thus, people in the United States tend to marry people of the other sex, and not marry turtles. But how is that?

It is a subtle question: it concerns not why we differ from our ancestors, but why the ''cultural programs'' of two people alive today are *similar*. And if we obtained those programs *solely* from our ancestors, then the question cannot be answered. A given individual—me, for example—learned his or her cultural program from relatively few people, like parents, teachers, or friends. My program, then, was copied from preexisting programs in those people. You too obtained your program from other people, but they were not the people *I* learned my program from. As our children and children's children acquire their programs, each of us— you and I—has become the founder of a particular lineage of cultural transmission. Your children learn your program, and mine learn mine. Even if you and I began with identical programs, the copying errors that creep into my lineage and into your lineage are probably different from each other, so that our lineages diverge *from each other*. Next, consider our great-great-grandparents (say). Even if their original programs were identical, the errors that entered your ancestral lineage differed from the errors that entered mine as they were transmitted to their children. By the time the process reaches you and me, we could *not* have identical programs. When we look back 300 years, say, and apply this process to *everyone* then alive, we see that today we do not and cannot have identical programs, simply because the errors and changes that entered your lineage were not the same as the changes that entered mine.*

So how is it possible that we speak the same language, eat the same foods, share our views on what love is, or can even marry each other? How comes it that both our lineages share in common the view that men marry women, and women marry men, rather than *your* people believing that men marry turtles and women marry each other, while *my* people believe that men marry men and women marry ferns? What keeps divergence within limits?

This is an old problem in biology, and was not solved until Darwin in 1859. In particular, the problem is identical to one posed by the Lamarckian theory of the inheritance of acquired characteristics. In fact, the "cultural transmission" idea is simply one form of Lamarckianism. Let me shift the ground from culture to animals in order to display the parallel, and to suggest that the question of "cultural transmission" can be solved only in a Darwinian and biological manner, not by present-day social science.

Consider an animal that can acquire traits and transmit them to its offspring. Now, however, the traits are anatomical and physiological, and the transmission is not via culture but through the germ cells—the egg and sperm. If, and it is a classic example, we want to explain how long necks evolved in giraffes, we imagine that ancestral giraffes had shorter necks, and that they ate leaves off trees. Doing so, they lifted their heads and stretched their neck muscles, and gradually, each individual giraffe's own neck grew slightly longer. The animal has then "acquired" this trait and, by the postulate of inheritance of acquired characteristics, transmitted a slightly lengthened neck to its offspring. They, in turn, stretched their necks upwards slightly and grew necks that were slightly longer than their parents. Again because

*A skeptical reader may now want to say, "Aha! *I* see the fallacy! You've forgotten that cultural mechanisms and processes exist that *prevent* such divergence!" But no good. These cultural processes are transmitted with culture. So errors can creep into those parts of the cultural program also, and eventually these "cultural-preserving" mechanisms also change between lineages. Once again the result is cultural divergence without limit.

we postulate that acquired characteristics are inherited, the next generation of giraffes had longer necks. Repeated generation after generation, eventually giraffes evolve very long necks indeed.

The problem is not a question of evidence for or against the inheritance of acquired characteristics. The problem is *logical*.

Consider, again, the original, short-necked giraffes. Some of these, we can easily imagine, were chased by various beasts of prey and ran away. Their legs thus were strengthened, and again by the postulate of the inheritance of acquired characteristics, their slightly stronger legs were transmitted to their offspring. They, in turn, ran away from predators, grew still stronger legs, and transmitted the trait to *their* offspring. Eventually there evolves a lineage of animals descended from the original giraffe that has strong legs indeed.

Next, imagine another giraffe in the original short-necked group. It was also attacked by predators, but, for some reason—accident, bad temper, good luck, it does not matter—instead of running, it turned to counterattack and bit the predator, thus driving it off. Now, once again by the postulate of the inheritance of acquired characteristics, it transmitted to its offspring its sharper teeth, stronger jaws, and nasty temper. In turn, its offspring also chewed on predators, causing further development of strong jaws, sharp teeth, and nasty tempers. Generation after generation, there evolves a *second* lineage of giraffes—and *they* have long necks plus powerful jaws, long sharp canine teeth, and virulently bad tempers.

However, now we look at still *another* giraffe in the original group. It survived predators' attacks by hiding timidly in the bushes, all curled up. And, obviously, from that giraffe we obtain still a third lineage of giraffes which curl up timidly and resemble clumps of dried grass when they see predators.

I hope the point is clear: the inheritance of acquired characteristics can indeed "explain" why giraffes have long necks, but by doing so it simultaneously requires that giraffes be diverse in every trait they possess. Some have sharp teeth and big jaws; others are timid and look like dried grass; still others gave up trying to eat leaves and started to eat termites instead; still others eat birds and have specially shaped hooves for picking up eggs . . . and so on until one produces an utterly imaginary menagerie of impossible beasts that do not resemble any living giraffe at all.

The problem again concerns divergence from the original. *All* theories of the acquisition and inheritance of anatomical, physiological, and behavioral traits run afoul of the same problem: What keeps divergence from becoming greater than is observed empirically?

To Lamarck's immediate followers, the answer was simple: God. A kindly and beneficient Deity, in His all-seeing Wisdom, reaches down and gently corrects the course of animal evolution. It is He, not anything intrinsic to the process of the inheritance of acquired characteristics, Who maintains each species in its proper form and shape. This, of course, is the assumption of the Divine creation of species, and, until Darwin, it seemed logically essential to Lamarckian thought. Unless checked by some *external* force or process, the transmission of acquired traits will necessarily produce immediate and extensive divergence from the original.

So, if we return to the transmission of cultural traits from the Ur-people down to today, we encounter a similar problem. What has prevented behavioral divergence from straying into every possible or thinkable pattern? Why don't men marry turtles and women each other?

Deus Ex Machina

It is easy to say that men do not marry turtles because men do not *love* turtles, and that the emotion and experience of love is restricted to members of the other sex, at least often enough to produce offspring. In this, again we see the idea that love is *essentially* a supernatural force, one that acts—as through Divine ordinance—to bring men and women together, and thereby assures that the behavior of modern men and women resembles the behavior of our ancestors. Men and women then acquire their notions of love and all its institutionalized appurtenances, like marriage, from a Divine source That has always acted consistently. In brief, God makes sure that human behavior does not diverge too far from the Divine plan for it.

An elegant and evocative example of this solution to the infinite regress appears in the classic Breasted and Robinson (1914) history of ancient times. Breasted and Robinson open with an implicit query: How does history *begin*? Consider a newborn child placed in the wilds of a tropical forest. He would not know what chairs are nor how to open doors (the images and pronoun are theirs). Nor would he possess tools or weapons or implements of any kind, or clothing. He would probably never have seen a fire or, if he had, know how to make one or cook with it. He would not even know how to speak, or that there was such a thing as speech. They then continue:

> All these things every child among us learns from others. But the earliest men had no one to teach them these things, and by slow experience and long effort they had to learn for themselves [for later reference, notice the parallel between earliest man and a child]. Everything had to be found out: every tool, however simple, had to be invented; and, above all, the earliest man had to discover that he could express his feelings and ideas by making sounds with his throat and mouth. At first thought the men who began such discoveries seem to us to be mere animals. Nevertheless the earliest man possessed, among other advantages, three things that lifted him above the animals [again for later reference notice that human beings were lifted *above* the animals]. He had a larger and more powerful brain than any animal; he had a pair of wonderful hands such as no other creature possessed, and with these he could make tools and implements; finally, he had a throat and vocal organs such that in the course of ages he would learn to speak. (Breasted and Robinson, 1914, pp. 1–2)

But "learning" from other people is not an adequate theory of history. Accordingly, Breasted and Robinson start history with a special kind of learning—

discovery—and presuppose a being that *already* has the human brain, hand, and capacity for speech. Nature endows him with these, as it endows the child with the same three gifts. Prehistoric man has simply not *yet* discovered how to use his capacities.

This is "man in a state of nature": as yet devoid of learning, knowledge, and culture, he is nonetheless *human*. In his mind, were we today able to read it, we would find, preexisting but inarticulate, those "feelings and ideas" that, today, we express by speech.

And where did this "natural man" come from? Robinson and Beard (1921) solve the problem when they discuss how 17th century men began "to distrust" (p. 74) the ignorant and superstitious past. Then, "[i]nstead of accepting the teachings of the theologians that mankind through Adam's fall was rendered utterly vile and incapable (except through God's special grace) of good thoughts or deeds, certain thinkers began to urge that man was by nature good, that he should freely use his own God-given reason, that he was capable of becoming increasingly wise by a study of nature's laws, and that he could indefinitely better his own condition and that of his fellows if he would but free imself from the shackles of error and superstition" (pp. 74–75). Thus, God *Himself* set that being on earth with the capacity for reason, speech, discovering fire, tools, and implements. Man could reason and, by reasoning, discover the *culture* that would lift him above the animals and the nature to which they, and, once, he, belonged.

The romantic novelist James Branch Cabell provided another very revealing version of how man originated in a state of "nature." Cabell begins exactly as do Robinson, Breasted, and Beard, including saying that reason lifted man upwards (n.d., pp. 42–44). Then, in a moment of suave spiritual weariness (Holt, 1923, p. xiii), Cabell pauses: "reason," he points out, is hardly an attribute for which human history is noted. Instead, he argues elegantly that human progress depended on emotional beliefs in several "dynamic illusions"—romance, the search for the ideal woman (and the belief that she exists), and, for the great mass of people, a search for the middle way in life. In Cabell's history, these force-producing illusions replace reason, and yet they lead us upward. Cabell is not quite serious in his proposal—it is more a literary conceit with which to enter the lists on the side of romanticism in the then heated war between romanticism and realism (a war not yet dead: see Appendix)—but, nonetheless, the logic is impeccable. Given "man in a state of nature," history can be explained only by a *Deus ex machina,* by postulating that the capacity for reason (or romantic self-delusion) *already exists* prior to all discovery, all culture, and all history. And where did these abilities first come from? In one form or another, the answer is always God.

These "solutions" and the themes that underlie them will return later in very surprising ways. But, for now, I want only to stress that the infinite regress of learning in fact stops if we postulate that God placed on earth a being human in all ways except for the possession of those forms of knowledge we call *culture*.

Nonetheless, it is peculiar argument. In fact, we postulate a Deity not for reasons of faith or revelation, but to escape a problem in logic that arises from an otherwise interminable regression. Without that solution, the theory of inheritance of acquired characteristics (be they anatomical *or* cultural) involves an impossibility: continuing and uncontrolled drift and divergence in behavior, anatomy, and physiology. The argument introduces the Deity solely to eliminate this possibility, and this "God" becomes the initiator, prime mover, and overseer of an otherwise impossible process. "God" is intrinsic to this argument, but is not really an Omniscient Deity so much as a logical device needed to save the argument from internal collapse. Quite independently of the question of God's existence, we can surely doubt the logical propriety of invoking God simply because an argument failed. Indeed, I believe we must set aside that explanation as no explanation at all.

Twice now we have been forced back from a simple explanation for the reaction of a man like Neal to a woman. First, the lover's own reaction—that love is magical, inexplicable, and transcendent—leads us only into domains of mysticism in which criteria of evidence fail. Second, the idea that men and women are socialized into loving someone fails because it leads us into an infinite regress from which the only escape is mysticism (and illogicality). Let us try a third time, raising the level of analysis from the individual to collectivities of individuals. By doing so, we discover a way to understand the lover that does not involve mysticism.

The Biosocial Approach

I would like to invite the reader to imagine a bowl filled with red and white beads—males and females, obviously, though it doesn't matter which color is which. If I am a red bead, then from my individual perspective in the bowl I see other red beads who look like me (more or less). As I look back on my own development, I realize that once I was not as bright red as I am now and was, in fact, once nearly indistinguishable from other beads that later developed into white beads.

So how can I explain my own color? One answer is that I was always "red," but it once didn't show. This view makes males and females *essentially* different, and sees sexual differentiation and gender acquisition as only a matter of transforming latent essences into actualities. When I became a red bead, it was because my "true nature" slowly came to the surface. Likewise if I am a white bead. A second possibility is that all beads, myself included, were originally pink (that is, "bisexual"). If so, then I became "red" only because agencies external to me differentially reinforced and encouraged me to move towards greater redness, that is, to become "male." During my development, then, external agents (other beads, of course) elicited from me only those parts of a *larger* potential repertoire that they deemed appropriate to "men." They saw me playing with dolls and discouraged me; they saw me fighting with other beads and encouraged me. With other beads, the opposite potentials were reinforced. In this view, one's sexual behavior represents only part of one's "true nature." A third possibility is that no baby bead really had any potential color, and that my redness was installed from without (rather than elicited), by processes of socialization and acquisition discussed above. In this view, one's sexual behavior is only what external agencies of socialization have installed in the person, who then does not really have an intrinsic sexual "nature" at all.

From the individual bead's perspective, each of these possibilities has its own attractions. I can conclude that I became a red bead because I was influenced by other red beads around me, a form of acquisition of male sexuality. But looking inward, I seem to feel that I am innately male, so the idea that I was always essentially a red bead has its attractions as well. Finally, I can agree that perhaps I was not originally "sexual" at all, but merely an asexual entity, into which others poured their ideas of what my sexual behavior should be. As I think of these alternatives, each seems plausible and implausible, and, of course, I cannot make up my mind about them. I end up as a confused red bead.

An objective observer, standing outside the bowl and looking in, can readily sympathize with an individual bead's conclusion that it acquired its color from other beads. Indeed, the observer may be able to describe the process of acquisition of sexuality better than the bead itself can. This process we call "nurture" or "learning." But the observer can also sympathize when one of the beads says that it is essentially red or white. This process we call "nature" or the "innate."

Next, imagine the beads themselves hearing these terms. Since they cannot decide, from their own individual perspectives, which process is more likely to be true, they see a *conflict* between these hypotheses. "Wait," one bead says, "you can't have it both ways. Either you're a blank bead—a *tabula rasa*—or you're a genetically determined bead!" And the beads argue fiercely among themselves about these possibilities and soon fall into two camps that war with each other.

The observer standing outside the bowl can only smile at this war among the beads. When the observer watches a baby bead develop from conception to physical maturity, he or she sees that the first influence on the bead was at conception, when it obtained its genes from external sources (specifically, its mother and father). The next set of influences occurred before birth, when the bead was developing in utero and its genes were turning themselves on and off. Then, later, parts of the bead were influenced by other parts, when, for example, development of sexual anatomy proceeded under the influence of hormones produced in other organs of the developing body. Then, still later, the bead entered the world as a baby, and external influences—nutritional, social, perceptual—continued to act on it. Finally, when the bead becomes sexually mature, the outside observer sees that its *entire* life was a long, very complex series of influences acting on it.

The beads, however, take a very different view. For them, an immensely important difference exists between influences occurring before birth and those occurring after it. The first kind of influence they call "biological," "natural," or "genetic." The second kind they call "nurture," "learning," or "acculturation," and they feel that these are essentially different from biology.

For them, the symbolic marker event that distinguishes these classes of influence concerns *the bead's relationship to its mother:* while it is in utero, it is subject to the direct influence of Nature, that is, the mother; but when it is born, it becomes subject to the direct influences of Culture, that is, the no-longer-female world of external rules and authority.

But the objective observer sees no such dichotomy between Nature/Nurture. In brief, that dichotomy is not a fact of development, but is part of a complex set of beliefs that Ortner and Whitehead (1981), among others, have seen as a symbolic way to divide up the world into Female, Natural, and the domains of genetics, embryology, and biology; and Male, Cultural, and the domains of learning, rules, and society. [Sabbah (1984) has written a brilliant analysis of these concepts.] Accordingly, when the beads argue whether or not sexuality is natural and inborn, or cultural and acquired, they are not discussing sexual development. Rather, they are arguing about which of their cultural symbols—Nature and Female or Cultural and Male—holds sway and predominance during the development of the child's sexuality. Theirs is an exercise in mythology, not science.

The alternative, which I will adopt in this book, is that no differences in kind exist between pre-natal ("biological") and post-natal ("cultural") effects on the child's developing sexuality. Rather, a series of developmental events occur all during the period from conception to adult sexuality. Each has its own character-istics and features, but at no point can we divide them up and call one set "learning" and the other "genetic." Instead, events before and after birth share a continuity that is invisible when, true to our own mythology, we divide up sexual development into "natural" and "cultural" phases (see, e.g., Chisholm, 1983).

(The view that Nature and Nurture are different agrees with how the parents and other adults see the process of development. *They* cannot teach or influence the embryo before birth, but can do so afterwards, so they conclude that Nature rules prior to birth, but Culture—that is, they themselves—rules afterwards. The devel-oping child has a different view: so far as it is concerned, influences occur on it before and after birth. For us, the child's viewpoint is more accurate, because we are asking how and why it becomes what it becomes.)

So, true to our own (adult) mythology, if we want to know why men and women fall in love, we might say "Why, it's just natural." Or, a man, say, sees a woman and finds her fascinatingly attractive. "Men are just naturally like that," someone might say. "I guess it's just part of a man's instinctive sex drive." By that, the speaker would mean not only that such reactions are somehow part of the "natural endowment" of men and women in general—that is, are "genetic"—but also that such reactions are inevitable, or are at least so common that they seem to be just part of being human. "It's natural, I guess," people say, "it just happens."

These are folk-explanations that belong to the immensely complex set of beliefs about what is right and proper—that is, "natural"—male and female behavior. But they are not biological explanations, simply because genuinely biological explana-tions of human behavior refer not to mythic and vague forces like Nature or Culture, but to specifiable and describable processes of development that lie behind behavior.

Comments about love being "natural" do not define, identify, or describe any physiological or developmental process that causes the man's reaction. Instead, these comments serve, sociologically, to *legitimate* the man's reaction. They say *It's okay for a man to feel that way.* Yet we can provide criteria for identifying when a reaction is of biological origin. Again, take the man who sees a woman and suddenly reacts to her.

An Example—Templates

The reaction is fast—within one or two seconds. There is no long period of consideration, introspective study of one's feelings or thoughts, no long discussion prior to making up one's mind about one's feelings. The processes of social intercourse and adjustment that might operate when the same man is thinking about a large financial investment, say, simply do not occur. Indeed, his friends and buddies may later argue against his involvement with her. "She's no good for you, Joe," they might say, but Joe pays little or no attention.

In this, Joe's reaction is like other rapidly triggered physiological responses, such as his reaction to (1) potential danger, e.g., someone popping out of a dark alley; (2) pulling his hand away from a hot stove; (3) seeing food when he's hungry; or (4) feeling happier when he comes in from the cold into a warm, cozy room. Even if very different physiological mechanisms produce these reactions, all are mediated or produced by quick-acting neural processes.

Second, his reaction to the woman is very specific. For Joe, *Delores* evokes his response, not women in general. He has had similar reactions to other women, but, as he would say, "Delores is *special.*"

Like most men, Joe cannot really describe what makes Delores so special. If you ask him, he will say, "Well, she's just so pretty. I can't take my eyes off her sometimes," and adds, "I've never seen anyone like her before."

Although Joe would not think of it this way, it is as if Delores fit a preexisting pattern in his mind. "The moment I saw her, I knew she was the girl for me," Joe says. But Joe is familiar *and* unfamiliar with Delores—it's as if he's "known her all his life," yet he "never met a girl like her before."

I suggest that somewhere in Joe's mind and brain there is a *template* for Delores.* For Joe, that template is a *prefigured gestalt* of an ideal woman, which a real woman named Delores happens to fit, or so Joe thinks. As time passes, Joe will try to make his image of Delores fit his template as much as possible. That will entail modifying the template a bit and will entail perceiving Delores in ways that are sometimes quite inaccurate. In brief, Joe sees Delores as fitting his vision of his "ideal women" even if he has to attribute to her characteristics she does not have, either in her own mind or in the minds of others who know her.

The seeming preexistence of this template and the desire to reshape the real person to fit it both suggest that the template is neurophysiologically quite real. Somehow—and what a triumph it would be to explain how!—the human brain

---

*My use of the word *template* comes from biology: a template is the original from which one makes the real object.

contains in neurophysiologically coded form a specific proto-image of a woman who, once seen, and I stress *seen,* will trigger off an immense network of thoughts and emotions that center on love, sex, intimacy—and marriage.

These thoughts and feelings are *not* an "urge to copulate." Joe's reactions to Delores are not totally sexual; he's had *that* feeling before and knows the difference between being simply sexually aroused and the surprising (to him) richness of his reaction to *this* woman. In fact, sex with her doesn't have to be "particularly good," as people say; Joe's reaction is global, not genital. Everything about Delores is fascinating, not just sex.

It seems biologically impossible that Joe's reaction to Delores is a product of "socialization" or "learning," if we take those words in their usual disembodied social scientific sense. No one ever *taught* Joe that he should or would react as he did to the characteristics Delores presents (or seems to present). Nor has Joe practiced this reaction before. For Joe, his reaction to Delores is notable because it is *unlike* his prior experiences with other women. For Joe, his reaction is genuinely unprecedented.

The objective observer sees that many men have had Joe's reaction. It is as if *most* men carried around with them a pre-figured gestalt that is specific to each man. Now, if we take the perspective of the individual, we will stress the individual differences between these internal visions of an ideal woman and conclude that a man's template for his ideal woman is solely a product of the vicissitudes of experience and development. Thus, we might argue that because the specifics of the templates differ in different men, the template itself was acquired from the different social world and background of each man.

However, for the outside observer, what is so remarkable is that so *many* men have such templates in the first place. To be sure, for one man, the ideal woman has dark hair, a slender figure, and blue eyes, while for another, she is a blonde with a lush figure. I will not disagree that post-natal processes external to each man helped fill in those details. The details of the template sometimes come from definable external sources—e.g., Wiggins, Wiggins, and Conger (1968) concluded that some men's preferences for large breasts derived from *Playboy* magazine. Some details of the template may represent a late and post-natal completion of the template.

However, for heterosexual men, underneath the person-specific details of the template is a configuration that is anatomically *female.* Such men seem to possess a primarily visual image of a woman prior to any experience with a real woman like her. They may construct the details of this woman—e.g., large breasts—from post-natal and external social sources, but something in the man's neurophysiology causes him to construct her as a female in the first place.

That ability, I suggest, is profoundly biological. It arises from genetic, developmental, and physiological processes operating from the earliest period of conception through embryonic development through post-natal and childhood experiences. This template is not somehow "encoded" in the genes, but is created by a slow developmental process involving genetic regulation of neural development and later neurophysiological construction of an increasingly detailed and recognizably female image of a woman—who, in Joe's case, happens to resemble a real woman named Delores.*

Finally, Joe's reaction to Delores is not only fast, specific, and unprecedented for Joe. It is also surprisingly and unexpectedly intense. Joe literally can neither ignore nor forget her. He watches her almost continuously (as people say, "He has eyes only for her"). He thinks about her, he wants to be near her, and his emotions all center on her. In Tennov's (1979) word, Joe is "limerent" about her, though everyone else says that "He's crazy about her."

Moreover, Joe's limerence is specific to Delores. *She* elicits these reactions. It is as if entire circuits in the brain were suddenly triggered when he saw her, circuits that preexist the encounter with the real Delores, but somehow seem to pre-figure her. Joe's startingly intense reactions cannot be anything except neurophysiological.

Thus, these circuits are specifically sensitive to one or a few women. When Joe sees such a woman across the room, those circuits fire with overwhelming intensity and speed. In a real sense, they have been waiting for her to appear. By the time Joe is in his mid-20s, he has probably had one or two such experiences. Indeed, many men describe their "highschool sweethearts" in just such ways—as females who elicit unforgettably intense emotions, profound involvement, and an unquestioned sense of *fit* between him and her. I suggest that this "fit" is quite real, and represents how men describe the locked-in connection between a real woman and the preexisting and neurophysiologically real template they have of her.

Women also have templates for men, and sometimes women's templates are as strongly visual as men's. But women's responses to men seem less tied to the purely visual. At least some women respond very strongly to *touch:* a woman once explained that she had fallen in love with a man while they were crossing a New York City street simply because he had tenderly and lightly placed his hand on the small of her back as they stepped into traffic. She is not unique. Other women have become fascinated by men who talk interestingly and attentively. These reactions also are all fast and surprisingly specific for certain kinds of men and male behavior

*My argument is a version of Laughlin and d'Aquili's (1974) idea of neuro-gnostic or, more specifically, neuroemotional development. In neurobiology, the basic idea is that all "intrapsychic events"—from experiences of mood to abstract thinking itself—are mediated by electrochemical activity of certain *parts* of the brain. In specific, biochemical activity of nerve cells in those brain parts is necessary (and, to some scholars, sufficient) for the intrapsychic event to occur. This theoretical identification between anatomically localized bio- and electrochemical processes and the "intrapsychic" experience itself is achieved by speaking, as I just did, of biological processes that "mediate" the psychological events. Given the mind/body dualism so widespread in Western thought, few writers will say "cause" instead of "mediate," but the idea of causation is not far from the surface. The idea is a very powerful part of modern biology; for clear introduction to a concrete example, see Prince (1982) for how trance can be mediated by brain chemicals called endorphins.

Several readers said that templates reminded them of Jungian thought. I find the possibility intriguing, but from what I know of Jung's ideas of an "anima" possessed by men, templates are not the same. Templates are images in the mind and brain, not fundamental aspects of personality. Thus, a man's template for a woman is not a visual image of the "feminine" components of his personality.

and, like men's visual reaction to women, are also very powerful. So, the neurophysiological reactions of a man like Neal are not restricted to a few men. Instead, they are quite general, among men *and* women.

Thus, love is an embodied process. *It exists not in the sex organs nor in the heart, but in physically and biologically real neural events occurring in the brain.*

Why Biology

The first implication is that we no longer have an infinite regress of learning. If Joe and Delores are each born with their own templates (even if not fully developed), the search for their origin stops with Joe and Delores themselves—that is, with the developmental biology that created their templates. The regress ceases because it becomes a problem in the developmental biology of the brain instead, even if we cannot yet identify which cells in the brain create the template. If, however, the template derives *totally* from external and post-natal processes, then by virtue of the drifting path of social change discussed above, there is really no good reason why Joe's social environment did not install in him a template for ferns. He could fall madly in love with ferns, and form a desultory relationship with a woman, adequate for the preservation of the species. But he does not: instead, most men fall in love with women. Something—and I am saying that it is biological—keeps the drifting path of social learning more or less on target, more or less restricted to a few options, more or less centered.

The result is that Joe now possesses a template for a *woman,* not for ferns. When Joe sees Delores, and when his indwelling neurophysiological mechanisms trigger off his intense, rapid, and fascinated reaction, he is aroused by a female of his own species. When she sees him, likewise she is aroused by a male of her species. Next, when they want to touch each other, move close, never leave each other, she will—if Delores is as interested as Joe is—very possibly become pregnant. The process is not random at all. It has been guided, so to speak, by a very real biological process existing in the brain. It has equally real biological outcomes: babies are conceived not through the union of Pure Mind, but through physical and biological intimacy.

However, this solution to the infinite regress of learning is bought by introducing biology into the discussion of love. The second implication of the existence of templates is that we *must* introduce biology if we are to understand what happens when men and woman begin to feel intimate with each other. If Joe's template is neurophysiologically real, think of the neurophysiological complexities of courtship, love, or a marriage ceremony! And because far more than mere templates *are* involved in love and all its expressions, biology becomes relevant to an extraordinarily wide range of events. To be sure, social learning theory, attribution theory, and the like are valuable—and called for—when discussing certain post-natal aspects of sexuality. Alone, however, these theories do not reveal the basic developmental processes that create the brain, but they presuppose that it develops with predispositions (e.g., ''templates'') to acquire knowledge enabling the organism to meet the two great Darwinian requirements for life: survival and reproduction.

However, once we see that birth does *not* mark a transition from Nature to Nurture, we can see that human development does not suddenly *begin* at birth. Rather, pre-natal embryological and genetic processes have immensely important biological roles in making us human. Second, we can see also that biological processes do not suddenly *stop* at birth, to be replaced by disembodied social or cultural processes. Instead, biology—as evolution, neurophysiology, and genetics—will be crucial for understanding how the tapestry of love unrolls outward from a man and woman's fascination for each other, and, indeed, crucial for understanding *all* that we sometimes feel are our proudest social and cultural inventions.

Chapter 2

Nature and Nurture

Indeed. But what can *biology* tell us about the immense range of variation in human behavior and culture?

It is not a simple question. Great controversy surrounds the role of biology in the study of human affairs. On one side is the Scylla that says that biology is irrelevant because all human behavior of any importance is learned (Nurture). On the other is the Charybdis that says that all human behavior is genetically determined (Nature). These sides war with each other, and adherence to one or the other view has generated intense polarization of thought rather than a recognition of the value and importance of the other's contribution. For example, consider sociobiology. It is a recent offshoot of traditional evolutionary thought and has made some interesting and important advances. Nonetheless, those advances have been swamped not only by the attacks of anti-sociobiologists, but also by the sociobiologists' own beliefs about the over-arching importance of the genes in determining human behavior. Perhaps it is a human impulse to defend one's ideas when they are attacked, but, rather like a nasty family fight, the sociobiologists have ended up defending some views that seem absurd in their genetic extremism. Likewise, social scientists have made important advances in understanding human culture, but they too have been swamped by absurdly insisting that biology plays no role worth mentioning in shaping human predispositions. The truth lies somewhere between these viewpoints.

It is between this Scylla and Charybdis that I intend to steer a path. I will show not only that biology and genetics offer immensely important insights into human behavior, but also that, when *combined* with social scientific ideas, biology produces new and potentially very valuable ways of seeing why people behave as they do.

The war between the Naturists and the Nurturists itself also provides some instructive insights. The issues are not really about genes and learning but about something very different: the proper relationships between men and women, and about the place each has in our culture and history. The Nature/Nurture controversy is a war about love and sex fought using the *language* of genetics, biology, and the social sciences.

But to reach that conclusion, we must first navigate past the rocks and whirlpools of the Nature/Nurture controversy itself. We must set the contributions and overstatements of each side into perspective and free ourselves to employ the insights of both the biological and social sciences without the extremism of either side of the Nature/Nurture controversy. We must learn the danger signs of extremism, the better to avoid it.

I will begin by discussing how anti-biological social scientists perceive biology and then turn to discussing how the biologically oriented thinker sometimes sees human behavior. While these viewpoints are often at war, they nonetheless share a common vision of how biology works, a vision I will call *ethnobiology*. It is a complex elaboration of the idea that women are somehow related to Nature and men are somehow related to Culture (or Nurture). Mirrored in the Nature/Nurture controversy of the sciences, we shall see a systematic over-valuation of men's activities compared to women's. Then, with these ideas in hand, I will develop the *biosocial approach,* which sees a reciprocal interleaving of genetic and cultural processes in shaping human behavior. The central concept will be *biosocial functionality,* which, throughout, will serve as a compass to guide us past the problems of how and why men and women look at each other and fall in love.

Simultaneously, we shall have a second conundrum. The differences between biological science and ethnobiological *myths* are so great that ultimately they themselves demand explanation. And the concept of biosocial functionality will help answer even *that* question. But first let us examine how social scientists see biology.

Ethnobiology

To the layperson, biology studies animals, plants, and microorganisms, or has applications in human health and well-being. Anatomy and physiology are needed in medicine, just as genetics is relevant for understanding inherited abnormalities and pathologies like phenylketonuria, sickle cell anemia, or psychiatric ailments like depression or schizophrenia. It sounds really quite peaceful and motivated by the highest ideals of humankind: devotion to pure knowledge and to helping the ill. Certainly, no one would expect that biology generates polemic and controversy, or that genetics produces unbridled fury.

Yet they do. The central problem concerns the roles of genes in shaping human behavior. Critics of "genetic determinism" have arisen from the social sciences, from philosophy, and from feminist scholarship. All of them see in biology a profound danger that doctrines of genetic causation will limit people's freedom to change their individual or social lives. The critics see those doctrines as condemning people to live lives controlled and manipulated by irresistible inbuilt biological determinants of behavior (Bock, 1980; Caplan, 1978). Moreover, from feminist writers has come a critique that sees biological ideas as menacing women's freedom in particular, and as reinstating counter-factual beliefs about "women's nature" that serve oppressive and repressive social ends (see, e.g., Bleier, 1984; Sayers, 1982; Lowe and Hubbard, 1983).

For these people, biology *is* genetic determinism, and *no one* should take such concerns lightly. In the wrong hands, "biology" has proved remarkably useful for supporting truly vicious programs of oppression and extermination, as the history of Nazi anti-Semitism proved all too well. Yet, behind these misuses of biology are ideas that do not come from biology at all, but, instead, from a racist ideology that permeated *every* aspect of Nazi thought. We must attack those ideas, but, simultaneously, must not confuse them with real biology or condemn biology for the perversions of Nazism or racism.

Social Scientific Ethnobiology

However, social scientific critics of biology have an additional reason for rejecting it as "determining" human behavior. Here the problem is subtler than rejecting Nazi pseudoscience, for the critics have *themselves* confused biology with a far older set of ideas about Nature and its all-powerful abilities to control us. These criticisms, and the vision of biology implicit in them, are best illustrated by some quotations.

The first is from William Simon and John Gagnon, whose sociological theories of sexual behavior (known collectively as "script theory") are central to modern social scientific thinking about men, women, and sex. In the following passage, Simon and Gagnon (1968) outline why they consider biology as fundamentally irrelevant to human behavior:

> We would like to argue, somewhat tentatively, that if sex plays a role in the conduct of human affairs, it is because societies have invented or created its importance, and not because of some *nearly irresistable urgency* stemming from the biological substratum. . . . For our present concern the importance of the foregoing argument stems from the position it implies—that it is talk about sex, both public and private, that creates the significance of the experience; hence we begin to understand some of the meanings and problems created by sexual experience when we understand the structure of definitions—*virtually none of which is a direct function of biology*—which create the significance of human sexual encounters. *It is obvious that the biological endowment has remained relatively constant over the millenia, yet the diversity in the importance of sexuality to either societies or individuals through history, across cultures, and between different populations in complex societies is one of the major hallmarks of the human record.* Perhaps what has varied then is talk about sex: the complex of symbols and meanings that transform mute nature into a sociosexual or psychosexual drama. (pp. 173–174, italics added)

In this, Simon and Gagnon clearly believe that if biology acts at all, it would produce *uniformity* in behavior and culture. But, since diversity exists, biology is irrelevant to human life, and the biological perspective is unnecessary and wrong.

This perception of biology persists throughout the social sciences. Of course, Simon and Gagnon are *denying* that biology affects human behavior. Yet the "biology" that they deny has certain properties which I want to analyze next.

First, biology is seen as a force or pressure. It acts *on* an organism to shape its behavior, either from outside (as an evolutionary constraint) or from within (as a genetic determinant of behavior). It is therefore not *part* of the organism but, instead, is extrinsic to its behavior.

Second, biology is seen as producing uniformity. It creates identity and similarity. Necessarily, then, it is not the source of variability, difference, or change. It is state, not process.

Third, this biology acts universally. If it acts—and most social scientists deny that it does—it would act on all people everywhere in the same way, thereby to produce the same results everywhere.

Fourth, it is inescapable. It permeates everything we do, so that if it did act, we would be helpless before its force and would become robots or automata.

Now, I know full well that Simon and Gagnon and other social scientists deny that biology affects human behavior. However, the properties of the "biology" that they deny arise not from real biology but from elsewhere.

The social scientist's perception of biology is folklore. To use a term from anthropology, it is *ethnobiology.** In fact, it has nothing to do with the *science* of biology.

The concept attacked by Simon and Gagnon (and therefore elevated into a vision of what biology is) is identical to the common English term "natural." We say, for example, that it is *natural* or part of his *nature* for a man to be jealous if his wife is having an extramarital affair.

An excellent example of this usage of *natural* occurs in an essay written by St. Thomas Aquinas (ca. 1260/1960), where he uses the concept of *natural* to condemn fornication:

> Likewise it must be against the good of man for the semen to be emitted under conditions which, allowing for generation to ensue, nonetheless bar the due education of the offspring. We observe that in animals, dogs for instance, in which the female by herself suffices for the rearing of the offspring, the male and female stay no time together after the performance of the sexual act. But with all animals in which the female by herself does not suffice for the rearing of the offspring, male and female dwell together after the sexual act so long as it is necessary for the rearing and training of the offspring. This appears in birds, whose young are incapable of finding their own food immediately they are hatched: for since the bird does not suckle her young with milk, according to the provision made by

*"Ethnobiology" refers to beliefs a people holds about biological matters. The term is formed on analogy with "ethnozoology" and "ethnobotany," which denote folk beliefs about the classification and taxonomy of animals and plants (Gray and Wolfe, 1982, 1983; Waldorf, 1983). Thus, by "ethnobiology" I mean the folk beliefs that we Westerners hold about living organisms and their place in the universe, about "human nature," and about the difference between human and animal.

nature in quadrupeds, but has to seek food abroad for her young, and therefore keep them warm in the period of feeding, the female could not do this duty all alone by herself: hence divine providence has put in the male a natural instinct of standing by the female for the rearing of the brood. Now in the human species the female is clearly insufficient of herself for the rearing of the offspring, since the need of human life makes many demands, which cannot be met by one parent alone. Hence the fitness of human life requires man to stand by woman after the sexual act is done, and not go off at once and form connexions [sic] with any one he meets, as is the way with fornicators. . . . . Hence, whereas it is necessary in all animals for the male to stand by the female for such time as the father's concurrence is requisite for bringing up the progeny, it is natural for man to be tied to the society of one fixed woman for a long period, not a short one. This social tie we call marriage. Marriage then is natural to man; and an irregular connexion outside of marriage is contrary to the good of man, and therefore fornication must be sinful. (pp. 220–221)

This passage not only attributes a moral lesson to nature, but also illustrates the ethnobiological notion of *natural* as a set of laws that determines what people and animals both do and *should* do. From this passage, we see that "nature" possesses some, and perhaps many, of the attributes of *divine* power and force.

Simon and Gagnon assume that this *folk* meaning of biology characterizes the real *science* of biology. In that they are not alone. Writing over 700 years after Aquinas, Jessie Bernard (1972a) describes something which she calls "human nature" but which is actually the ethnobiological vision of Aquinas and of later folklore:

Is there anything about marriage that is demanded or prescribed by human nature, or even proscribed? Are some forms "unnatural" or contrary to human instincts?

Neither "human nature" nor any of our instincts demand any special form of marriage. Just how "natural" marriage is can be gleaned from the diverse forms it has taken and the enormous literature on how to come to terms with it that has been necessary. [Here she implies that if marriage were "natural," it would be the same everywhere.]

The variety of ways in which husbands and wives can relate to each other in marriage, and have, is so staggering as to boggle the imagination. Human beings can accept almost any kind of relationship if they are properly socialized into it. . . . There is literally nothing about marriage that anyone can imagine that has not in fact taken place, whether prescribed, proscribed, or optional. (pp. 304–305)

Though Bernard does not mention Aquinas, she *does* accept the idea that biology or the "natural" is a universal force that would—if it acted—produce uniformity and be inescapable. Thus, while Simon, Gagnon, and Bernard all *deny* that such powers influence human behavior, they all *characterize biology as such a force*.

The idea is hardly restricted to theologians and social scientists. It is also common usage:

Although I admit the possibility of people who don't know how to boil an egg, I find it hard to credit someone over the age of three not knowing how to sweep with a broom. It may indeed, like the ability to blink your eyes without anyone ever telling you how, be a genetic trait. (Eisen, 1971, p. 150)

The image is sardonic, but the idea is the same. The word "natural" connotes an overwhelming and inescapable power. You do *not* need to be told how to behave "naturally": it just happens. It is unlearned, unpracticed, just automatic. It is *genetic,* an idea I suspect that Chaucer's Merchant would have understood perfectly, for—even though he has been gone these 600 years—he too opposed "influence" and "nature" (Chaucer, ca. 1400/1957, *The Merchant's Tale,* p. 122, line 1968).

Granting that biology does *not* produce irresistible and universal fixity, but change and diversity (as discussed in the next chapter), it follows that biology has nothing to do with the ethnobiological concept of "natural." Thus, when Gagnon, Bernard, and others deny to biology any power or influence over human life, they deny a *folklore* version of biology which they believe is identical to the modern *science* of biology. Although their argument refutes—successfully, it seems to me— the idea that an inescapable, universalizing, and uniformizing Nature controls human existence, their argument does *not* refute the crucial possibility that biology, *as understood as a science,* plays an immense role in shaping human behavior and culture (as biologically oriented historical writers have long known: e.g., Karlen, 1984; Zinsser, 1935).

A Struggle for Control

Nonetheless, it is not simple ignorance of biology and genetics that underlies the social scientist's rejection of biology. Instead, hidden in that rejection is a vision of the world itself and of the proper relationship of people to each other and to God. This vision itself is important, because it provides the *terms* in which the Nature/ Nurture controversy is fought.

Rational vs. irrational. Thus, when social scientists reject biology in favor of culture, they set the *rationality* of culture, learning, knowledge, and mind over the perceived *irrationality* of nature. In part, the issue is of control: in the views we heard above, Culture is of *human* manufacture. And, because it is created by *us,* it is therefore potentially under our rational control. But, likewise, Nature—which social scientists gloss as "biology"—is not so easily controlled, and is not necessarily rational at all, at least not by *human* standards. Nature must be *brought* under control—by technology, by science, by rational thought as opposed to superstition that sees evil or dangerous living forces in natural events. Raw Nature must be tamed and made to serve human needs.

In part, this viewpoint rejects an older Natural theology, in which Nature was the second Book of God, the Bible being the first (see, for example, the quotations with which Darwin began *The Origin of Species,* 1859, p. 3). In that Natural theology, the forces of Nature are not themselves evil, but contain lessons for humankind *about* good and evil. The seeming irrationality of Nature represents the Higher rationality of a God Whose infinite wisdom controls everything, nature and humanity alike. Here too Nature has power, but it is power which we should listen to, understand, and, ultimately, obey.

Thus, by denying that "Natural" forces inescapably control us, social scientists see humankind as creating *itself* and, by its own efforts, emerging from the state of Nature finally to tower *over* Nature. It is an ideology of human transcendence and a victory of human speech over forces that are, as Simon and Gagnon put it, *mute*. In this, Culture, not God, has given humankind dominion over the fish of the sea, over the birds of the air, and over every creeping thing that creeps upon the earth. The message is virtually Faustian: The seeking, enquiring Mind finally *overcomes*.

Even so, social scientific rejection of biology involves more than a rejection of natural theology in favor of a secular doctrine of human power. A new hierarchy is also established. When social scientists elevate the human above the merely "animal," they want to believe that Culture is above Nature, superior to it, commanding it, but ultimately independent of it. ("We have worked hard to demonstrate the *dominance* of social, psychological, and cultural influences over the biological . . . ," Simon and Gagnon, 1970, p. 31, italics added.) And yet, as we look at these ideas, we see that they are expressed in *metaphors*—and they are metaphors with deeper meaning than one might suspect.

I want to give an example of these metaphors, taken from Alexander Alland's *The Human Imperative* (1972). Alland, an anthropologist, knows how important human biological evolution is, and even calls himself a "Darwinian social scientist" (p. 153). But Alland also writes that "[i]n part, man adapts biologically to his environment in a non-biological way—through culture" (p. 22). Despite his Darwinism, Alland nonetheless sees biology as fundamentally *different* from culture, and sees culture as *replacing* biology in human evolution. Thus, he says that in human evolution, genetics has "given birth" to a "new and more efficient form of code system," culture (p. 152), reminding us of Breasted and Robinson's metaphoric identification of human prehistory with the *childhood* of humanity (see Chapter 1). Although Alland wants to see both biological and cultural processes creating human behavior and society, he finally places culture "above" biology, again like Breasted and Robinson. When he speaks of culture as *freeing* human beings from the slower biological processes of adaptation (p. 152), his view comes surprisingly close to the "superorganicism" of A. L. Kroeber, for whom culture represented something *above* the merely organic, the merely biological. Anthropologists (e.g., Bidney, 1967) have roundly criticized Kroeber's idea of the superorganic, but even so, like most social scientists, Alland has not integrated biology and culture, but has placed them into a *hierarchical relationship*.

Now, I am not picking on Alland: he is truly sympathetic to the importance of biology. However, Alland is not alone in his view that biology gives rise to culture; for example, Rappaport (1971, p. 32) expresses the same thought, as have other anthropologists. Nor do these images of biology exhaust or even summarize Alland's or Rappaport's anthropological contributions. Nonetheless,

Alland has expressed an important vision of how biology and culture relate to each other.

Metaphors of man and woman. These metaphors—that culture is above biology, that biology gives birth to culture, that culture is ultimately independent of biology—are curious indeed. And, even more curiously, I have heard them far more often from men, including male social scientists, than from women. And why is *that?* Why do such men so often argue that if it existed, the "force of biology" would lower us to the merely animal? Why do they so often insist that if it existed, the "force of biology" would act on everyone in the same fixed and unalterable ways? Why do they argue that if it operated, "biology" would control our every act?

When a man denies that biology has any importance while simultaneously asserting that if it did act, it would be inescapable, he is really quite right. For him, and for most men in the highly technological modern West, biology has been the domain of *women*—childcare, preparing food, nursing and caring for the old and ill. For such men, biology has no power because women take care of it for them. But, simultaneously, such men know full well that if women did *not* intervene between them and biological reality, biology *would* have overwhelming force and power.

The rejection of biology as irrelevant to human affairs mirrors precisely the traditional man's ideas of what is and is not important: women, not men, deal with biology, and it is woman's work, to be dismissed as demeaning and unimportant. It is ultimately simple: just mute nature.

We now see why biology is so crucial for understanding what happens when a man and woman talk and touch: their interaction can lead to intercourse and, *for the woman,* pregnancy. The immense power of biology over human life is writ very large over that interaction.

Men, following Simon and Gagnon, may want primarily to deal with definitions, symbols, psychosexual dramas, words, and other matters of the spirit and intellect. Women must live those dramas *as well as* feed the baby.

"That's *her* problem! Biology has no power over me!" the man says, thus simultaneously devaluing biology, women, *and* those parts of women's culture that have centered on the biological realities of life. When a man—social scientist or not—denies that biology is relevant to human affairs, he disdainfully dismisses the biological facts that women have dealt with for many years of Western history. He says that biology is the same everywhere: "Aren't babies all the same everywhere?" he asks. He says that biology is secondary to symbols and words: "After all," he says, "*men* talk, create sociological dramas, and define symbols; the women are only cooking and feeding the children." To think otherwise, such a man would have to admit that women, not men, have intervened between human life and the biological processes of courtship, intercourse, pregnancy, birth, childcare, nutrition, and taking care of the ill. In a word, women have historically *sheltered* men from experiencing the immense power of biology to affect human existence.

So there is much more than the importance of talk and sociosexual drama in the ethnobiological notion that culture varies while biology remains constant. Implicitly, the idea that a fixed Nature is subordinate to a variable Culture represents a historically old devaluation of both women and sexuality. It was no accident that Aquinas thought it ethnobiologically obvious that women alone are inadequate for raising children to full human status. For Aquinas and for all ethnobiologists, Culture—the allegedly masculine world of social and cultural rules—must ultimately supplant and rule the world of Nature, the allegedly feminine world of biology. At root, the image is profoundly hostile and carries with it a Western vision not of the science of biology, but of social and economic enmity between men and women projected *onto* biology. The idea of a fixed biology subordinate to a variable culture is a myth of Western cultural and historical origin which takes us directly to beliefs about how men and women should relate to each other in a social hierarchy in which men, not women, enact roles of social and economic power. In brief, in these ideas of Nature and Culture, we see the division of labor by the sexes.

Feminism

But also from social scientists comes another reason for rejecting biology, this time from feminist scholars who recognize the all too clear danger that arguments about "woman's nature" can disguise *justifications* for retarding women's social and economic progress and condemning women to roles concerned only with sexuality, motherhood, childcare, nutrition, and nursing (e.g., Bleier, 1984; Lowe and Hubbard, 1983). Although these justifications are, like Aquinas', ethnobiological and not biological, many arguments relegating women to such "natural" roles (e.g., Gilder, 1975) are expressed in biological language and take their seeming power from alleged biological facts (as they did in the late 19th and early 20th centuries: Newman, 1985).

However, other feminist scholars accept the idea that a woman's "nature" exists, but argue that it is superior to man's "nature" in its greater sensitivity, nurturance, capacity for love, and ability to achieve genuine emotional rapport with other human beings (e.g., Griffin, 1981; Sayers, 1982). [This viewpoint is similar to the views of one of the founders of sociology, Georg Simmel (1919/1984).]

In these feminist voices, we hear the *woman's* side in the Nature/Nurture controversy. The predominant view is that "biological" (actually, ethnobiological) arguments must be rejected because they embody the male viewpoint that woman is closer to Nature and is *naturally* inferior to man, who creates Culture. But, like the men who see Nature (or women) primarily as vessels of fertility, real or symbolic, these feminist scholars accept the *terms* of the Nature/Nurture argument while rejecting its conclusions. In brief, feminism has *also* often accepted the idea that Nature and Culture are inherently different, or even opposites, and that between them there is conflict rather than collaboration. Once again, we have encountered mythology, and, with it, a profound argument about the *place* of men and women in society.*

Biological Ethnobiology

But it is not merely social scientists who take sides in the Nature/Nurture controversy. Biologically oriented thinkers—biologists and biologically inclined social scientists—have also entered the fray.

An historical interlude. Typically, but not unexpectedly, biologists interested in human behavior and culture have stressed the power of biological processes to shape human life. In this, they have been joined by scholars from anthropology, philosophy, history, psychology, sociology, among other fields.

The idea that biological, psychological, and cultural processes mutually affect one another has a long history. In brief, it began with enlightenment thought, moved through Rousseau (e.g., the Noble Savage, an idealization of Nature and biology) and related speculations about "man in the state of nature," and then, with Darwin, took a sudden turn from philosophical speculation towards science. Darwin was profoundly concerned to show that all human behavior, from a "moral sense" to customary ways of expressing emotion, has rudiments in animal behavior. However, unlike Aquinas or Rousseau, he was not interested in drawing ethical or moral lessons from Nature, but in showing that humankind *evolved* from primate ancestors and is connected to animals by *real* linkages of inheritance from our ancestors. For Darwin, humanity's place in the world was no longer static, created once and for all by the Divinity, but *dynamic:* human history merges undetectably with human evolution, as non-human gradually *became* human. [Thus, Darwin criticized the British philosopher John Stuart Mill for rejecting the connections that "transmitted mental qualities" provide between humanity and nature (1874, p. 95).] Darwin saw humanity's place in Nature as no longer atop the ladder of creation (the *scala natura*), but as connected to Nature as a branch is to a tree. We are then organically, necessarily, and intrinsically *part* of Nature.

Such ideas easily attached themselves to 19th century historical and sociological speculation that equated "evolution" with "progress" [e.g., Spencer and even Marx (Heyer, 1982)]. But Darwin's idea that human evolved from animal also easily connected itself to *other* speculations: in particular, the idea that at least some human behavior and motivation exists because of the "animal within us." These were the "instincts": forms of thought, activity, and emotion (like sex) that are inherited with little change from our animal forebears. It is as if the tree of life contained common and basic similarities in all its branches.

A profoundly illuminating example of how important the instinct concept once

---

*A woman reader commented at this point that these feminist scholars want to wrest their share of culture—and power—from men, without disputing that cultural power is different from and more valued than biological power. Her concerns mirror ideas expressed by many feminist writers (reviewed by Sayers, 1982).

30   *Sex Signals: The Biology of Love*

was occurs in Bertrand Russell's *The Problems of Philosophy* (1912/1959). It again leads to a fork in the road.

Russell, one of the great mathematicians of history, defines instincts as "beliefs" which appear in the mind not by argument, as they would in a mathematical proof, but as ready within ourselves as soon as we begin to reason (p. 24). For example, when we look at a table, we immediately believe that something about it exists external to ourselves, even if our senses provide us with only an incomplete or inaccurate understanding of what the table *really* is (pp. 17–26). If we expand Russell's characterization of "instinct" to include feelings and forms of behavior that appear "ready in ourselves" without thought, we have as good a definition as any. [See Havelock Ellis (1928, pp. 1–65) for other contemporary definitions.] So, for Russell, who was deeply concerned to find the logical origins of mathematics [as opposed to its psychological origins in a person's unconscious thoughts (Hadamard, 1949/1954; Poincaré, 1956) or its anthropological origins in the mathematician's culture (White, 1947/1956)], the "instincts" provide the *givens of logic itself.* For example, we see the sun rise each day, and "[t]he mere fact that something has happened a certain number of times causes animals and men to expect that it will happen again. Thus our instincts certainly cause us to believe that the sun will rise to-morrow . . . " (p. 63). Even if such beliefs occasionally prove false, nonetheless, for Russell, we *instinctively* believe that Nature is uniform and is not lawless chaos. The leap from an observation to a generalization is *natural.*

But Russell's recourse to the "instincts" was not naive theorizing. Rather, it depends on a paradox: one cannot prove logic valid by using logic without begging the question. The validity of logic must *precede* its use in any argument. To end the infinite regress of learning based on learning, or of logic based on logic, Russell flatly rejected the existence of specific "innate ideas"—for example, the notion that "space" is known to us without experience, as the German philosopher Immanuel Kant argued (Russell, 1912/1959, pp. 73–74, 85–87). For Russell, the "instincts" do not provide us with innate ideas or any sure idea of their truth, but, instead, with the capacity to "see"—that is, infer from experience—the truths of logic without proof (p. 74). It is a third-order attribution to the instincts: ideas are not innate or instinctive, and neither is logic itself. Rather, the capacity to *infer and believe* logic is instinctive. Russell ends the regression just as did Breasted and Robinson, by postulating an organism for whom the validity of logic is naturally evident (pp. 111–112), and from which it can build everything else, including a mathematics that itself *derives* from logic (p. 25; compare Russell and Whitehead's *Principia Mathematica*; see Nagel and Newman, 1956).

Russell's ideas are both subtle and powerful, because they are dynamic, not static. Barring the word *instinctive* and its old-fashioned implications, Russell's argument was probably quite correct (Piaget, 1952/1963; Laurendeau and Pinard, 1970). The idea that an organism is *biologically* able to learn what it must to survive and reproduce has recently created an extremely promising synthesis of Darwinism and social scientific thought (in learning theory, from Seligman, 1970; Rozin and Kalat, 1971; Garcia, McGowan, and Green, 1972; in linguistics, from Chomsky,

1965, e.g., pp. 47–59; for sexual development, Goldman and Goldman, 1982). However, these developments came after Russell; for him in 1912, the instincts themselves provided humankind with an avenue to discovering truth.

And his argument also led him to mysticism, just as it led Breasted and Robinson to a *Deus ex machina*. For Russell logic ultimately leads to the apprehension of a "suprasensible" (p. 92) world of realities that transcend this world, as Plato also argued. This we might call the "Russell–Plato" position, which begins with a being whose instincts let it infer logic, and for whom reasoning and rational thought alone then lead it to a timeless world of universal ideas of pure *being* utterly unlike the world of our daily *existence*. It is the world of pure mathematics, pure qualities, pure forms and truths. And, Russell adds, "[w]e may hope, in a mystic illumination, to *see* the[se] ideas . . . " (p. 92; italics original). Then Russell, the great mathematician, suddenly becomes lucid, and philosophical jargon drops away:

> The world of being is unchangeable, rigid, exact, delightful to the mathematician, the logician, the builder of metaphysical systems, and all who love perfection more than life. The world of existence is fleeting, vague, without sharp boundaries, without any clear plan or arrangement, but it contains all thoughts and feelings, all the data of sense, and all physical objects, everything that can do either good or harm, everything that makes any difference to the value of life and the world. (p. 100)

It is a beautiful vision. Unfortunately, instinct theories are like dry sponges: they absorb whatever you pour into them and let you build whatever you believe into your argument from the outset. Then, as assumptions, those beliefs wait, only to arise later in the guise of conclusions. Because the idea of instinct does not come from biology, it can easily escape from the facts of biology, and one can call "instinctive" whatever one believes is essentially true of human beings—for example, the idea that human beings are reasoning beings *by nature*, who are led, by pure reason, to the Platonic domains of pure truth.

But it is *not* necessary that there exists a world of pure ideas. We need only postulate that the world—*this* world, not a suprasensible one—has its own regularities and uniformities and then, with Darwin, argue that any organism which infers the wrong rules will therefore fall off cliffs, mistake ferns for suitable mates, or otherwise will be quite generally misled in ways that threaten its survival. After a while, what remains are organisms that *can* infer, more or less accurately, what the world is likely to do—even if those organisms call those inferences "logic" and want to see in them avenues to higher truths. This argument might be called the Russell–Darwin position, and I adopt it throughout the book. But that position *depends* on modern biology and, in particular, on the ideas mentioned above that animals in fact learn what they need to learn in order to survive and reproduce.

However, for Russell, it remains true that the instincts—with which Nature itself has endowed us, if only we use them—allow us to reach a magnificent vision of all reality, from earth-bound existence to the domains of pure idea. I suggest that

Russell *wanted* to find that world and so built access to it into the very "instincts" with which his argument began. Even though his argument powerfully and fascinatingly prefigures later developments in biology, yet, in a very real sense, for Russell, logic *is* the mystical eye that sees such truths. And if the reader suspects that *I* have built into my own arguments my preference for the complexities of the real world, so it is: that world is, I suggest, the only world to which science can attain, even if we must therefore leave perfection to others.

And yet, for other early 20th century thinkers who accepted the instinct concept, matters were hardly so perfect or so sublime. In particular, Freud accepted a version of Darwinian instinct theory when, for example, he described the Primal Horde as the "biological" origin of the Oedipal complex and its concomitant rages and furies. In this, Freud depended heavily on parts of Darwin's *The Descent of Man* (see Freud's *Totem and Taboo,* 1918, pp. 162–164). But for Freud, Darwin's idea of an organic and dynamic connection between humanity and Nature was frozen into an iron-hard and unbreakable instinctual *force:* having inherited our "instincts" from animals, we are unable to break that connection. At root, we *remain* animals, with animal instincts below the surface of culture, learning, and rationality. Once again, we recognize the ethnobiological idea that Nature is *irresistible,* yet somehow beneath Culture. And, in contrast to Russell's vision, sometimes Nature is dangerous.

As intellectual interest in Freudianism declined during the 20th century, instinct theories were sharply criticized and finally rejected by most social scientists. But even so, some thinkers remained fascinated by the idea that humankind is connected to Nature by descent, if not by instinct. In psychoanalysis, Géza Róheim proposed a subtle version of Darwinian Freudianism (e.g., Róheim, 1934/1974), but after him, the idea seemed to disappear like a stream vanished underground.

After World War II, the idea of an inherited and irresistible basis for human behavior resurfaced in the European ethological thought of Konrad Lorenz and Niko Tinbergen. Even though their ideas arose before the war (in association with psychoanalytic tradition: documented, e.g., by Bowlby, 1980; and illustrated, e.g., by Rancour-Laferriere, 1980; Sarwer-Foner, 1972), I suspect that after the war, the grim determinism of ethology with its innate aggression and apelike beings embedded below the rational surface of culture fit particularly well with the devastation of Europe during the War and with the same alienated spirit that appeared in existentialism (e.g., Camus). If, as Lorenz argued in *On Aggression* (1967), warlike aggression is inherited and is therefore an inevitable component of human existence, the idea at least seemed to explain, if not mitigate, the ghastly genocides of the war. Men assuredly have a darker side, and even if one rejects instinct theory, it is an explanation of sorts to say that evil *is* within us, at least potentially.

Again, the issue is of control over human life. Do we or do we not control our own behavior, history, culture, and fate? Are we, at times, puppets in the hands of Natural forces, which, surfacing as instincts, drive us uncontrollably to mass murder, genocide, and continued senseless violence of all against all? The sociologist Philip Slater cuttingly characterized Lorenzian ideas as a biological argument for " . . . a kind of innate human surliness, based on some no-longer-functional instinct" (1977, p. 94). Then, as usual for social scientists, Slater pointed to the "extraordinary cross-cultural variability in human belligerence" (p. 94) and dismissed Lorenz's ideas as flawed. Alas, Slater missed the point. Perhaps if one survived World War II, it is easy to believe that deeply evil forces act on humankind from within to produce nothing so sweet or innocent as "innate surliness," but, instead, the mass murders of Auschwitz, Lidice, or the Russian Front. Ethology—and its genetic determinism—did not arise at an optimistic time in European history. In the face of *those* events, perhaps it is easy to say, *Yes, there is innate evil in men.*

Biological romanticism. But there is another thread in the argument that biology plays a major role in shaping human behavior. It is gentler and less violent and arose, I suspect, not from the ethologists' despair over the fate of humanity, but from romanticism and from poetry and art. In general, biologists, more than behavioral or social scientists, are attracted to this vision of Nature, for biologists tend to see in Nature processes of immense grandeur and beauty, which create *and* destroy, and which act from the smallest molecule to the vastest reaches of the universe. In this vision, *nothing* escapes the touch of Nature, and everything obeys its rules.

We have again the idea that an infinitely wise Deity acts through Nature. But, by and large, biologists (unlike their more grim cousins, the ethologists) are fond of nature and its beings, and so see little in Nature—or God—that could be socially dangerous to human society. They usually do not think of Nature as a force that leads us to kill and rape, or as a set of repellent ideas about the irresistible genetic determinism of the more evil forms of human behavior. Indeed, such biologically oriented thinkers often simply do not understand why anyone would *object* to saying that Nature has immense power in people's lives: for them, Nature is a creator, the source of order and beauty in this world, and the origin of all living things, connected into a magnificent Darwinian fabric of evolved and evolving life. In that view, *of course* human existence obeys the rules of Nature!

But, equally, few biologically oriented thinkers are over-willing to admit to such romantic personifications of Nature. For them, "romanticism" is the sentimentality of the Harlequin novel or the tale-spinning fancies of poets who lack contact with the real world. Usually, most biologists (like social scientists) see themselves as sober pillars of scientific rationality who depend on evidence, detailed observation, and scientific precaution. And I readily admit that much biology *is* motivated by the highest ideals of scientific truth. But still, biological romanticism exists and has deep connections to old ethnobiological ideas about a kindly and wise Nature.*

But biological romanticism can cause serious trouble. If social scientists often

*I am using *romanticism* here in its aesthetic sense of a vision that personifies Nature, and, to quote Keats, sees it as the source of truth *and* beauty. The Appendix discusses the aesthetics of social and biological sciences in more detail.

confuse ethnobiology and biology, so too biologists are often ignorant of the social sciences and of the immense complexity of human behavior and culture. Equipped with detailed knowledge of genes, physiology, evolution, and similar high-powered concepts of a full-fledged science, biologists can plunge into discussion of human behavior seemingly unaware of their own naiveté concerning the most elementary principles of social science, and have an alarming tendency to fall off intellectual cliffs into various absurdities and overstatements. Moreover, for many social scientists, biology is *already* a complex mythology about Nature, Culture, and forces that work for good and evil, so that the biologists' romanticism and personification of Nature simply adds to the confusion.

Accordingly, the biologist who thinks seriously about human behavior is often completely puzzled when social scientific critics of biology call it "reductionistic." Perhaps unaware of how badly biology has been misused in the social sciences, the biologist plaintively wonders why it is reductionistic to see human culture as connected to all life and to the great fabric of all existence. The answer is that the *terms* of the discussion change drastically as one passes from one to the other side of the Nature/Nurture controversy. Totally different visions of Nature motivate social scientists and biologists, and where one sees horror, the other sees beauty. Obviously, they see different parts of human life.

So there is much more to biological thought about human behavior than sheer ignorance of social science or malice intended to reduce humanity to murderous, crazed animals. If—an oversimplification I make for purposes of discussion—social scientists tend toward rationality and want to see rational and therefore rationally preventable causes for human behavior, then the biologically inclined thinker sees beauty, synthesis, and integration among all forms of life, from microorganisms through people.

So far, however, I have asked the reader's indulgence in accepting the idea that some biological models of human culture and behavior are romanticized. I turn next to some examples of the *biological* ethnobiology that underlies these models. In them, we shall see biological facts entangled with familiar stories and beliefs about human nature, and, in particular, about how men and women should relate to each other.

The hunting model. I will begin with the so-called "hunting model," in which human evolution and behavior are seen as inevitable results of a long-ago commitment to hunting animals and eating meat (Perper and Schrire, 1977). According to this model, pre-human habitats dried up during the late Miocene and early Pliocene (5 to 6 million years ago), the forests dwindled, and our ancestors were forced onto the savannahs. To survive, they had to hunt animals for food. In consequence, these previously vegetarian beings began to make tools and weapons for killing and dressing game. At the same time, intelligence and brain size increased. Simultaneously, the larger food supply made possible larger and more complex societies. One result was a division of labor by the sexes, with males hunting and females rearing the young and gathering food near the base camp. As a result of larger brain size, infants took longer to mature, prolonging the period of dependency on females. Hunting males therefore assumed responsibility for their home-bound females and young by ranging afar to return with game. Such females evolved constant sexual receptivity—losing a limited period of estrus receptivity to males and instead becoming receptive throughout the whole menstrual cycle—so that males returning from the hunt would have been welcomed home by sexually receptive females. In this, we see the beginning of the nuclear family formed by father, mother, and their young.

In this model, "biology" and "evolution" play large roles, and we see how early evolutionary events "shaped" *all* subsequent human behavior and social organization. Indeed, these events catapulted our ancestors into the path of becoming fully human. Hunting created an entire *trajectory* of biological, social, and sexual evolution.

This example illustrates how "biology" often appears to the social scientist: as a profound causal force that initiates and directs evolution with an unseen hand. And, seeing the story begin in violence and end with the nuclear family, the social scientific critic of biology sees it as justifying aggression as "biologically" inevitable and as rationalizing the nuclear family with its repressions over women as "biologically" given and determined. Then, perhaps believing that the story represents biological *science,* that critic moves on to reject biology as necessarily serving to justify war and sexual repression.

However, this story hides something which does not arise from biology at all but from a more familiar source (Perper and Schrire, 1977). In 1961, Robert Ardrey published *African Genesis.* It described the hunting model at some length and, in a striking series of metaphors, showed that the hunting model mirrors Creation according to Genesis. For Ardrey, human evolution began in the lush forest galleries of Miocene Kenya, a place he called "Eden." In those forests lived vegetarian primates whose survival was at stake as the forests shrank when the drier Pliocene began. They were "Eden's outcasts." Their expulsion from the forests onto the savannahs was the irreversible loss of Eden. Then by an "incredible accident"—that is, a miracle—they began to prey on and kill the rich herds of game that dwelled on the Pliocene savannahs. As Ardrey put it, " . . . there, faraway under vasty skies, Cain killed for a living" (the quotations are from Chapter 9).

In this model, hunting is the equivalent of Original Sin. And not merely the equivalent, but sin which derives from our origins and which we inherit by reason of our origins. If we are aggressive *because* we hunted and killed for a living under those vasty skies, we owe our aggression to our origins, and by definition the sin is original, that is, of origin. *African Genesis* begins "Not in innocence, and not in Asia, was mankind born. . . . "

That, and the very title of the book itself, suggests why the hunting model is so familiar. Under the "biology" and "evolution" of the hunting model is a myth Westerners know very well: Creation according to Genesis. Eden was lost. Killing followed hunting, and men work by the sweat of their brow. Women bring clinging babies into the world in pain. We struggle against the temptations of "constant receptivity" because Eve's sins are visited upon us as adultery and infidelity. In Ardrey's own words, we are "Cain's Children."*

It is a familiar story. But it is not biology at all. In fact, humans are not carnivores, but omnivores. Biologically, the hunting model is erroneously one-sided. For example, we require vitamin B_{12} to live, and meat is a good source of B_{12}. But equally, we require vitamin C to live, for which plants, particularly fruits, are the best source. The hunting model can be refuted both physiologically and archaeologically (Perper and Schrire, 1977; Bleier, 1984, chapter 5, pp. 115–137).

However, to a social scientist who knows only a little about biology, the biological language of the hunting model qualifies it as real biology even though it is not. The hunting model is only an elaborate theological argument in which the Biblical story is *expressed* in the words and terms of biology. In this, biology has provided metaphors of Nature which are used without reference to biological reality. Biology here is surface language, not content.

Meiotic longings. The next example may be less familiar. It comes from the psychological philosopher Giora Shoham (1983) and concerns the urge to join sexually with another person in intense emotional and physical intimacy. How can we explain such urges? Shoham builds his mythology upon meiosis, the biological process that separates chromosomes during the formation of the gametes, the egg and sperm. His argument sounds very scientific.

During meiosis, the number of chromosomes in the sperm and egg is reduced by one-half, from "diploidy" to "haploidy," as biologists say—from 46 to 23 in humans. When fertilization follows sexual intercourse, the original diploid number of chromosomes is restored when the 23 chromosomes in the egg and the 23 in the sperm join to give 46 chromosomes in the newly fertilized egg. As the fertilized egg develops into an embryo (and, later, into the infant and adult), the diploid number (46) is retained until meiosis again occurs in the adult gonads as haploid eggs or sperm are produced.

For Shoham, the sexual fusion of haploid egg and haploid sperm is a kind of re-union driven by a longing to restore the sundered diploid original: what he calls the "violence" of meiotic chromosome separation is undone when the haploid gametes fuse to restore diploidy in the fertilized egg and in the adult into which it develops (pp. 22–24).

His idea is basically simple. Certain cellular and molecular events serve as the ultimate cause of the immensely complicated process of *sexual* union and re-fusion. The activity of the chromosomes during meiosis and fertilization provides a metaphor for human sexual union.

Since perhaps few readers can tell if Shoham's metaphor is true or false, let us consider it a bit further. Shoham postulates that the gametes themselves somehow

---

*The parallels exist whether or not writers accepting the hunting model "agree" that it represents Genesis. These are *formal* or *structural* parallels. Compare Landau (1984).

experience an urgency to undo the separation that brought them into existence. Let us grant this idea, for then we see that it cannot explain sexual behavior at all. The people who interact sexually—the *adult* individuals who fall in love and who make love—are not, themselves, haploid at all; unlike the gametes, which *are* haploid, the adult is *diploid*. The adult is already re-fused, his or her cells already in a state of chromosomal re-union, and any force intrinsic to haploidy that seeks re-union has been neutralized. Why, then, should adults experience an urgency to undo a separation that was undone the moment the egg from which they developed was fertilized?

To be sure, to some readers, Shoham's ideas may seem *prima facie* nonsense because he attributes motivations to the chromosomes. Quite true. But a fair-sized sociobiological literature says that the *genes* are selfish little creatures, eager only to reproduce themselves (Dawkins, 1978). Furthermore, the idea antedates both Shoham *and* sociobiology. Ultimately, it comes from Plato's concept that sexual union occurs because men and women are driven to reestablish a once existing state of bisexual perfection (Plato, *The Symposium,* 1956, pp. 353–358). Moreover, Shoham's ideas probably draw on the Judaic tradition that all people contain sparks of the Divinity, with Whom they yearn to reunite (Schachter and Hoffman, 1983). But still, under this metaphor is a belief about human sexuality: it allows us to connect and re-connect ourselves with others, thereby to undo the violent separations that created us at birth or at creation.

Again, while Shoham's story is expressed in the *language* of biology, it is not biology no matter how evocative it is as myth or metaphor. Although the non-geneticist—Shoham *or* Plato—may want to believe that genes or chromosomes can think, feel, and hold and enact human-sounding strategies, biologically they cannot. The capacities to think, feel, and develop strategies belong *biologically* to the brain and nothing else. By *personifying* the genes—which are stretches of DNA, nothing more—these ideas are only a form of genetic mysticism, not connected by lines of evidence to the real science of genetics.

Nor did the image of the personified gene escape the unidentified artist who illustrated the cover of *The Selfish Gene* (Dawkins, 1978). The painting shows a bird feeding its nestlings in a tree, but the bodies of the birds are covered with dozens of *human* eyes which stare directly, watchfully, and intelligently at the viewer. By contrast, the birds' *own* eyes are merely the eyes of birds. It is a striking and accurate aesthetic translation of Dawkins' idea of an ever-watchful, ever-selfish internal and *personified* genetic eye. Even though Dawkins has tried to justify his analysis in technical detail (1982), Symons' comment in *The Evolution of Human Sexuality* still holds: the rhetoric of selfish genes " . . . exactly reverses the real situation: through metaphor genes are endowed with properties only sentient beings can possess, such as selfishness, while sentient beings are stripped of these properties and called machines" (Symons, 1979, p. 42). It is an excellent summary—and it reminds one of the philosopher Leibniz (1646–1716) saying that material objects consist of colonies of souls (Russell, 1912/1959, p. 15).

Genetic Determinism: Genes as People

My last examples of ethnobiology concern genetic determinism, the belief that the genes (or "heredity") irresistibly control and shape our behavior. Of course, genetic determinism is a kind of biological determinism, but the latter term is broader. For example, Freud was a *biological* determinist when he said that libidinal or sexual instincts control aspects of human life and that they vie with "civilization" for power over our behavior. But *genetic* determinists speak explicitly of genes as controlling behavior (the jargon is to speak of "genes *for* a behavior"). Genetic determinism is a refinement, so to speak, of biological determinism: it locates Natural forces specifically in the genes.

Currently, the best known set of genetic determinist speculations about behavior are found in sociobiology. To some people, "sociobiology" refers to *any* argument that uses biology to explain human social or individual behavior, and such people would call this book *sociobiological* even though sociobiology is only one *kind* of biological argument (which I do not use). Sociobiology has produced some important genetic and biological ideas, but much of it is biologically weak precisely in its overstated emphasis on genes that control behavior.

Historically, sociobiology is a recent offshoot of evolutionary biology and not of the social sciences. When it originated in the early 1960s, sociobiology focused mainly on evolutionary problems of animal behavior—e.g., the evolution of altruism and of mating strategies—but, increasingly, it has attracted certain social and behavioral scientists who seem to want to reintroduce instinct theories into the social sciences (thus, sociobiology often appeals to Freudian instinct theorists).

However, other social scientists, such as Robin Fox and Lionel Tiger, initially saw in sociobiology a way to connect human social behavior to its biological antecedents. [Their term was "zoological," which they used before sociobiology was a clearly recognized field (Tiger and Fox, 1966).] Contrary to popular reviews of their work, Tiger and Fox never accepted (and still reject) the iron-clad genetic determinism of other writers, e.g., Edward O. Wilson, author of *Sociobiology: The New Synthesis* (1975), who is himself a biologist. Sociobiological thought also appeals to some primatologists and physical anthropologists, whose first-hand knowledge of non-human primates has convinced them that there are some profound similarities in the social behavior of *all* primates, human and non-human. Nonetheless, sociobiology gradually slid towards postulating genetic determination of human behavior, towards an omnibus of repetitive pseudo-philosophizing (see Geertz, 1984), and towards efforts, discussed later, to explain infanticide, rape, and nepotism by referring to genes that force us to behave in morally reprehensible ways (at least as we Westerners judge such things). In this, Nature is no longer the source of Good. When these allegedly genetically determined urges and instincts surface, they seem to reveal a darker side of Nature, no longer glorious, beautiful, or romantic, but grim and deadly. It reminds one of the grimness of post-World War II European ethology, and for the same reason. We too lost a war (Vietnam), and perhaps some—not only sociobiologists—seek to explain its horrors and its drastic and continued social effects by speaking of the "genes" and of a Nature turned destructive—for example, when Hunter S.Thompson speaks of "the rancid genes and broken chromosomes that corrupt the possibilities of the American Dream" (Thompson, 1968/1979, p. 213).

Yet sociobiology has produced some valuable *scientific* ideas. One of its basic biological concepts—Robert Trivers' (1972) idea of "differential parental investment"—is very important, and I will use the concept later, in Chapter 7. But parental investment is also far more complex than some "sociobiologists" may realize. Likewise, sociobiological concern with mating and reproductive behavior has provided insights into the different roles of males and females in choosing mates, a theme that will appear and reappear throughout this book. However, many other sociobiological ideas, especially those related to "altruism," are biologically nearly senseless, as I want to discuss next.

Nuclear as natural. Basic to much sociobiology is a concept called "genetic relatedness" (Hamilton, 1964a, 1964b; E. O. Wilson, 1975). Usually, it is measured by r, the "coefficient of genetic relatedness," which is given as 1/2 between parent and child or between siblings; 1/4 between grandparent and child and between aunts/uncles and nieces/nephews; 1/8 between greatgrandparent and child, and so on, ever decreasingly, until one reaches $r = 0$ for non-relatives. The layperson of course wants to know what these numbers mean, and the simplest *sounding* explanation (which, however, is wrong) is that 1/2, 1/4, 1/8 . . . represent the fractions of genes that two related individuals share in common with each other. In this simple interpretation, parent and child would share 1/2 of their genes, and so on (as explicitly stated, for example, by Dawkins, 1978, p. 151; and by Alexander, 1974, p. 373).

The idea is plausible because we all believe that we are more "closely" related—by blood, as people say—to our parents than to a third cousin or, of course, to a stranger. Thus, this reading of r represents our own ideas of who our relatives are, and how closely we are related to them. In r, we see the nuclear family of our own English-speaking tradition—father, mother, and their children.*

But the sociobiological interpretation of r has important consequences. Given the nuclear family as Natural—that is, presuming that $r = 1/2, 1/4, 1/8 . . .$ measures how many genes two related individuals share by virtue of

---

*When sociobiologists speak of nepotism as "genetic," we can also conclude that they see the genes elevating our traditions of kinship and the obligations it entails to the status of Natural (which, of course, leaves the status of other kinship systems somewhat unclear; see, e.g., Alexander, 1974, pp. 372–374; Alexander and Borgia, 1978, p. 467, where they speak of *genetic* mutations that generate and increase nepotism towards members of the nuclear family). Some biologists (e.g., D. S. Wilson, 1977) early on doubted the universality of sociobiological thought, but not surprisingly, their critiques focused primarily on purely biological issues. And, although D. S.Wilson later discussed the imputation of kindliness to Nature (1983, pp.160–163), the projection of the nuclear family onto Nature remains central to sociobiology. However, "nepotism" is hardly so simple. Indeed, the study of economic and political duties and perquisites among kin forms one historical root of sociology (e.g., Max Weber). And a great deal more than the "nuclear" family is involved when people exchange goods and services—a fact basic to anthropology itself.

common *familial* descent—then it follows, in one sociobiological version of how altruism evolved, that if I perform an altruistic act which will virtually certainly cause my death—like trying to rescue someone from a burning and collapsing building—then altruism can evolve only if a specific mathematical relationship holds between r and the *number* of people I save (Hamilton, 1964a). In brief, I must rescue $1/r$ people, for, otherwise, the argument implies that altruism can neither evolve nor persist. The only biological explanation for the evolution and persistence of altruism is the preservation of one's own genes—and the genes which are identical to them in other individuals (who, for sociobiologists, must be relatives). So, in sociobiology, I must rescue two parents or siblings (because $1/r = 1 \div 1/2 = 2$), four grandparents or grandchildren, and so on (e.g., Eberhard, 1975, p. 6; Barash, 1977, pp. 80, 85–87).

The crucial implication is that if r is measured in this way, then altruism will occur only between close kin, and the closer the better. In this theory, altruism cannot evolve between non-relatives (strangers), since r between them is theoretically 0, and I would have to rescue 1/0 or an infinite number of people. This implication is false. Volunteer firemen and rescue workers all rescue strangers. So do men in war, even at great risk and without pay.

Thus, if sociobiological theory is correct, then it cannot apply to human behavior, not because of its pseudo-philosophical speculations—the usual target of anti-sociobiological writers—but because it generates the wrong predictions about people. Thus, Mary Jane West Eberhard (1975) wrote, apparently in complete seriousness, that "Theoretically, the most willing lifeguard [at a beach] should be a physically fit eunuch or post-reproductive individual . . . with few living relatives . . . "(p. 8, col. 1). Although this "prediction" does follow from the usual sociobiological reasoning about genetic relatedness, it too is obviously false.

The reason is that this sociobiological explanation of r is wrong, and although the preceding argument may be mathematically valid, its basic premise is not. The number r is *not* the fraction of genes two individuals share in common. Instead, r is the probability of inheriting a certain gene from an ancestor, or of any two individuals having inherited the same gene from a common ancestor. For example, say that my maternal grandfather possessed a certain gene A1, my maternal grandmother had gene A2, my paternal grandfather gene A3, and my paternal grandmother gene A4. If these genes are what is called "alleles" of each other, then I have a 1/4 chance of inheriting gene A1, a 1/4 chance of inheriting gene A2, and so on.

But that does *not* mean that I share 1/4 of my genes with a given grandparent. The reason is that the genes A1, A2, A3, and A4 might all be the same. For example, if my grandparents all had blue eyes, like their children (my parents), then they, my parents, *and* I all have the same gene(s) for blue eyes.

In genetics, people in such descent groups (or extended families) may all share some 90 percent or more of their genes regardless of their degree of "blood relatedness." Indeed, people who are not "related" at all may share upwards of 60 percent of their genes. (Such genes are called "monomorphic," which means that everyone in the population possesses the same gene, for example for blue eyes in a completely blue-eyed population.)

The error is in assuming that the phrase "degree of genetic relatedness" means in *genetics* what it would in common speech: merely how "close" two people are according to our American scheme for reckoning kinship (as illustrated, e.g., by Fox, 1967, pp. 256–261, esp. Diagram 71). But *r* measures no such thing. Thus, this sociobiological explanation of altruism depends in large part on a misinterpretation which is obvious *genetically*. It is not, however, obvious to the non-geneticist, for whom the North American kinship system, and the family and sexual relationships upon which it is based, are all "natural." These sociobiological conclusions about altruism therefore more closely resemble what we believe is "right" and "normal" than anything derivable as universal truths from the principles of genetics.

Aware of these difficulties, some sociobiologists have proposed a subtler version of the argument (e.g., Trivers, 1971), although the model I have discussed is still usually assumed to characterize most sociobiological thought (see, e.g., Andersson, 1984, for a detailed and highly technical empirical critique of the *r*-calculation just described, plus evidence that it is in fact inapplicable in some purely biological contexts). In this version of the theory, sociobiologists speak of *individual* genes that cause a person or animal to behave altruistically (e.g., Trivers, 1971, p. 36; Alexander and Borgia, 1978; Dawkins, 1982. p. 191), and apply the *r*-calculation to those genes, rather than to *all* the genes the altruist possesses. It is now technically valid to apply the *r*-calculation, but only at the cost of arguing that genes in fact *do* cause altruism. I hope the reader will bear with me for an additional technicality, for here we encounter a subtler, but far more important, problem.

The original *r*-calculation does *not* depend on postulating a "genetic" basis for altruism. It simply said that more genes identical to mine would be passed on—which is the basic criterion for success in all evolutionary thought—if I behave "altruistically" toward my near kin. Even if I had *learned* to behave in self-sacrificing ways, the reward was that genes identical to mine by descent in my family were rescued. The problem, of course, is that altruism is not displayed only along family lines, but still, there is no need here to postulate genes *causing* altruism.

Now, in order to avoid the fact that altruism is *not* solely directed toward close kin, the newer *r*-calculation says that altruism *is* genetic. Here the layperson or biologist who knows little of the sciences of human behavior can make a profound mistake. It concerns the definition of altruism itself. To be sure, a self-sacrificing rescue of a drowning person qualifies, and *perhaps* a "gene" causes that behavior (though I frankly doubt it). But such activities do not even *begin* to exhaust the range of behavior patterns that human beings deem altruistic, and will perform even at considerable cost to themselves and their offspring.

An excellent example is religious faith. A traditional Jewish mother may take considerable time and effort to teach her children to behave in ways obedient to the teachings of Judaism, and she will assuredly argue that it is spiritually and culturally beneficial to them to learn those teachings. In brief, she behaves altruistically, for she is motivated by a desire to do good as she sees it, even at a cost to the *child* that results, for example, if the family lives in a pogrom-ridden, anti-Semitic society. In this case, we have an altruistic act that does *not* seem to "improve the fitness" of the child, and yet is proudly mandated by Judaism.

If, next, we apply the sociobiological argument that altruism is genetic, we must postulate that this woman's desire to teach her children a specific creed and faith *is* "caused" by a gene. However, not even the most assertive genetic determinist, sociobiologist or not, would argue that a religious woman's behavior is "genetic." And, if they did, then the argument begins to squirm towards some nasty implications: are such "genes" the same in a Jewish mother as in a non-Jewish mother, and, if not, then—perhaps?—the non-Jewish "genes" are just the tiniest bit *better* than the Jewish "genes"? Because this argument applies to *any* minority at risk in *any* society (e.g., early Christians), the social scientist—and the layperson— may begin to see such arguments as not only biologically senseless (there exist no "genes" for specific forms of religious behavior), but also as socially *dangerous* in their biological falsity.

E. O. Wilson's sociobiological "explanation" of religion deserves comment (Wilson, 1978, pp. 169–193). No one would doubt that religious faith and behavior both "exist" mentally and neurophysiologically, as somehow encoded in brain anatomy and physiology, nor doubt that genes play roles in brain development (p. 177). But even though Wilson says that the genes are "remote" from religious practice (p. 178), he nonetheless believes that " . . . ecclesiastic choices are influenced by the chain of events that lead from the genes through physiology to constrained learning during single lifetimes" (p. 177). An unkind reader might say that he really *does* mean that the choice of ritual and religious convention (his definition of "ecclesiastic," p. 176) is ultimately caused by an individual's genes. If so, is he saying that Jewish "genes" are different than Muslim "genes"? But perhaps Wilson himself does not really know what he means here, or in this entire chapter. Either way, such ideas, especially about "constrained" learning, demand much more care in thought and expression than Wilson provides in this section of his book.

I am not accusing sociobiology of anti-Semitism or of other racist doctrines. But I *am* saying that many biologically based sociobiologists are often naive about human behavior and its complexities, and certainly *seem* naive about the implications of their ideas if those ideas prove wrong. Not even romanticism or a desire to see Nature as all-powerful can excuse ignorance of those implications.

Infanticide: Nature as economics. My last example of a sociobiological argument illustrates how certain social and economic processes are projected onto Nature, which is then seen as their ultimate cause. It concerns infanticide, a behavior pattern of widespread but sporadic occurrence in animals and humans. (I am here defining infanticide as the deliberate killing of an infant, rather than as neglect that leads to its death.)

The example is taken from the Martin Daly and Margo Wilson analysis of human infanticide (1984, pp. 487–502). Immediately, I must say that I am *not* accusing these scholars of insensitivity to the moral issues raised by infanticide. Rather, I cite them because they develop with great clarity some implications of the sociobiological thought of R. D. Alexander (1974, 1979).

Their starting place is the general evolutionary principle (accepted in all evolutionary thinking) that the characteristics of an organism evolve and persist only if they "contribute to reproduction, or more precisely to genetic replication, hereafter called 'fitness'" (p. 487). Indeed, this principle is the most powerful touchstone of evolutionary biology. Daly and Wilson wish to apply this concept by asking if human infanticide, contrary to intuition, might contribute to reproduction. Of course, they recognize that parental "solicitude" (p. 488) makes excellent sense, but are there times at which infanticide might paradoxically *increase* the chances of passing on one's genes?

Drawing on Alexander's theoretical work, Daly and Wilson see this possibility in three cases: first, the child is not the offspring of the putative parent; second, the infant is of low "fitness," for example, hopelessly deformed; and, third, the parent has alternatives for conceiving and raising other, more fit offspring. Alexander's ideas thus represent a kind of eugenics that says that, although it is morally tragic, it *is* to the parent's advantage to kill certain offspring under certain circumstances.

Daly and Wilson examine these possibilities in a cross-cultural sample of 60 non-Western, non-industrial societies. In these, infanticide occurred in 39, but in only 35 of these cases did the original report give reasons for infanticide. The ethnographic data from these 35 societies then showed that infanticide typically occurs for reasons corresponding to Alexander's ideas. In 21 of these 35 societies, "deformed or very ill" infants are killed, while in 29 of 35, infants were sometimes killed when there were "inadequate" parental resources, such as the birth of twins when the mother cannot feed both (Table I, pp. 490–491).

No doubt many readers are horrified that parents would kill offspring for such reasons, but let us set aside that horror to examine the *logic* of Alexander's argument. Again, the layperson may not see a problem here, specifically, the confusion of genetic or evolutionary explanations with *economic* explanations. In the calculus of reproductive success explicitly adopted by Daly and Wilson, what counts is offspring produced, for only through them are one's genes transmitted. In simple numbers, two children are better than one. In that case, it follows that twins are better than single births (two for the price of one, so to speak). *If* this genetic calculus applies to human infanticide, then twins should be welcomed, not subject to infanticide. Infanticide then can be seen as a problem of *economics*—of resources commanded by the mother and available to her in a given cultural system of distribution—limitations on which may make it impossible for her to feed both or to raise them to adulthood. In brief, an economic problem of the distribution of goods and wealth (with associated cultural tradition) has been confused with genetics, so that Nature, here represented by the "genes," is seen as benefiting from infanticide. So when Alexander wrote that " . . . human parents have evidently been sacrificing or using part of their offspring to increase their reproduction via others" (1979, p. 368), we might agree, but not because this "increase" arises from the principles of genetics. It does not. Such needs are economic and may even be the counsel of despair arising in the face of starvation.*

I am not suggesting that infanticide could be eradicated simply by feeding people better, although that would not hurt. Rather, I am saying that custom ultimately connected to economics may sometimes make infanticide seem necessary to some people. But even so, infanticide operates *against* the genetic calculus that makes offspring a genetic benefit, and not, as Alexander seems to believe, in the *same* direction as genetics. (Daly and Wilson conclude that infanticide in an industrial society, Canada, in fact does not afford genetic benefits.)

There are similar problems with explaining infanticide of deformed or ill children, or of children of uncertain parentage. To be sure, some eugenic or reproductive benefit *might* accrue to killing off hopelessly deformed children, but is this really infanticide? In non-industrial societies, ill or deformed children may inevitably die in any case, so that hastening death may be tragic, but *economically* necessary. (Compare Eastwell, 1982.)

Finally, "uncertain parentage" actually means uncertain *paternity* (as Daly and Wilson know). If genetic or economic benefit results when the husband of an adulterous wife kills the child born from his wife's extramarital relationship (e.g., he reasons that it doesn't have his genes, so why should he support it?), then the *woman* certainly will not draw the same conclusion. After all, the child *is* hers, and it therefore contains her genes. Again, in the calculus of genetic success, she should *not* want her child dead. If the man (or men) does want to kill it, then this form of infanticide occurs because the woman cannot resist her husband's infanticidal impulses. The problem has become one of inequality of *power* between men and women, and not of the "genes" acting to cause men *and* women to kill children according to an austere calculus of "fitness."

Sociobiology does not actually *explain* economic behavior by referring to genetic processes acting under it, but simply *equates* economic and genetic processes. However, in reality, as infanticide illustrates, genetic and economic processes can be in stark opposition. Hence, when sociobiologists believe that genetics explains economic or social behavior, they have *projected* economics onto Nature, and then found in Nature the same economic principles with which they began. The effect is that Nature takes on the power and intentionalities of human activity. In a word, sociobiology *personifies* Nature.

Ethnobiology: Nature as Divine

Over and over, stories, myths, and personifications like these are presented as representing the biology and genetics of human behavior. But often such ideas are

---

*Pre-Revolutionary China illustrates the immense importance of agricultural disaster and starvation in producing infanticide and child neglect. To understate, the economics of food production and distribution has much greater immediate power over human life than the "genes" of the sociobiologists. See, e.g., De Leeuw, 1933/1979, pp. 69–190, especially pp. 87–105, but see also Belden, 1949.

simply biologically wrong, *even though* they represent what we might think is "natural." However, because these beliefs are couched in the language of biology and science, they can mislead someone who has no way to understand *why* such myths are biologically impossible.

These people include many social scientific critics of "biology." If these critics do not know biology, they cannot tell the difference between stories like these, in which "biology" merely serves as a language for speaking in myths about "Nature," and biological hypotheses that make excellent biological sense. In brief, because *some* biological stories are myths, social science has rejected all biology even though it cannot distinguish real biology from an ethnobiology that sees in biology a virtually Divine and universal force.

This conclusion is very important. It forces us to examine any biological explanation of human behavior on its own biological merits. The hunting model is false not because it is a version of Creation; after all, that particular version of Creation *might* be true. It is false because biologically meat has no transcendent, overwhelmingly important role in human physiology. Shoham's metaphor of chromosomes longing to re-unite is false because it is a biologically inadequate description of human cytogenetics. Sociobiological explanations are often false because they are based on oversimplified or even inaccurate genetic ideas as well as naiveté in the social sciences.

And yet, if there was nothing more to it, biological *science* might long ago have been integrated into the social sciences. After all, ignorance is *not* invincible. However, the obstacle against applying biology and genetics to human behavior is not merely ignorance. Instead, for both social scientific critics of biology *and* the proponents of biological ideas discussed above, biology is a complex and full-fledged mythology with a structure all of its own. The Naturists and Nurturists are not arguing about the properties or qualities of "biology," but about whether a specific mythology about Nature applies to human behavior and culture.

Paradoxically, that mythology, which I have been calling *ethnobiology,* is accepted on both sides of the Nature/Nurture controversy. Naturists and Nurturists both agree that Nature *can* act irresistibly and universally, and that if it did act, it would produce fixity and identity in behavior. The argument is solely about whether this all-powerful Nature does *in fact* act on human beings, with the Nurturists denying it and the Naturists saying it does. The properties of this much vexed "Nature" are not questioned.

But we must raise such questions. Historically, our ideas of Nature arose *before* industrial technology and modern biology had solved many real medical, agricultural, and nutritional problems. The powers and properties of nature once had immediate and practical consequences where today we see only theoretical issues about Nature. And it is easy to personify Nature when its weather controls the crops that provide you with food, when its unknown parasites, bacteria, and viruses control the life of your children, and when its equally unknown biochemistry controls whether or not you die of vitamin deficiencies. It is also easy to personify Nature when your life involves cattle, horses, and wild animals that have to be hunted to provide food. We are, today, impressed—and amused—by the names the English language once had for groups of animals (e.g., a "cete" of badgers) but forget that knowledge of these "terms of venery" once marked the gentleman (Lipton, 1977, pp. 1–4). Nature was once central to human existence: prior to technology, we were embedded in nature, not metaphorically, but concretely and in reality.

But why has Nature retained its power over our modern thinking? Why hasn't concern for Nature dwindled as have the names for groups of badgers, foxes, and deer?

An important part of the answer is that connection visualized between Nature and God. If by "human nature" a speaker means those qualities of humanity that are *essentially and intrinsically* human—that make us what we *really* are, aside from accidents of upbringing—then it is still easy for us in a post-industrial age to seek the source of that "reality" in forces that have acted on us, to shape us, as clay is shaped by a sculptor or, perhaps, by a Sculptor. No one concerned with the Nature/Nurture controversy can underestimate the importance of such metaphors for Divine action. Moreover, in metaphors like Breasted and Robinson's it is easy to see human prehistory as the *childhood* of humanity and, in metaphors like Alland's, to see human beings as children of Nature. Feminist theological concern over the "gender" of God is then far easier to understand (e.g., Ochs, 1977), for it no longer pertains simply to issues of women as priests or religious officiants, but, in metaphor, reaches towards efforts to understand creation itself.

However, concern about Nature also centers on its use to legitimate various social and economic arrangements between men and women. It is one thing to debate whether such arrangements have *Divine* sanction, but it is quite another to say that those arrangements are *genetically* ordained. We must not simply project onto Nature our own mythologized perceptions of men and women and then "discover" them in Nature. We must view cautiously—*very* cautiously—comments about animals, such as the following from a Cambridge University (Great Britain) primatologist that "[m]ales could, in principle at least, choose to mate with a few large (but heavily competed for) females or many small (less desirable) ones. [He is referring to heavily egg-laden and therefore large female toads.] There is some suggestion that something comparable might be operating among humans: males may choose between courting (socially) highly desirable females (with limited chances of success) or courting less attractive (but more easily 'conquered') females . . . " (Dunbar, 1983, p. 428). We cannot so glibly assume that Culture dominates Nature or that men conquer women.

Nor, in the 20th century, can we any longer so glibly assert that Nature is the second Book of God and that biology is its moral or intellectual interpreter; although the first statement might be true, the second assuredly is *not*. Modern biology does not seek moral lessons in Nature, as did Aquinas; nor does it seek the real nature or meaning of human life; nor—emphatically—does it assert that biological processes act universally and irresistibly to yield fixity of behavior, as social scientists so often believe. And since that conclusion differs so much from common belief, I want next to explain it and thereby begin to suggest how we can build a *genuinely* biological social science.

Chapter 3

The Biosocial Approach

I submit that most scholars have been asking the wrong questions about human behavior and biology. When they focus on Nature *versus* Nurture, they thereby create conflict between them. That conflict is understandable when we see it as a metaphor for conflict between men and women for social power and recognition. Nonetheless, one still wonders what happened to the original question: What biological principles *do* apply to human behavior and culture? As long as we remain confined by myths and by passionately held and argued beliefs, that question vanishes in silence and disappears as the polarized factions—Naturists and Nurturists—fight each other. But if we cannot be content with the ethnobiological mythology of some *biologically* oriented thinkers, neither can we be content with the *social scientist's* dismissal of biology as an unacceptable doctrine of universal causation. Progress in understanding the real relationships between biology and culture can be achieved *only* by avoiding these polarized extremes and their rhetorical overstatements.

I will next outline some biological principles that seem to me basic for avoiding the Scylla and Charybdis of the Nature/Nurture controversy. This *biosocial* viewpoint sees reciprocal relationships between genetic, evolutionary, psychological, *and* cultural processes as central to human evolution and culture. My thinking has been strongly influenced not only by Darwin and his biological followers, but also by social scientists interested in creating linkages between biology and social science, e.g., the theorists Donald Campbell, William Durham, Robin Fox, Marvin Harris, Solomon Katz, Roy Rappaport, Donald Symons, Lionel Tiger, and Andrew P. Vayda, among others; and, among feminists, Wollstonecraft and de Beauvoir (of course) and, in particular, Janet Sayers (1982). These necessary obeisances made, let me turn to the biosocial approach itself. To begin, what *is* biology?

Structure and Function

Modern biology is complex, subtle in its underlying philosophy, and formidable in its terminology and literature. It cannot be summarized. Nonetheless, certain biological concepts—structure, function, variation, and diversity—are basic.

I will begin with *structure* and *function* because the social sciences also use these terms, and the possibilities for confusion are very great. By "structure," a biologist means a physically real part of an organism. The kidney is a structure because I can point to it in a dissected animal.

This definition of structure differs sharply from the social scientist's. When social scientists speak of *social structure,* they are not referring to an object to which one can point. Rather, social structure is an abstraction, and means that human social behavior displays regularities and obeys certain rules (e.g., Lévi-Straussian or Piagetian structuralism). In biology, the study of structure is the study of objects, not abstractions.

For a biologist to speak of a *structure,* that part of the body must have its own *function.* The kidney is a structure because, among other things, it excretes water and salts and helps maintain water balance in the body.

However, the idea of a deep relationship between structure and function is deceptive because it is easy to analogize with more familiar things. Everyone knows that objects have parts—e.g., a clock has gears and a mainspring. But such analogies are dangerous.

A clock with all its parts is the product of a designer, an engineer, a craftsperson. We therefore easily say that the *purpose* of the mainspring is to store energy and drive the clock hands, simply because the clock designer used a mainspring for that purpose. Next, when one says that the mainspring *functions* to drive the clock hands, it is obvious that the concepts of purpose and function are closely related (as discussed, e.g., by Aronson, 1984, pp. 37–38).

However, biologists sharply distinguish purpose and function. The concept of purpose inevitably seems to suggest a designer, perhaps a Divine Designer, a God Who is the Clockmaker of all life. Now, biologists feel that it is unwise to make theology and a belief in God essential for understanding biological phenomena. Biology is biology, and God is God. They should not be confused. Accordingly, biologists prefer to describe phenomena without building into their descriptions a tacit assumption that God exists. Thus, God may or may not be the Great Designer; either way, kidneys contribute to the survival of the organism. The biologist therefore speaks of function and not of purpose.

As a result, biology can study empirically what kidneys actually do: they excrete salts and water, and *thereby* function to maintain salt and water balance.

But *function* refers to far more that what an organ "does." In biology, function refers *only* to how any component, characteristic, trait, or property of an organism *contributes to the organism's ability to survive and reproduce.*

Again, the concept is empirical. In principle, it is always possible to design an experiment or observation to determine if the characteristic actually does "function" as it is alleged to do. Moreover, biologists in general share both this definition of function—it originates with Darwin—and the recognition of the overwhelming importance of the concept. Biology has no "functionalist" schools of thought that oppose or distinguish themselves from other schools. Instead, the concept of function is the central integrating thread of *all* biology.

This concept of "function" is very widely applicable; it is not restricted to a few organisms or organ systems within an organism. It applies to *any* characteristic of an organism. An organism like a cat, a fern, or a bacterial cell possesses specific characteristics—whiskers, fronds, cell walls. We can *always* ask if and how that characteristic contributes to the organism's survival and ability to reproduce, that is, how it functions. These examples are of anatomical characteristics, but function also applies to processes. We can ask what functions are served by breathing, photosynthesis, transport through the cell membrane, or—even!—behavior. And when we do, the question is always: *How does this characteristic contribute to the organism's ability to survive and reproduce?*

Biological and Social Scientific Ideas of Function

For the non-biologist, *function* has connotations that can shadow one's thinking to cause confusion. Some distinctions are needed.

The first is illustrated by Marion S. Goldman's sociological analysis of prostitution on the Comstock silver lode of Nevada in the 19th century. She writes:

> The definition of prostitutes as deviant human beings not only legitimated respectable women's status, but also contributed to the solidarity and clarification of behavioral rules for everyone within the respectable community. Thus prostitution served general social *functions* for Comstock as a whole. (Goldman, 1981, pp. 9–10, italics added)

By "functions," she means not how prostitution contributed to survival or reproduction, as it might had the prostitutes had children. Rather, she means that for Comstock society, prostitution had social consequences that contributed to how people defined their own respectability.

This type of sociological analysis is very useful, for the division of women into two groups according to their sexual behavior is deeply embedded in North American traditions. Indeed, the differences between *respectable* and *not respectable,* or between *proper* and *improper,* are centrally important for understanding the sexual strategies women use (discussed in Chapters 5, 6, and 8). But only rampant confusion will result if such sociological meanings are confused with the *biological* meanings of function.

Second, the biological concept of functionality does *not* imply that a functional behavior is necessarily "good" or makes one "happy." A woman who has an "illegitimate" child may be considered "bad" by moralists and may suffer psychologically and socially. Yet, by definition, her behavior was as biologically functional as it would have been within different social circumstances—e.g., marriage. The biological definition of function is independent of the social and moral rules that make one and the same event sometimes "good" and sometimes not. (See the discussion of illegitimacy in Chapter 5.)

Third, the biological concept of function is profoundly different from the concept of *motivation*. Thus, kidneys have neither brains nor minds to hold or enact "motivations." Yet, when the kidney excretes liquids and salts, and when urination voids them, these processes serve the survival of the organism no matter what motivates the individual to urinate, simply because, physiologically, life requires an appropriate salt–water balance. The biological function of the kidney can therefore be defined without reference to behavioral or social scientific definitions of "motivation."

So it is with sexual intercourse. No matter what motivates an individual towards a sexual interaction—be it love, boredom, a yearning to fuse with another person, or sudden fascination—intercourse has a *biological* function in the production of offspring. Now, in the late Medieval Catholicism of Aquinas, an apperception of this biological function of intercourse was elevated into a moral, that is, *motivational, law.* Indeed, ethnobiological thought generally confuses biological functionality with motivation, even though a given human—or a pair of them— might be motivated to a sexual interaction for reasons of pleasure, bonding, love, a release of boredom, repression of anxiety, or a dozen and more additional possibilities. Only sometimes do people have intercourse expressly motivated by a desire to have children.

A behavior pattern does not have to be motivationally goal-directed to be biologically functional. One need not have intercourse *motivated* by reasons of biological functionality: the biological function is served by the behavior no matter what one's motivations and intentions are, or what social meanings or consequences the behavior has. In brief, biological functions are motivationally over-determined, but they retain their functionality nonetheless.

Behavior and Function

These distinctions between biological function, social effect, and personal motivation are a starting point of the biosocial approach. *At root, much of human behavor and culture is biologically functional even if people do not have any conscious knowledge of those functions, either personally or socially.* In brief, much may elude people about the *biological* functions of their behavior (especially when biology is confused with Nature!). But still, those functions exist, for behavior and culture may contribute to survival and reproduction in ways people do *not* consciously recognize.

Furthermore, around those biologically functional behavior patterns has grown a complex system of *cultural* explanations, motivations, and institutions. It is as if one could peel back culture to find a kernel of biological function at its center instead of nothing.

We can now ask the crucial question of the biosocial approach. To what extent are culture and human behavior *independent* of biological functionality? Does culture exist in a domain utterly free of biology and its functions, or do matters of biological functionality permeate even to our most elevated and precious cultural beliefs and institutions, those so often seen as *non*-biological? Can biological functions related to survival and reproduction be found at the root of *most* human behavior?

All social scientists would admit that *certain* kinds of human behavior—e.g., urination—have biological functions. But the question before us is subtler. Consider marriage, for example: it certainly is socially created and culturally shaped, and, equally certainly, no "genes" cause us to marry. Moreover, a woman can have an out-of-wedlock child as easily as having an in-wedlock child. But in the biosocial approach, we ask: Does marriage itself, as a social institution, as a religious ceremony, and as a personal and public celebration of love, nonetheless still serve biological functions? If so, what are they? In the biosocial approach we seek such functions especially when they seem hidden below culturally and socially learned behavior. The biosocial approach asks how far into culture do the tendrils of biological functionality reach.

I am also asking *how* human behavior patterns might serve such functions. It is obviously inadequate to say that "Intercourse produces offspring, and that is one of its biological functions." Of course. Rather, we must ask how gender role acquisition, the rules and paradigms of courtship, the modes and forms of love, the kinds and types of marriage, and even the division of labor by the sexes all have served and still do serve not only social but also *biological* functions. We must sift through the motivational, situational, and cultural complexity of these varied customs and habits to find, if possible, the biological needs that they meet.

Biosocial Functionality

The word *function* sounds quite bland, as if biological functions were somehow automatically taken care of by the body, that is, ensured by a kindly and wise Nature that endows its children with innate knowledge of what is biologically best for them. But when we define function by reference to survival and reproduction, the concept suddenly gains very sharp teeth. When the "biological functions" performed by an organism cease or go awry, the organism *dies*. Thus, despite the immense importance of the psychological and sociological dramas of our lives, biology—for example, in the form of food—comes first. True, in a vastly wealthy United States, our daily bread is not a major issue for most people. Yet, when we belittle biology, we behave like a young child whose mother feeds him: food is just there. "Biology doesn't affect *me*," he then (and later) believes. But if the economic and technological apparatus that meets our biological needs were to collapse, we might be less sure that we are above the merely "biological." Technology serves both to solve biological problems *and* to hide their existence and power from us.

However, throughout human history and throughout the history of all organisms over millenia of evolutionary time, biology has ruled life. These ruling biological processes do not operate or control us through "instincts" or other ethnobiological concepts. Instead, biology lays down the absolute and inescapable prerequisites for life to continue.

I want to give an example because, for the layperson such biological influences are often invisible. Although it concerns nutritional biochemistry, it nonetheless illustrates the central biological concept of this book: *biosocial functionality.*

A Nutritional Example: Vitamin C

Below the skin, and elsewhere in the body, is a protein called "collagen." It gives the skin and blood vessels their slight elasticity (when one pinches the skin momentarily and it snaps back, it is because collagen is elastic). Collagen also anchors the teeth to their sockets in the jaws, and has other functions as well. But collagen is not "just there," produced by magical processes of mute nature. Instead, collagen is synthesized by the cells of the body, like all proteins. And thereby hangs a tale, well known to biochemists (e.g., Stryer, 1981, pp. 186–187, 192; Lehninger, 1975, pp. 641–642), but probably not to others.

Cells synthesize collagen by assembling certain components of the diet, the amino acids, into a specific sequence (rather like assembling a chain of pop-it beads of different colors: one after the other). The order of amino acids in collagen is given by the sequence of what are called nucleotides in a specific portion of the DNA of the cell. Because the nucleotides in this region of DNA are arranged in a given order, they "encode" the sequence of amino acids in collagen (in a complex process that need not concern us). Since the DNA is the genetic material, the amino acid sequence of collagen is "genetically determined," a phrase that means *only* that there is a one-to-one relationship between the amino acid sequence of collagen and the nucleotide sequence of this region of DNA.

After the amino acids of collagen are assembled, one of them, called proline, is transformed into another amino acid, called hydroxyproline (as if we now put a little lump, called a hydroxyl group, on certain pop-it beads after having inserted them into the chain). Again, however, proline is converted to hydroxyproline not by some sort of magic, but because another biochemical process achieves the conversion. That process involves specific enzymes and a substance called ascorbic acid.

And where do *they* come from? These enzymes too are synthesized under the genetic control of the DNA (just as collagen itself is synthesized). Ascorbic acid is another matter. Most mammals synthesize ascorbic acid by still a *third* biochemical process which begins with dietary sugars and ends with ascorbic acid. This process too involves specific enzymes—*all* cellular biochemistry involves enzymes—and one of these enzymes has the specific function of converting something called gulonolactone into ascorbic acid, which can then be used during collagen synthesis.

It is such a complex-sounding system that one wants to take it for granted. But *that* would be a mistake. Unlike most mammals, human beings do *not* possess a stretch of DNA that encodes the enzyme which makes ascorbic acid from gulonolactone. Therefore, we are genetically unable to synthesize ascorbic acid. But collagen synthesis *still* requires ascorbic acid; without it, collagen will not be synthesized, and blood vessels and other structures that contain collagen will not function. For example, the ligaments holding the teeth in their sockets in the jaw are not maintained, and the teeth fall out (scurvy), and, finally, blood vessels weaken, collapse, and do not heal when damaged. The result is death.

All human beings therefore need a supply of ascorbic acid (vitamin C) from the diet. It is not that it would be *nice* to get ascorbic acid, or that once one is finished enacting the psychological and sociological dramas of life, one might get around to satisfying the demands of mute nature. If we do not obtain vitamin C, collagen synthesis does not occur, and we die.

No matter how involved we are in our daily dramas, these facts operate: find vitamin C or die. It is not that vitamin C prevents colds, nor anything else quite so optional. It is essential for life.

Moreover, these facts have held for all human beings who ever lived. With the force of logic, it follows that these people all *did* find sources for vitamin C. No doubt very, very few knew the biochemistry of collagen synthesis. Nonetheless, that biochemistry exists regardless of any conscious knowledge of it. Find vitamin C or die.

And when, over millenia, people *did* find it, are we to dismiss their actions as mute nature and of secondary importance to psychological or sociological drama? Even if certain social scientists might wish to do so, this example illustrates very well *how* biology works and *why* it has immense power over us. Biological processes lay down the inescapable and absolute requirements for life.

Now, no rule of Nature or biology guarantees that we *will* meet those reqirements. Yet, when we do—for example, when people eat fruit, motivated by the pleasant flavor or by far more complex social and psychological reasons—the biologist understands that no matter what these psychological or sociological processes are, *they are nonetheless biologically functional*. The tendrils of biology reach very far indeed into the daily dramas of life.

The vitamin C example thus serves as a paradigm for defining biosocial functionality. The laws of biology cannot be escaped, for they involve concrete and material genetic, cellular, and physiological processes. Accordingly, limits are established on behavioral variation. No individual can survive without vitamin C, and no society of individuals can set that fact aside through learning, custom, legislation, convention, or tradition. Any such custom would condemn its believers to death. In this, we find the reason behavior cannot vary infinitely widely over history or cultures, as the infinite regress of learning (in Chapter 1) implies it otherwise could. Behavior is biologically constrained, not by the mysterious Genes of the ethnobiologists, but by real and concrete facts that form the necessary conditions for life to continue. And when, often in ignorance of how the details of social phenomena meet these needs, we enact our seemingly purely cultural rituals and behavior patterns and thereby *meet* the requirements of biology, we may speak of *function* in the full biological sense for those cultural phenomena, or, in brief, of *biosocial functionality*.

Above all—and this is crucially important—the concept of biosocial functionality allows us to set aside the furious artillery of the Nature–Culture controversy. Instead of proclaiming that "Biology is an abhorrent doctrine of genetic causation," as social scientists say, or that "Biology is a true doctrine of genetic causation," as sociobiologists say, we can look for the biological *functions* of individual and cultural behavior, in whatever places and ways those functions might exist. If this replacement challenges the tyranny of customary modes of thought, as Bertrand Russell said (1912/1959, pp. 147, 157), then so be it. It may prove to be no small matter.

Adaptive Diversity in Courtship

Biologists call solutions to the biological needs of life "adaptations." The vitamin C example shows that adaptations can be quite varied—e.g., one can eat oranges *or* take vitamin C tablets from a bottle *or* do both. In fact, it is a centuries-old principle of biology: organisms of different species, or even one organism (e.g., a person) in the course of its own lifetime can meet the biological needs of its life in *extraordinarily* diverse ways.

For example, birds' wings are anatomically quite different from bats' wings or the wings of insects. Yet, in each organism, the function is the same—flight.

This principle is also central to the biosocial approach. Although nutritional physiology provides one avenue towards understanding human biosocial adaptations and their functions, *this* book is about love and sex. In contrast to ethnobiology, which sees biology—as Nature—answering reproductive needs through moral instincts, the biosocial approach begins with reproductive needs that must be met if life is to continue, and asks what biological, psychological, and cultural adaptations fill those needs. The biosocial approach sees the immense diversity of courtship and marriage customs not as evidence for cultural variation superimposed on biological fixity, nor as evidence for the moral or social superiority of one custom over another, but as evidence for diversity and inventiveness in how humans have solved the universal problems of sexual reproduction.

And universal they are. Human beings do not reproduce by budding, or by sending out runners like strawberry plants, or by telepathy. If people *en masse* were to cease their sexual activities and interactions, there would be no more people. However, nothing says that an individual will reproduce, no more than biology says that he or she will obtain vitamin C. Instead, biology lays down a contingency for any species: *reproduce or die.*

Around this inescapable biological need for reproduction have grown in different societies some immensely complex systems of habit, custom, ritual, belief, feeling, and institution—infant betrothal, chaperoned meetings, Polynesian nightcrawling, brother-sister marriage among ancient Egyptians, polygyny, polyandry, and our own customs, which range from lengthy engagements through meeting people in singles bars. For some people, the importance of such cultural variation is *moral,* for they believe that variation creates choices among forms of behavior.

Here, however, the importance of such variation is *scientific*. The biosocial approach begins not with moral questions, but, instead, seeks to trace out in sexual behavior the effects of an absolute and inescapable fact of reproductive biology: men and women must meet, court in one way or another, touch, and eventually make love or else vanish forever (Harrison, 1983, chapter 1, p. 11).

And do our *own* sexual customs serve biological and biosocial functions? Given how frequently moralists condemn modern sexual habits (e.g., the "promiscuity" of the singles scene) and given how frequently people despair of finding either mates *or* love, the question is not so simple. For example, the seeming chaos of a singles bar—the noise, the marketplace sexual atmosphere, the mercurial attachments and disattachments between people: are these things merely symptoms of license, decay, and collapse, indicators of a profound moral and social malaise, or does the singles scene serve quite real biosocial functions? We must not presume, in advance, that we know what biological functions a bar might serve, or what the biosocial functions of "promiscuity" might be (they are discussed in Chapter 6, where "promiscuity" will become something quite different).

When we ask about the biosocial functionality of courtship in North America of today we see culture and learning connected intimately to biology, but *not* through "genes" that cause, control, or encode human happiness and love. The linkages between biology, learning, and culture are far more complex than Nature versus Nurture. The biosocial approach does not promise simple answers—such as saying "The genes make us do it"—but, in its complexity, the biosocial approach is far more realistic than either pure genetic or pure cultural determinism.

The Biological Capacity for Behavioral Variation

But once again, we encounter an echo of ethnobiological thought. If courtship behavior serves universal biological functions, shouldn't courtship be universally fixed and unchanging in all societies and time? Doesn't "biology" require that all human behavior be the same everywhere? If marriage and courtship customs vary, isn't that variation evidence, as Bernard argued, for the *non*-biological origin of those customs? The answer is *No*.

When I was first taking biology courses, we had to watch amoebas. They are delightful little creatures, constantly extending pseudopods this way and that, moving slowly towards food, engulfing it and digesting it, always crawling about in the thin layer of water between the microscope slide and the microscope itself. Amoebas are single-celled beings—no brain, no language, no culture—only the single cell which *is* the amoeba. The amoeba is forever changing. It is not constant, its shape is not given, its behavior not fixed. Inside it, its physiology is also constantly changing, as its pseudopods extend and retract, as its digestive enzymes dissolve food and convert it into the protoplasm of the amoeba. The amoeba's life *is* its biology: not universal constancy among all amoebas everywhere, but *change*—continual, ever-recurring change.

Old-time biologists had a quaint phrase for the capacity of living organisms to change. "Irritability," they said, "is a property of living protoplasm." By that, they meant that the capacity to respond to the environment is inherently a *biological* fact: a feature of life itself (e.g., Burton-Opitz, 1928, p. 42; Giese, 1957, p. 385). The implication—and it is far-reaching—is that biology does not produce fixity *at all*.

But for some people, biology produces the fixity of dead pickled organisms in jars. Or, in a far more macabre image (from a sociologist), "[t]he physiologist cutting down a freshly hung man and slicing off his head feels curiosity more than horror" (Cuzzort, 1969, p. 322). There is profound hatred of biology in that phrase. It is also false.

Biology is not the science of death, but of shifting behavior, shifting shape and form, shifting activity, and of the processes that regulate those changes, to make them orderly and functional, rather than random, pointless squirmings. Difference and change are the fundamentals of *all* biology. I want to describe an example from my own work. Though it concerns copulatory interactions of rats, its implications are of great importance for thinking about *human* courtship.

Diversity in Animal Behavior

Copulatory behavior in rats is very unlike human sexual behavior. In specific, the interaction begins when we place a female rat with the male. She is in estrus (i.e., "receptive" to the male) and will allow him to mount her and, finally, to ejaculate. (Female rats not in estrus will ignore males or fight them off.) The sequence begins with the two animals approaching and sniffing each other. After a few moments, the female will suddenly dash away from the male in a stiff-legged run called a "hop and dart." The male follows her and, in a moment or so, mounts her, though without ejaculating yet. The mount takes only a few seconds and, after he has dismounted, the two animals separate briefly. She then again hops and darts, he follows her, and again mounts. During some of these mounts, he achieves penile intromission, but again does not ejaculate. This pattern of separations followed by mount (with or without intromission) occurs repeatedly for some minutes, until the male finally mounts, intromits, *and* ejaculates. This sequence is called a "copulatory series," and it begins with the animals nuzzling and ends with the male's ejaculation.

When observed superficially, the sequence seems remarkably stereotyped. But, when observed carefully, it becomes apparent that each sequence is somewhat different. In one series, the male may intromit 8 times; in another series at another time, he may intromit 12 times. In one series, the total time from start to ejaculation might be 2 minutes; in another, it might be 10 minutes. Another difference concerns the physical proximity of the two animals. When we tethered one of the two animals and allowed the other to visit the tethered animal, we found that the number of visits the freely moving animal makes to the tethered animal also varies (Krieger, Orr, and Perper, 1976; Perper, 1978; plus unpublished data). Some males will approach a tethered female and remain with her during the entire sequence, but other males approach, intromit, and then depart, only to visit the female again and again, until ejaculation. Likewise, females differ considerably: sometimes, a female will stay with a tethered male and other times she will repeatedly move towards and away from him.

To the casual observer, these variations are really quite slight and seem unimportant. Who cares what rats do? After all, the sequence itself is similar from time to time; it always involves a set of visits, mounts, intromissions, and departures, terminated by the ejaculation. But something very important lurks behind the seemingly trivial quantitative variation in the sexual behavior of these rats.

What explains all these variations? Could they be produced by changes in *partners?* Thus, if male A copulates first with female 1 and later with female 2, will his behavor change with a new partner? Likewise, does the female's behavior change with a new partner?

We found that *every* component of the animals' behavior changed when the partner was changed, and changed quite consistently. With certain females, the males had fewer intromissions and took less time to ejaculate than with other females. With certain females, the male would visit and stay with them, but with other females, he would depart after each intromission. Likewise, some tethered males consistently elicited high frequencies of visiting and departing by females, but with other males, the same females would not depart.

Throughout the entire experiment, we observed such effects over and over: what the animal did depended on who the partner was.

We obtained some dramatic examples of this ability to change behavior. When the male is tethered and the female free to visit and depart, she typically visits only briefly, and he can intromit only if she stays with him long enough. However, the total number of intromissions achieved by the tethered male varied quite considerably—from 15 down to three or four. To what was this variation due?

We quickly found that the number of intromissions depended upon *two* behavior patterns of the female. The first was the number of visits she made to the male. For example, one female might visit a given male six times, and he might intromit five times and then ejaculate. Another female might visit him 12 times, and he might intromit eight times before ejaculating. Now, this is a peculiar result. Imagine that the male has "programmed" into him a requirement for a fixed number of intromissions before ejaculating, say, 10. Then, when the female had visited only six times, and he had only six intromissions, he would simply wait for her to visit another four times, to reach his predetermined number of intromissions and ejaculate. But that did not happen: the male's behavior depended on what the female did. In a word, the males were *adjusting* their behavior in response to the female's behavior.

The second factor causing variation in the number of intromissions was how long the female stayed away from the male. If she stayed away 90 percent of the time (say), then the number of intromissions was reliably *lower* than the number obtained with a female who stayed away only 35 percent of the time, say. Again, the male's behavior was changing according to what the female was doing.

Female rats also changed their behavior according to who the male was. For example, some males elicited many hops and darts whereas other males elicited far fewer from the same females. Likewise, the number of visits the females made to a tethered male depended on who the male was.

There are two kinds of mutual responsiveness here. First, if the female does A, then the male does B in response. That is one level of responsiveness. Second, however, if the *next* female does C, the male does *not* wait around until she finally does A so he can respond by doing B. Instead, he *adapts* to the new female and responds to her by changing his *own* behavior—that is, now he does D. We have here the capacity to respond and the capacity to *change* the response.

So, in these rats, the males respond to the females and the females to the males. There is a loop or cycle between the two animals, and each mutually and reciprocally influences the other. It is *not* that one animal—the male *or* the female—is somehow in charge, and the other simply passively responds. Instead, the interaction is dyadic. Even if the casual observer thinks that the sequence is stereotyped and is read out of preexisting tape, *the sequence is actually created interactively moment by moment.*

I stress the word *created.* At the beginning of the interaction, neither animal possesses a predetermined quantitative pattern of behavior. Instead, moment-by-moment each *alters* its behavior in response to the other. Their behavior is determined not by indwelling or preexisting tapes, but by the process of the interaction itself.

We performed many experiments like these (and some with gerbils: Waring and Perper, 1979, 1980). The results were always self-consistent. No matter what behavior pattern we looked at, it arose interactively and was *not* pre-determined. The animals were capable of exquisitely fine-tuned adjustments of their own behavior in response to other animals' behavior.

I stress these observations because they show that behavioral variation is a fact of *biology.* Rats have no culture to teach them to behave in different ways at different times; they have no symbols with which to communicate and with which to change each others' attitudes and behavior; they have no language that instructs them how to behave in different ways; they have no minds (at least as far as we can tell) that enable them to conceive of rules of behavior that specify when to behave this way and when not. Instead, rats have only their "biology"—*an immensely complex set of physiologically real capacities and abilities to respond to the environment and change their behavior accordingly.*

Yet the result is really quite curious. If these were people, we would say, "Of course! People influence each other all the time!" But rats are not people. Yet they also respond to each other and influence each other. Thus, I suggest that when people interact, our capacity to change and adjust our behavior as our surroundings change is a fact of biology.

An example familiar to many social scientists is "experimenter demand" (Orne, 1962). Subjects in an experiment try to guess its purposes and the results the experimenter wants, and then unconsciously but cooperatively try to provide those answers. The phenomenon irritates and frustrates the laboratory scientist, who doesn't want such "invented" responses, but the subject's "real" response. However, the phenomenon is *much* more than an experimental nuisance, for it illustrates the organism's capacity to adjust its behavior according to the requirements of its environment—or to what it *perceives* those requirements to be.

Yet the conclusion that these capacities are biological may puzzle someone who is mired in the Nature/Nurture dichotomy: "But if so, then you are saying that human behavior is not learned, and that is false!" *Of course* human cultural behavior is learned! But the human capacity for learning is a property of our living organisms, and, in particular, arises from the physiologically real processes of thought and mental activity in the brain, rather than being alterations in Disembodied Minds.

These ideas have a remarkable implication: we cannot explain human behavioral variation by referring to a fixed biology plus a variable and superimposed culture. *There is no such thing as "fixed biology."*

Because the capacity to modify one's behavior is *inherently* a property of the living organism, it follows that human behavioral diversity and capabilities for change are examples of a true biological universal: the property of living matter to alter and adjust to the conditions of its existence. To the biologist, human culture and all its rich diversity are all forms of "irritability": vast and complex, but still inherently biological.*

---

*Some readers may feel that I am "reducing" human behavior to biology. Typically, one "reduces" problem A to problem B to find its solution in the simpler domain of the logic or facts of field B. *But there is nothing simple about biology.* If it is "biological" to write poetry, that fact does not make poetry "simple." It means that the neurophysiology of writing poetry is *very* complex. True, ethnobiological thought is often simplistic, and its recourse to Nature or the Genes is often done reductionistically. But again I stress that ethnobiology has nothing to do with biology—nor always with facts, as Eberhard's ancient eunuch lifeguard without any family illustrates quite well.

Second, I am aware of the difficulties of seeing all human behavior as necessarily having a neurophysiological basis. For some readers, "mind" and "brain" partially overlap, and both have their own separate domain of existence. Philosophically, I take the opposite stand and suspect that our theories of mind and brain are *both* primitive—really only one step beyond speaking about phlogiston as responsible for fire, or about the four humors as responsible for mood. Indeed, it is in the study of the brain and how its neurophysiology produces mind that we perceive the last tendrils of Medieval thought, for the notion of separable mind and brain is not merely dualism in Descartes' sense, but dualism in the Medieval sense of body and soul, of lower and higher faculties. Yet I know all too well that for some readers *any* kind of biology is always reductionism, and no words from me will convince them otherwise.

Aronson's (1984) discussion of scientific reduction (which I read after writing the comments above) may clarify my intentions. In a specific *technical* sense of philosophy, my program is in fact "reductionist." Aronson says about scientific reduction that it asserts " . . . that the entities and properties which are the subject matter of the reduced science(s) [here, the social sciences] are identified (the same as) with the entities and properties referred to in the reducing science [here, biology]" (p. 215). Thus, "culture" and "learning" (which are conceptual entities and processes in the social sciences) are *identified* with conceptual entities and properties in biology, namely, with the biological capacities of individuals to respond to changes in their environment by creating adaptive social and individual solutions to those changes. Accordingly, the verb "to reduce" does *not* mean "to trivialize." Instead, as Aronson, and I, use it, *to reduce* means *to map* the two sciences onto each other, so that concepts and ideas in one are, in essence, the same as concepts and ideas in the other. Even though each science retains its own

In fact—and it ought to make us more modest—we are only highly evolved, talkative, and sociable amoebas, who crawl about this way and that. However, we *also* sometimes believe—like the delirious but intelligent clavichord so sardonically described by Diderot (ca. 1782/1956, p. 108)—that we possess disembodied Minds and Ideas which raise us above the *merely* physical, the *merely* biological. But we are misled. We refuse to see that if the sounds we make when we are played are those of a clavichord (or a person!), it is because, internally, we have the hammers, strings, and sounding boards that shape our sounds and make them different from those of an oboe, an electric guitar, or an Aeolian harp. But the music a clavichord makes is not fixed; it could be Bach or jazz-rock. In analogy, so too with culture: if we have culture, it is because the human brain and body cause us to create and transmit culture with all its diverse themes and variations according to the functional needs of our lives. But sometimes we too think like Diderot's delirious clavichord, and also wish to stand above mere mechanics—mere biology!—and to imagine, instead, that ours is a disembodied music that is, ultimately, independent of biology.

Biological Activity, Not Passivity

Thus, the biosocial approach involves much more than recognizing that culture adapts human beings to the conditions and necessities of life. Although such statements are a cornerstone of anthropology, they can be taken too far, and lead us to see people as essentially *passive* vehicles for enacting learned cultural rules (see Appendix). If biology teaches us anything, it is that the organism is *active* and brings to its social life a set of biological capacities to change and adapt itself to the altering conditions of its life.

This biological capacity is not restricted to copulating rats. For example, individuals of the small, herb-like plant *Potentilla* produce long stems and broad leaves when grown in moist shade, but develop shorter stems and thinner leaves when they grow in moist but sunny soil (Grant, 1963, pp. 120–122). All gardeners will recognize this ability of plants to change their growth habits under different conditions, though they may not know how universal the capacity really is.

Such biological capacities for variation are incompatible with the ethnobiological idea that genes program behavior or, if left to their own devices, produce behavioral fixity. In fact, genetic effects on *molecular* biological activities are magnified to produce not fixity, but the capacity for adaptive variation within biologically adaptive limits.

What the genes do: I. Molecules and magnification. In social scientific and sociobiological ethnobiology, if a behavior pattern like courtship is "genetic," then

viewpoint and terminology (p. 218), these viewpoints now see phenomena previously thought to be unrelated as having a "common ontology," which, for Aronson, refers to a set of assumptions, principles, conclusions, and ideas about nature and its rules that are shared in common by the two sciences. There is now a common explanatory ground, so to speak, in the new ontology. For more details of how reduction has been achieved in the sciences, and for further discussion of this "ontology," the reader is referred to Aronson's book, especially Chapter 8.

it is "read out" of a genetic tape stored somewhere in the body, just as a tape player plays out music or words stored on a tape. In this view, there is no room for behavioral variation or diversity because the tape never changes. It is part of the fixed "genetic endowment" of the organism, "encoded" into its genes. Variation in courtship or marriage can then arise *only* if "culture" or "learning" superimposes itself on the tape, to cause it to be played out differently in different situations or times or even to drown it out completely. Once, say in 1910, behavioral and social scientists could make such attributions to heredity, but in the past 30 and more years since the development of molecular genetics, we now *know* that genes do not, and cannot, produce such fixities.

The vitamin C example above illustrates quite well that one role of the genes in behavior is very different from that of personified little beings living somewhere within our bodies. Genes are very small molecules of DNA that typically function by providing a molecular pattern for encoding the amino acid sequence of enzymes or other chemically related molecules, like collagen. In biology, this is the only meaning of the phrase "genetic code": a set of relationships between certain nucleotide sequences in DNA and certain amino acids to be assembled into proteins.

The meaning is easy to elaborate into a vast metaphysical "story" in which DNA is the "code of life," but such stories are biological nonsense. Genes do not think, feel, or embody instincts. They cannot be selfish. They are chemical molecules, *nothing more*. In ethnobiology, the genes are treated as the prime movers of life, a role they *cannot* have biologically.

Yet the genes *can* affect behavior. Since they are like very small parts of a huge machine, usually their individual effects are small (though cumulative). But when something goes wrong with a gene—like the genetic inability of human beings to synthesize the enzyme that makes ascorbic acid—then a long train of events begins that ends with effects on behavior: human beings need foods that contain vitamin C. But no geneticist would predict, *in advance,* how a given gene will influence behavior: the chains of causation between chemical molecules and behavioral action are too complex (geneticists call such chains "pleiotropies"). Would one guess that because collagen is made (in part) when proline is converted into hydroxyproline that it is functional—and not merely a pleasure—to eat citrus fruits? Hardly! Though a charlatan might claim that such chains are easy to see, and a non-geneticist might believe that genes are simple, it is tedious, hard work to analyze the chain of causes and effects between genes and behavior (Fuller and Thompson, 1978; Scheller and Axel, 1984; Katz and Schall, 1979; Fuller and Simmel, 1983).

Nonetheless, pleiotropies like this exist. Analyzing them is somewhat like looking at the machine that goes *pocketa-queep, pocketa-queep* in Thurber's *The Secret Life of Walter Mitty* and determining which of its cogs, gears, wires, and transistors is awry. Only in fantasy does Walter Mitty do so immediately. Unfortunately, however, many ethnobiologists think one can simply look at the biological engine that is our body and see all the connections between its parts. It is also unfortunate that many social scientific *critics* of sociobiology accept such ethnobiological fantasies as biology and genetics when they are not.*

But, even so, we can describe how genes do and do not affect behavior, at least in principle. First, they do not "determine" behavior in the sense of "encoding" it, because it is physiologically impossible for the sequence of nucleotide molecules in DNA to contain enough biological information to do so. In analogy, one cannot look at a television set and say, in imagination, that *that* transistor—that one and no other—is responsible for or "encodes" everything the set does, from receiving football games and telecasts of operas, to humming quietly and blankly when it is tuned between channels. DNA is chemically *very* complex, but not even DNA is complex enough to "encode" our behavior.

No, genes do *not* "program" behavior. Instead, they create the *need* for one or more given behavior patterns. Thus, our genetic inability to make ascorbic acid eventually causes a dietary need for it. But the genes do not murmur "Eat oranges." Rather, they create a need that can be *satisfied* by eating oranges or lemons, *or* by taking vitamin C supplements from a bottle. Such needs are quite powerful—after all, life depends on meeting them—but the genes do not "encode an instinct" for eating oranges. *That* concept is ethnobiological, for it attributes to Nature a sort of near-Divine Wisdom for shaping our lives towards survival and (sometimes) happiness. *Biologically*, genes are simply small memory storage devices which typically encode the sequence of amino acids in proteins. When the genetic "memory system" fails—as in the case of the human genetic inability to make ascorbic acid—life does not necessarily cease. The organism *compensates* by finding ascorbic acid in food, if it can.

It is sometimes said that the genes contain the "wiring diagram" for our bodies and therefore for behavior. The analogy is pleasant, for it makes the genes seem familiar and simple. But this analogy is also false: like transistors in a television set, the genes are simply molecules within the body. They do not "contain" the wiring diagram, or act autonomously to orchestrate or direct the development of the embryo.

Instead, anatomical and behavioral development occurs through what biologists call "epigenetic" programming (*epi-* means *on top of*), in which the genes are turned on and off in the properly functional sequence as the embryo grows. Although epigenetic programming is both complex and subtle, the major idea can be explained without too many technicalities.

In essence, when genes are activated, they function as governors or regulators

---

*When is it genetically legitimate to speak of "pleiotropic genetic determination" of behavior? Broadly, there are two procedures for identifying and analyzing genetic pleiotropies. One, "from gene to behavior," is illustrated in the text, and requires that the "gene" in question be known to exist by rigorous molecular or biochemical tests. The vitamin C example meets these criteria. The second, "from behavior to gene," is the classical procedure and is far harder, but very elegant when done successfully (e.g., Truslove, 1956; Thiessen, 1965). Given the widespread ethnobiological desire glibly to impute behavior to the "genes" without much evidence at all, the explicit use of these criteria should probably be adopted by writers who discuss the genetic bases of human social behavior.

to prevent (pre- or post-natal) development from going too far off course, a process classically called "canalization of development" or "developmental buffering." [The idea is not new in biology: Dobzhansky, 1970; Waddington, 1962; Rendel, 1967; Lerner, 1954/1970; Mordkoff, Schlesinger, and Lavine, 1964; see E. B. Wilson (1925) for the classic statement of the problem and its general solution, and Mitton and Grant (1984) for a recent review.] Canalization explains why organisms do not display the unlimited variation of the kind that plagues the Lamarckian theories of Chapter 1: certain combinations of genes (which differ in different species) function together to establish limits on how a particular organism can develop.

An analogy, though it is very rough, is a door stop that prevents a door from slamming into a wall: a small piece of metal can have large and quite functional effects on how the door "behaves." A very dramatic example of how physiology limits change concerns food and weight gain. If, between the ages of 15 and 45, a person eats 2 pounds of food per day, then in these 30 years, the person has eaten $2 \times 365 \times 30 = 21,900$ pounds, or nearly 11 *tons* of food. Yet people do not swell up to the size of trailer trucks; they just swell up a little, gaining perhaps 10 to 20 pounds. The reason, of course, is that food is broken down, and its nutrients are used to replace the carbohydrates, fats, and proteins that the body utilizes in its daily activities. Collectively, these processes of digestion, replacement, and excretion all depend on enzymes and therefore on the *genes* which specify the structures of those enzymes. In brief, the maintenance of body weight within a fairly narrow range (compared to *total* intake) depends on complex, gene-controlled physiological mechanisms which limit development and change. Those limits are established dynamically, by processes of intake and replacement, rather than by mysterious "Genes" that know how much we should weigh.

Since Darwin, biologists have concluded that evolution itself creates and maintains these genetic limits on development. However, evolution does not operate through the Lamarckian's vision of a kindly God Who prevents variation from exceeding certain limits, but through the concrete conditions of life that confront an organism. (In evolutionary jargon, genetic limits on developmental variation are maintained by processes collectively called "normalizing selection.") And why should such limits exist? In biology, we convert that question into another about function: what functions do these limits serve? The answer is that these evolved and gene-regulated developmental processes are responsible for producing the adaptations of an organism—a bird's wings, a cat's claws, or the human brain. Thus, "canalized" limits on developmental variation function to preserve the life of the organism by restricting developmental variation to what has proved functional in the evolutionary past (at least within the limits of the possible—after all, nothing is perfect). And, if the reader will forgive me if *I* personify nature for a moment, it stands to reason that quality control during development is necessary if the final product is to be optimal! But even without personification, it is by now clear in biology that the genes perform very important functions when they prevent development from wandering too far off course, in either anatomy *or* behavior.

Furthermore, physical anthropologists and primatologists are discovering increasingly striking similarities between humans and our closest primate relatives (Fox, 1980). For example, during copulation, pigmy chimpanzees gaze intently into each other's eyes (Hrdy, 1981, p. 137). Such similarities must somehow be inherited, for no one claims that *cultural* transmission accounts for them (Fisher, 1982; Hrdy, 1981; Fedigan, 1982; Zillmann, 1984). In the back of our minds we must always recall that human behavior is not as unique or as unprecedented as we might proudly want to believe. For example, I suspect that the development of sexual templates, like those mentioned in Chapter 1, is "canalized"; that is, templates can develop in primates in only a few directions (thereby to exclude ferns and include other primates, such as other people).

But, for now, it seems wiser not to speculate too far or too fast. Instead, I will begin with the concept of biosocial functionality, and with the idea that, whether we know it or not, many human social and individual behavior patterns have served immensely important biological functions. That idea, and neither the intricate technicalities of modern genetics, nor the ethnobiological concept of genes that embody Natural wisdoms, motivations, hopes, and ideas, will be the central thread of my analysis.*

What the genes do: II. Altruism once again. Finally, what of altruism? How can an organism sacrifice its life (or risk doing so) to save another life? (By "altruism," I now mean an act that rescues another individual from certain or near-certain death, rather than the far more complex forms of altruism involved, for example, in religion.)

The problem of altruism is crucial to evolutionary genetics: if evolution depends on transmitting one's genes, how is it possible for an individual to *sacrifice* those genes to save another life? Such activities seem to make no *genetic* sense, even if they are considered the highest forms of ethical behavior. If we have thrown out the "genes" as prime movers of all behavior and if, simultaneously, we see learning and behavioral diversity as deriving from biology itself, is there anything left over with which to explain how altruistic capacities evolve?

The question is important partly because sociobiology prides itself on being able to explain the evolution of altruism (with its postulates of genes for altruism and the *r*-calculation). The least the biosocial approach must do is provide ideas towards an explanation that is self-consistent and neither personifies the genes nor slights culture.[†]

Genetically, altruism can evolve only if the altruist and beneficiary have genes in common. If I decided to save the life of a rosebush, set on fire by some accident, and I burned myself to death in the attempt, no one would speak of "altruism" and, in fact, no genetic benefit would come to me. Rosebushes and people are so genetically dissimilar that my effort would simply cost me all my genes (i.e., my

*This decision may upset the evolutionary biologist and geneticist. However, the problem is evidence: we lack the kind of information needed to draw firm conclusions or even form reasonable hypotheses about the genetics of the human behavior patterns I am discussing.

†My argument starts from assumptions similar to those of Trivers (1971) but does not assume that altruism has strong "genetic" components in animals (p. 36) or humans (p. 48).

life). If enough people (madly) tried to rescue burning rosebushes at such high cost, eventually the survivors would decide that there was no advantage to *that,* and such "altruism" would disappear.

So, we of course assume that the altruist saves the lives of other *people.* But there is a subtlety here. We are not discussing modern life, but the ancestral conditions of human existence when altruism *first* evolved in its human or proto-human forms. In *those* days, our ancestors did not live in large communities, but in small groups that wandered here and there, or remained in one area, hunting and gathering and trying to survive (Lee and DeVore, 1968). Genetically, all such small groups will become inbred; that is, after a while (six to eight generations living in isolation from other groups), group members can share upwards of 90 to 95 percent of all their genes with everyone else. They are virtually a clone, in other words.*

Moreover, small inbred groups like these develop some purely genetic adaptations. To simplify somewhat, the existing genes function particularly well with other groups of genes in the population [geneticists call such groups of genes in one individual a "coadapted genome," where "genome" refers to all the genes an individual possesses (Shields, 1982; Mayr, 1970; Dobzhansky, 1970; see also Mitton and Grant, 1984)].

If, now, the effect of *learned or acquired* altruism is to rescue such coadapted genomes in other members of the same small population, then, for the altruist, altruism sustains no large cost compared to the *benefit* of rescuing, say, only two such coadapted genomes possessed by two other individuals. If the average degree of genetic similarity is 90 percent between all the genes of the altruist and beneficiary, then by rescuing two beneficiary genomes, the altruist has a net benefit of 1.8 in saving identical genes if altruism does not kill the altruist, or of 0.9 if it does. If *three* such beneficiary genomes are rescued, even at the cost of the altruist's life, then the net benefit in identical genes saved is $(3.0 \times 0.9) - 1.0$ (for the altruist itself), to give a positive balance of 1.7 genomes rescued. Clearly, the process is not *genetically* disadvantageous for the altruist, even if no one *wants* to lose his or her life.

In this, the genetic "target" of altruism is no longer genes "identical by descent" in other individuals [as originally proposed by Hamilton (1964a, 1964b) and which implies that altruism can evolve and persist only if it is directed to the nuclear family]. Thus, altruism need *not* be directed to "close kin" in order to have

---

*"Inbreeding" does not mean "incest," and, as I am describing it, does not have the bad "eugenic" effects typically attributed to incestuous inbreeding. As a technical note, Li (1955, Chapters 15 and 16) stresses that genetic similarity will increase in any small, closed population, *no matter what* breeding system is operating. See also Selander and Johnson (1973), Stern (1973, Chapter 28), Bodmer and Cavalli-Sforza (1976, p. 426). The data are quite classic, but are still acceptable (Shields, 1982, p. 85). Since this is a selection argument, the existence of selectively neutral (e.g., electrophoretic) variation does not undercut the discussion. By definition, selection "sees" selectively neutral alleles as equivalent, and the altruist can rescue any selectively neutral variant with equal advantage (or disadvantage). Furthermore, if the 5 to 10 percent figure underestimates heterozygosity, the argument in the text is strengthened, provided that coadaptation is maintained, as discussed next.

a genetic benefit. Instead, it can be directed to *anyone* who was born and lives in the altruist's own community of birth and rearing. In such communities, known genetic mechanisms, inbreeding and coadaptation (Shields, 1982; Bateson,1983b; see also Ford, 1964, e.g., Chapter 15) can relatively quickly produce sufficiently great genetic similarities between altruist and any possible beneficiaries to make altruism *genetically* advantageous.

But here we encounter a second subtlety. In effect, when an altruist rescues another individual, he or she has preserved an *already* existing genome in the other individual. It is as if the altruistic act merely undid whatever disaster or calamity threatened the beneficiary's life. It is as if it never happened. Of course, that result is positive, but we must observe that this kind of altruism merely preserves already existing genes and individuals (the same comment applies to the sociobiological explanation as well; see Michod, 1982, pp. 41–42). A second process must occur if altruism is to evolve further than merely preserving existing genes.

That process is reproductive, and in part concerns the 5 to 10 percent of the genes that *differ* between the altruist and beneficiary. In small populations, inbreeding typically does not produce 100 percent genetic identity, because certain genes function best when they are heterozygous, not homozygous (such genes are called "heterotic"). Without technicalities, this phenomenon can be illustrated by sickle cell anemia, the defect in hemoglobin that is widespread in parts of Africa and among American Blacks. Together, two sickle cell genes are typically fatal, but one sickle cell gene plus one normal hemoglobin gene, while producing potentially dangerous problems, simultaneously confers elevated resistance to malaria. Thus, the heterozygote, with its combination of a sickle cell and a normal hemoglobin gene, is at an advantage in malarial environments compared to either homozygote (the person with two normal hemoglobin genes or with two sickle cell genes).

Thus, if the altruist "calculates" the costs and benefits of altruism, the full calculation goes as follows. First, the altruist preserves the 90 percent of the beneficiary's genome that is identical to the altruist's own genome. Second, the altruist rescues genes that *differ* from his or her own, but that can have advantages when combined with the altruist's own genes. However, such "combination" can occur only reproductively, either if the altruist mates with the beneficiary or if the altruist's offspring can do so. In this case, altruism rescues the "heterotic" genes that can confer enhanced survival and therefore reproductive capacities to members of the next generation (for example, by conferring disease resistance, although other possibilities also exist). In total, the altruist has advantageously preserved *100 percent* of the beneficiary's genes, composed of those that are identical to the altruist's plus those that differ but can confer later reproductive heterotic advantage.

Moreover, if we are considered *social* organisms—and our ancestors certainly must have qualified!—then any two individuals can make the same "calculation" when they encounter someone in danger, so that each can advantageously try to rescue that individual. Trivers' "reciprocal altruism" (1971) thus occurs between genetically virtually identical individuals, whose genetic "interests" are very similar, and the problem of "cheaters" who fail to reciprocate is reduced or eliminated. Collaborative or social altruism then becomes possible, with its reduction in risks for each altruist individually. And, from *that* can emerge proto-cultural and cultural rules for codifying when, how, and with whom one is altruistic.

Thirdly, however, reproduction itself is paradoxically a form of altruism. To be sure, reproduction ensures the transmission of the genes in parent A, but biologically only half the genes in the offspring come from parent A. The other half come from someone else, so that reproduction serves also to transmit *parent B's* genes (more precisely, one-half of them). It is as if parent A had rescued those genes in parent B, this time not from death by drowning, say, but from reproductive oblivion. Accordingly, when they reproduce together, parent A "rescues" parent B's genes, and vice versa. Moreover, geneticists who study the evolutionary genetics of reproduction have stressed that reproduction also has potential or real *costs* (again, like altruism). For the female especially, those costs can be high. Pregnancy puts considerable metabolic demands on the mother, e.g., for increased protein, calcium, and iron intake, as well as posing dangers of death at childbirth or immediately after. (Prior to modern medicine, those dangers were *very* real.) It stands to reason, as Darwin first noted, that females should be fairly choosy about their mates and, as I will stress later, about the social and emotional circumstances of mating. After all, the female has a good deal to lose if she makes a mistake. But, as Searcy (1982) has recently commented, if females *can* choose their mates, it is to their genetic benefit if they pick males who carry genes that confer heterotic advantage (Searcy, 1982, especially pp. 63–65). In turn, such genes confer *added* benefit to the offspring, for example, in disease resistance. Thus, when an altruist rescues from death those 5 to 10 pecent of heterotic genes in another individual, he or she does more than merely *preserve* them: altruism makes them available to the next generation. And, because those genes help confer disease resistance (say), everyone benefits: the altruist, individuals who can mate with the beneficiary of altruism, the resulting offspring. In brief, small, inbred populations represent precisely the contexts in which learned or acquired altruism will have large genetic benefits.*

My intention here is to clarify some qualitative aspects of the early evolution of human altruism, not to analyze its later development into its full-fledged cultural forms. The analysis is simply not subtle enough to do so. But, on the other hand, sociobiological explanations for altruism do not explain religious altruism either. However, whereas modern sociobiology apparently can cope with religion only by postulating genetically "constrained" learning (as did E. O. Wilson, 1978, p. 177),

---

*A critic skeptical of the biosocial approach should note that it is *not* underlain or premised on the preceding analysis of altruism. For the geneticist, I will add that my informal and brief sketch centers on recognizing that "altruism" does no more than preserve existing genetic material and that if altruism—of *any* origin: cultural, genetic, *or* biosocial—is to have further genetic benefit, it must enhance reproductive success. One way it can do so is by preserving heterotic alleles for future sexual selection, but there is, obviously, a balance between natural selection against too great heterozygosity, sexual selection favoring it within limits, and genetic drift (Bateson, 1983b).

biosocial explanations are free to understand religious altruism as cultural elabora-
tions of simpler and far older forms of altruism that, in ancestral days, concerned
practical and secular realities, not spiritual benefits. (I return to some biosocial
functions of religion in Chapter 8).

Moreover, two closely similar, coadapted genomes will develop in a social
environment that is similar (by hypothesis) for the two of them. That environment
should then produce organisms—people—able to learn very similar *cultural* rules
for altruism and its reciprocation (Mauss, 1925/1967)—with immense effects.

Thus, the story is told that when Carl Friedrich Gauss was a boy—he later
became one of the greatest of all mathematicians, reckoned the equal of Newton and
Archimedes—he was rescued from drowning by an unknown laborer (Bell, 1956,
p. 297). If we ask what benefit accrued from that act, are we to be content by saying
that genetically there was none, merely because the boy and his rescuer "shared"
no genes by recent or familial common descent, that is, that $r = 0$ between them?
That calculation misses something, I think; and what it misses is that that act of
altruism preserved the life of a genius from whose later discoveries *all* modern
mathematics arose. Must we not calculate the genetic consequences of that laborer's
altruism to include the effects of mathematics on the modern world itself? In *fact* the
answer is *yes,* even if those consequences are both positive and negative, in
life-saving technology and in potentially world-destroying weaponry; *yes,* even if
the thought lacks simplicity of the sociobiologist's r-calculation; and *yes,* even if the
laborer knew not the effects of his act.

The point, I hope, is clear: in a system of communicative, social, and talkative
beings, like people, the effects of altruism are greatly amplified and far transcend
any simple calculus of genetic relatedness by *family* descent. Altruism of this kind
affects *everyone,* merely because everyone shares sufficient genes (perhaps greater
than 90 percent) to cause them to be born human and, thereby, to become members
of a social community in which a seemingly simple act amplifies itself and
reverberates through the culture that those shared genes themselves make possible.
And that fact is implied by my argument above, which sets "altruism" not into a
world of isolated and mutually indifferent lines of genetic descent, but into a world
of beings who are similar genetically and culturally. No man nor woman is an
island, not even a genetic island, isolated from others by a barrier called "$r = 0$."*

---

*If a sociobiologist reader now exclaims, "But then we cannot explain the genetic origin of altruism,
nor explain how it spreads genetically!" the point is that altruism need not spread "genetically" nor be
of "genetic" origin. Specific forms of altruism can be learned by an organism, provided it has the
general, genetic capacity to do so. And, in turn, that capacity can evolve in the small groups discussed
in the text.

Although the general topic of homosexuality is beyond the scope of this book, the altruism argument
has important implications for the evolution of male homosexual behavior. Weinrich (1976) suggested
that non-reproductive male homosexuality (as opposed to bisexuality) can evolve if such males contribute
otherwise to close kin, e.g., economically. His argument is hardly changed if "close kin" becomes the
"whole kin group," as in my discussion. Pillard and Weinrich (1984) have recently found evidence that
male homosexuality runs in families, though they do not speculate whether for genetic or non-genetic
reasons. If so, and if such descent groups existed in the evolutionary past, then community or group

Finally, this argument does not personify the genes. Instead, like *all* evolutionary arguments, it recognizes that, for a behavior pattern to evolve and persist, there must be genetic benefits in enhanced survival and reproduction associated with it (e.g., by preserving heterotic genes). But such genetically advantageous behavior patterns do not *themselves* have to be of "genetic" origin to have those genetic benefits. Indeed, learned behavior—like altruism—may have evolutionary and genetic advantages so large that those advantages ultimately lead to the evolution of organisms *better* able to respond to their environments by adaptive and appropriate changes in behavior (Chapter 2, page 31).

These conclusions are at the biological heart of the biosocial approach. In the remainder of the book I will apply them to modern courtship behavior, as it can be seen in the United States and Canada today. We shall need no elaborate ethnobiological apparatus of selfish genes, r-calculations, or such personifications of Nature. Nor shall we confront a never-ending regress of learning that takes us back to the beginning when men and women lived, idyllically or not, in a state of Nature. Those are the trappings of mythology, sometimes romantic, sometimes not, that sees human beings not in their biological complexity, but as enacting roles in a great drama composed around an ineluctable war betwen Nature and Culture, Male and Female. Instead, we shall see a thoroughgoing interpenetration of biological and cultural processes, based, ultimately on the organism's biological capacity to adjust and alter itself in response to the needs of its life and to create and transmit culturally the functional solutions to those needs.

Biology and Courtship

When Bernard wrote that there is literally nothing about marriage that anyone can imagine that has not in fact taken place, she used such diversity to argue that no biologically real universal exists in or about marriage. But it is not so. Men do not marry turtles, nor do women marry ferns. Typically, they marry each other. And why is *that?*

Underneath the immense diversity of custom, habit, and terminology of human courtship and marriage exists an irreducible and inescapable biological reality. Men and women must find each other, court in one way or another, and mate. Under the diversity of courtship and marriage, there exists a universal that is not produced by a Nature which creates all-powerful instincts to mate, played out genetically, fixedly, and stupidly. Instead, it arises—universally—because humans reproduce sexually. So it is not marriage, as Westerners know it, that exists universally; instead, the diversity of institutions concerning courtship and mating all serve one and the same universal biological *function*—reproduction.

Thus, when men possess templates for women, and women for men, it is

bonds between them and other descent groups may have provided a basis for the evolution of a generalized capacity for "homo-" or "bi-" sexual behavior in men (Green, Simon, and Harry, 1984).

reproductively *functional*. Not merely do people not fall in love with ferns or turtles, but they are able to bond emotionally, physically, and socially with a biologically appropriate partner—one with whom sexuality virtually guarantees reproduction, at least in the days prior to contraception.

Functionality vs. Functionalism

Here, however, a philosopher may again see a problem. "Well, that's very interesting," he may say, stroking his beard (most philosophers are men; only some have beards). "It sounds like you're saying that these behavior patterns, templates, traditions, and habits exist *because* they have functions. That's an old argument in philosophy—it's called 'teleology.' Teleological arguments date back to Aristotle, and they imply that something exists because it has an *end* (or 'final purpose') for which it is the *means*. The problem is that such arguments reverse time's arrow: they place the 'cause'—or the purpose served—in the future or ahead in time of the act that serves them."

But let me interrupt. What the philosopher says is true, but nothing could be further from my argument. Biology does *not* imply that templates or other components of courtship exist *because* they might have "functions" in some vague future state. Biological discussions of function are not teleologies which explain the means by the end or by referring to "final purposes." Nor are biological discussions of function mere abbreviations or sketches of more complex theories of motivation, desire, or need, as certain philosophers of science seem to believe (e.g., Hempel; see Aronson, 1984, pp. 37–38). Instead, templates exist because the brain contains groups of cells that somehow "represent" or "are" the template. In brief, the template exists because the brain contains certain real (if presently unknown) anatomical structures.

In general, when biologists seek to explain why any functional characteristic of an organism exists, they first seek structures that serve that function, and next seek the origin of that structure in the embryological development of the organism. Behind embryology, biologists seek the set of developmental and genetic processes, like canalization, which regulate the development of that structure. Then, finally, they seek the evolutionary processes that have led to the species possessing those genetic limits and not others. Throughout, biologists want to explain functionality by systematically anchoring their search in the material and observable processes of physiology, development, genetics, and evolution, rather than in unobservable *future* states or advantages.

But we have a subtlety here. Many social scientific explanations are "functionalist" not only in proposing that social behavior has social functions [as in Goldman's (1981) discussion of Comstock prostitution], but precisely in saying that behavior exists *because* it is functional. Though such teleologies are fairly common, my argument is not teleological in this sense either.

First, in biology, my approach would not be called "biosocial functionalism" (as a functionalist might think), but would simply be called a functional analysis, without much stress on the word "functional." Because biology does not have schools or traditions of "functionalist" interpretation set into opposition with other perspectives, historical (evolutionary), developmental, or genetic, the idea of "biosocial functionalism" suggests a fragmentation that precludes historical and developmental analyses. But the biosocial approach itself invites such analyses, because there is a second reason to reject the idea that love exists "because" it is functional.

Consider homosexual love. If one is a "functionalist"—for example, if one (erroneously) takes my argument to imply that love exists "because" it leads to reproduction—then gay and lesbian love is inexplicable. Indeed, for the anti-homosexual, it is worse: functionless *and* inexplicable. However, consider the existence of templates. If some people have homosexual templates [as I suspect is true from observing in gay bars and from the literature (McWhirter and Mattison, 1984)], gay and lesbian love can flow from gay templates and courtship, just as love can arise between men and women. In all cases, the result is bonding between two people; often the result is sexual involvement; if the couple is male and female, then, barring contraception, the result is reproduction. The last result is biologically functional (by definition), yet has not caused love or templates to exist in the first place. That puts the cart before the horse: the couple is in love because their neurophysiology works that way, right now in the immediate present. In brief, templates exist *and* can be functional; they do not exist *because* they are functional. (This is one of the great differences between biological functionality and social, psychological, and emotional motivation, intentionality, or purpose. Love thus provides an excellent example of why biologists so sharply distinguish function from purpose.)

Next, we ask how the couple's neurophysiology permits templated bonding and love. Indubitably (though speculatively), the answer is that the capacity to develop templates is inherited (that is, brain development is the result of genetic pleiotropies and canalization). Then, the offspring of people with templates also have templates, fall in love, and once again reproduce, and so on, endlessly.

In sum, the chain of effects goes genes, complex pleiotropies and canalization of brain development, templates, learning of sex rules, fascination, courtship, love and its cultural forms, sexual intercourse, reproduction—and the genes are transmitted once again. For homosexuality, using Weinrich's (1976) model, it goes genes, pleiotropies, canalization, homosexual templates, learning, fascination, courtship, love and bonding, altruism to the kin group, so that *they* reproduce. Whereupon homosexuality can be inherited either culturally or genetically (through kin) or both.

The final result is that the argument is not teleological. No final purposes drive this system, nor need they. The system exists because it is *self*-reproducing—in two words, because it is alive and embodied.

Nowhere does biology imply that functions exist "because" they serve ends— or Purposes. No ethnobiological Genes sit behind the scene planning the future or being drawn to it as to the last act of a play. Instead, biology turns to present-day reality rather than seeking explanations in domains it cannot reach, such as the Mind of God, That sees everything in one instant—including the final curtain.

But this is not an *easy* solution to the Nature/Nurture controversy. First, this notion of function is biological, not social scientific. Thus, marriage serves many social scientific functions, e.g., to produce legitimate heirs to the family fortune. Such "functions" can more or less readily become detached from the underlying process of courting and mating and the behavioral adjustments they entail. These "functions" are, as it were, historical and cultural adornments on the basic biological process of courting and mating.

Second, nor do women behave "naturally" when courting and mating, while men behave "culturally." *Both* are partners in a courtship, and are simultaneously performing social, cultural, *and* biological activities. *Both* partners respond to each other. It is only *we* who construe the categories *male* and *female* as representing a difference between variable Culture on the one hand and fixed Nature on the other. In brief, we use *male* and *female* as symbols when we believe that men learn to be sexually aggressive and that women are—naturally!—sexually hesitant, reluctant, or coy.

That dichotomy, which makes men active and women passive, has no obvious basis in biological functionality. Biologically, it need *not* be that men should be active and women passive. It could be the other way around, as long as the two people meet, court, and eventually make love. We can readily anticipate that courtship may involve extensive variation in who does what, and in who starts what. In the biosocial perspective, diversity should be the rule, *for biology does not "encode" fixed behavior patterns, as ethnobiology has it.* Biology requires only that on the average, meet we ultimately must.

Accordingly, Bernard's argument against biology obscures the real role of biology in influencing our sexual behavior. There is no principle of adaptive or functional universality in biology. Just because it is adaptive and functional for amoebas to extend pseudopods to engulf food, it does *not* follow that other organisms—e.g., people—must or should have pseudopods. Marriage and courtship can exist here in one cultural form, and elsewhere in another. The *real* biological principle is that the functional needs of life can be met in a variety of ways, and those ways can change as the organism itself responds to changes in its own life and environment.

So, in contrast to ethnobiology, the real *science* of biology leads us to predict diversity in courtship, even in the life of one individual. But it cannot be random diversity—e.g., of men courting turtles in a world of higgledy-piggledy. Such diversity should be *functional,* and should allow men and women to meet, court, and make love in ways that are suited to different times and places, to the diverse habits and customs of the lovers and their emotions. If, on the one hand, diversity funnels down towards a core of biological functionalty, then it also funnels upwards from biological functionality, to allow people to *adapt* their behavior to the varied conditions of their lives.

But even though I have asserted that biology produces diversity, and that diversity is often functional, assertion is *not* evidence. We must now turn to the real world. What actually happens when men and women meet, become intimate, and slowly or suddenly find themselves fascinated with each other? How can we be so sure that all the diversity and richness of love *does* surround a core of biological functionality?

So let us now return to the lovers themselves, entranced with each other, their eyes filled only with each other. For them, biology is far, far away. But, for us— observers and not lovers—it is really quite close. We are about to watch courtship, to see how a man and woman negotiate the path from unfamiliarity to intimacy. As they do so, we shall also see how some biologically very real principles of sexual reproduction color and shape their every act. So, let us turn to the lovers, in their entrancements, their eyes filled only with each other.

Chapter 4

The Course of True Love:
The Courtship Sequence

LYSANDER: The course of true love never did run smooth . . .

—*A Midsummer-Night's Dream*,
Act I, Scene 1

Lysander was right, of course. The observer sees that courtship is filled with little bumps that can cause courtship to grind to a halt. These I call *escalation points*, and I will describe them presently. But the lover has different eyes. Details that are everything to the observer the lover buries in a merged fabric in which both wonder and terror inhere—the way she moves, the way he touches her, the way they turn angrily from each other. These events all create intensely experienced meaning quite different from what an objective observer sees. The lover reshapes experience around these emotionally vested details and distills from them an emotional center, to create an idealized rhythm and flow that, in memory, irresistibly moves towards its appointed end, be it consummation or rejection. To the lover, love is a torrent fed by the melted waters of glaciers that run and dash and fall ever downward to the sea. The rest the lover discards, and is henceforth like the poet who vests in actions an otherwise absent continuity and who vests in words an otherwise inexpressible symbolic reality. The torrent of language that flows from love is concentrated stuff indeed:

> Who could resist? Who in this universe?
> She did so breathe ambrosia; so immerse
> My fine existence in a golden clime.
> She took me like a child at suckling time,
> And cradled me in roses. Thus condemn'd,
> The current of my former life was stemm'd,
> And to this arbitrary queen of sense
> I bow'd a tranced vassal; nor would thence
> Have mov'd even though Amphion's harp had woo'd
> Me back to Scylla o'er billo(w)s rude.
> For as Apollo each eve doth devise

75

A new appareling for western skies
So every eve, nay every spendthrift hour
Shed balmy consciousness within that bower.
—Keats, Endymion (1818/1962a, p. 157)
Book III, lines 453–466.

Magnificent language that contains an ever-renewed epiphany and exaltation of intense inner experience.

In thrall to that mood, who could analyze courtship? For the lover, courtship and love are hope and desire embedded in enchantment. Analysis of love kills it, people say; love is a mystery, sacrosanct in success and failure both. Indeed, for many people, love's greatest wonder is its *loss* of objectivity. When love's appareling magic is expressed in the exalted and transcendent language of love, it affirms the lover's conviction that his or her every act is an unprecedented miracle of intimacy.

Examples of this process abound in literature, and sometimes in the most unexpected places. In A. Conan Doyle's *The Sign of Four* (1930), Dr. Watson sees Mary Morstan, his future wife, for the first time: her blonde hair, her small, dainty form, her sombre grayish-beige dress and turban, its dull hue relieved only by a suspicion of a white feather. He muses on her smiles and the rich tones of her voice, and, within ten pages of Sherlock Holmesian adventure, they are holding hands. "A wondrous thing is love," Watson thinks to himself. The story is fiction, but the process is not—indeed, the description is accuracy itself.* The behavioral descriptions I am about to give do *not* arise from literature, but from observation and interviews (see Appendix). In fact, not until *after* these observations did I realize how precisely some writers describe men's templates—such as Watson's—and the behavioral events of love. Nonetheless, some readers will be horrified by my referring to poetry and literature. "That's not scientific evidence!" they will cry. "It's just *anecdote!*" Yet, literature embodies some of the most profound concerns people have about sex, love, and each other. True, Elizabeth Bennett's story in *Pride and Prejudice* (Austen, 1813/1945) or Chaucer's Wife of Bath or even Dr. John Watson himself may be literary "inventions," but they are also profoundly true psychologically, emotionally, and observationally.

In parallel with the exalted transcendence of love and its expression exists the actual behavior of the lovers. By that I mean what the two people actually do when they are together—their looks, their touches, their movements. If we are to understand love, and *especially* if we are to understand its biology, we must focus on the lovers' behavior. To do so, I will focus on a specific process: the behavior of two people when they first meet, begin to talk, and begin to feel close and intimate. (The Appendix describes how we made the observations.) I will describe what happens when a man and woman meet at a party, a singles bar, or elsewhere—and I can assure a dubious reader that the process is more significant than it may seem!

*The description of Mary Morstan is on page 94, Watson's musing is on page 97, and love appears on page 107 immediately after she "seizes his wrist."

When a man and woman meet, they enact a set of behavior patterns that simultaneously are visible to the external, objective observer and that have profound internal meanings to the participants. There is an "inside" and an "outside" to these interactions: the inside represents the lovers' feelings and beliefs, and the outside represents their actual behavior. To understand love, we must translate back and forth between love as the poet describes it and behavior as the video camera sees it.

The reason for this dual view is that, despite the exalted language of love, there exists a quite regular sequence of events during such meetings. At this stage, courtship is really quite similar from time to time, from person to person, and from place to place. My comment is not cynicism, however; I am not saying that the lovers are deluded into believing that their feelings are special when they are not. For them, love *is* special, and unique, and wonderful.

Yet courtship does have a remarkably similar form from time to time and place to place. Courtship is not a fixed series of events somehow "encoded into the genes." But it is a *process* that comes into existence as two people construct their own behavior in response to each other, and in response to quite specific signals and cues. This sequence is created *dynamically* very much in the way our rats create *their* interactions—in mutual responsiveness and in a cycle or loop of signals sent and received, sent and received.

So let us turn to the courtship sequence itself, and to the actual behavior patterns that two people enact when they first meet. For simplicity, I will first describe a *successful* sequence—the two people will succeed in passing through a series of *escalation points* I mentioned above, and will achieve the beginning of intimacy.

The Core Sequence

When the two people are strangers, courtship begins as one person *approaches* or moves next to the potential partner. An approach occurs when a man sits next to a woman in a train. More often, though, the woman makes the approach, for example, by sitting next to a man in a bar.

The person approached has two options. He or she can turn slightly, look, move (e.g., make room), or otherwise respond to the other person's presence. Alternatively, the person approached might simply ignore the person who is approaching. Thus, the man at the bar might not look at the woman who sat next to him. The woman approached on the train might continue to read her newspaper.

But if the person approached does turn slightly, or look—e.g., the man turns and looks at the woman, or she glances up from her newspaper—then, quite reliably, conversation opens, usually about banal topics—the bar itself, traveling, trains, and so on.

As they talk, the two people now *turn* to face each other. Depending on the couple, turning can take anywhere from 10 minutes to 2 or more hours. However, it is usually slow and gradual—first the head is turned, then the shoulders and torso, and finally the whole body. With each turn and shift, again intimacy is increasing.

If all goes well, the two people will end up facing each other and will remain facing for the rest of the interaction.

Simultaneously, two other processes are starting. The first is *touching,* and again intimacy increases. Women often make the first touch, typically lightly and fleetingly, involving nothing more intimate, for example, than the fingertips placed on the man's hand, or the palm placed flat on his arm. Such touches are quickly withdrawn. However, sometimes men touch women and will *not* withdraw the hand—for example, he puts his arm around her shoulders, or he fingers her hair. The interaction will then often stop quite quickly.

The person touched has only two options. He or she can respond positively: by leaning towards the other person, by smiling, or turning more completely, or by reciprocating the touch. Or the person touched may try to ignore it. The interaction then typically ceases. But let us assume the touch *is* acknowledged positively, perhaps by a touch given in reciprocation.

As the two people talk and continue to turn towards each other, they now touch each other increasingly freqently. They are now perhaps half- or three-quarters turned towards each other, and are beginning to look at each other. Such looks wander over the face, hair, eyes, shoulders, neck, and torso. As the sequence progresses, the couple will look more and more frequently at each other until, finally, they virtually never take their eyes off each other.

Such gazing is very different from the looking that occurs during casual conversation, or that occurred during the beginning of the sequence. It is more intense, more constant, and it does not shift as the two people take turns speaking [as it does in casual conversations (Exline, 1971; Cook, 1977)].

The second process is even more remarkable: they start to move in *synchrony* with each other. For example, they both lean forward, reach for their drinks, lift them, sip, place the glasses back on the bar or table, all simultaneously. Or, if sitting next to each other on a train, the woman on the right leans her right arm on the arm-rest and turns to look at the man to her left, while he leans his left arm on his arm-rest and turns to look at her on his right. It is as if a mirror had been placed between them.

Synchronization develops throughout the entire sequence. Yet few people spontaneously notice synchronized body movements and postures. Initially, it may involve only a brief (and perhaps accidental) movement made in common and followed by rapid desynchronization of movement. [Givens (1983, p. 2) provides an example.] As time passes, more and more movements occur in synchrony, especially after the first exchange of touches. Initially, synchronization involves only arm and head movements, but progresses to more complex series of simulta-neous motions such as drinking in unison. Later, synchronization includes simul-taneous shifts of weight and swaying movements that result when the hips, legs, and feet of the two people move in synchrony. This is complete or "full body" synchronization, and involves all movements made by each person.

Full-body synchronization is striking. It is fluid, continuous, and ever-chang-ing. Apparently, it was first described scientifically by Scheflen (1965), and is illustrated further by Morris (1977, pp. 83–85). Givens also describes it (1983, pp. 40–43). I shall stress synchronization, for it is the best indicator that exists of mutual involvement.

The whole sequence, from approach to synchronization, can take from 15 minutes to over 3 hours. Once synchronized, however, people can stay in synchrony seemingly indefinitely—until the bar closes, until they finish dinner and drinks and must leave, until their train reaches wherever it is going; to put it another way, until the business of the outside world intervenes and causes their interaction to stop. Intimacy has grown stepwise and mutually. Together and in response to each other, the two people have created their own world.

The courtship sequence can be summarized diagrammatically (Figure 1). Because we assumed that the two people started as strangers, the sequence begins with an approach and its acknowledgment (e.g., a turn and look). When they begin to talk, the two people thereby involve themselves with each other ("intimacy"). As they turn towards each other and as they look increasingly attentively at each other, intimacy increases (the rising curve labeled "Turn"). But even if the two people started with their shoulders in the wide "V" that Americans typically adopt when talking to a stranger, they can turn only so much—that is, to face each other fully—and no more. Likewise, they can look only so much and no more. Intimacy mediated by turning and looking eventually, therefore, levels off (as the plateau in the curve indicates). Next, when they touch, their intimacy can increase further (as shown by the rising curve labeled "Touch"). If the interaction continues past the first touch, the two people are now talking, looking at each other, and beginning to touch regularly. Synchronization is progressing to involve more and more body movements, and it too increases their mutual involvement (the rising curve "Synchronization" is shown with a dotted line to indicate that synchronization may begin at different points for different couples). Finally, they enter full-body synchronization and are looking at each other nearly continuously, touching each other regularly, talking face-to-face and moving in full-body synchrony with each other. Generally, in a public place, intimacy does not increase further, though sometimes the couple will start to kiss each other.

In virtually any sense of "intimacy," a fully synchronized couple is intimately involved and will ignore a great variety of external stimuli. Loud bar noises or trains stopping and starting may make them look up in unison and then back at each other. The two people have built an enclave of privacy around them, into which the external world only rarely penetrates.*

Couples who know each other somewhat, like a dating couple sitting facing each other across a restaurant table, also go through a similar sequence. Though they cannot turn to face each other, initially they may look past each other (e.g., at the

---

*The reader eager to compare these observations with laboratory studies of non-verbal behavior and "intimacy" should be warned that the transition from the laboratory to a "natural setting," such as a singles bar, is *extremely* difficult. Indeed, in a study designed partly to replicate this one, Jones (1982) could not confirm several laboratory-based hypotheses in the field. The relationship between laboratory and field studies of intimacy is discussed further in the Appendix.

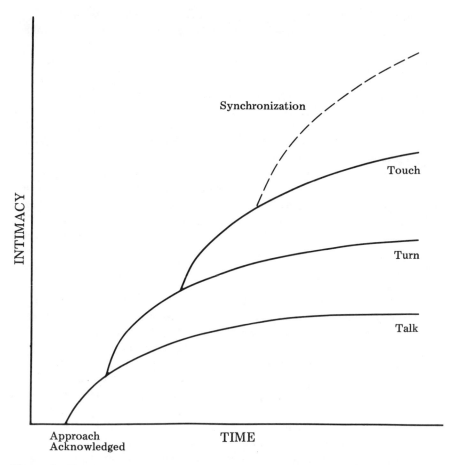

Figure 1 The development of intimacy during the courtship sequence. The interaction begins with an approach and its acknowledgment, followed by the opening of a conversation. The two people slowly turn to face each other, and then one person touches the other for first time. Meanwhile, synchronization is gradually developing (the dotted line indicates that synchronization begins at different times with different couples). In some couples, a touch will occur very early in the sequence; typically, however, such interactions do not proceed very far, as the text explains.

restaurant), and will talk about unemotional subjects (such as their dinner order). But later they may begin the intensified gazing, touching, and synchronization that characterizes the later stages of the courtship sequence.

We observed this sequence—approach, talk, turn, touch, synchronize—nearly everywhere we went. It occurs in bars, parties, trains, supermarkets, church socials, and in the United States and Canada. However, since few people are familiar with the entire sequence, several examples may help illustrate it concretely.

Three Examples of the Core Sequence

EXAMPLE 1

An airport bar in New York City, a weekday afternoon in summer 1980.

A blonde woman entered the bar and stopped at the doorway to look around (as nearly everyone does when first entering a bar). She was wearing white slacks and blouse, open at the neck, and was carrying a gift-shop shopping bag jammed with parcels. She threaded her way past the tables towards the bar itself, which was crowded with men standing or occupying all the barstools. When she reached the bar, she stopped in the middle of four men (myself included), unable to reach the bar itself. The men looked at her. After a few moments, she reached into her purse, but fumbled with the gift-shop bag and dropped several parcels and the bill she had taken from her purse. The four men helped pick up her packages, and one man retrieved the bill and offered to order her drink. She agreed, and, after he had ordered and returned to her, they stood about 2 feet apart, their shoulders at right angles. They began to talk about traveling (she was waiting for a departing flight). Then the man went back to the bar to get her drink. When he returned, he had half-turned towards her. During the next 15 minutes, they turned to face each other completely, as they talked about her purchases. They were presents for her family and herself, she said; it was her 30th birthday, and she had bought herself a present. As the conversation continued, they began to synchronize their drinking, lifting and lowering their glasses in unison. He asked where she worked, and she said a jewelry company, and, taking a sample earring from her bag, pointed out that it was similar to the earrings and necklace she was wearing. The man, now facing her fully, reached out his hand and took the earring she was holding (thus touching her hand). Simultaneously, she turned her face slightly and tossed her hair to reveal the earring she was wearing. He looked at her face, necklace, hair, and earrings, and then at the earring she had handed to him. After this, they looked at each other more and more frequently, and the conversation turned to birthdays, families, marriage, getting old, and similar personal subjects. He looked nearly continuously at her face, hair, and necklace, while she focused almost solely on his face and eyes. They began to shift their weights back and forth (the onset of full-body synchronization) as they simultaneously began to talk about the problems of her marriage. They stayed in synchrony until her flight was announced, some 15 minutes later, when she took both his hands in hers, clasped them, leaned close, and thanked him for a nice time. Their faces were now about 6 inches apart. Then she turned and left the bar.

Initially, when she approached the bar, she *de facto* also approached the men who were standing around it. Obviously the action was deliberate, for she might have chosen to sit at a table and wait for table service. Her fumbling with her purse and packages virtually guaranteed that the men would notice her. (A woman acquaintance of mine read this story, laughed, and said, "Why didn't she drop a handkerchief?") The man ordering her drink treated her approach as an opportunity to talk to her. The conversation became more personal (the problems of her marriage) only after considerable non-verbal intimacy had developed (turning and touching). Thus, the intimacy of a conversational topic *by itself* does not cause the development of non-verbal intimacy, but, instead, verbal and non-verbal intimacy develop in parallel, if they develop at all. Certainly, as conversational intimacy increased, so did non-verbal intimacy in its final form, full-body synchronization. The entire interaction took approximately an hour.

EXAMPLE 2

A neighborhood music and dance bar in New Jersey, late in the afternoon in spring 1980. The bar's usual clientele are in their 20s and 30s.

> A casually dressed young woman had been sitting at one end of the bar for about an hour, facing the doorway some 25 feet away. A tall young man wearing a ski jacket came in and sat at the other end of the bar. The woman looked directly at him, and after a few minutes, he got up and, taking his drink with him, sat four seats away from her. They looked at each other, and he almost immediately moved next to her, on her left. His right arm rested between them on the bar, with his shoulders parallel to the bar itself. As they talked, he turned his head to look at her. Over the next 2 minutes, they turned to face each other completely. He took his arm off the bar and pivoted on his barstool to face her. She turned simultaneously (a form of movement synchronization). He held his drink in his right hand, and she her drink in her left, in mirror synchrony. He had braced his feet on a rung of his barstool and, within another 2 minutes or so, she placed both her feet between his on the rung of his barstool. They continued to lean closely together, until, quite suddenly, she leaned forward, put her arms around his neck, and kissed him.

The entire interaction took approximately 15 minutes from his entrance into the bar to her kissing him. It was the fastest interaction we have recorded, but, nonetheless, the two people went through the entire core sequence.

EXAMPLE 3

A New York City singles bar, early evening in winter 1982–1983. The observations were made while I was collaborating with a television camera team to obtain footage for a show on my research. The cameraman, Robert Wells, had set the camera to include the door of the bar plus a black-haired young woman sitting alone at a barstool some 15 feet from the door.

> The 40-minute sequence began when a man entered the bar, looked around, and then focused on the young woman. He walked over to her, hung up his

overcoat, and sat next to her. She turned slightly to look at him (thus, his approach was acknowledged). They almost immediately began to talk, looking first towards the bar and then more and more at each other. Simultaneously, they began to turn to face each other. After about 35 minutes, her hand was on the bar, holding her drink, and his arms were half-folded on the bar in front of him. She started to lift her glass, and he immediately followed suit, so that by the time their glasses were fully lifted, they were drinking in synchronization. They remained in synchrony for the remainder of our observations.*

These examples are typical of our observations. They illustrate not only the core sequence itself, but how different people in different settings actually enact it as they begin to become intimate.†

The examples also illustrate that while this kind of "intimacy" is not the intimacy of a couple married for 20 years, it nonetheless represents the development of an intense mutuality of shared attention between the two people. Indeed, people in full-body synchronization seem fascinated with each other, and will *remain* in synchrony, rather than reaching it and then leaving the bar together. Thus, the sequence is not instrumental, in the sense that people enact it simply because they want to hurry on to sexual intercourse. Fully synchronized people do not seem goal-oriented, unless one says that a desire to *stay* in synchrony is a goal. The sequence creates an intimacy that exists *right now*, and even if they do indeed later have sexual intercourse, it is their *present* involvement, and not some future state of sexual bliss, that they prolong.

Synchronization is extremely common. It occurs between men who know each other well, and between women talking. It also occurs in married couples, who typically fall into synchronization the moment they sit and start to talk (e.g., in a restaurant). Such couples thus behave very differently from the courting couple: they synchronize quickly, touch without hesitation, and turn towards and away from each other casually and quickly. The comparison shows that when a courting couple synchronizes, their behavior closely resembles the already-established intimacy of people who know each other well.

Surprisingly few people know that the sequence, and synchronization in particular, is as common as it is. People are more familiar with its individual components, like the approach, touching, or looking, than they are with the fact that these actions occur in a regular and orderly sequence over time. Men especially seem unfamiliar with the temporal structure of the core sequence, although women are often more familiar with it. Givens (1978, 1983) has provided some details about

---

*The synchronization sequence was aired on "The Last Word," ABC, 29 January 1983.

†Adam Kendon's documentary film "The Wedding Reception," which was made as part of a study of non-verbal behavior by Birdwhistell and his colleagues, and which is held in the film archive at The Eastern Pennsylvania Psychiatric Institute in Philadelphia, shows the beginning of the sequence at frames 66700 ff, and shows synchronization developing between a man and woman at frames 91000 ff. A flirting couple is shown in synchronization around frame 86000.

the early stages of the sequence; otherwise, it seems unreported in the scientific literature.

However, visual artists—photographers, painters, cameramen, and dancers—are often familiar with the whole sequence, synchronization included. Illustrator John Tenniel shows Tweedledum and Tweedledee in mirror synchrony (Carroll, 1960, p. 242), and James Thurber shows three couples sitting at a bar in mirror synchrony in *Midnight at Tim's Place* (1960, p. 10). The American cartoonist G. B. Trudeau (1982, p. 61) depicts movement synchronization between Rick Redfern and Joanie Caucus to accompany Rick's suggestion that they get married (a suggestion Joanie herself made, sometime back). I can assure the reader unfamiliar with synchronization that Trudeau's depiction is absolutely accurate. [The observation that visual artists are familiar with the core sequence may be similar to Rosenthal et al.'s (1979) comment that artists do well on their standardized PONS test of sensitivity to non-verbal behavior.]

Emotionality

But let us now return to the lovers. For them, what is important is what the courtship sequence means *emotionally,* and not that it possesses a specific temporal form. For the lover, the sequence is merely an outwardly visible embodiment of a series of individual actions that express emotional desire or communicate emotional closeness. Thus, for the lover (to the extent that he or she even thinks of such things), the sequence is ultimately the product of the emotions. These, the lover believes, create the courtship sequence *automatically.*

For example, a woman looking deeply into a man's eyes vests her attention with profound emotional meaning and understands the man's return gaze as proof that he too may feel love. She probably does not much care *when* "looking" enters an objectively described sequence of courtship behavior. For the lover, the externally visible sequence is an unimportant epiphenomenon on top of the truly significant flux in his or her *internal* emotional state.*

In this mood the lover floats in a world of intense personal reality, and emotion builds almost magically (I am drawing here on a certain class of interview results). Mosher (1980) uses the perceptive word *trance* for similar states during sexual intercourse. Where the observer sees "synchronization," the lover experiences a process so fantastic and so precipitous that it seems to transport the two people from the here-and-now of this world into a private and timeless universe of each other. In that state, the lover does not experience the sequence as such, but rather only those emotions that surround the events of the sequence as a kind of halo.

Accordingly, the lover does not understand the events of the sequence as having any real similarity to everyday behavior. The woman gazing in her lover's

---

*In psychological terms, love is primarily an intrapsychic experience for the lover, to which all its external and especially interpersonal qualities are referred. In some cases, these intrapsychic experiences can come near fugue states, as shown by Tennov (1979), Barthes (1978), McWhirter and Mattison (1984), Peele and Brodsky (1975) and Greer (1971, pp. 145ff).

eyes experiences not a normal activity—which, dispassionately, could be simply called "eye-contact"—but a *remarkable* activity. The lovers see allure, not anatomy, in each others' eyes. The lover reifies this flux of feeling, and projects it onto the objectively visible components of the sequence. In consequence, for the lover, the sequence *is* the sense of growing closeness, of incipient transcendence, or, even, the disappointment and betrayal that occurs when the sequence fails to complete itself. For the lover, the emotions are a fully sufficient cause and explanation for the sequence and its development. The lover sees the inside of the sequence—its emotion and meanings—as necessarily producing its outside—the behavior patterns that the observer sees.

The lover is partly right. When we ask why an individual performs a specific act, such as looking, reaching, or touching, we can certainly agree that the person's internal state (be it emotional or intentional and cognitive) caused them to look or reach or touch. The lover wants—that is, *intends*—to achieve emotional closeness, and the relationship between act and internal state is then clear: the act serves the intention and emotion very well.

But in vassaldom to these emotions, the lover *also* believes that if people look, then turn, then touch, then synchronize, it is somehow simple. Love and intimacy have grown, and with their growth, the two people express love increasingly openly. Thus, for the lover, changes in feeling *cause* changes in behavior. Where the observer sees emotional intimacy increasing as behavior changes, the lover believes that the growth or decline of the emotions drives changes in behavior, not the other way round.

In this, the lover thinks locally. He or she sees the world and its past as if they existed *now*. The lover feels a touch *now*, and does not calculate objectively when or how it emerged during a 2-hour sequence of non-verbal communication. For the lover, the beginning of the sequence has become fuzzy, as increasingly it is seen as the precursor of the touch, and the touch is seen as the inevitably foreordained consequence of the past. Thus, the lover extends the boundaries of the present moment, its touch and emotions, into time past and future, thereby to reshape the world which, in memory and in anticipation, has been appareled with the adornments of the present. Thus, the lover *mystifies* the creation of intimacy. [Barthes (1978) has described in detail this curious and really quite extensive reinterpretation of the lover's world. It involves not merely the sense of time, but the very idea of causation itself.]

And, believing in the primacy of love, in its cradling and reshaping power, the lover ultimately has *no* explanation for the sequence. The ultimate origin of the sequence is referred off to a mysterious domain of emergent feeling: "It just happens. It's good chemistry, that's all, and it doesn't follow any formula." By seeing behavior as *dependent* on emotion, the lover places personal feeling at the center, and explains everything else as if the universe circled around that center.

Now, quite curiously, a social scientist might agree with the lover, at least in attributing the origin of the courtship sequence to the participants' internal states. A sociological script theoretician might argue that the courtship sequence is a "scripted" performance built on a set of expectations (a "script") that is known in advance to the participant and that specifies not only one's own behavior, but also how the partner should behave. On the basis of this internal script, each person's behavior adheres as much as possible to the scenario laid down in advance by the script. A social psychologist might then add that the sequence is also built around a series of changing attributions that one person makes about the other. For example, the woman sees the man turning towards her, and attributes to him an increased degree of sexual interest (that is, she "labels" his behavior). She therefore responds in kind to him. Furthermore, a clinical psychologist might see one participant's latent or hidden motivations expressing themselves during courtship, and therefore helping to shape its ultimate course.

These views have some validity. Attributions, expectations, motivations, and emotions like love assuredly all exist, and the lover's internal state might cause him or her to perform a *specific* action (e.g., a touch). However, such internal states seem to produce the local event, like a momentary touch, rather than establish the *sequence* in which those actions occur. If we liken courtship to a chain, then the lover's internal state might help create each link of the chain, but not the *order* in which these links are assembled to produce the overall sequence itself. Thus, we cannot agree with the lover that a near-magical flux of feeling gives the sequence its form, nor with the social scientist's more dispassionate sounding claim that internal states and intentions control or drive the courtship sequence.

The reason is simple. Courtship involves *two* people. Emotions, expectations, attributions, and motivation exist, but they exist personally—within *me*, for example. To be sure, wishing may cause *me* to act in a certain way, for example, to reach out and touch my partner. But how do *my* wishes cause my partner to reciprocate the touch? After all, my partner might have other wishes that might cause him or her to behave in some other way.

If the emergence of the courtship sequence depends entirely on one participant's internal state, then unless the *other* person's internal state is identical, the behavior of the two people will desynchronize (because, by hypothesis, their internal states drive the interaction). Moreover, the idea that internal emotional or cognitive states shape the courtship sequence makes the sequence, and synchronization in particular, at least twice as complicated as the phenomenon itself. We must now explain not only why our behavior is identical but also why our internal states are identical.

Nor does courtship run on a mutually agreed-upon agenda, as if it were a business meeting moving towards a decision about some marketing plan, or a theatrical performance of a play whose lines and movements have been memorized and rehearsed for weeks or longer. No lover—at least not in our study—ever entered a courtship saying, "I wish to seduce this woman. Therefore, at 10:17, we shall be half-turned. At 10:25, she shall touch me for the first time. At 11:26, we shall simultaneously lift our glasses, and she shall tilt her head sideways and smile at me. . . . "

No such agendas exist. Outside a stage performance, it is impossible that any human being, let alone a *pair* of human beings, plan so carefully and in such detail to play out a series of actions as complex and as synchronized as courtship. The theatrical metaphor may appeal to certain social scientists, but, as an explanation for the origin of the courtship sequence, it does not help.* The same holds for the ethnobiological notion that the core sequence is "encoded in the genes." It *cannot* be, for no biological mechanism exists to read out genetic information in such detailed synchrony between two people even if that information existed. The courtship sequence is *created* and does not preexist, either as a script or as a "genetic" program.

Because courtship involves two people, the origin of the courtship sequence cannot be sought in the feelings of *one* person, no matter how strongly the lover's own attention is focused on them. Nor can it be sought in one person's scripts, expectations, motivations, or attributions, no matter how tempting social scientific theory is for that purpose. Nor is ethnobiology adequate to explain the sequence. Rather, we must look at the detailed, step-by-step *interaction* of the two people to explain first why people behave as they do—when they look, turn, touch, or synchronize and respond to each other—and, second, what the biological functions of the entire courtship sequence itself are.

Escalation and Response

If the courtship sequence does not exist in the participants' minds as a foreordained internal state, script, or program, then the only possibility is that it is *constructed* during the moment-by-moment interaction of the two people. Two processes are crucial in the moment-by-moment creation of the sequence, and especially in determining its success or failure. These are *escalation* and *response*, and both refer to how intimacy changes during courtship.

Broadly, *escalation* refers to an overture made by one person that would, *if accepted*, raise the level of intimacy between the two people. The initial approach is one example. If it is accepted, it obviously will involve the two people in a conversation. Turning to face the other person also increases intimacy, for it focuses the two people's attention on each other. Touching, especially for the first time in the interaction, can increase intimacy powerfully. I shall speak of an "escalation point" for any event in the interaction where one participant makes such an overture.

The concept of escalation lets us avoid fruitless arguments about the lover's motivations for performing a certain act. If person A touches person B, the outsider might want to believe that the touch, and therefore the increased intimacy it created,

---

*The proper domain of script and attribution theory is not the microscopic realm of reaching or touching or of behavioral synchronization, and I am perhaps being unkind to suggest that they do apply to it. They deal with more global problems, such as why a person selects a certain kind of mate (e.g., Lewis, 1973; Stryker, 1977), what is meant by femininity (Garcia, 1983), and what is believed about sexual behavior in general (Gagnon and Simon, 1973). For such purposes, these theories are quite useful, though they cannot explain how and why behavior changes during the courtship sequence.

was intentional. Indeed, a lover might agree. But the lover might *also* say that the touch occurred simply because he or she "felt like it" without premeditation, prior intention, or an explicit desire to create "intimacy." Since we cannot read the lover's mind, we do not know why the lover touched. But such touches do occur, and have observable effects on the other person. Accordingly, escalation refers *not* to motives that someone might attribute to behavior, but solely to observable behavior itself.

Second, at an escalation point, the partner's behavior is far more crucial than at other times in the sequence. Intimacy does not develop merely because person A *extends* an overture that would increase his or her intimacy with person B. That overture must be *accepted* by person B. At an escalation point, the *partner's* behavior determines whether the interaction will continue: an overture that will increase the couple's intimacy must be emotionally *acceptable* to the other person. If it is not, intimacy cannot then grow.

But it is not sufficient merely to *feel* accepting of the other person's overture, for example, to *feel* happy when the other person extends a hand and touches you. Though a lover might believe that such happiness is communicated automatically by a lover's telepathy that transcends mere behavior, intimacy is not generated mystically. The person extending a hand towards you does not know if you feel warm and happy about it, or if you are indifferent and are simply ignoring him or her.

At an escalation point, an overture must not merely be emotionally acceptable. It requires overt behavioral response. Thus, the concept of response refers not to how person B feels about the overture, but to what person B *does* about it. For example, in *The Sign of Four,* Miss Morstan takes Watson's hand, and he continues to hold it (p. 107). When Doyle thus makes Watson *respond* to her escalation, he shows himself to be an acute observer, for it is generally true that at an escalation point, person B *must* respond to the overture, or the interaction will eventually grind down and halt ("de-escalate").

Enmeshed in subjectivity, the lover cannot explain why the sequence sometimes fails and can say only, "Well, I guess the chemistry just wasn't right." What the lover cannot see, but the objective observer can, is that intimacy develops step-by-step. It moves through a series of definable and observable escalation points, at which an overture is made, accepted, and reciprocated. And when the overture is *not* reciprocated, then the interaction ceases.

So, the observer has a distinct advantage over the lover. The observer can literally *observe* in the patterns of escalation and response, something that the lover only feels and may not be able to express: the knowledge of how and when the courtship sequence *fails.*

Some Examples of Success and Failure but Mostly of Failure

The courtship sequence does not unfold smoothly. Instead the *partner's* response to an escalation determines its success, and that is never guaranteed.

The next two examples illustrate escalation and response for the approach. In the first, the young man did not respond to the woman's approach, and she soon left. In the second, he *did* respond.

An extremely popular New Jersey singles and dance bar, mid-evening in spring 1979.

A casually dressed young man was standing on the top of three steps leading down to the dance floor. Drink in hand, he was watching the band and the people dancing. Behind him, a woman wearing a burgundy-red dress came over to the top of the stairs, stopped momentarily and glanced at the man, and then walked down to the step below him, to stand slightly ahead of him and to his left. She began to move her hips in rhythm to the music and simultaneously moved her feet in dancing motions. The young man continued to stare at the band. She continued to sway and move her feet. He continued to stare at the band. After about a minute, she glanced at him again, stopped moving, turned, and walked up the stairs to stop some 5 feet away, behind a railing that separates the dance floor from the rest of the bar. There, she moved neither her hips nor her feet. (Later, we saw her talking to two other men, proving that she was willing to interact with men that evening, though she never again approached the young man just described.)

By not responding to her overtly, this young man *de facto* rejected any overture she was possibly making. To say this, we need assume nothing about her motivations, for it does not matter *why* she approached him: an interaction cannot proceed if the person approached simply ignores you. Nor do we need to know anything about his state of mind—that "He was shy," for example. True, but he might have been indifferent to her, or somewhat drunk, or . . . whatever. Either way, his non-response prohibited any interaction from developing with her.

In contrast, an interaction did begin in the next example.

The bar of Example 3, early evening in spring 1979.

A woman with dark hair and a white jacket came into the bar, stopped at the doorway, and looked around. As she scanned across the people in the bar, she saw a tightly built bearded man standing alone a few feet in front of her. She focused on him for a moment, and then walked directly toward him and stopped a pace or two ahead of him to watch the band and dancers. As she stood, she swayed slightly in rhythm to the music. He turned towards her, looked for a moment, and then spoke. She immediately turned to look back at him. Her eyes flickered briefly across his face, and she answered him. They then began to talk.

These virtually identical examples illustrate escalation and response quite clearly. When the man did not respond (in Example 4), the interaction could not proceed, and when he did (Example 5), it did.*

The approach is not the only escalation point of the sequence. The whole sequence is filled with them. At each escalation point, the recipient of the escalation must respond overtly and positively, or the interaction will fail. Moreover, passing the first escalation point—approaching and talking—is no guarantee that the two people will pass the *next* one, which involves turning.

EXAMPLE 6
_____

The bar in Example 5, early evening in spring 1979.

> A woman entered the bar, walked to the bar iself, and sat next to a man. Neither greeted each other, indicating that neither knew the other. She ordered, and then looked at the man next to her. He looked back (that is, he responded to her approach) and they began to talk. She gradually turned to face him, nodding as they talked. Initially, she looked at him nearly constantly, her elbow some 6 inches from his. However, he did not turn towards her, and the conversation kept faltering. She would turn away and back and would again begin talking, but he neither turned nor looked extensively at her. Eventually, she folded her arms across the bar, and, lifting one hand, placed it on her face (on his side). She then moved away from him on her barstool, and the interaction broke off permanently.

This is the "crossed T" configuration. It is unstable: either both partners eventually turn, or the interaction ceases. Turning is an escalation. When it occurs, the partner must respond actively to it. To do nothing when the partner turns will cut the interaction short.

In the following example, the man rejected several escalations. We were sitting immediately next to the couple, at the corner of the bar, so that we could observe quite clearly as well as overhear their conversation (which they were not attempting to hide).

EXAMPLE 7
_____

A motor hotel bar in New Jersey, early evening in fall 1979.

> The couple came into the room together (so they obviously knew each other), and seated themselves at the bar. She had dark hair and a blouse open to reveal her cleavage (and, apparently, no bra). He was older, with white-grey hair and a white shirt open at the neck. After they sat, ordered drinks, and lit cigarettes,

---

*Certain male readers may not believe that the mere approach of a woman represents an escalation of any kind at all. "She was just there," a man might say. However, women often explicitly describe approaching a man as a hint that he should talk to her.

she began to talk about her decision to leave her husband. He tried to persuade her not to do so, but she indicated that it was all settled. Now that her mind was made up, she indicated, she felt that now she could do anything. "I feel so *free*," she said.

At first, she leaned directly towards him, sitting half-turned to face him, and looking at him nearly continuously. He sat leaning back in his chair, smiling and nodding, but without reciprocating her leaning. Several times she leaned fully towards him, thereby pulling the fabric of her blouse tight against her breasts and widening her cleavage. He did not look down. Nor did they ever synchronize, though they occasionally nodded together, and, once, both raised their arms simultaneously.

Slowly, their conversation ceased. Finally, they both sat silently, with her now facing the bar, leaned back in her seat, and with him leaning on the bar itself, looking around. After a while, she said she wanted some water, and since there was water in her hotel room, she was going to her room. She then left. He remained at the bar for the next hour or so.

By leaning forward and exposing her decolletage, she created an opportunity that *could* have led to increased intimacy. Her conversation also created such an opportunity. Because he did not respond when she escalated the interaction, he rejected any overtures she might have been making.

There are two additional, but important points here. First, his manners were good, at least as such things are judged. He acted towards her in a friendly and attentive way—he listened, joined in the conversation, and seemed interested in what she was saying. But these responses are not appropriate for escalating *courtship*. For example, he could have leaned towards her, touched her, complimented her appearance, or assured her that she was attractive. He did none of these things. Thus, regardless of his motives, his non-responsiveness ultimately led to the breakdown of the interaction.

Second, if we compare this interaction with that between the blonde woman and the man in the airport bar (Example 1, p. 81), we see that the topic of conversation *by itself* does not produce non-verbal intimacy, or determine whether the couple will focus on each other intimately. The two women spoke about very similar problems. But in Example 1, the two people were mutually involved, while in the present example, they were not. This too is quite typical: even though conversational intimacy usually increases as the sequence proceeds, the topic of conversation itself does *not* produce intimacy. Even though the topic remains trite and banal, non-verbal intimacy can build swiftly. Intimacy depends on the escalation and response sequence, and, as Example 1 implies, conversational and non-verbal intimacy build together, in parallel with the onset of full-body synchronization.

The next example illustrates how touching also represents an escalation that, if ignored, will lead to the cessation of the interaction.

EXAMPLE 8

A neighborhood tavern in New Jersey, late afternoon in fall 1980.

A tall woman with very long blonde hair was sitting opposite a man at a table. They apparently knew each other, and she was talking animatedly. She leaned forward and back while moving her arms, hands, head, and hair. At first, he leaned back in the chair, legs spread and hands clasped behind his head (a common male posture). Thus, they were not in postural synchronization. Then he leaned forward, placing both arms on the table. Both were looking directly at each other. She too leaned forward and touched him lightly on the arm. He did not move. Within a few moments, she again touched his arm, but again he did not respond. She leaned back, and over the next few minutes began to lean forward less and less frequently. Thus, movement synchronizatiion broke down completely. She started to look around the bar, got up, left the table, and went to the bar to talk to several people. The man remained at the table by himself.

Just as surely as the man rejected the women in the burgundy-red dress when he did not look at her (Example 4), this man too rejected the woman's overture. In fact, of all the escalation behaviors we have observed, touch is perhaps the most important. A touch not reciprocated will nearly always lead to the rapid, complete cessation of the courtship sequence.

In summary, the courtship sequence develops through a series of discrete steps, marked by observable escalation points: the approach, looking, turning, and the first touch. At an escalation point, an overture made must be accepted emotionally and responded to overtly. The sequence ceases when the couple fails to negotiate any of these escalation points. Successful interactions pass through all these escalation points and lead, ultimately, to full-body synchronization and intense, shared attention.

Thus, the reader need not feel a grim sense of failure after reading the examples in which the escalation-response sequence did not complete itself. The course of true love may not run smooth, but it *can* be travelled.

Some Implications, Practical and Otherwise

People vs. Rats

Somehow, these sequences seem similar to what our rats did. Clearly, it is not that people and rats enact the same behavior patterns. Humans simply do not possess the episodic interaction pattern of rats, and rats simply do not write lovers' poetry. But in both forms of courtship, the two individuals are reacting to each other and, in a successful interaction, the behavior of each is shaped by what the other does.

Furthermore, these behavioral reactions and shapings occur—even in love-struck human beings!—without either participant necessarily knowing what behavior patterns they are enacting. Some people are quite conscious of their behavior. But knowledge is not necessary for the courtship sequence to occur. For example, few people know that synchronization exists, but many people can in fact move in synchrony with someone else.

The emotional and intensely symbolic relationship between the man and woman is paralleled by another form of interaction that seems purely behavioral. It is mediated by the looks, turns, and touches just described. Now, for the lover, it is not that a gaze "means" love, for few lovers are so remote from their own behavior that they can label their actions so neatly and scientifically (an assertion I make despite what is called "symbolic interactionism" in social psychology; e.g., Stryker, 1977, p. 150). When they are with each other, the lovers do not *want* to dissect or label their behavior. Instead, for the lover, the gaze *is* love, and, if returned, will communicate love. For the other person, the gaze is also love, and he or she reacts to it with a reach, perhaps, or a touch.

Moreover, the word *parallel* means just that. The kinds of behavioral communication produced by a touch or by synchronization do not occur at some "lower" or "animalistic" plane of life above which exist the lofty dimensions of the emotions. Instead, *two* channels of communication are open between the lovers. One is the set of shared emotional meanings that they can discuss with each other—for example, whether to sleep with each other or, even, to marry. But such meanings are elicited in the lovers' minds by a second channel of communication which operates through the *embodied* touches, leans, reaches, gazes and, above all, the synchronizations I have been discussing.

Accordingly, the outsider watching the lovers sees that emotional and behavioral communication are *integrated* even if the lovers themselves do not consciously know that they are moving in synchrony with each other. And here we reach a profound difference between rats and humans.

As far as we know, rats (and most mammals) simply do not possess the neurophysiological capacities to create emotionally meaningful categories like "love." For them, there is no multiplicity of channels to integrate—they respond, react to each other, modify their behavior without simultaneously expressing or symbolizing those events emotionally. But humans communicate both behaviorally *and* symbolically and must integrate those channels if they are to communicate at all.

Thus, human courtship is *not* a matter of "animal instincts" but is based on neurophysiologically real abilities to process the behavior and its emotional meanings simultaneously. It is as if the brain of the rat deals only with behavior, while the human brain deals with both behavior *and* meaning. The human brain thus closes the loop between behavior and feeling. A touch is made behaviorally, and in immediate parallel the feeling grows: "I love her." And *that* is what makes us so different from non-human animals like rats: *the ability first to create and next to integrate emotional symbols and meanings into the flow of behavior that connects us to other people.*

So, again we encounter the biological concept of function. The courtship sequence is profoundly functional in the biological sense. By definition, it contributes to the participants' capacities to reproduce. *The integration of emotional and behavioral communication during courtship is therefore one function of the human brain itself.*

Even if chimpanzees, orangutans, and gorillas perform behavior patterns during courtship that are strikingly reminiscent of human behavior [for example, mutual gazing, touching, embracing, the grazing of lips (Hrdy, 1981, p. 137)], human beings are not simply "apes in disguise" when they court. In humans, these primate behavior patterns have become elaborated behaviorally (e.g., are more extensive and complex) and have become attached to emotions that have symbolic meanings. Human behavioral communication is not "animalistic," an idea that once again returns us to the Nature/Nurture dichotomy. If we call behavioral (non-verbal) communication "protocommunication" and liken it to the communication of a man and his dog [as Bernard explicitly did (1972b, pp. 97–110)], we have *dualized* human experience and, by dividing it into Natural *and* Cultural, or into animalistic *and* symbolic, we have set our total experience at war with itself, rather than seeing that in behavioral and symbolic communication are *human* capacities to respond, or not, to what another person is doing.

Accordingly, courtship is neither a fixed series of symbolic events encoded in people's sexual scripts, nor a fixed series of "primitive" behavioral events encoded into the genes. Courtship is an *interpenetrating* biological and cultural process that comes into existence as two people respond to each other and *simultaneously* create their behavior and construct the feelings and meanings that lead to behavioral synchronization *and* emotional intimacy. Courtship is biological and emotional and behavioral all at once, without any seam or division between what otherwise might appear to be very different universes of human experience. They are all simply facets of one and the same process.

Theory and Practice for Lovers and Scientists

One can talk endlessly about interactions like these. Some people will see the courtship sequence as a paradigm for studying interpersonal communication (Knapp, 1983); or as a stage on which inequalities in male–female power relationships are played out (Henley, 1973); as a model for how people create their own couple-identity (Lewis, 1973); as a microcosm for how meaningfulness itself is created (Poole, 1975); or as representing the play of sociological principles that range from approval-seeking (Rosenfeld, 1966) through status (Mehrabian, 1969) to a full panoply of interpersonal rituals and norms (Goffman, 1971, e.g., Chapter 5, pp. 188–237; Goffman, 1963, e.g., Chapter 8, pp. 124–148).

These viewpoints and interests are all important. But I want to ask some different questions.

If the courtship sequence is not pre-programmed in the genes or in the mind, what accounts for its stability? Why don't different lovers enact very different versions of the sequence? Why does the sequence cease if one person tries to become too intimate too quickly? These are practical questions for the lovers, because nothing has greater importance than the future of their relationship.

So, momentarily, let us set aside the idea that a person's *individual* motivations and desires drive the courtship sequence. Objectively, courtship involves *two* people who form a dyad in which each person sends and receives signals. The lovers are linked together in a *loop* of communication, not a hierarchy in which one person alone sets the pace and tone of the interaction. When our focus shifts to the dyad, then the origin of the courtship sequence may be easier to find.

Predicting the Outcome

For the scientist, this objective viewpoint has a great advantage over the lover's own subjectivity. The couple's behavior at an escalation point enables the observer to predict (in the sense of anticipate or foretell) if the interaction will continue towards intimacy. By "predict," I do not mean from *a priori* theoretical grounds, but "predict" *right now*—that is, at 9:18 this evening—if the couple will remain together over the next period of time.

For example, a man has just met a woman, and he touches her, but her shoulders stiffen slightly. We can *at that moment* predict that the interaction will gradually cease. Likewise, if *any* escalation is refused, we can make a similar prediction. Over and over, we could confirm such predictions, and over and over we found that courtship continues only if the couple does successfully and mutually negotiate each escalation point.

The lover might find such predictions useful, at least at escalation points. Thus, he touches her and she stiffens and turns away. The observer knows that the interaction is probably doomed, but does the man know? The answer is *No,* not if he believes that courtship is simply the mechanical enactment of behavior patterns like touching. And believing that, he simply pays no attention to how his overture was *received.* If, later, he is rebuffed, it is because courtship is dyadically created, not driven unilaterally by one person's will or desire.

However, under other circumstances, such sequences of mutual escalation and response can be quite stable, rather than terminating rapidly. Thus, he touches her hand as they sit facing each other at a table, and she leans forward slightly and smiles. The observer can now predict that the interaction will continue—an escalation point has been passed—at least until the *next* escalation point (no one can predict the complete outcome; we think we do so only in hindsight!)

These "predictions" differ from the prediction one might make if one looked at the sky, saw wispy clouds, and "predicted" rain. Then we depend on *correlations* between events, that is, on the purely empirical observation that wispy clouds are often a *sign* of rain. However, such correlations do not arise from knowing what *causes* rain, but depend on empirically observed associations between events, or even on pure folklore. But when the observer watches a touch being reciprocated and predicts that the couple will stay together for a while at least, the prediction is closer to the causal level partly because touch is not a *sign* of intimacy as much as it *is* intimacy in a sociosexual encounter. Its reciprocation therefore reveals that intimacy is mutual, at least to some extent and for now. Predictions the observer makes at an escalation point about the immediate future (and that the lover *could* make) are not merely correlations between otherwise arbitrary events, like wispy clouds and rain. Instead, they work so well that they seem to pertain to real causal events below the growth of intimacy. And what might these causal processes be?

Feedback and the Stability of Courtship

As it turns out, we can "model" the interaction quite well by understanding that courtship is dyadic and involves the reciprocal exchange of signals between the two people.

But first, a word about scientific models. Their purpose is not to explain everything about a phenomenon like courtship, but to stress certain of its aspects which arise logically from the premises of the model. A model is certainly never complete and is not even necessarily true. Nonetheless, if we understand the details of courtship better with the model, then it is useful, and we can suspect that it contains the germs of a genuine causal explanation for how intimacy develops during courtship.

I suggest that courtship involves behavioral "feedback" between the two people. A familiar mechanical example of feedback is a thermostat and a furnace. If it gets too warm, the thermostat opens, and the furnace shuts down. The temperature drops. The thermostat then closes, the furnace turns on, and the temperature rises. The cycle continues over and over, and the result is that room temperature remains within preset limits.

"Self-regulatory" systems like this are very common both in engineering and biology. They depend on the transfer of signals back and forth between the two components of the system (e.g., the thermostat sends the furnace an electrical current—a "signal"—when the temperature drops below the preset limit). These signals than alter the state of the receiver (e.g., the current from the thermostat switches the furnace from *off* to *on*). In many ways, courtship resembles systems like this, simply because the two people send signals back and forth and respond to them.

In rough analogy, courtship is like a feedback system in which limits are gradually reset as the couple moves towards intimacy. At first, the limits are set low for each person—they are only talking. They may have plans and hopes for each other that involve much more than talking, but the behavioral limits on intimacy are not yet set so high. As they become interested in each other, the limits change for both of them. One person—the man *or* the woman—turns somewhat, and the other person responds. They have moved past an escalation point, and the limits on intimacy are reset upwards. One reaches out and touches, and the other reciprocates.

The limits are again reset upwards, towards greater intimacy, and they continue to touch each other. They look at each other more and more, in gazes that are reciprocated and therefore create further intimacy. If all goes well, the limits again shift upwards. Finally, they are *very* interested indeed.

Signal Exchange in Courtship

With some refinements, the thermostat–furnace analogy can provide the start for a very useful way of understanding courtship and the escalation–response process, although the process is hardly as simple as a mechanical thermostat sending an electrical current to a furnace. Imagine two people sending signals and responses back and forth in their conversation, looks, and touches. Sometimes the sender hopes the signal will convey interest or, at other times, lack of interest. Sometimes the signals are more intense than at other times—a lingering look, for example, as opposed to a quick, casual glance. Sometimes signals elicit very strong positive or negative responses, and sometimes they seem to be ignored. Despite these complexities, I suggest that their mutually exchanged signals link the two people together into a complex but understandable self-regulated feedback system.

Although the idea of behavioral feedback is hardly new in either animal or human research, I want to develop some of its implications for understanding courtship. [My argument is based on ideas presented by Beach (1976); see also McClintock (1983) and Argyle (1969, pp. 127–215, e.g., p. 181).] Not only is behavioral feedback characteristic of animal behavior, but it is based on the biological fact that all organisms respond to their environment by changing their behavior. So, with behavioral feedback, we can build into the model one premise of the biosocial approach.

Let me begin simply. If person A—a man, say—starts, his first signal triggers a response from person B, which in turn triggers a response from A, which triggers a response from B, and so on. It is as if they merely reflect signals back and forth, like a pair of mirrors. (Such conversations are called "making small talk.") But in courtship, the signals not only change but also become more intense as time passes. For example, person B leans forward towards the man—for her, leaning represents an increase in her interest. Or person A may increasingly often look at the woman's face and hair—which, for him, also represents an increase in how intensely he expresses his interest.*

---

*Certain readers will object *strenuously* to my saying that behavior varies in "intensity." "*Feelings* can differ in intensity," they might say, "or even some physically measurable *component* of behavior, like pressure measured in dynes per square centimeter, can be called 'more' or 'less' intense, but behavior patterns *per se* cannot be so compared." Alas, these are quibbles. The English language itself makes it easy to compare the intensity of two behavior patterns—for example, a *gaze* is less intense than a *leer* or an *ogle*. Nor is the difference simply that of duration: a gaze prolonged does not become a leer. Moreover, when questioned, people will spontaneously compare intensities of courtship behavior—for example, when a woman says that a man "comes on too strong," she is not really trying to measure how strongly she herself feels (and when she does, she might say "I *really hate* it when men come on too strong"). Thus, "intensity" is often in the eyes of the beholder, and is relative to the person's feelings

So, imagine person B receiving A's first signal (e.g., he looks at her from across the room). She must now decide not only if she *will* respond (a yes/no decision), but also decide how *intensely* she will respond. For example, she might simply smile, or she might walk over and say, "Hi! I've been wanting to meet you!"

How might person B make such a decision? Many factors enter her decision: her sexual status, her belief that he is good-looking, her present level of boredom as she stands at the hors-d'oeuvre table or at the bar. So, we boil all these factors down to what can be called a "response curve," which, in effect, says respond *strongly, moderately, hardly at all,* with all degrees of intensity of interest in between. (Different people have different definitions of intensity. For one woman, a smile returned to the man may be quite intimate while, to another, a smile may be simply polite. These might be called differences in behavioral style.)

But the woman's response to the man is not determined *solely* by how interesting she finds him or by her own behavioral style. Her reaction also depends on the intensity of the *man's signal to her.* Thus, she may like it if this man seems very friendly at first—that is, if *he* is intense, she will respond intensely, but if he is not, she will respond less intensely. For example, she might feel shy and want him to make clear overtures of friendliness, or she may simply like "self-confident" men. [Or, as Mme. Verdurin said when speaking of Odette's feelings for Swann in Marcel Proust's *Swann's Way,* " . . . but he's always shy with her, and that makes her shy with him," n.d., p. 326).] But another woman with the same man might *not* want him to "come on too strong" as she perceives it and will respond coolly to a strong expression of interest. For example, she might not like it one bit if he touches her, even briefly, and she will move back or look away from him when he does. The intensity of his signal in part determines the intensity of her response.

Furthermore, her response depends not on what *he* may have intended, but on her *own* assessment of how strong his signal is. And, for her, with this man at this moment, the relationship between intensity of signal received and response returned is precisely what I am calling her *response curve.* It shows how this woman responds when there are changes in the intensity of the man's signals to her. Thus, in Figure 2A, the woman responds strongly to an intense signal from a particular man, but less strongly to a less intense signal. In Figure 2B is the other woman. She responds coolly to the same signal from the same man, but more strongly when he is less intense. The differences between them is represented by the differences in the *slopes* of their response curves for this man. Thus, the two curves show how each woman

at that time. No universal scale of behavioral intensity need exist for us to believe a woman who says that she dislikes men who "paw" her but "doesn't mind too much" if a man touches her when she dances. For her, "pawing" *is in fact more intense* than "touching during dancing." It is therefore a major mistake to assume that "intensity" means merely what it would in old-fashiond physiological psychology—e.g., how strong a pinch must be (in dynes per square centimeter) to elicit a given degree of response. In courtship, "intensity" is personally assessed and has symbolic and emotional meaning that cannot be measured in dynes per square centimeter. Nonetheless, it is very real to the participants. Thus, the only "intensity scales" that count are internal to the man and woman who are interacting, and, empirically, they *do* distinguish behavior by its global or overall intensity.

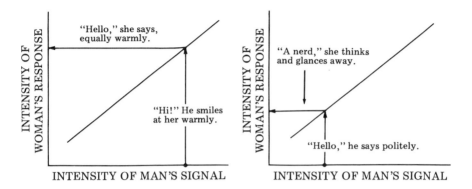

(A) FIRST WOMAN

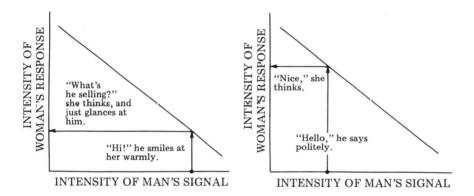

(B) SECOND WOMAN

Figure 2 Response curves for two different women. The first woman (2A) responds warmly to strong signals, and does not respond strongly to less strong signals. In contrast, the second woman (2B) is the opposite. She responds most warmly when the man's signals are not "too pushy." Actually, these curves are not mathematical *lines,* but are *bands* or *zones* that cluster around the lines drawn on the figures. Moreover, the bands can curve more or less sharply. But I hope the reader will allow me some simplifications for discussion's purposes.

will respond to whatever signal the man sends. (He has no idea which way either woman's curve slopes.)

Of course, a woman's response curve can change with different men or even vary with time. However, the idea of a response curve enables us to see how a stable and regular sequence of behavior can be produced interactively, rather than by saying "the genes made her do it." It goes as follows.

The encounter has begun with his first signal. She has decided how to respond and has reciprocated his signal, e.g., by smiling at him. Now it is his turn. He too has a response curve that shows how *he* will respond to the intensity of her signal. Again, men differ in their response curves. Some men like it if this woman's behavior is clear and overt, and will respond more intensely if her signal is also intense, e.g., if she comes over to him when he looks at her and smiles (Figure 3A). But other men do not like women who are "too aggressive," as these men say (Figure 3B). For this man, the stronger this woman's signal, the *less* intense his response. Again, these differences are represented by the difference in the slopes of the men's response curves. But, either way, the woman has smiled, and he now responds, e.g., by smiling back or by walking over and starting to talk to her.

Now their response curves are paired with each other. She assesses the intensity of his behavior and responds with a degree of intensity given by her response curve. Then *he* responds to *her* . . . and back and forth it goes, to give the opening of the courtship sequence. Now, however, the two people are not simply reflecting or mirroring each other's responses, but are changing their responses, according to the person's response curve and the perceived intensity of the partner's behavior.

Response systems like this have some surprising and enlightening properties. In particular, progress through the courtship sequence depends on the precise slopes of the response curves of the two people for each other. In words, this means that how intensely a person responds to the partner can determine the immediate future of their interaction.

Settling for Less—or More

Sometimes, however, the result differs from what the two people themselves might believe—e.g., that what counts is what one feels internally, or that it is not one's response that counts, but self-initiated "sexual aggression." Let me illustrate.

The first example can occur between courting couples or even between married individuals. I observed it dramatically when a young man approached a young woman, sitting at a table in a bar. She had loose blonde hair, and was wearing a white, off-the-shoulder top. They greeted each other with a light hug. He sat nearly fully facing her and looking at her face, hair, and upper body. Quite frequently he would lean towards her and touch her shoulder or hair. She would then draw back slightly. Though she never reciprocated his touching, she continued to talk animatedly, and turned towards him. With time, his touches and looks grew less frequent until finally he had stopped touching her. Simultaneously, their conversation grew

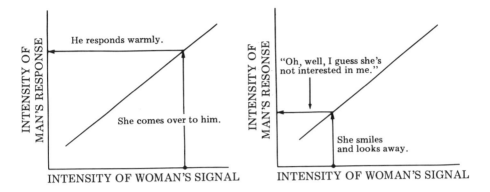

(A) FIRST MAN

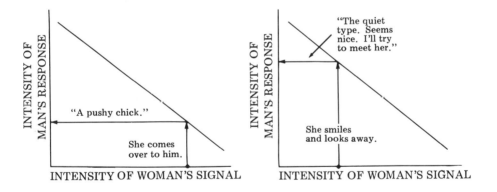

(B) SECOND MAN

Figure 3   Response curves for two different men. The first man (3A) responds warmly when the woman sends strong and clear signals, and does not respond to less strong signals. In contrast, the second man (3B) is the opposite: he does not respond warmly to "pushy women" or "pushy chicks," as he might say, but, instead, prefers quieter and less "aggressive" women, as he again might say. If one writes "woman" instead of "man," Figure 3 is the same as Figure 2.

less animated and he finally stopped talking, looked around the bar for a while, and then got up and left.

The example illustrates how an observer can predict the outcome of an interaction. She did not respond to his escalation (touches and looks) and the interaction eventually ceased. However, the observation also suggests how two people's response curves can lead to a gradual decrease in signal intensity (de-escalation) through behavioral feedback between them.

Let me illustrate the principle by using a dialogue created to resemble the observations that is quite typical of real interactions.* In it, the man sees the woman, whom he does not know, and is very interested.

He starts by walking over and giving her a "big hello." She does not know him, and does not like such openings from any man, but she is interested "sort of, maybe." So she responds coolly; that is, their response curves slope in opposite directions (Figure 4).

HE: Hi! *(Big smile, looks in her eyes.)* [He is very interested in her; perhaps she is close to his template. Point 1 in Figure 4.]

SHE: Hello. *(She doesn't smile and barely glances at him.)* [She thinks that he is coming on too strong, so she does not respond strongly. Point 2.]

HE: *(Somewhat disappointed.)* Uh, hello. What's that you're drinking? [For him, not at all an intense response. He was going to say that she is pretty, but decided against it. Point 3.]

SHE: [Now that he is less pushy, she feels a bit more friendly.] Just a glass of soda. I don't like alcohol much. *(She smiles, looking at him a bit longer.)* [Point 4. Her response has become a bit more intense than at point 2.]

HE: *(Looks at her again, lifts his glass, moving it between them, i.e., a slight reach towards her.)* Oh, I don't either really. It makes me do things I might regret. *(Smiles at her again, shifts his weight towards her slightly, again looking at her while he moves his glass slightly towards her.)* [Point 5.]

SHE: [Again, he has become too pushy, so she responds coolly.] Really? We don't want *that* to happen. *(Glances away briefly, then turns slightly towards him.)* [Her response is now more friendly than at point 2, but is less friendly than at point 4. Point 6.]

HE: [Again, somewhat disappointed, but at least she is still talking to him.] Oh, it won't. *(He looks away from her and then back, and pauses briefly.* My name is Jim, by the way. What's yours? [Now he has become far less intense than originally and has moved towards a "polite" conversation. Point 7.]

As their interaction and dialogue continue, their reactions converge towards the middle of the range, in fact, towards the region of intersection between their response curves. They will remain in the middle range, because if he *again* becomes

---

*The dialogue gives an observable sequence of behavior plus ascriptions of feeling and motivation that are confirmable with interviews.

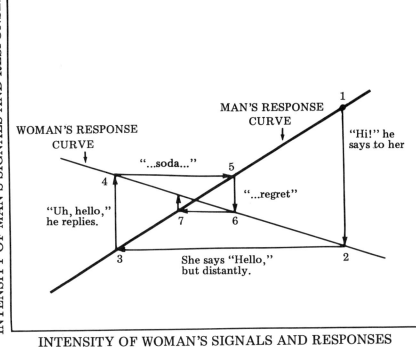

Figure 4 A man and woman talking in a quickly stabilizing interaction. His warm overture (1) elicits a cool response (2), which cools him off (3), to which she responds more warmly (4). And so it goes until they reach the mid-point. The man sends signals to the woman parallel to the Y-axis, and the woman sends the man signals along the X-axis. Anyone who wants to simulate such interaction systematically will find that the X and Y axes must be reversed for the man and woman. No one else need worry about it.

more intense in expressing interest, she will respond coolly (as she did in lines 2 and 6), which, in turn, will cause his level of expressed interest to drop (as it did at lines 3 and 7). It is like the thermostat and furnace. If his response becomes too hot, her reaction cools him down, but if her response becomes warmer, so will his, which, in turn, causes *her* to become cooler. Finally, they simply cycle back and forth near the middle.

This outcome is inevitable, given their response curves for each other and the feedback loop between them. But neither person necessarily likes it. He is expressing less interest than he felt initially, even though he may still find her very attractive. He is not expressing his *actual* level of interst. For her, their final range of intensity of expression is *higher* than her initial level, and she may be expressing *more* interest than she actually feels.

Next, for him, the swings and shifts in her responses—from quite cool (points 2 and 6) to fairly warm (point 4)—are very great indeed. He may not understand why she "blows hot and cold," and may conclude that her emotions are not under rational control. (One male informant spoke of women in "moodswing" for such situations; he meant it as unfriendly.) Finally, she may decide that he usually "comes on too strong" rather than alternating between interest and disappointment. For both of them, there is something of incomprehensible frustration and futility in the whole exercise.

But the shifts in intensity are not incomprehensible at all. They follow directly from the fact that each person adjusts his or her own behavior according to what the other person just did. When the response curves slope in opposite directions, the result is feedback that stabilizes the interaction around a middle ("thermostatted") range.

A similar process can occur between a husband and wife concerning sexual intercourse. If one responds too strongly for the other's tastes and preferences, the partner therefore tries to "cool it off." The two people can enter a similar pattern of cycling back and forth in sexual intensity and behavior. Again, they ultimately will stabilize around a middle range of sexual activity.

However, if nothing keeps the two people together (like a marriage or even the lack of other prospects), then they will probably separate. Perhaps each now thinks that the "chemistry just wasn't right," or even that members of the other sex are "just peculiar." From their *individual* viewpoints, their feelings make sense, but the objective observer sees the two people as part of a system in which signals are sent back and forth. And, for the observer, the outcome is therefore predictable.

True Love, Once Again

It can be depressing to think about. Sometimes, however, the two people are better matched—for example, the slopes of their response curves for each other are both positive. Then, each overture can generate a somewhat more intense response, which in turn generates more intensity, in reverberating and escalating increments.

I call the following dialogue the "earring scenario"; it is based on a real exchange between a man and woman. I report it in the present tense to illustrate how an interaction can steadily become more intimate and emotionally intense. The woman ("she") had long dark hair and was wearing a light blue hat with a floppy brim that partly covered her face. She was "strikingly" pretty. The man ("he") was sitting three seats away. Each was talking to a companion (arranged she, female friend, male friend, he) and they could see each other past the two people in the middle. He had been gazing directly at her for a while. The conversation began when she got up and walked towards him (an approach). As she did, he turned towards her, looked up, and said:

HE: I'm sorry, I was staring at you. I hope you don't mind. You're a very beautiful woman.

SHE: *(Stopping and turning towards him.)* Thank you. I like being appreciated. *(She looks at him with a slight smile.)*

HE: *(He gazes at her face and hair.)* Those are pretty earrings. Where did you get them? I'm Bob. What's your name? *(He turns more towards her, continuing to look up at her face and hair.)*

SHE: *(Turning still further towards him, tilting her head slightly so her hair brushes her shoulder, and looking in his eyes.)* I'm Elizabeth. Why don't you guess? *(She touches one earring briefly, brushing her hair aside momentarily.)*

HE: *(Continuing to look at her face, hair, and earrings. Returning his glass to the bar behind him, he turns back to her.)* Well, I'm not sure. An artist friend made them?

SHE: No. *(Smiles slightly while continuing to look at him.)* You get another guess.

HE: I give up. *(They are looking directly at each other, now nearly fully turned.)*

SHE: I made them. *(Smiles again.)* How did you guess that I was an artist? [Et seq.]

To be sure, some readers might dismiss the dialogue as unmitigated romanticism, but both it and the processes it involves are quite real. And it shows nicely how signals sent and received can *amplify* each other, rather than reaching a less than satisfactory stopping point somewhere in the middle range (as in the preceding dialogue). Figure 5 shows the earring scenario in diagrammatic form.

But Figure 5 also reveals several subtleties that might otherwise escape our notice. The first implication of Figure 5 is that the slopes of the response curves determine whether or not escalation occurs. Again, we might believe that escalation depends on one person being assertive ("aggressive") and therefore overcoming the partner's reluctance. However, this impression is false. When one partner does *not* welcome the other person's more intense overtures, we do not have escalation at all. Instead, as the first dialogue showed (and the data demonstrate), then there is gradual *diminution* of intensity as the interaction cycles downwards. When the two response curves both slope upwards, as in the earring scenario, then each person responds more and more positively to the other's overtures in the stepwise increments that help give escalation its name (Figure 5). If escalation depends on feedback, then the courtship sequence *must* be mutual if it is to achieve intimacy, and true love cannot grow from force.

The second implication is perhaps less expected. Escalation will occur only if the interaction is initiated by the person who sends *less* intense signals. In an escalating interaction, the first signal must go from the *lower* response curve to the *higher* one. The point is illustrated by the earring scenario because he began the interaction by merely *gazing* at her, but she responded by *approaching* him. Such a gaze is ambiguous: he might simply be bored with his male friend and be staring at a conveniently located person. His gaze does not commit him to any form of interaction. But when she took his relatively ambiguous signal as an opportunity to approach him, she responded more strongly—she upped the ante, so to speak. His

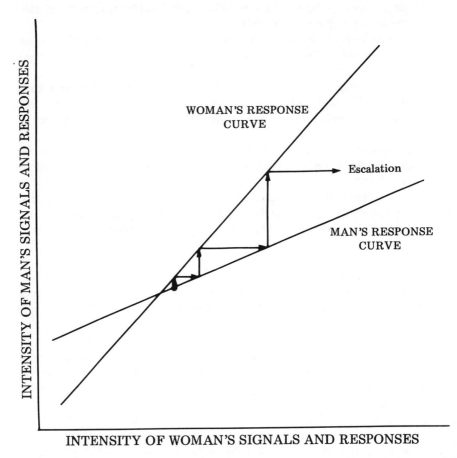

INTENSITY OF WOMAN'S SIGNALS AND RESPONSES

Figure 5 The earring scenario. The man starts by looking at her. Whereupon, she responds more warmly each time he extends an overture to her. Soon, they will reach an escalation point—for example, she might offer to "show" him one of her earrings, and after taking it from her ear, give it to the man while touching his hand. The axes are the same as in Figure 4.

opening line is also relatively unintense—by apologizing to her while giving her a genuine compliment, he gave her the chance to put an end to it all if she wanted to. ("Oh, you were?" she could have said. "I really didn't notice.") But again she responded more strongly, by overtly thanking him and welcoming his appreciative attention. Likewise, her question "Why don't you guess?" is simultaneously flirtatious and inviting, for it promises an on-going conversation. In fact, *throughout* the scenario she responded strongly, thereby eliciting his stronger and stronger responses.

It is a surprising conclusion, especially for men who believe in "coming on strong'' to women. Yet, if the man's response curve is higher than hers, the interaction will deteriorate. I will illustrate this by again using the opening of the earring scenario.

HE: I'm sorry, I was staring at you. I hope you don't mind. You're a very beautiful woman.

SHE: *(Stopping, and looking at him in surprise. She has been wondering who this is who has been watching her so intently.)* I beg your pardon?

HE: Uh, I'm sorry. I was staring at you just now—I mean, I hope it didn't bother you—?

SHE: That's quite all right. Things like that happen. *(Smiles politely.)* Excuse me. *(Leaves.)*

She has shut down the interaction firmly but still courteously. And he has no recourse but to accept her refusal. The example also shows why it is often unwise for a man to compliment too extravagantly a woman he has just met: if her response curve for him is lower than his for her, it will turn her off, not on. Men, take note.

Finally, interactions that "start out well, but never get anywhere" can be modeled by assuming that the couple's interaction begins below the point of intersection (rather than above it, as before). Then signal exchange occurs intensely at first, but soon converges to the middle range and does not become more intense as long as the response curves remain unchanged. And, sooner or later, one partner becomes bored or frustrated, bringing the interaction to a halt.

Other interactions can also very realistically be modeled by using these response curves. Indeed, modeling them is so easy that I suggest that the courtship sequence and escalation are in fact built step-by-step by behavioral and emotional feedback between the man and woman.*

*Two cautions about these feedback curves and dialogues should be made. First, a reader familiar with social scientific, especially sociological, theories of courtship may find my approach "mechanistic," "oversimplified," and so on, in contrast to the very general—indeed, global—theories of writers like Duck and Miell (1983). Those reactions may underestimate how counter-intuitive feedback can be, compared to Duck and Miell's intuitively obvious discussion. But the response curves in the text are quite compatible with more general social scientific theories, despite their unfamiliar appearance.

Second, the dialogues are underlain by two principles which act in real conversations with the escalation–response process. The first is "answerability," which means that Person B can easily answer or respond to whatever Person A has just said. The requirement for answerability is actually quite stringent. For example, in the following "dialogue," set in a bar between two strangers, each line is in fact not answerable at all. Instead, the sequence sounds forced.

HE: Hi. My name is Eddie. I used to work in a store downtown.
SHE: Wow.
HE: Umm, I was wondering, I mean, like . . .
SHE: Yeah! Right!
HE: How 'bout a beer?

But what happens next? Obviously, a conversation can become only so intimate and no more. I suggest that when the escalations go offscale, so to speak, then the two people find *new* ways to express intimacy (as shown in Figure 1). For example, in the earring scenario, the man and woman are quickly nearing the ceiling of intimacy that flirtatious *talk* can provide. So, soon, one will touch the other. Then a new ascent of intimacy will occur, until they are at the ceiling of intimacy that touching can provide in public. Simultaneously, they have begun to synchronize their movements, and are now sending and receiving signals so fast that the exchange is virtually simultaneous.

So courtship behavior is *not* a wild excursion into lust or a descent into the "animal" level of existence of a man and his dog. The process is regulated, and the lovers are not out of control, even though they may not know how delicately and even cautiously they are negotiating their way through a series of stepwise and reciprocated increases in mutual intimacy.

Cartoonists like Gilbert Shelton ("The Fabulous Furry Freak Brothers") and R. Crumb ("Fritz the Cat") have used dialogues like this to mimic two stoned, counterculture types trying to communicate with each other. Otherwise, however, the dialogue is unrealistically arbitrary, a conclusion I state from many hours of observation (see Appendix). A real woman would be far more likely simply to turn away from the man, or perhaps say "So what?" and then turn away. In a real courtship interaction, at least one line of dialogue made by each participant must be answerable, for otherwise the interaction will cease (by definition). The two examples in the text show how interactions can be built line by line, even though a reader may believe that the entire sequence preexisted in the participants' minds (or scripts). "Answerability" is person-specific, but the principle nonetheless remains.

The second principle is that emotional intensity escalates by small, gradual increments in dialogues like these, rather than growing by large jumps. In the following dialogue, invented for two strangers in a bar, the man's second line is much too strong, and her response is downright strange.

HE: Hi. My name is Eddie. What's your name?
SHE: Hi. I'm Janice.
HE: Janice, I have felt myself drawn to you from afar. You are the most beautiful woman in the world. [Too strong, even if she does fit his template. The line is also an emotional and conversational *non sequitur* compared to line 1.]
SHE: I like mice. Do you like mice? [In this context, utterly unanswerable. *Perhaps* an inventive woman might use the last line to shut him up, but otherwise the sequence sounds like the Theatre of the Absurd, *Alice in Wonderland,* or a bad parody.]

The skeptic may feel that each line is *conceivably* answerable. That is true in the same way that "boy the see run" is a *conceivable* version of "see the boy run," but nonetheless the first word-string disobeys empirically well-founded rules of English syntax. Conceivable, yes; English, no. Likewise, the two dialogues above are conceivable but break observable rules of "flirtatious speech."

Thus, by being able to write realistic and accurate dialogue, we can show that "speaking flirtatiously" involves definable rules of linguistic behavior that control how a dialogue develops line by line. These rules concern linguistic structures "above" the level of the sentence, so that the grammaticality of each *individual* line is not an important issue. Rather, these rules for dialogue construction reveal that dialogues are *not* arbitrary strings of sentences tacked one onto the next in an arbitrary but "conceivable" world. Some rules concern how quickly and in what ways a person can express emotional or sexual interest, but others, like answerability, are more purely formal or linguistic. Space limitations prevent further analysis here of these really quite difficult problems, e.g., of defining what a "well-formed" dialogue is.

Moreover, once the couple has reached the level of intimacy represented by synchronization, the cycle of signals, reactions, and signals can continue seemingly indefinitely. Once they are synchronized, each reciprocates the others' actions, so that if a lean and touch from him elicits a warm and reciprocating touch from her, then her touch in turn elicits a second touch from him. Back and forth, each responds to the other and elicits the same response in return. The pattern mirrors itself, and the observer sees full body synchronization.

But the *lovers* make no such analyses. For them, the world has changed. Now, everything focuses on the other person, and the outside world has faded away. Encradled in a mirrored process of response followed by response, experience is reshaped into an idealized rhythm and entrancement. The past vanishes from memory as the two people merge in a world of continuity that sees not anatomy, but allure and enchantment.

On to Biology . . . and More

And, after a while—marriage or that evening—courtship *can* lead to sexual intercourse. Of course, we cannot conclude that couples go through the courtship sequence because they intend to have sex or marry each other. After all, they *have* just met. [Yet the thought of marriage sometimes occurs to a participant *very* early in the sequence as in the quote from Neal in Chapter 1, or in Watson's reaction in *The Sign of Four* or—if you prefer "science"—in the women studied by Silverthorne et al. (1976).] Nonetheless, *no* future involvement can exist if the couple does *not* pass through the courtship sequence. In North America, it is a necessary prerequisite for anything that might follow.

Second, people make love by looking at each other, touching, moving together—in short, with all the actions that we have already encountered as "escalation points." Thus, the precise behavioral features of the escalation points are not arbitrary: they mimic quite precisely what people do when actually making love.

Third, however, the couple's behavior during the sequence is not "fake" intercourse. By the time the two people are fully synchronized, they have communicated to each other *behaviorally* that they can look, touch, move, and interact intimately. In this, they have created the behavioral preconditions for sexual intercourse, and together have swept away any *behavioral* obstacles to moving and touching intimately.

Fourth, I would like to speculate that by the time they are fully synchronized, each person is physiologically prepared for intercourse. (Compare Symons, 1979, p. 179.) If they are not overtly *sexually* aroused, nonetheless each is prepared to become aroused quickly [a state that Whalen (1966) called "high arousability"]. I suspect that the trance-like state that full body synchronization engenders and represents may involve neurochemical changes like those in other trance states, and specifically may involve a class of brain chemicals called endorphins. [Prince (1982) provides a very readable introduction.]

So, in contrast to the biological fixity envisioned by some social scientists and sociobiologists, we have no need to call on the "genes" or other mysterious internal forces to explain how the lovers reached intimacy. Of course *they* may want very much to believe that their love was preordained in the stars, in that ole black magic, or even in the genes. But the outside observer must be less romantic: the development of intimacy is neither magical nor programmed by an inner genetic eye that oversees our search for happiness. Instead, intimacy develops through the exchange of real and embodied signals sent back and forth and which, if the model here is correct, involve feedback with its possibilities of escalation and de-escalation.

The courtship sequence and the escalation–response process each illustrate the biological capacity to alter and adjust one's behavior in response to what is happening externally. Not only does behavior *itself* change (e.g., touching occurs and becomes more frequent) but people can alter *how* their behavior changes. Thus, one and the same woman may have two very different response patterns to two different men: with one, she may (perhaps unconsciously) allow her behavior to become more intimate as time passes, but with another, her behavior will become less intimate. And these capacities to adjust behavior are biosocially functional: if completed, the sequence and its behavioral components are the precursors to intercourse and, barring contraception, impregnation.

And finally, the two people may now be *emotionally* ready for intercourse. Thus, if the observer sees that the courtship sequence prepares the couple behaviorally and perhaps physiologically for intercourse, for the lovers, it is a great deal more. The lovers apparel this process in the cradling magic of each other: a love that they have created around themselves by their exchanged and reciprocated looks, touches, gazes, and synchronized movements.

Finale

. . . The evening has finished, and its dancing and music and entrancements have ended: even if with difficulty, the course of true love has found its home. In the bartender's prosaic "*Last call!*" we hear echoing the end of an older play of love, Theseus' last speech in "Midsummer-Night's Dream," as he addresses his new wife Hippolyta:

> The iron tongue of midnight hath told twelve:
> Lovers, to bed . . .

And here we reach a paradox. We would, of course, like to conclude that if our lovers are behaviorally and physiologically prepared to have intercourse, and if they are as entranced with each other as they seem, then they would simply proceed to make love. But that they do not *necessarily* do.

Why does the courtship sequence not automatically lead to intercourse? Assuredly, some people do proceed to have intercourse as quickly as possible, but not all do. An evening spent entranced with one's partner simply does not guarantee that intercourse will necessarily be forthcoming in the immediate future.

Something has intervened to sever what seems otherwise to be the virtually inevitable connection between courtship and intercourse. The eager lover may find those barriers painful, but they exist. And, to understand those barriers and their very real functions, we must understand the *woman's* role in creating sexual intimacy, and how that role interacts with *social* rules about sex.

Chapter 5

Proceptivity

In this chapter, I argue that women play an active role in initiating and maintaining the courtship sequence and that women will treat, and historically have treated, men's behavioral and emotional responsiveness to them as adequate reason for sexual intercourse. Each of these flat-footed statements has an observational and theoretical side, as well as practical implications. Some theory may show how these ideas pertain to the plight of the lovers as we left them in the last chapter.

My conclusions about women's active roles in courtship come from observation, not theory. However, theories exist in biology about female sexual initiative, and to the biologist, the facts will seem quite familiar. Nonetheless, social scientific theory is much less willing to see women taking active, self-initiated roles in courtship. If we are to bridge the gap between biology and the social sciences, we must resolve those differences. Accordingly, I will begin with certain social scientific theories about women's sociosexual passivity, reluctance, and repression. Only sometimes are those theories true, and once again, the conclusion will be that when social scientists and biologists work separately, each sees only parts of the whole truth.

Sexual Repression

It is a weary truism that we in the West repress sexuality. Freud, for example, told us in great detail how the child learns to control its sexual impulses, often with difficulty (and downright anxiety!), and how civilization itself depends on preventing the darkly destructive forces of sexuality from shredding the fabric of society. Many feminists have argued that traditional forms of marriage and family oppress women sexually, deny to them their birthright of genuine female sexuality, and keep them to the millstone of monogamy, servants of a patriarchal system of inequality. Likewise, the Church Fathers, and their modern commentators, tell us that sexuality is repressed because it *ought* to be, except in its proper place in the procreative act.

112

It is a commonplace that society exerts enormous power by suppressing and controlling people's sexuality. Who could disagree with an opinion so widespread? Clearly, no one.

So it should be easy to explain why our lovers do not instantly proceed to sexual intercourse—their sexuality has been repressed and suppressed, has it not? Held down somehow, it is kept bottled up until the marriage bells ring, or until he professes undying love and she yields. Even in a modern world of seeming promiscuity, it remains easy to speak of the repression of sexuality and to see the iron hand of tradition laying itself on the shoulders of the lovers to remind them that even if they want to, they really shouldn't.

In this vision, women have a special role as sexual gatekeeper. They hold back as the man presses for intimacy; they hesitate while he is ardent; they say *No* or *Not yet* while men extend their every effort to bed them.

> A girl was in theory a superior being, more modest of thought, more pure of body, and ineffably more elevated in moral perception, than a boy might hope to become. Such was the theory nurtured in just one compartment of his mind. (Cabell, 1932, p.76)

"Good girls don't," as they say.

Thus, two forces come together to prevent our lovers from intercourse, do they not? One is the social repression of sexuality to which we are all subject and the second is feminine reluctance, the purity and modesty of which Cabell speaks in this remembrance of his youth in Virginia.

However, we should not be *too* hasty. Cabell continues; his implicit "but" rings very loud:

> In practice a girl was so much desirable flesh which protested dutifully, without even pretending to mean a word of it, in the while that a boy kissed and touched and investigated, in a pleasant routine of very gradual approach, and which by-and-by he gently tilted over, and accompanied, into recumbency. (op. cit.)

It is the *contradiction* between the assured morality of the first voices, which all agree that sexuality is repressed, and the somewhat puzzled recognition of feminine participation, which Cabell records, that must concern us. The "hypothesis" of sexual reluctance, be it general or of feminine origin only, simply does not account for the full range of sexual experience. True, sometimes women say *No* or *Not yet*, but sometimes they do not. Sometimes women say *Yes*.

How shall we address this contradiction? Some men, like Cabell, simply say that women are peculiar beings whose feelings change this way and that without any clear rule or sense. *Così fan tutte*—women are like that. And for most men, women often *are* mysterious creatures.

Yet such male "wisdom" and folklore hardly explains the contradiction between traditions that say sexuality is repressed and the experience that often it is not. In brief, something else is happening between men and women besides the mere playing out of socially approved moral roles of modesty, purity, and chastity. Indeed, something *far* deeper.

The Myth of the Reluctant Woman

Once again, let us begin with myth. Women who are not reluctant are called *promiscuous, wanton,* or *forward.* These moralizing works record disdain for such women and embody a virtual definition of the word "proper":

> The truly feminine woman does not project her sexuality. She is modest. It goes against her nature to project herself sexually. . . . The radically provocative woman is often the very opposite of feminine. (David Mace, quoted in Packard, 1968, p. 62)

Images of Potiphar's wife float across our memories (Genesis, 39) . . . and, in fact, many people *do* believe that the woman's sexual reluctance *defines* her as a "good" woman (see, e.g., Green and Sandos, 1983; Walster et al., 1973—or Thomas Mann's *Joseph in Egypt,* 1938).

Female sexual reluctance has intrigued social scientists, including Margaret Mead, Robert Bell, Jessie Bernard, and many others. Their work provides a detailed model explaining why women supposedly adopt the strategy of refusing men.

These scholars have argued that "masculine sociosexual aggression" and "feminine reluctance" are with good reason believed central to all that is perceived as natural, proper, or at least inevitable sociosexual behavior (e.g., Mead, 1949; Bell, 1966; Laplante, McCormick, and Brannigan, 1980; Bernard, 1981, especially pp. 469–471; Korman and Leslie, 1982; Goodchilds and Zellman, 1984, p. 238). In brief, they argue that these essentially moral beliefs have profound personal and social *functions.* Now, these "functions" are not defined biologically, but sociologically. That is fine, as long as we do not confuse the biological and sociological concepts. And we must not, for "functionalist" explanations of female sexual reluctance have shaped much scholarly writing about the woman's role in a sexual encounter.

However, the contrary idea has developed in biology, starting with Darwin's (1874) description of how *females* choose their mates, through Frank Beach's (1976) much more recent demonstration that female mammals *actively* solicit males sexually. By now, a large biological literature exists on both topics (to name a few, Bateson, 1983a; Searcy, 1982; Campbell, 1972; McClintock, 1983; Baum, 1983; Fedigan, 1982). It is a curious and striking difference from the social scientist's usual view—perhaps it represents a real difference between human "sexual morality" and simple "animalistic" behavior? By now, I hope the reader is growing suspicious of all such attributions to Nature and Culture, but, nonetheless, the idea of a "natural" morality is basic to some social scientific analysis of women's sociosexual behavior.

Social Functions for Women's Sexual Morality?

For example, writing of the young woman in the world of 1949 and before, Mead argues:

> The first rule of petting is the need for keeping complete control of just how far the physical behaviour is to go; one sweeping impulse, one acted-out desire for complete possession or complete surrender, and the game is lost, and lost ignobly. The controls on this dangerous game . . . are placed in the hands of the girl. The boy is expected to ask for as much as possible, the girl to yield as little as possible . . . [and] the boy expects the girl to keep it within bounds. (Mead, 1949, pp. 290–291)

Working within this social scientific functionalist mode of analysis, Mead next argues that *moral* rules for limiting sexual involvement reduce, or prevent, the risks of pregnancy for the woman (p. 290). In this functionalist view, the medical, social, and legal risks of pregnancy are so great that women seek to control the man's ardor, to limit it to non-copulatory sex, and, accordingly, to play a game with him in which if he wins she loses. In this scenario, the woman senses the man's sexual interest, but knows that she must not permit intercourse. Her "moral" decision thus protects her against the risk of pregnancy. Mead put it well: the young woman "is the conscience of the two" as they parry back and forth "in a game that is never finished and at which she may always lose" (p. 290).

In 1966, five years after oral contraception was introduced, the sociologist Robert Bell could still agree with Mead: "The male role, as generally defined by both sexes, is to be the aggressor in areas of sexual intimacy. The assumption made by both sexes is that the male will generally push for more intimate levels of intimacy unless he is stopped by the female" (Bell, 1966, p. 102).

In a functionalist vein like Mead's, Bell later argued that the well-known recent increase in premarital intercourse among young women is a direct consequence of the relaxation of hitherto potent dangers. Thus, Bell and Coughey (1980) suggest that sanctions against premarital intercourse have slowly eroded in part because "the fear of pregnancy was much greater before the availability of contraceptive methods and legal abortion" (p. 357). They also saw feminism as causing a decline among women in feelings of personal guilt that once were associated with premarital intercourse. [Clayton and Bokemeier (1980) review other sociological theories about the rise in premarital intercourse as well as document its existence; see also Zelnik, Kantner, and Ford (1981).]

Bell and Coughey (1980) agree with Mead that feminine sociosexual reluctance and hesitation arise from women's perceptions of social and medical risks associated with yielding to male sexual ardor. Moreover, even though women have increasingly begun to use contraception, thereby reducing these "risks," nonetheless, as recently as 1982, social scientists have argued that little has *really* changed in how men and women play the sexual game. Korman and Leslie (1982) began an analysis of sexual aggression by saying

> Current tacit sexual mores, although changing somewhat in the wake of the "sexual revolution" and the "woman's movement," dictate a double standard of behavior for males and females. Males are "supposed" to be sexually aggressive; females are "supposed" to be passive and submissive. . . . Mores also dictate that it is the duty of the female, lest she gain the reputation of being too "easy" or "loose," to limit sexual advancement by the male in order to gain his respect and affection. The male, on the other hand, is encouraged through peer pressure of the "masculine subculture," replete with "bull sessions" that encourage verbal exchange of sexual exploits . . . to actively seek sexual experience and knowledge with females. . . . (Korman and Leslie, 1982, pp. 114–115; all quotation marks in original; references in original deleted)

For these scholars, the sexual game has not changed since before oral contraception: men start and seek sexual intimacy; women resist and hold back. However, as risks to women have decreased following the introduction of effective, female-controlled contraception, more and more women can give themselves to Mead's "complete surrender" with so little risk that, in essence, they can *accede* to the man's desire for sexual intercourse.

For the moralist, the result has been a rise in sexual promiscuity and permissiveness that comes directly from contraception and its loosening effects on general morality. In this, the moralist agrees that the vigor of the state depends on the morality of its women, an idea that seems to have originated with Aristotle (Pomeroy, 1975, p. 39). Accordingly, if our lovers do proceed to intercourse, it is because contraception (or even legal abortion) *reduces* the woman's risks and has, in collaboration with feminism, created a social ambience of increased female permissiveness. Or, if they do *not* do so, then, presumably, lingering doubts about pregnancy or about morality itself remain with her, sufficient to stimulate her to enact the role of reluctance these scholars see as so central to femininity.

Some Problems with the Model

Despite the attractions of such social scientific functionalist thinking, things are not so simple. Associated with an increase in premarital intercourse has been a widely publicized apparent increase in teenage *pregnancy* (Zelnik, Kantner, and Ford, 1981). For example, *The New York Times* (de Witt, 1980) carried Kantner and Zelnik's report that teenage (ages 15 to 19) pregnancy rose from 9 percent of all teenage women in the United States in 1971 to 16 percent in 1979. Out-of-wedlock births to teenagers more than doubled from 92,000 in 1960 to 249,000 in 1977 (Vinovskis, 1981, p. 211). Since there has been no obvious concomitant groundswell of national approval for teenage pregnancy, these figures suggest that the likelihood, and therefore the "risks," of pregnancy have *increased* rather than decreased in recent years.

Moreover, these figures actually seem to reflect two processess. One is a decrease in birth rates for women between the ages of 18 and 19 years, and the second is a plateau in birth rates for women between the ages of 15 and 17 years (Vinovskis, 1981). By further subdividing the figures for teenage births, Vinovskis (1981) showed that from 1960 to 1964 and from 1970 to 1974 the proportion of births *conceived* out-of-wedlock remained at about 50 percent of all births to teenagers in both periods, but the proportion actually *born* out-of-wedlock increased as the proportion of births legitimized by marriage dropped from 65 percent to 35 percent. Thus, the increase in out-of-wedlock births among teenagers seems largely to be a consequence of more young women not marrying after becoming pregnant.*

So, despite words of wisdom from experts—and many words they have been (Kinsey et al., 1953, p. 307, ft. 23)—it is difficult to believe that the risks of pregnancy frighten, or have ever frightened, at least some teenage women from having intercourse. Among such women, the premarital conception rates have changed little since oral contraception was introduced. Thus, the apparent increase in teenage pregnancy arises not because moral and cultural rules of sexual behavior have been relaxing, but, in part, because these pregnancies—*and the sexual behavior that led to them*—are no longer so frequently hidden behind the marriages that were once deemed necessary to legitimate them.

In brief, it is not *sex* behavior that has been changing: *marital* customs have changed (Cargan and Melko, 1982; Clayton and Bokemeier, 1980).

Engagement and Other Forms of Social Commitment

Of course, for some women, concern over intercourse may still center on marriage. Indeed, it seems intuitively plausible that upwardly mobile women might not willingly risk pregnancy and birth outside of marriage—if abortion is not an option, it ruins one's career and has other equally great risks. If so, then concern and anxiety over the social consequences and medical dangers of *pre-* or *non-*marital pregnancy, and not pregnancy *itself*, might explain why women are reluctant about intercourse and explain why our lovers do not immediately make love. By reducing those risks, contraception could have led to a general rise in intercourse among well-educated younger women who see it as their autonomous *right*, as women, to have intercourse without the bondages of marriage. If so, then feminism—for example, the publication of Simone de Beauvoir's *The Second Sex* in 1952 and of Betty Friedan's *The Feminine Mystique* in 1963—played an immense role in

---

*Vinovskis, Zelnik, Kantner, and others have compared pregnancy frequencies among Black and white teenagers, finding higher rates among Black teenagers than white teenagers. Nonetheless, the frequencies in both groups are sufficiently high to make the discussion in the text relevant in general. (See, e.g., Vinovskis, 1981, Figure 3.)

preparing women for the population-wide sexual freedom that the newly available oral contraceptives provided in 1961,

This explanation of female reluctance shifts the ground from the ethnobiological assertion that women "naturally" fear the consequences of intercourse, to consider instead the social and emotional characteristics of sexual behavior itself. For example, Mead (1949, p. 291) wrote that a woman's sexual reluctance represents an in-built "natural" response to the "cautions of her body." These are oddly biological determinist phrases for an anthropologist as famous as Mead for her anti-biologism. Yet Mead's words remind us of how deeply embedded in our thinking are ideas of women's "natural" sexual morality.

So, the shift in focus away from myths of Nature is sensible. I doubt if the behavior of a woman seeking to avoid intercourse with an over-ardent man embodies a natural, collective consciousness of men's biological sexuality as dangerous and something to be avoided. In brief, I do not believe there could ever exist a "natural" aversion among women to sex.

How could it? Such women, if they existed, would simply not have children (for intercourse produces them!) and would therefore quickly be outnumbered by the daughters of women without such "natural" aversions. Biologically, then, the idea that women are "naturally" sexually reluctant is nonsense.

However, female reluctance about intercourse probably has sometimes involved a real concern that the man's intentions be honorable, to use an old-fashioned phrase. Some women do not avoid intercourse *per se*, but only intercourse with the wrong man at the wrong time. In brief, we must see that women are *selective*, and that reluctance is always contingent. To be sure, the idea is commonsensical, but the concept that females are sexually selective and that such selectivity is *biologically* functional has some startling implications.

Above all, biology itself now forces a crucial distinction on us between a woman's selectivity among men who might become her *husband* and among men with whom she might have *intercourse*. In literature, D. H. Lawrence's (1932/1959) Lady Chatterley is a good example, for she could not marry Mellors, even though she could make love with him. Sociologically, the field of *marital* eligibles may be far smaller for any woman than her field of *sexual* eligibles. Biologically, however, intercourse with either (or both) sets of men may produce offspring. Thus, what is important biologically is not marriage *per se*, nor the rules which define certain men as potential husbands, nor the moralities that define intercourse as licit only after certain marital ceremonials. Rather, what is biologically important (and, as we shall see, functional) is that women are selective among potential *sexual* partners regardless of the social characteristics of their relationship. Lady Chatterley does not have an affair with just anybody, but with a man who is very special to her.

So, our focus has changed. Perhaps female reluctance is more a matter of what the woman herself thinks and feels about the man than a matter of the risks of pregnancy and social ruination. I doubt very much that women are merely the passive vehicles for enacting the ideals of reluctance. What if she *likes* him, and has repeatedly found herself as entranced and as involved with him as our lovers were in the last chapter?

And, as the tale is told, it was not long after a young woman named May spoke her words of love that she *made* love:

> . . . for here I him assure
> To love him best of any creature,
> Though he no more had than his shirt.

But it is no Keatsian or Cabellian romance: this is the voice of Chaucer, speaking in the later 1300s (Chaucer, ca. 1400/1957, "The Merchant's Tale," lines 1983–1985, p. 122, spelling modernized). The process is old indeed: under some conditions, the woman's fascination and love are enough to lead to intercourse.

Such interactions and the emotional and behavioral rapport they create seem more than enough to offset the alleged risks, dangers, and melodramatically tragic consequences that older and wiser heads see in precipitous love-making. Now, I am *not* saying that women who engage in premarital intercourse are incapable of planning for the future, or have impaired senses of autonomy, or are unable to integrate attitudes and behavior, as some researchers seem to say (e.g., Kornfield, 1984; Resnick, 1984; Shah and Zelnik, 1981; Zabin et al., 1984). To the contrary, they may have excellent capacities for planning and for integrating attitudes and behavior. But who cares? Here is the most wonderful person in the world, and, with him the courtship sequence has moved ahead, obeying its own behavioral rules, and the world has changed. And perhaps, this woman thinks, having this man's child might also be wonderful. Maybe she *wants* to get pregnant.

Private and Public in Conflict

That possibility may horrify someone for whom the decision to become pregnant can *properly* be made only after marriage and is then a major part of the normative plan for the life cycle (Chapter 8). In effect, that belief says that pregnancy involves much more than the man and woman and whatever they may feel for each other at the time of intercourse. Instead, the belief is that the community *too* is involved, and that its moral and sociological rules for regulating intercourse and pregnancy *take precedence over* the individual's desires. In this, pregnancy can properly be achieved only after the couple has passed social inspection, so to speak, and has undergone the appointed *public* rituals of the wedding and its symbolism (Chapter 8).

Thus, we have reached the crux of the matter. By itself, the courtship sequence seems to create all the preconditions needed for intercourse and impregnation, but rules and processes external to the couple and their exalted experience of love now intervene to alter the course of their behavior. These rules range from strategies of mate selection to the far more extensive symbols of the wedding and its place in the life cycle, and will increasingly concern us as the argument develops.

However, for now, the couple knows only that their sexual interest in each other—and very possibly their mutual desire for her impregnation—have encountered obstacles that are not of their own making. Here, people often speak of "public opinion," but the real point is a growing conflict between *personal* intimacy, created by the courtship sequence, and *public or community* intervention in the couple's behavior. From this conflict grows a series of compromises which, in essence, defer the consummation of intimacy in regular and repeated intercourse until certain social events have occurred. Community rules thus regulate, not repress, the sexual behavior of the couple.*

It is at about this point in the overall courship sequence that field ethnographers begin to pick up on the rules of courtship. The reason is partly built into anthropology and partly into courtship. Anthropologists typically are interested in communities—villages, groups of nomads, and so on—and in the cultural rules by which those communities operate. On the other hand, the initial stages of courtship often occur in privacy or semi-privacy or are camouflaged under "normal" social interactions. As a result, courtship does not fully enter the attention of the community—and therefore the visiting anthropologist—until it has progressed quite far towards sexual intimacy and, therefore, towards the possibility of marriage with all its social effects and consequences. Overall, the result is that the ethnographic literature often contains only passing and brief references to the stages of courtship that occur prior to community notice. It is an unfortunate fact, because it makes it hard to compare Western and non-Western courtship behavior.[†]

Prior to community notice, the courting couple interacts in their own culturally approved ways—on streetcorners, at parties, at dances (Shepherd, 1966, pp. 67–80; Carter, 1977), in the fields, in singles bars, in brief, any place where *overt* community control is absent. But marriage is not merely copulation: it is a *biosocial* phenomenon, and soon courtship can involve complex economic negotiations and exchanges among kin, and community preparations for the wedding ceremony [e.g., Price, 1984; Carter, 1977; see Bolton's (1977) very useful set of decision trees illustrating these aspects of courtship].

Then, with these community processes under way, the specialness of a man to a woman is not merely a private emotional experience, as it might be in an extramarital affair or in a hushed-up teenage pregnancy. Sometimes, a man's

---

*A reader who confuses biology and ethnobiology may misread me here to say that a "genetically encoded biological imperative" to reproduce has expressed itself in the couple's behavior, and that the community has acted to restrict that imperative. To be sure, such "imperatives" exist, for otherwise there will be no more people. But it is not the genes whispering within us that create the desire for intercourse: no upwelling of dangerous and anti-social instinct leads our lovers to each other. Instead, the combined emotional and behavioral intimacy of the courtship sequence assures that reproduction eventually occurs. The end result is the same—the biological need is met—but the genes, selfishly or otherwise, have not made them do it.

[†]I am not blaming anthropologists for tending to ignore the early stages of courtship. Indeed, those stages may be impossible for an outsider to observe, especially if the outsider is him- or herself beyond the courtship years. After all, if a boy and girl are "flirting" out in the fields, one can hardly ask to join them and watch! Observing in singles bars, on the other hand, is far easier.

specialness to the woman is symbolized publicly. In specific, an engagement says to the world that *This is my man*, and it reveals publicly and socially that a bond exists between them. But that bond is not *merely* formal, official, or conventional, as it would be if only the community established it, but has also grown *personally* between the two people themselves. Engagement says in a social and symbolic language for all to hear that emotional and behavioral intimacy exists between the two people. In it, the woman says, "Of all the potential *sexual* partners I have, I have chosen *this* one." Engagement, then, is the public *marker event* that says *Our intimacy has become real.*

So, for the couple, it follows that engagement and even marriage are only the external wrappings, so to speak, on the deeper and far more private process that creates a specialness and an intimacy that grows from the behavioral interactions I discussed in the last chapter. Engagement does not *create* that intimacy; it merely symbolizes that it already exists. It follows that *emotional and behavioral intimacy, not a wedding ring or its social equivalent, leads to and, for the couple, legitimates sexual intercourse.**

The feminist writers Nanette Davis and Jone Keith point out (1984, p. xiii) that much literature on teenage pregnancy is written from the "social control perspective," which assumes that such pregnancies are *necessarily* bad and deviant. However, I strongly agree with Pope's comment (1967, p. 555) that this moral preconception is no sure guide to understanding how and why pre- and non-marital pregnancies occur. As he points out, it begs the question to argue that the relationship is abnormal simply *because* it results in non-marital pregnancy. Indeed, with Pope, I submit that that many of these pregnancies do not occur in deviant, abnormal, or unusual social circumstances.

Regardless of the *public* status of the relationship between a man and woman, and of conflicts between that status and personal feeling, the kind of behavioral intimacy that develops during the courtship sequence leads the lovers to *feel* good about each other. They *want* to touch each other, look at each other, kiss each other . . . and more. And, as a result, they do (Clive M. Davis, 1980), even if individuals of proper moral temperament are thereby outraged.

An Historical View of Premarital Pregnancy and Intercourse

There is, I suggest, considerable evidence that this view is correct. A man does not become emotionally special simply because he is suddenly known publicly as one's fiancé (or husband). He is special because his emotional involvement with her has been signaled to her by the kind of behavioral communication discussed in the last chapter and because he has publicly signaled his commitment to her by

---

*The sociologist Ira Reiss (1981) has argued that, for certain people, love redeems sexuality from guilt. I agree, but am expressing a somewhat different thought here. It does not matter whether or not our lovers feel guilty about sexuality; instead, after a certain level of behavioral and emotional intimacy has developed, intercourse becomes very likely regardless of whether or not the lovers later need to justify their behavior by calling it "love."

engagement or its honorable equivalent. He has said, in private and in public, *I am your man.*

And, as would be expected, the frequency of premarital intercourse among *engaged* women has been high for many years in the United States. Citing Hamilton, Kallen (1934) concluded that 61 percent of married women born between 1891 and 1895 had had premarital intercourse (which probably implies with their fiancés). In Kinsey et al.'s 1953 figures, by age 45 approximately 50 percent of all women in their sample had had premarital intercourse (Kinsey et al., 1953, p. 330, summary table). Among these sexually active women, at least 46 percent had had intercourse with their fiancés (Kinsey et al., 1953, p. 331, summary table), to give about one-quarter of the women in this sample as having had intercourse with a man whose intentions were, in fact, "honorable." In Bell and Coughey's (1980) summary for college women, in 1958 intercourse was between two and seven times higher among engaged women than for dating women (Bell and Coughey, 1980, p. 355, Table 1; both frequencies had increased greatly by 1979). We can conclude that for "traditional" times prior to effective oral contraception, at least some women actively entered into intimate sexual relationships with men even though they were not married to them.

If risks deter women from intercourse, these numbers make no sense. Moreover, in the 1953 sample of Kinsey et al., 56 percent of 5,727 women indicated that fear of pregnancy was *not* a reason for refraining from intercourse, even though this "fear" plays a central role in the "functionalist" model of women's sexuality discussed above. In that sample, an additional 23 percent of the women indicated that such fears would only "more or less" restrain them (Kinsey et al., 1953, p. 344, Table 91). Thus, only 21 percent of this sample feared pregnancy sufficiently to assure their sexual abstinence.

Indeed, historically, it has happened before, both in the United States and Great Britain. In 18th century England, the wedding did not mark the beginning of socially legitimate intercourse— betrothal did. Neither the man's nor the woman's "honor" was compromised if she showed up for the wedding some months pregnant [Stone, 1979, pp. 397–398; this is what John Money (1980, pp. 57–58) calls the "Nordic" pattern of betrothal; see also Stiles, 1871/n.d., pp. 11–13, note].

Moreover, illegitimacy rates have varied cyclically over history. Thus, Stone documents a sharp rise in out-of-wedlock births in English history from a low of less than 10 per 1,000 births in the 1650s to over 60 per 1,000 by the 1770s [Stone, 1979, Chapter 12, page 390; in fact, the rates rose throughout Europe (Berlanstein, 1980)]. Even later in English history—between 1845 and 1848—Mayhew and Hemyng (1861–1862/1968, pp. 468–469 of Volume 4) gave the average illegitimacy rate in England and Wales as 67 per 1,000 births, but the rate was dramatically higher in certain counties—for example, 99 per 1,000 in Salop and 100 per 1,000 in Hereford, both on the Welsh border; 105 per 1,000 in Norfolk in the Northeast of England, to a high of 108 per 1,000 in Cumberland on the Scottish border. (Even the lowest rates—in Middlesex County, which includes London, and in Cornwall— exceeded the low rates for the 1600s: 40 per 1,000 in Middlesex and 47 per 1,000 in Cornwall.)

Though these "crude rates" of illegitimacy are far from ideal for demographic investigations (see Berlanstein, 1980), they indicate a *very* high rate of out-of-wedlock intercourse and pregnancy among some women in these regions. An illegitimacy rate of 100 per 1,000, say, implies that 1 of 10 people chosen at random from the total population will be illegitimate. The rate is *not* the frequency of out-of-wedlock births per *woman*. If—as an example only—a woman has an average of five children in her reproductive lifetime, then of the ten children of two women one could well be "illegitimate." Thus, 50 percent of the women could have borne children out-of-wedlock at some time in their lives (either before their first marriage, between marriages if the first husband died or left, and so on).

These regional differences in illegitimacy rates in the English counties have been retained into the 20th century. The Northern Counties, Cumberland among them, had very high rates of marriages of pregnant women. For example, in one Cumberland County parish between 1920 and 1951, 40 percent of all brides were pregnant (Hair, 1980, p. 199).

My purpose is not to reconstruct Cumberland county demography, nor to reconstruct the history of out-of-wedlock births. Instead, the point is that these lean and spare statistics hide an *extremely* high rate of out-of-wedlock intercourse and pregnancy. Given that not every act of intercourse leads to pregnancy, these figures probably disguise a far higher rate of pre- and non-marital intercourse.

United States history shows a very similar pattern of historically cyclic changes in illegitimacy rates. The lowest rates occurred during the 1600s and middle 1800s, with the highest rates occurring during the late 1700s and today (Smith and Hindus, 1980). For one township in Massachusetts, Hingham, between 1741 and 1780, from two-thirds to three-quarters of women were pregnant when they married (Smith and Hindus, 1980, p. 208). But, crucially, most of these women were also pregnant at the time they filed their intention to marry, that is, at the time of their *official* engagement. [This pattern is not restricted to New England (Pope, 1967).]

Our digression into history now begins to bear fruit. First, neither contraception nor feminism is *alone* sufficient to explain why women will have premarital intercourse. Rates of intercourse were high at historical times when neither effective contraception nor a widespread and generally accepted feminist ideology existed. Furthermore, the figures show that if women have tended to resist intercourse, it cannot be because they fear pregnancy, either inside *or* outside of marriage. True, it may *sound* plausible to say that women resist men because they "naturally" fear men's sexual ardor or they fear the social and medical consequences of pregnancy, and that they enter into nonmarital relationships only because effective contraception is available or because feminist ideologies have recently liberated them from the bonds of older, traditional repressions of female sexuality. To be sure, for some modern women, both these fears and these changes in ideology and technology may play significant roles in the decision to have or to resist intercourse. But ideology and technology do not *generally* explain why women will quite so readily make love with men to whom they are not married, especially since even now startlingly high percentages of young women do not use contraception [between 30 and 60 percent, depending on age (Vinovskis, 1981, Figure 5)].

Second, we can now separate two aspects of the growth of intimacy. On the one hand, behavioral and emotional intimacy increase between the man and woman as they interact with each other over and over. It begins with their being relative (or complete) strangers and ends with regular and repeated intercourse. This sequence is *private*, in the sense that it involves only the two of them. However, on the other hand, external to the courting couple and their intimacy exists a *social* world in which live other people who have beliefs— and rules!—about intimacy and about when it ought to be recognized *publicly*. In that external world, people hold to rules that say that public ceremonials, like a betrothal or a wedding, *ought* to mark certain stages of the couple's otherwise private movement towards intimacy.

And history teaches us that the timing of these public ceremonials and the couple's own movement towards intimacy have varied considerably with respect to one another. At some times and places, public ceremonials like the wedding occur very late—for example, after the couple has been living together for a while, and she is pregnant. At other times and places, the wedding is placed *earlier* in the sequence—for example, prior to first intercourse, as in the traditional ideal that the bride should be a virgin.

But, either way, the couple themselves have moved towards sexual intimacy, no matter where the ceremonials of intimacy are placed by tradition, by common consent, or by culture. Thus, we see that ceremonials of intimacy—be they an engagement party, a formal betrothal, a house-building or a house-warming for the newly intimate couple, or a wedding—are a kind of external social *adornment* on the growth of intimacy. They celebrate the existence of intimacy at times that society says it ought to be celebrated. Such ceremonials are, so to speak, the next layer of the culture external to the biosocial reality of the courtship sequence itself, and represent the increasing involvement of other people in the lovers' hitherto private lives. But those ceremonials do not *create* intimacy—the couple does.

Thus, we can conclude—with some force, I believe—that purely social scientific functionalist explanations (like those with which I began this section) fail to explain not only the growth of intimacy but also the woman's role in creating it. If anything, arguments invoking a fear of pregnancy ought to have had their greatest power *before* effective contraception was available. In *those* days, women should have avoided intercourse like the plague! But history, and women, say *Nay*—at least at certain times and places. So too fail the functionalist explanations of sexual morality—that it serves to protect women against the dangers of sex. Indeed, if morality functions sociologically to prevent illegitimacy, then it does not function particularly well.

So we are left with a conundrum and a puzzle. In fact, it is James Branch Cabell's puzzle: why do these morally perfect and ideally asexual beings so quickly and enthusiastically enter into sexual relationships with men? Everything, it is said, is against our lovers—sexual repressions that reach back into childhood, male-dominated rules that repress women sexually, an indwelling and built-in natural fear of pregnancy and intercourse, sexual moralities that set forth iron-clad *Thou shalt not until marriage*, terrors and dangers of social ruination, shame, and disgrace, thunderings from pulpits both real and televised against the scourge of promiscuity, sex educators who teach responsibility in making reproductive decisions. Clearly, only the most extraordinarily and profoundly dysfunctional and alienated sociopaths could *possibly* ignore such powerful injunctions, pressures, and rules!

No, clearly, it is impossible. Our lovers could never go to bed with each other!

But, of course, they do—if not the first night, then sometime later. And, very possibly, she becomes pregnant. And how is that? What, precisely, could have such power that in a few days it can overthrow the immense forces of morality, education, religion, fear, common sense, and sexual repressions that date from childhood?

The answer, as we shall soon see, is far more than the fact that the woman *loves* the man, or the fact that the courtship sequence has its own power over people's sexual behavior. The answer concerns the *woman's* role in initiating and maintaining the courtship sequence itself.

An Ethnographic Short Circuit

The anthropologist Michael Agar (1982) recently wrote that ethnographic research progresses only when the researcher encounters what he perceptively calls an "ethnographic break": not a piece of good luck, but a startling break between what the ethnographer thinks he knows and what the actual data reveal. It is a kind of short circuit, and when it happens the control panels of the mind start blinking their red lights on and off. Something doesn't fit together.*

On the one hand, we all know the myths of female sexual reluctance and male sexual ardor. We all know that men court and woo women, not the reverse. But, on the other hand, over and over, women, not men, initiated the first contact—as I described in Example 1 of the last chapter. She approaches *him*, as he stands looking at the band, as he fills his plate at a buffet party, as he waits for an airplane or a train. Put next to one another, the belief and the data *do not agree*. Something does not fit.

This short circuit is deep indeed. In mid-1983, I asked a woman in her 70s how things had been when she was a young woman. "How did you let a man know you were interested in him?" I asked.

She smiled, as she sat in her blue velvet living room chair in her retirement community apartment, and looked at me, head tilted slightly. She placed her hand on her neck and slowly twirled an imaginary necklace between her fingers. "We had our little ways," she said softly, looking directly into my eyes. Indeed so, I thought appreciatively—for, by then, I had over and over again seen women the age of her granddaughters do precisely the same things.

---

*I am saying "short circuit" instead of "break" because I found that "break" sounds like a piece of good luck, a meaning Agar did not intend.

EXAMPLE

A dinner party I attended, spring 1980, in New Jersey.

As we sat eating, someone asked me what I did. I answered that I studied how men and women meet. Since that is not the average dinner conversation answer to such a question, soon the other guests were talking about their experiences. One man, in his mid-20s, said that for 18 months he had been a salesman, traveling on the road, never in one place for more than a few days or so. After a while, he had wanted to meet women pretty desperately, he said, and would end up at the bar of whatever motor inn he was staying at. He didn't have much success meeting women, he indicated, until he figured out what to do. "I'd go to the bar," he said, "and sit down with an empty barstool next to me. Sooner or later, a woman would join me."

We all laughed. It seemed a reasonably clear confirmation that women sometimes initiate such things. But what of the *morality* of such actions? Maybe a forward woman in a bar, perhaps even a prostitute . . . . Our hostess said that *she* would never have the courage to approach a man. Then she stopped and almost blushed. Her husband was smiling at her.

"Well," she said, "I once did approach a man. That's how I met my husband." She had been at a party and asked the hostess who that attractive man was. A scientist, she was told, so she went over to him and asked, "You're a scientist. Do you know how abalone shells swim? I've watched them, and I can't figure it out." After 45 minutes of discussion, it turned out that neither of them could quite figure it out, but they had gotten off onto other topics, and, what with one thing and another, here they were hosting our dinner party.

Something is profoundly false in the belief that men are the sexual aggressors and women are sexually reluctant, coy, or hesitant. True, women sometimes do say *No* or *Not yet*, but sometimes—in fact often—they not only say *Yes*, they actively seek to *open* a relationship with a man.

However, to the biologist, the fact is not particularly surprising. In 1976, Frank Beach employed the word *proceptivity* for the female mammal's ability to initiate and escalate a sexual interaction. Beach concluded that proceptivity is extremely common in female mammals, and subsequent research has confirmed his conclusions. Proceptivity is now standard usage in animal sex research (e.g., Baum, 1983).*

*According to *Science Citation Index*, Beach's 1976 paper was cited 21 times in the animal behavior literature in 1983 alone. I gave some examples of proceptivity in rats in Chapter 3—the female's stiff-legged hop and dart is one, and so is her visiting a tethered male in his side of the test apparatus. Proceptivity is not the same as *proception*, a term John Money uses for a certain stage in courtship (1980, pp. 73–76). Proce*ption* involves invitation, solicitation, seduction, and being attracted and attractive, and refers to actions performed by both men *and* women. In contrast, the term procep*tivity* refers *only* to female behavior, and forces us to focus specifically on *female* behavior, rather than lump it with male behavior.

There is no doubt that women are proceptive. In fact, in our observations, over half the time the woman—not the man—initiated the courtship sequence by approaching the man. [Jones (1982) independently reached very similar conclusions.]

Like escalation, proceptivity refers to behavior. A woman who is interested in a man but who does not express it in her actual behavior is not being proceptive. Instead, she is being passive, like someone who *feels* love but does not respond to his or her partner's overtures. Only if, for example, the woman tries to catch the man's eye, or goes over to stand next to him, or opens a conversation with him, has she behaved proceptively. Thus, the "little ways" mentioned by the older woman above are all proceptive, for they represent the woman's autonomous initiation and escalation of her interaction with a man. Thus proceptivity may be defined (for human, not animal, behavior) as any behavior pattern a woman employs to express or signal interest to a man, or to arouse him sexually, or that serves to maintain her sexual or sociosexual interaction with him.

Proceptivity involves much more than the initial approach. A woman is proceptive if she turns to a man while they are sitting, if she leans toward him or reaches towards him, or—quite dramatically—if she touches him. Indeed, whenever the woman escalates the courtship sequence, at any of the escalation points mentioned above, she is being proceptive.

Some social scientists have recognized that women are highly proceptive, as Ford and Beach said long ago (1951, pp. 93–103). More recently, Clinton Jesser (1978) found that most women in his college sample reported asking directly for sex from their partners, or used non-verbal signals to indicate their interest. Likewise, Naomi McCormick (1979) found that college women writing essays on how to seduce and reject men could describe at least ten different strategies for seducing men. Using in-depth, open-ended interviews with women of a variety of ages and social backgrounds, Heather Remoff (1980, 1984) concluded that women possess extensive repertoires for expressing sexual interest in men. These strategies ranged from brief, non-verbal cues to detailed, long-range plans that led to marriage. Finally, several writers have concluded that some men recognize and appreciate women's proceptive overtures (Green and Sandos, 1983; Hite, 1981, p. 1119; Novak, 1983; Tennov, 1979, p. 214). Proceptivity is quite real, no matter what myths say about women being sexually reluctant.*

---

*It is not hard to find passing references to proceptive behavior in the ethnographic literature [e.g., in Sally Price's first-rate study of Saramaccan women, in Suriname, South America (1984, especially Chapter 3, pp. 39–59)], and in other sources, ranging from the Kama Sutra (Vatsyayana, 1961, Part V, Chapter III, pp. 186–188) through Marco Polo's enfuriatingly brief comment that women in Tangut (modern Kan-su, in Northwest China) make overtures to men, and that men sustain no sin if they respond! (1298–1299/1958, p. 91). Nonetheless, though the existing data clearly support Ford and Beach's conclusion that in no society is sexual initiative solely the prerogative of only one sex (1951, pp. 101–103), there seems to be no *systematic* description of proceptivity for any non-Western society. In fact, despite many references to women's sexual "aggression" and "assertiveness" in the popular literature of the modern United States, the present study, plus Remoff's (1980, 1984), may be something of pioneering efforts. If so, I certainly hope that they stimulate others, especially ethnographers, to look for and systematically analyze women's roles in initiating courtship and intercourse.

It is female *autonomy* that gives proceptivity its immense importance. Even if a woman is proceptive only once in her life—a very unlikely possibility—but it is with a man who later becomes her husband or with whom she later becomes pregnant, her behavior has had immense reproductive and social impact. Multiplied by millions, these individual acts of proceptive autonomy may represent the real bases for mate selection, as opposed to myths and beliefs that *men* initiate sexual encounters and woo reluctant women. And, if so, then courtship and mate selection operate under rules *very* different from the game of female reluctance described by Mead and others, and so common in the folklore of love and courtship.

Conservatism and Forwardness

However, despite studies like Jesser's or McCormick's, colleagues of mine—usually men, of course—felt (or hoped?) that proceptivity was much less widespread than I believed. "Sure," they might say, "what do you expect? Women in *bars* come on to men, but that's because they're sexually liberated! Traditional women would *never* do such things—they would think it was improper!"

For such men, proper women are never "forward" (as shown by the quotation from Mace near the beginning of this chapter). Indeed, for such men, the word "proceptivity" is only a fancy way to say "flirtatious," "kittenish," or "coquettish." These terms are as heavily loaded with moral disapproval as *promiscuous* or *wanton* are, for they refer to a perceived inability of women to behave consistently or steadfastly with a man. Such women are *teases*, my male colleagues were saying.

And, as a type, such women abound in literature (which, notably, has been written mostly by men):

> Though shee were true, when you met her,
> And last, till you write your letter,
>   Yet shee
>   Will bee
> False, ere I come, to two or three.
> (John Donne, 1650/1952, p. 9, lines 23–27)

It is an old story. Even in ancient Rome:

> Lesbia says she'd rather marry me
> than anyone
>   though Jupiter himself came asking
> or so she says,
>   but what a woman tells her lover in desire
> should be written out on air and running water.
> (Catullus, ca. 50 B.C./1966)

Although these images are hostile (an understatement; I will discuss something of men's feelings in a later chapter), fickle women are also the stuff of parody. Molière's *Le Bourgeois Gentilhomme* (1670/1957) contains in Act III a scene in which, first, Lucile and Nicole pursue Cleonte and Coveille, who refuse them. The tables then turn, and Cleonte and Coveille pursue Lucile and Nicole, who now refuse *them*. It makes great stage business, especially since it is hard to tell who is more foolish, the men or the women. But still we see the image of women as sexually silly, flighty, and inconstant. Such are, in myth, the "wiles," "guiles," and "manipulations" of women.*

Now some women *do* employ their sexual allure to curry favor among men or to achieve advancement in male-dominated domains such as politics, finance, or the entertainment business, and did so even before Mary Wollstonecraft (1792/1967) made such female behavior the centerpiece of her attack on male social power over women's lives. But, if, *today*, we still believe that proceptivity is nothing but flirtatious coquetry or the manipulative use of feminine allure for social or economic purposes, we shall never understand women's roles in courtship. Indeed, we shall not understand that the courtship sequence itself is typically *built* a proceptive step at a time.

But my colleagues *were* raising an important point. It might well be that proceptive women are sexually liberated, or treat sexuality casually. A few exceptions here and there, maybe—like the older woman I just mentioned—but it *is* possible that proceptivity is an historically recent consequence of the sexual revolution and its changes in sexual ideology and technology, and that it is restricted primarily to liberal or liberated women. No doubt, then, the sexual behavior and proceptivity of such women would be distasteful or even abhorrent to the vast majority of sexually conservative women in our society. In this view, we once again encounter the idea that there exists an innate female sexual morality—for that is what both Mace's and Mead's arguments boil down to—which somehow ensures that *most* women behave *non*-proceptively with men. In that case, the rise in illegitimacy rates mentioned before are easy to explain: they represent a *breakdown* of these innate moral mechanisms, as history slides into periods of promiscuity in which women are vulnerable to men and to their ardors and seductions. The historian Lawrence Stone put it well:

> The rise in pre-nuptial conceptions therefore represents primarily a shift in community standards of honour; the rise in bastardy represents social disintegration and a collapse of all standards of honour, primarily among social groups too poor to afford or comprehend such things. (Stone, 1979, p. 398)

It is then simple. If our lovers now proceed to make love, it is because our society *too* is proceeding to social disintegration and a collapse of the standards of honor.

---

*Writing of Susan Brownmiller's *Femininity*, Rita Mae Brown (1984) said that for Brownmiller, femininity is " . . . a complex of duplicity, narcissism, and subservience designed to win and hold a man" (p. 8). This is a brilliant summary of the traditional view of woman as sexual manipulator.

Indeed, in microcosm, we see a whole morality play writ out small when our lovers touch, and look, and want to make love—a morality play that signals death, doom, and destruction for all that is fine and good, especially for those elites *not* too poor to comprehend such things. The sky is falling, says Chicken Little.

Proceptivity and Conservatism

Like so much written about sexuality and morality, this vision of incipient social collapse is nonsense. And I say that not because it is my *opinion*, but because two colleagues, David Weis of Rutgers University in the United States and Margot Crosbie of the University of Windsor in Ontario, Canada, and I gathered data to the contrary. I want next to describe this study, for it showed us as clearly as possible that proceptive behavior is *not* restricted to sexually liberal women. In fact, proceptivity is the common possession of most women in our sample, conservative or liberal, from the United States and from Canada. Once again, myth has intervened to shape our ideas and perceptions about women and sex.

The U.S.–Canada study had two purposes. One was to measure the sexual liberalism and conservatism of a group of college-age women, so that we were sure that our sample contained representatives of both groups. The second was to determine how these young women would seduce and reject men. Would there be any relationship between conservatism and proceptivity—for example, would only sexually *liberal* women behave proceptively? Would sexually conservative women reject the idea of seducing a man, and say that it was *his* prerogative to make the first overtures? Would there be an association between proceptivity and sexual freedom—that is, would proceptive women be happy to engage in what is euphemistically called "recreational" sex, in contrast to non-proceptive women?

Since the results make no sense unless the reader knows what we did, I will describe our procedure in somewhat more detail.* To find out how women would seduce and reject men sexually, we asked them two essay questions. These questions were borrowed from the work of Naomi McCormick (1979), who also provided us with essays written by forty women in her study (which was done on the West Coast of the United States). The essay questions put the essayist into a realistic situation, since we were not interested in vague, theoretical answers. The seduction question read as follows:

> Imagine that you have known someone of the opposite sex for about three weeks. You have dated this person once, but so far there hasn't been any kind of sex between the two of you. Now, you are on a second date with this person, and you feel really turned on by them. How would you influence this person to have sex with you (of course, we mean going only as far as you want it to)?

We then read (and read and read and read!) the answers, until we could categorize

---

*The full details of the study are now in preparation for scholarly publication.

every theme and strategy the essayists used. Next, we could compare these descriptions with our observations of what women *actually* do: that is, we could tell how accurate and how realistic the answers were. If a woman said that she would stand on her head, we could, of course, dismiss her answer as idiosyncratic (if not pathological) but, by the same token, we could also tell if a woman was describing accurately all the touches, looks, reaches, and so on that we had observed during the *real* courtship sequence itself.

We also asked the young women to describe how they would reject a man sexually. The question read as follows:

Imagine that you have known someone of the opposite sex for about three weeks, and that you have been out on one date with them. Now, you are on a second date with them, and feel that while they are really turned on by you, you know you're not interested. How would you influence this person to avoid having sex?

This question is nearly the same as the seduction question, but now the woman knows that she is *not* interested. What strategies and techniques does she use to communicate her lack of interest?

I will discuss the seduction strategies in this chapter, and the rejection strategies in the next.

Then, using a specially designed questionnaire, we measured the sexual liberalism and conservatism of the women in our U.S. and Canadian samples. To make a long story short, we found that the sexually conservative women tended to be highly religious and devout, tended to disapprove of premarital intercourse both for themselves and for other people, even when in love, tended not to date for sexual purposes, and tended not to ask men out for dates. In brief, we found a pattern that is recognizably "conservative" by U.S. standards. We also found that the same profile of conservatism held for Canadian women: Canadian conservatives were very similar to sexually conservative women from the United States.

In contrast, sexually liberal women were the opposite. They tended to be less religious and less devout, tended not to disapprove of premarital intercourse either for themselves or for other women, tended more to date for sexual purposes, and tended to ask men for dates. (This set of associations is well known to sex researchers, e.g., Mahoney, 1980.) In brief, we found a pattern that is recognizably "liberal" by U.S. standards—and, once again, Canadian liberals resembled their U.S. counterparts very closely.

We also found—and this should surprise no one who know anything about Canada—that, on the average, the Canadian women were *much* more conservative than the U.S. women (see also Mackie, 1983; Herold and Goodwin, 1981; Whitehurst, 1977). Nonetheless, there were some quite liberal Canadian women, just as there were some quite conservative U.S. women. All in all, these women's beliefs ranged from the extreme conservatism of the very devout young woman who felt that premarital intercourse was *always* immoral, to the extremely liberal young woman who professed little or no religious belief and felt that sex was just plain good fun.

In this procedure, the seduction strategies were obtained from the *essays*, but the conservatism–liberalism scores were obtained from the *questionnaire*. In this, we hoped to measure two independent components of these women's sexual attitudes and behavior. The questionnaire measures the woman's attitudes, norms, and the ideals that shape her thinking about what is morally and explicitly right and wrong sexually. However, the essays measure something else—the woman's actual knowledge of how to influence men sexually, and her ability to communicate sexual interest (if she so wishes). The essays concern how the woman would *behave* with a man. Thus, together, the questionnaire and the essay questions elicited attitudes *and* descriptions of behavior, and those need not be the same thing.

So how do these women describe seducing men? Are they proceptive or not? Second, what is the relationship between proceptivity and conservatism? Do sexually conservative attitudes, as measured by the questionnaire, imply that the woman is behaviorally conservative, as inferred from her essay results?

The answers should surprise no one who has read this far. The vast majority (87.2 percent) of the essayists—from the United States and from Canada, whether liberal or conservative—were highly and explicitly proceptive. In fact, many essayists could describe the courtship sequence in exquisite detail.

Here are some examples. Now women are speaking in their own voices, and, ultimately, the essays are convincing. Proceptivity exists as an articulate and central component of female sexuality, no matter what myths about Natural moralities and bodily cautions say to the contrary.

Some Examples of Proceptive Strategies from U.S. and Canadian Women

The seduction question was answered by 117 essayists. Of them, only *four* (3.4 percent) said that they would *not* try to influence the man. Five more women (4.3 percent) said that sex would occur without her influence, but did not attribute an active role to the man. An additional six women (5.1 percent) said that they would "do nothing" under these conditions, but also did not attribute an active role to the man. Totaled, only 15 of the 117 essayists did not describe proceptive strategies. In brief, 102 of 117 or *87.2 percent* of the essayists spontaneously described how they—not the man—would initiate and escalate the interaction.

ESSAY F1

21-year-old U.S. woman, seeing one man seriously, not particularly devout, with only 8 percent of the combined U.S. and Canadian sample more liberal than she.

I attempt to influence the mood of my date by suggesting that we go somewhere quiet, relaxing, and secluded. If my date likes this suggestion, I usually let him suggest the place in order to get a better idea of where his head is. If he asks for suggestions as to where to go, I inevitably suggest MY PLACE!

Once we've gotten settled wherever we decided to go I try slipping in compliments wherever I can. These are usually about my date's physical appearance and how it/they turn me on, e.g., Your eyes have such a mysterious gleam, they really are captivating, or Your smile is so warm and comforting it just makes me melt. Then after careful evaluation of my date's reaction to all of this I proceed in one of two ways:

a) If his response is positive, I escalate the level of intimacy through more intense eye contact and more but subtle body contact. This is almost always sufficient to eventually make my date suggest or attempt sex.

b) If his response is either negative or apparently indifferent I will back off a bit and wait for him to make the next move. If he takes too long to do this to suit me, I'll try putting on romantic or soft music and suggesting we dance or I'll offer a body massage to sort of break the ice. I find praying and hoping useful at this point. [Emphasis and subheadings original]

Hers is a virtually analytical plan to communicate sexual interest to him. She is not simply listing strategies or seductive devices; she describes a *sequence* of events that progresses from the beginning of the date through dancing. At each of the escalation points she so carefully describes, *she* takes the initiative.

Moreover, she has contingency plans for the man who does *not* respond to her. With such a man (under heading b) she makes her overtures more and more obvious, hoping that he will respond. Such men are not inventions: they are the men we so often observed not responding to women's overtures. In fact, such men appeared so often in the essays (43.5 percent of the U.S. essayists mentioned them) that we finally named them *Recalcitrant Males*. The essayists write of them with impatience and even irritation, as the following essay illustrates.

ESSAY F2

21-year-old U.S. woman, seeing one man primarily, a fairly devout Catholic, with 60 percent of the combined sample more liberal than she.

Invite up to apartment, turn down lights, fake TV watching or put soft music on. Drink wine or smoke joint—get person relaxed. Kiss. Tell how much you like person and how attracted you are to them. Kiss neck. Try to lay down on couch, floor. Kiss more intensely. If other person has arm around you casually move so that hand may touch your breast. Rub back or thigh. While laying down roll to a position for pelvic thrusts. And if he doesn't get the hint by then forget it.

Essayist F2 is fairly conservative, but she is also highly proceptive. In fact, hers was one of the most sexually explicit answers we recieved. And, like Essayist F1, she too will not go on forever: at a certain point, the man must respond, or the proceptive sequence will stop.

ESSAY F3

18-year-old U.S. woman, not seeing anyone, an extremely devout Catholic, with 90 percent of the sample more liberal than she.

> This is a toughie. I've never been in this situation before. I think I'd be very free in my manner and very affectionate, hoping he'd catch on and take over from there.

Except in imagination, she is *not* now "in this situation." Yet she too can visualize autonomously expressing interest and, like the other women, then wants the man to get the hint.

The following essay is a good example of the detail that these women included in their answers. For this woman too, proceptivity is a coordinated sequence of signals whose purpose is to awaken the man's interest.

ESSAY F4

19-year-old U.S. woman, seeing one man seriously, a very devout Catholic, with 79 percent of the whole sample more liberal then she.

> I think the way you dress that evening could help in arousing the man. I would wear suggestive clothes (not too suggestive). For example tight designer jeans and a low cut blouse. This might help to arouse him a little. All night long I would try to touch him (a slight touch on the arm, or even pretend you're going to read his palm). I know it sounds corny but it's touching. Also gear your conversation towards a slight sexual conversation. Dancing is great! Really just give the appearance that you're looking for some action. It's easy to detect. Eye contact is essential. A held glance says, Hey, I like you.

For some women, the endpoint of proceptive action is intercourse. However, other women can be highly proceptive even if they do *not* want to make love with the man.

ESSAY F5

26-year-old U.S. woman, now married, somewhat religious Episcopalian, with 43 percent of the whole sample more liberal than she.

> If we were traveling by car anywhere I would slide over closer to my date. I would try to keep the conversation going because it relaxes people and makes the atmosphere more intimate. I don't think I'd go as far as going to bed with this guy because no matter how physically attracted to him I might be I just don't know him well enough. I'd try to snuggle up to him or lean against him

because then he'd put his arm around me. If I wanted to be kissed, I'd make the first move and kiss him. I like to have control over any intimate situation. It makes me feel more receptive.

In contrast to the Reluctant Female of myth who controls the situation because she is *not* receptive to the man's overtures, for this woman, having control *increases* her receptivity. Even though she has established a limit on their intimacy (at least until she knows him better), she is not playing games. She *wants* him to respond to her overtures. In fact, her phrase "because then he'd put his arm around me" illustrates proceptivity with paradigmatic clarity: the woman starts, and the man responds. Her answer thus underscores something implicit in the previous examples, that the *woman* has initiated and escalated the interaction.

To be sure, some essayists did mention the idea of male "sexual aggression." Here is an example, written by an extremely conservative woman.

ESSAY F6

20-year-old U.S. woman, seeing one man primarily, a somewhat religious Catholic, with 99 percent of the whole sample more liberal than she.

Well, if I had known this person for 3 weeks and only dated him once before in those three weeks, he may not be as attracted to me as I am to him, so it may take *some* influencing [emphasis original]. But then again being female I don't believe the girl should make the first move, since there has been no kind of sex between us yet. So if he's interested he'll make a move and this being our second date only, I wouldn't go any farther than french kissing no matter how turned on I was. If I wanted to influence this guy to kiss me, I would probably sit close to him as he talked to me and smile a lot so he realizes that I am turned on and liked him a lot. If he started to kiss me I would maybe try to prolong a simple kiss into a french kiss with maybe a little body pressure putting my arms around his neck. I would do this to let him know that I liked him without actually saying it, and any future dates and further involvement would have to be up to him.

This is a striking answer. Immediately after saying that it is not her place to make the first move, she describes what she would do to get him to kiss her. She seems to see no contradiction between her idea that a man should start and her ideas about how to start herself. Indeed, the essay suggests that for some women the purpose of proceptivity is to get the man "to make the first move," that is, to make what is conventionally *called* the first move (Weber, 1984, p. 49, gives another example). But despite such terminological niceties, in fact *she* starts the interaction.

Her essay contains a second theme that concerned these women. Some, like Essayists F1 and F2, will engage in a long series of proceptive actions before stopping, while other women, like Essayist F6, will send only a few proceptive signals. These women differ in *when* they want the man to take over (a phrase used

by the essayists themselves, e.g., F3): for some women, the man must respond
overtly very quickly, while other women are more tolerant of masculine non-responsiveness. The difference is not that some women are proceptive and others are
not: rather, some women stop signaling sooner than others. For example:

ESSAY F7

*19-year-old U.S. woman, seeing one man primarily, without formal religious
beliefs, with 60 percent of the whole sample more liberal than she.*

> I would influence this person by asking how he viewed the relationship at this
> point. I would feel out what he says then I would give little hints like: how
> would you like to come over to my place or to your place for a drink. I then
> think he would get the hint and act accordingly. If he doesn't, then I would
> simply drop the subject and he'd let me know when he's ready.

Thus, for these women, proceptivity does not serve to exert an over-arching,
manipulative power over the man which would reduce him to a puppet. To the
contrary: these women hope that their proceptive overtures will sooner or later elicit
his sexual response. They *want* the man to become aroused.

ESSAY F8

*21-year-old U.S. woman, not seeing anyone, without formal religious beliefs. with
40 percent of the sample more liberal than she.*

> Since I am female it would be much easier for me to influence my date to have
> sex with me than for a male to influence a female. . . . Since this person did
> ask me out there must be some sort of attraction to begin with. Knowing that
> he was attracted to me would certainly make the situation easier. The first
> "problem" is to find the right location, preferably someplace quiet, private,
> and dimly lit. I believe in the gentle approach—I would *not* pounce on him. The
> first move would be to play with his hair and the back of his neck. Then I would
> thank him for taking me out and kiss him the on the cheek (near his mouth).
> Then I would kiss his mouth and run by hand over his chest. If he doesn't know
> what to do then or doesn't want to go any further I wouldn't know what to do.
> I would probably drop it and not pressure him any further.

ESSAY F9

*21-year-old U.S. woman, not seeing anyone, extremely devout Catholic, with 80
percent of the sample more liberal than she.*

> I would never outright ask this person to have sex with me and I would not be
> the first to start kissing, necking, or manipulating his body in any way. If no
> response towards having sex was given to my hand holding, my arm around

his, my arm around his back or my smiles and my dancing and excited eyes, I would not go any further. If this person wasn't as turned on by me as I was by him, then trying to influence him to have sex with me would not make him feel comfortable and would end up not being a satisfying experience for both of us.

Even if her conservatism restrains her from kissing him, or causes her signals to be fairly subtle (compared, say, to those of Essayist F2, who is *also* fairly conservative), it is still not *she* who feels uncomfortable or reluctant about sex. She wants this man to understand, respond, and reciprocate the interest she feels and expresses. Proceptivity *invites* the man's sexual response.

The Canadian essayists were just as proceptive. The first example is by a quite liberal woman. Note how similar her answer is to those of U.S. women.

ESSAY F10

29-year-old Canadian woman, seeing one man primarily, without any formal religious beliefs, with only 5 percent of the entire sample more liberal than she.

Show my enthusiasm for the other person by smiling, laughing, sharing intimate information about my life (not too intimate). Also touch his arm and stroke his head. Do things like that to let him know what I'm thinking. If he takes me home without mentioning the idea of having sex at all and I feel I really want to I'd say something like "I'd love to stay with you tonight."

As Jesser (1978) and McCormick (1979) found for U.S. college women, here is a woman who will directly *say* that she is interested in intercourse. Her forthright request is mirrored in the following essay, written by a quite conservative Canadian woman.

ESSAY F11

18-year-old Canadian woman, not seeing anyone, an extremely devout Catholic, with 82 percent of the sample more liberal than she.

I would take the stand and express how I feel and what I'd like to do. The main thing here is communication. Without it, a relationship can fall apart. As long as both parties know what is expected and what isn't, the relationship is safe and it will probably last longer also.

And sometimes proceptivity can be very forthright.

ESSAY F12

18-year-old Canadian woman, seeing one man seriously, for whom intercourse is for marriage only. A total of 97 percent of the whole sample was more liberal than she.

—move closer
—start kissing
    & take it from there.

This was her entire answer. It can stand as a summary of all the essayists' proceptive strategies and of the sequence that these women, liberal and conservative, U.S. and Canadian, visualize when discussing their strategies.

Proceptive Women and Responsive Men

Our essay-by-essay analyses—not only of these 12 examples, but also of 90 more answers—force us to reject completely the idea that only liberal women are proceptive, or that only such women assume it as their prerogative to influence men sexually. Although popular belief may hold that women are hesitant, passive, reluctant, or coy when expressing interest in men, the women studied here flatly contradict such mythology. Regardless of sexual "conservatism," these women take the initiative themselves: they do not need to defer to, or rely on, men to begin the sexual encounter.

The conclusion has all the more force for being based on essays written by women who quite often felt that intercourse should be reserved for marriage or for some other equally monogamous and committed relationship. These women are *not* sexual libertines, a statement that holds with *special* force for the Canadian women.

Yet this conclusion may seem debatable, especially given the feminist critique of Western society as based on a ruling principle of *male* sexual power (e.g., Firestone, 1970; Brownmiller, 1975; Greenspan, 1983; Korman and Leslie, 1982). To be sure, the essayists place a high premium on female action and are also calmly and confidently articulate about their strategies. But is there a problem of viewpoint here? Do these essays acccurately depict the sociosexual encounter, or are such reports of proceptive behavior merely fiction?

Perhaps the essays refer only to a fantasized world in which women play an active role that is, in harsher social reality, denied to them by a deeper and far more real masculine dominion over the sociosexual encounter and all that occurs during it. Writing of both her own life and of the English novel, Rachel Brownstein (1982) expresses the possibility well: "One hidden ruling *fiction* is that women are the shapers as well as the shapes of men's desires" (p. 14, emphasis added). Perhaps the descriptions of proceptivity contained in these essays are only a complicated set of rules for speaking in conventional fictions about powers that women do not have. Perhaps the proceptive heroine—of whom Elizabeth Bennett in *Pride and Prejudice* is one example in women's writing—exists only in an escapist dream of a world in which women have sexual prerogatives that they lack in reality. Perhaps describing strategies for seducing men is only an opiate for sexual helplessness. Perhaps in *reality* these women are subject to the kind of prepotent male sexuality described by

Mead and others, which simply sweeps proceptivity to the side and renders it irrelevant.

Although these possibilities *sound* plausible—they fit both the stereotype of the reluctant woman and the vision of certain feminist writers—in fact the answer is *No*. The essays are neither fictional nor invented: their descriptions correspond *precisely* to what we have observed in bars, at parties, and in more formal social settings. The sequence envisioned by these women parallels the courtship sequence quite exactly, even to the details of the escalations made by women and rejected by recalcitrant men. The essays are extremely accurate, no matter how alien that conclusion may seem, given the traditional idea that *men* are the sexual initiators or that women are—naturally—sexually reluctant.

Nor can we argue that the "proceptivity" of these essayists arose merely because we tricked them with an essay question that was structured to elicit actively seductive strategies. Nothing required the detailed length or the careful analyses so often provided. In fact, the few completely non-proceptive essayists show that the question could be answered by referring to "traditional" male aggression themes. But the great majority of the essayists did not opt for such "traditions." Instead, they simply and accurately described how women, not men, initiate and escalate the sociosexual encounter.

Moreover, the essayists often made shrewdly realistic assessments of men's *inabilities* to respond to sexual overtures (e.g., the Recalcitrant Male). Not only do the men in these essays not initiate the encounter, they often do not even respond to what the woman sees as a clear invitation. In these essays, men are not sexually authoritative, powerful, or even particularly confident people. Rather, they often seem fragile and timid, and require gentle handling lest they become afraid. Underneath these essays is often the sense that many men are not at all sexually assertive, even when they could be, and even though the essayists might want them to be. When Essayist F8 writes that the *man* might not know what to do after she has kissed him we can hardly conclude that she is envisioning the all-powerful, confident male of folklore.

Moreover, the great majority of these women unquestioningly accept the premise that they have the autonomous *right* to initiate a sexual encounter with a man. Not one woman, in an interview *or* an essay, said "I know I shouldn't do such things, but . . . ." Though sexual conservatism may *sometimes* limit the extent of the woman's proceptivity (Essayist F9 as compared to Essayist F2), even the most conservative women—like F12—see it as their prerogative to influence men sexually in some way. Proceptivity is underlain by a belief that is virtually ideological: the essayists assume that *of course* women can influence men sexually, and do it all the time. These women are not sexual radicals, rebelling against norms that would have women wait passively for the man's overture. To the contrary: such "norms" never even *enter* the great majority of the essays. These women accept their proceptivity, and the privileges it implies, calmly and matter-of-factly.

If anything, these women are disappointed when men do not respond to them. In the romantic sociosexual drama these women are describing, the ideal man understands the woman's behavior as well as understanding its emotional and sexual meanings and intentions. Like an actor, he picks up his cue from the actress: as Essayist F5 put it, " . . . then he'd put his arm around me." And, if he does, she now sees him as the kind of man she wants—responsive, attentive, and understanding.

We can now comprehend better the logic of why women terminate these encounters. (Recall the women in the last chapter who left non-responsive men.) Some women do not take an initial non-response as a complete rejection, but continue to signal the man. Continued signaling makes sense, however, only if the woman believes it is within her power to make her signals ultimately effective. In essence, these women *forgive* the man for not getting the message, at least initially. However, other women will stop if the man does not respond after only one or two proceptive overtures. In neither group, then, is there any place for the utterly passive man. These women all see it as part of masculinity—or, better, perhaps of *attractive* masculinity—that the man will or should eventually enact an ardent but *responsive* role. Without that response, none of these women will continue indefinitely: not even Essayist F1 will go on forever. And when that response is not forthcoming, then the encounter ceases.

In this, one sees the man who recognizes the woman's needs and desires, be they for an emotional partner in a prolonged romance, or for passion and for a man who sweeps her willingly off her feet—of whom perhaps the best example is Porphyro in John Keats' *The Eve of St. Agnes* (1820/1962b). By understanding this vision of responsive masculinity, we begin to understand the historical and cultural background for proceptivity. It is not rooted in traditions of meek submissive passivity. Rather, it is connected to traditions that put female autonomy to the center. Writing of Samuel Richardson's *Sir Charles Grandison* (1753–1754), Brownstein (1982) says of Sir Charles that "[c]ritics have grouped him with the 'men of feeling' who begin to be written about in novels of his time, but he is a heroine's hero not for being overemotional, but because of *his capacity for responsiveness*" (p. 116, emphasis added).

Brownstein's point transcends literature: the essayists are envisioning precisely such a heroine's hero. These are not the Recalcitrant Males of whom the essayists speak so often, but are men who respond to proceptive signals, who understand the woman's intention and meanings, who enact a clear role in the proceptive romance, and who therefore validate the woman's behavior and interest. These men are *therefore* attractive.

As the Kid Goes for Broke: The Proceptive Tradition

Our observations in bars and analyses of essays apply only to today. True, liberal and conservative women can be highly proceptive, but has all of this happened only because the old, traditional rules have collapsed? "Certainly," the moralist might say, "only a weakening of male vigor could have led to the women making the overtures. The man's natural place has always been to woo the woman, just as natural to him as modesty and reluctance are to her. Things seem different nowadays because those time-honored traditions have been replaced by the unnatural forms of female behavior."

However, I suspect that the Wife of Bath would *still* sneer at the idea that women were naturally passive, deferential or submissive in their dealings with men. And since the 1300s, the Wife of Bath's voice has echoed back and forth in history to prove that proceptivity is no recent invention, no product of moral collapse, nor of contraception, nor of a diminished fear of pregnancy. Indeed, proceptivity is deeply embedded in Western tradition.

My favorite example occurs in *Sir Gawain and the Green Knight*, a late Medieval English poem about Gawain, the great lover of the Arthurian myth cycle. At one point, Gawain find himself the guest of Bercilak and his wife in a castle deep in the forest. As he lies abed one morning—his host has long been up and about—

An English forest, ca. 1400 A.D.

> . . . he heard stealthily come
> a soft sound at his door as it secretly opened
> and from under the [bed] clothes he craned his head,
> a corner of the curtain he caught up a little,
> and looked that way warily to learn what it was.
> It was the lady herself, most lovely to see,
> that cautiously closed the door behind her,
> and drew near to his bed. Then abashed was the knight,
> and lay down swiftly to look as if he slept;
> and she stepped silently and stole to his bed,
> cast back the curtain, and crept there within,
> and sat her down softly on the side of the bed,
> and there lingered very long to look for his waking.
> (Translation by J. R. R. Tolkien, 1975 p. 55–56)

Though I find it irresistibly satiric that Gawain, the great lover, hides under the covers, the lady may not have thought his behavior so amusing. But she waits until he finally pretends to awaken and then overtly tries to seduce him.

Gawain pleads various excuses and finally manages to escape from this highly proceptive lady, but she returns the next day. However, Gawain is not a buffoon in this poem, or a figure of comedy. He is a proud and dangerous man, unafraid of many things. Nor is *Sir Gawain* about courtly love, a romance centering on how women seduce men. In places, it is a dark poem indeed, in which Gawain's very human fear of dangers both natural and supernatural is opposed to his sometimes foolhardy courage (Benson, 1965; Tolkien, 1975). And sometimes women too can seem very dangerous, a theme which will reappear later in the book.

Normally, of course, such heros of epic are righteously incorruptible, so *Sir Gawain* embodies something of parody in this scene. But Bercilak's wife has some sisters in these epics, and some *do* gain their ends.

One example is Belissant in *Ami et Amile*, a *chanson de geste* written in Old French ca. 1200 (Calin, 1966, pp. 57–117). First, Belissant declares her love to Amile and is refused (proving that Recalcitrant Males are not recent, even if this one is a count refusing a princess). She later tries what the essayists would no doubt call "the direct approach": she comes to his bed at night, notices that he is asleep, gets into bed with him, and *enver le conte est plus prez approchie*—which is to say, she drew very close to him [Calin (1966, pp. 81–82) gives both the Old French and modern English texts of this scene]. And, rather like the young man in Essay F5, whose lady snuggles up to him, Amile also responds. Soon, he is in love with her, and they marry, have children, and live happily ever after—once they have waded their way through a plot that, among other things, incorporates leprosy, at least one miracle, and a version of the folktale *Faithful John* (Calin, 1966, pp. 64–67).

No, there is nothing recent about proceptivity. Even the details in these epically proceptive strategies are like the essayists': after all, they are but versions of "Move closer, start kissing & take it from there." Rosalind would have thought so too when, in *As You Like It*, she follows Orlando into the Forest of Arden simply because she loves him. Like Belissant and Amile, they too marry.

The implication is that, if anything, proceptivity is increased when Mr. Right comes along. Here is example—but it is not from poetry.

INTERVIEW

A 33-year-old woman (interview by Dr. V. Susan Fox)

> She began by saying that he later told her that he had been afraid to come over to her. "He didn't approach me," she said, "since he thought there was too much competition. So he didn't bother with it."
>
> But she did want to meet him. "So I started going in [the bar] hoping he'd be there because I had to make some kind of contact with this guy . . . I was sitting at the bar, looking particularly good that night. That was the day of minidresses, the mid 70s. I was wearing a red dress that had a V-neck. It was pretty simple, full sleeves and fit—sort of an A-line form: it was gored, but not very full and stopped about mid-thigh—high heels, hair down, eyes expertly made up but not too much, a piece of tasty [sic] gold jewelry which had belonged to my mother, so it looks nice. He got up and went to the men's room, or to make a call, or to do something, and I sidled up to the bar—just bellied right up there—and sat down in his chair and drank his Beefeater on the rocks with the extra twist of lemon which tasted just like a Christmas tree. It was a good move, and I've never regretted it. And he came back, and of course he had to say *something* because his drink was gone. And I said, 'This is just like a Christmas tree.' He was shy. But he said, 'Yeah, that's the juniper berries. . . . ' "

They then went on to a 6-year relationship.

These are not strategies designed by flirtatious coquettes for playing games with men or for acting reluctant. Nor is the following, taken from James Joyce's "A Painful Case," in *The Dubliners* (1914/1977).

A theater in Ireland, ca. 1900.

One evening, he found himself sitting beside two ladies in the Rotunda. The house, thinly peopled and silent, gave distressing prophesy of failure. The lady who sat next to him looked round at the deserted house once or twice and then said,
—What a pity there is such a poor house tonight! It's so hard on people to have to sing to empty benches.
He took the remark as an invitation to talk. He was surprised that she seemed so little awkward . . . . (p. 109)

Four times Joyce says that the house was empty. The two women had to choose to sit next to him. And is it a case of life imitating art when the woman in the following example made a similar choice?

An Episcopal church, Princeton, New Jersey, early one winter's evening in 1979.

A male friend and I had gone to a concert at the church. Most pews were empty, so we sat as close to the small orchestra as we could, on the center aisle. As we waited for the concert to begin, I looked around and watched the people entering, taking programs, and seating themselves.

A red-haired young woman came in, got her program, and walked up a side aisle. When she reached our pew, she slid in and sat about four feet from us. She did not turn to look at us, but merely opened her program and began to read. I turned back to my program and also started to read. In a minute or so, she turned to us and asked if we knew the music. We did and began to talk.

With as much of the church as empty as the theater Joyce described, this woman also had to choose to sit next to us. Later, in the reception that followed the concert, she and my friend began to talk and soon had turned towards each other and synchronized.

It is an old process, this proceptive approaching and touching . . . *very* old.

Rome, ca. 80 B.C.

. . . at a show of gladiators, when men and women sat promiscuously in the theatre, no distinct places being as yet appointed [for them], there sat down by Sylla [the usual spelling is Sulla] a beautiful woman of high birth, by name Valeria, daughter of Messala, and sister to Hortensius the orator. Now it happened that she had been lately divorced from her husband. Passing along behind Sylla, she leaned on him with her hand, and plucking a bit of wool from his garment, so proceeded to her seat. And on Sylla looking up and wondering what it meant, "What harm, mighty sir," said she, "if I also was desirous to partake a little in your felicity?" It appeared at once that Sylla was not displeased, but even tickled in his fancy, for he sent out to inquire her name, her birth, and past life. From this time there passed between them many side glances, each continually turning round to look at the other, and frequently interchanging smiles. In the end, overtures were made, and a marriage concluded on . . . . (Plutarch, n.d., p. 572)

The translation used by Pomeroy (1975, p. 175) says that Valeria picked a piece of lint from Sulla's cloak. I like the image because I have seen modern women do the same thing with men they like; indeed, men's clothing seems to collect a good deal of such lint. Valeria's opening line is really quite clever: Sulla's enemies had said that his victories in battle were due only to good luck—*felicitas*—and not skill. Pomeroy also suggests that Valeria's behavior represents something new in the history of the late Roman republic, but I suspect, though without proof, that proceptivity was not an invention of Roman women in 80 B.C. or thereabouts, *especially* since Plutarch's description quite accurately captures the opening of the courtship sequence as we saw it in the last chapter.*

The results dovetail quite neatly: observation, essays, and literature all lead in one direction. Proceptivity is not an invention of poets, writers, or of women's immodest or silly daydreams. Women can be proceptive at all stages of their interactions with men, from the opening approach, through each of the escalation points of the courtship sequence to explicit invitations to intercourse. "As the kid goes for broke," Joanie Caucus thinks to herself right after her evening declaration to Rick Redfern that she cooks a good breakfast (Trudeau, 1977, p. 91). Her statement would have surprised neither Bellisant nor Valeria, and neither of *them* would be surprised to find that today women still tell their boyfriends that they want to make love.

Conclusions

Despite a widespread belief in universal and natural female sexual passivity and reluctance, proceptivity is an ancient and highly developed form of women's sexual behavior. We have observed it in real interactions, have obtained detailed and explicit descriptions of it from women in interviews and in essays, and have read about it in literature and history. Women for whom premarital intercourse is acceptable and women for whom it is not can be proceptive and extremely articulate about how women initiate and escalate their sexual interactions with men.

Nor is proceptivity feminine "wile," "guile," or "manipulation" of male sexual interest. Proceptivity represents a range of skills and behavior patterns that

*A point of scholarship must be made here. Strictly, we can conclude only that *Plutarch*, writing in the first century in Greece, could describe proceptive behavior accurately, and not that the historical Valeria was proceptive or, for that matter, even existed. Nonetheless, Sarah Pomeroy (1975) accepts Plutarch as giving valid evidence about Sulla's times, and, independently, Ovid confirms that Roman women around the beginning of the Christian era were also highly proceptive (1949, Book I, 27ff et passim). So I have set this scene at about 80 B.C.

can serve a range of purposes, from social through emotional to ultimately matrimonial. These women are not sex-kittens, bludgeoned by fear into obstructing male ardor by coquetry or by a complementary desire to seem properly modest. Indeed, followed to its logical end, female sexual reluctance—and the social norms that create and reinforce it—would lead the woman to reject all suitors, even those who would have proved quite reasonable mates.

Thus, women's behavior simply does not ride only on the coattails of a single set of internalized and repressive norms, pre-formed in the beliefs of others, and transmitted lock, stock, and barrel to women. Instead, with the right man—one in whom they are interested and whom they find attractive—these women will openly express their interest, and, even if some women stop signaling sooner than others, the difference is in degree, not in kind. Virtually all the essayists are proceptive, as, I suspect, have been countless millions of women in history, even if they are less famous than Belissant, Valeria, or Joanie Caucus. Nor is there a hidden agenda in proceptivity: it is what it seems—an open, genuine expression of interest in a man.

Moreover, these women embark, and have embarked, on their proceptive romances without the faintest overt traces of reluctance, hesitation, or doubt. It is the woman's *right*, they are telling us, to seek responsive men who understand and reciprocate their interest. Nor is proceptivity built on the premise that men really are, or should be, the sexual initiators. To the contrary: these women have created their detailed, analytically organized proceptive plans because men are often recalcitrant or inattentive to their signals. Proceptivity is therefore not a rigid set of cookbook devices for seducing men in general, nor a predetermined recipe for sexual promiscuity to be followed with any man who happens to come along. Rather, proceptivity is intrinsically a set of contingency plans tailored to communicate interest to a particular man—the heroine's hero, as Brownstein (1982) calls him.

It is no small thing. Even when men have social status, wealth, and power, the proceptive tradition has given women a complementary right to evaluate them independently of whatever power relationships may hold generally between men and women. In this, we see a potentially profound connection between proceptivity and feminism, for *both* envision male-female relationships that center not on male sexual prerogative, but on the woman's privilege to choose a man according to her *own* desires, needs, and interests.*

Nor does proceptivity mean that a woman will (or must) express interest in every man she meets. The essayists indicate quite clearly that proceptivity is associated with a complementary privilege to reject a man's overtures completely or to limit them and stop short of intercourse. We must *not* assume that proceptivity is mere cringing submission to masculine power, nor flirtatious allure that represents

---

*The connection is not accidental between the proceptive ideal of the responsive man and the emergence of archetypically sensitive men in the fiction of the mid-1700s. When Richardson wrote *Sir Charles Grandison*, he did not create him independently of the lives of *real* women. Irene Brown (1982) demonstrates that Richardson knew and admired women like Mary Granville who, in the early and mid-1700s, was among the first women in the English-speaking tradition to develop systematically a vision of a woman's right to a rational and egalitarian relationship with a man of her own choosing.

the collapse of morality and honor in classes too poor to comprehend such things. When a woman is proceptive, it is because she has *chosen* the man to whom she expresses her interest. And if he responds to her, then the sequence begins, and— if not tonight, then soon—synchronization leads to making love. Now, to be sure, a *male* reader must not presume that if he raises his glass in synchrony with a woman, they will spend the night together! Yet, if he is responsive to her—if he is *this* heroine's hero—then intercourse *will* occur. Under these circumstances, the lovers *will* make love.

The moralist's vision of women imbued with nature's innate modesty is inadequate to explain what really underlies the shifting customs of birth and marriage, not only for today, but for all the Cumberland Counties of Western history in which women took "risks" impossible to explain by the simplistic, reductionist view that women are, of course, "naturally" terrified of pregnancy. These moralizing images are too thin, too unreal to capture the proceptivity of a woman like Valeria, or Bellisant, or Joanie Caucus—or of the women quoted above.

No, it is not powerlessness or fear of prepotent masculinity that motivates these so highly proceptive women. It is not to play cat-and-mouse with a man that they smile, laugh, snuggle closer, touch, look lovingly, and kiss him. With the full weight of a 2000-year-old tradition behind them to legitimate their proceptivity, they do so because they *like* him, biological masculinity and all. No analysis of courtship can ignore *that* fact.

Chapter 6

Three Faces of Reluctance

Yet proceptivity is not the whole story. True, myths exist of deities like Pan, before whose sexuality all female reluctance fades, but few of us operate in a world that includes such beings [and the exceptions tend to live in books, like *The Crock of Gold* by James Stephens (1912/1967) or *The Circus of Dr. Lao* by Charles Finney (1962)]. Sometimes women *do* say *No*, and very clearly. Moreover, even if I am critical of Mead, Bell, and others, scholars of their stature are not so easily *completely* misled. Even if we can criticize their ethnobiological functionalism, we cannot ignore them when they say that women are sexually reluctant.

So, again we have a puzzle. How can a woman sometimes say *Yes* and sometimes say *No*? How can she coordinate strategies that seem contradictory? To some men, like John Donne or Catullus, the answer is that women do not possess any strategies at all—they are simply fickle *by nature*.

Yet women *do* have strategies, and my first purpose in this chapter is to show that myths of a natural female inconstancy are just that: myths. I also have two other purposes: first, to show that very real biosocial processes underlie women's reluctance and rejection of men and, second, to show that proceptivity and reluctance make excellent biosocial sense together. Indeed, as strategies, proceptivity and reluctance do not contradict each other at all: together, they form the basis for *how* women select their men.

The Rules for Smart and Proper Sex

I want to begin with a useful distinction. Drawing on his field work in Trinidad, the anthropologist Morris Freilich (1980) suggested that sexual behavior is guided by *two* complementary belief systems, one embodying the normative rules, judgments, and standards for proper sexual behavior, and another embodying strategic and practical rules based on shrewd commonsense and experience. These he called the "proper-sex" and "smart-sex" rules, respectively.

Now, the word *rule* does not refer to "rules of etiquette" or to the rules found in legal codes, but rather to cultural principles and premises that underlie the behavior of any individual in a particular society. And, for sexuality, these principles are quite extensive.

The proper-sex rules contain the moral and attitudinal "shoulds" of sexuality, for example, the idea that a woman "should" be a virgin when she marries. An example of an extremely powerful proper-sex rule is that a woman who is married and living with her husband (happily, we may assume, and in good health) would *never* give up her newborn baby for adoption. She and her husband might decide on abortion, certainly a difficult decision, but putting up the child for adoption seems out of the question. (I want to thank Martha Cornog for this example.)

In turn, the smart-sex rules pertain to the principles of behavior that arise, for example, when the woman is *not* a virgin at marriage. Thus, the color of the bride's wedding gown: the proper-sex rule is that she can wear pure white only if she is a virgin. The complementary smart-sex rule is that if she is not a virgin, then she can wear white if she also wears something that is *not* white. The somewhat old-fashioned example illustrates an important point: *both* sets of rules depend on tradition and custom, and on the constant reshaping of tradition to fit circumstances [Handler and Linnekin (1984) discuss how "tradition" is constantly reworked].

The proper-sex rules are particularly important in understanding women's sexual reluctance. The most traditional rule is simple: she *should* say *No*, clearly and firmly.

For the moralist, virginity has always been "precious balsam in a fragile glass" (Atkinson, 1983). It is to be defended to the death. When a woman breaks this proper-sex rule—for example, she bears an out-of-wedlock child—the moralist sees her behavior bringing chaos and disorder into the way "things should be." Then, as Stone (1979) says, behavior that deviates from propriety indicates that the social fabric in disintegrating. Ultimately, it is devil's work.

But Freilich had no such moralizing intentions when he distinguished proper- and smart-sex rules. He wished, instead, to show how *together* they allow people to deal with sexuality. Thus, sexuality does not represent propriety and honor struggling against a drunken bawd's ethic of bastardy: it is regulated by two *systems* of rules that work in *complementarity* with each other. In brief, the proper-sex rules deal with "dignity and duty," as Freilich put it, while the smart-sex rules deal with survival and shrewd solutions to problems that arise in the real world.

In actuality, the proper-sex rules therefore embody far more than rejections that defend virginity against all men. Instead, the proper-sex rules operate in most day-to-day social congress between men and women and are quite adaptive, not merely repressive or moralizing. Thus, a woman may readily find it appropriate not to express sexual interest at certain times, e.g., in a business meeting. The proper-sex rules *regulate* the occurrence of sexual activity and restrict it to certain people at certain times and certain places.

But sometimes such rules are inappropriate—for example, when the woman has just met an interesting man at a party. Then the proper-sex rules yield to the smart-sex rules which enable her to express forthright interest in him.

Accordingly, one and the same woman may possess different strategies and rules that are appropriate for different situations. An extremely conservative woman—like the older woman mentioned in the preceding chapter or the very conservative women in the U.S.–Canada study—may well be shrewd and knowledgeable about men, and may even willingly impart her knowledge to her daughters, knowing that they too must be able to communicate interest to men. Likewise, sexually liberal women may deeply respect the rules of sexual propriety and behave quite reservedly when the situation warrants. Thus, women are not tied to a "natural" modesty, no matter what the moralist might say (or hope). Instead, the smart-sex rules permit women to *modify* the norms of propriety to fit the fluctuating requirements of their lives.

The proper-sex rules are valuable in another way. For example, if a woman is confronted by a man whose ardor far exceeds hers—a pushy type, as people say, or a masher—then those rules give her the *privilege* of saying No. She need not simply yield to him, for the external and traditional authority vested in the proper-sex rules acts in *concert* with her internal desires, and reinforces her personal decision.

However, at other times, the proper-sex rules can openly conflict with the smart-sex rules. Though the norms of propriety are quite clear, they do not answer a crucial question. Given that a woman is likely to marry or form some other essentially monogamous relationship, how does she know what kinds of overtures to reject? True, she might always draw the line at intercourse, but why there? Why not earlier? Carried into the real world, the proper-sex rules sometimes seem inapplicable.

What if he is her only suitor—or boyfriend, if you prefer? What if she is an adamant virgin—Herold and Goodwin's (1981) phrase for a woman who will not have premarital intercourse—but she perceives herself as too "unattractive" to find someone else in case he leaves? He, we may conclude empirically, finds *her* attractive, even though he too may undervalue his own appeal. But she may *not* believe that she can "do better." Underlying the now clichéd story of *Marty* is a profound question that cannot be answered if only the norms of total rejection are in operation. Sometimes, the proper- sex rules must be replaced by the smart-sex rules. They then temper the woman's reluctance and permit her to become involved (with or without intercourse) with a man whose interest exceeds hers as she *presently* perceives her feelings. And, by freeing herself to make sexual and emotional decisions on a case-by-case basis, she minimizes the chance that she might mistakenly reject a man who is actually acceptable to her—or might prove so, if given time and a chance.

Thus, reluctance is *not* a simple, one-dimensional matter. Throughout, it is modified by smart-sex considerations and by quite real problems for which propriety alone has no answers.

Outright Rejections, Heroic Deeds, and Good Opinions

Yet the formal rules of reluctance are quite real. Indeed, they are the stuff of romance, for they define several *modes* of rejecting the man—or of giving him a chance.

One is prototypically, if sardonically, embodied by Belinda in Alexander Pope's *The Rape of the Lock* (1717/1954, pp. 680–688). In rhymed couplets, Belinda simply tries to kill the baron who snipped off one of her tresses, even though it seems that he loves her (Canto V, lines 87–102). Hers is an outraged and coquettish fury: his behavior is utterly improper, utterly unacceptable, even if the much calmer Clarissa does not agree. When Clarissa says " . . . she who scorns a man, must die a maid" (Canto V, line 28), we hear the voice of sanity which understands that ironclad rules for rejecting men are not reasonable reproductive *or* emotional strategies. Nonetheless, Belinda's behavior *was* appropriate to her time and station in life, even if it brought down Pope's greatest powers of irony. Against her fury, Clarissa's calm advice to Belinda goes unheeded: no second chance for this fellow!

However, apart from this poetically overwrought extreme, a second mode of reluctance also exists. In certain Old French *chansons de geste*, the hero must achieve honor and victory in battle before she will marry him: he must win his city in order to win his lady (Calin, 1966, pp. 3–56, see e.g., pp. 26ff). Aragorn cannot wed Arwen in *The Lord of the Rings* without first returning to become king, even though they are betrothed (Tolkien, 1955). It is unthinkable—and hence never mentioned— that either lady consummate the betrothal *prior* to such victories. But we need not delve into epic to find the same contingent reluctance. For example, in the *Anne of Green Gables* stories, set in Prince Edward Island, Canada, around 1905–1915, only after Gilbert Blythe saves Anne Shirley from drowning and, later, refuses a job so that she can have it, does he become, for her, something other than a silly nuisance who teases her about her hair (Montgomery, 1908). So, too, in Jane Austen's *Pride and Prejudice* (1813/1945), Darcy finally proves himself to the hesitating Elizabeth Bennett by anonymously providing for her sister Lydia's marriage. It is in his character to do so, and he is not motivated by a crass desire to impress. Nonetheless, when Elizabeth finds out about it, her last doubts disappear.

These romances remove love from this world and translate it into a world apart, in which the test of the man's suitability as a husband is shifted from the personal feelings of the woman and transferred to deeds performed in a world external to her. If he vanquishes enemies, he is a good potential mate, an equation whose very illogicality forces us to see that it only serves rhetorically to stress that he is special—*very* special. And when she realizes *that*, then her reluctance fades.

Of course, without feminine reluctance, there would be no plot. But still, not many men have opportunities to conquer cities, rescue drowning girls, or provide for marriages from immense fortunes. Despite tales of suitors who court princesses by slaying dragons, ridding the land of plagues, or finding the jewelled hearts of strange beasts in far-away lands, to set men such tasks in reality is simply to get rid of them. In fact, the courtship of Elizabeth Bennett's sister Lydia is far less the stuff of romance. George Wickham is hardly Darcy: in fact, he is just a man, drawn perhaps to a pretty face and a ready adventure, which may explain why Elizabeth's father calls him his favorite.

Indeed, by providing Elizabeth with Darcy and his fortune and country estate, Austen contrasts Elizabeth's romance and its heroines and heros with Lydia and Wickham's reality and its reasonable accommodations and practical solutions. Lydia stays with her new husband for a while, and then they drift apart, to leave Lydia, it seems, living quite contentedly in the great city of London.*

And in *The Lord of the Rings*, Lady Éowyn, the slayer of the evil Ringwraith himself, falls in love with Faramir, not a king or hero, but merely a wounded captain with whom she holds hands as the enemy's tower Barad-Dûr crumbles into ruins (Tolkien, 1955, volume 3, book 6, chapter 5). The same is true, of course, of Princess Leia in the *Star Wars* trilogy: she falls in love with an ex-smuggler whose greatest heroism consists of foolhardy courage and a fast ship, and whose life *she* saves in the end. "I love you," he says to her immediately before she rescues him by disintegrating several Imperial troopers. "I know," she says.

So it is not clear what it means to be reluctant about a man. One model is Belinda, for whom the man's behavior *a priori* establishes his suitability. If he breaks her rules of coquettish reluctance, that's the end. Forget it. A second model is Elizabeth Bennett, and, with her, many women in fiction, for whom the gradient of ascent to love is steep. *Her* man must pass many tests indeed before her reluctance fades. But Lydia is a third model: she is less demanding, less romantic, and she loves far less in a world of heros then does Elizabeth. So does Éowyn, and so do Hermia and Helena in *Midsummer-Night's Dream*. *Their* men are just men, not heros. The good opinion of their women is all they need to earn. Once more echoes the voice of a young woman in love:

> . . . for here I him assure
> To love him best of any creature
> Though he no more had than his shirt.
> (*The Merchant's Tale*, lines 1983–1985,
> Chaucer, ca. 1400/1957, p. 122)

And our digression into theory and literature proves useful. There is no single tradition of "reluctance" for dealing with the too-ardent man: instead, reluctance is a continuum ranging from coquettish fury through outright rejection to the commonsense practicality of saying "wait and see." The proper-sex rules of rejection and reluctance *are* supplemented by other rules, at least in fiction. If some rules spurn the man or set dragons to slay, others are less exalted.

And so, what of real people? How do *real* women deal with men whose interest

---

*There is a stylistic reversal here worth noting. If the man of heroic romance wins the lady by winning his city, then, in Austen, the woman wins *her* city by leaving the man. There is truth to it. After all, Scarlett O'Hara goes through three husbands to keep Tara, the family estate.

exceeds theirs? What forms of reluctance do they display, and how do they weave these rules and traditions into their behavior and its meaning?

U.S. and Canadian Women Writing About How to Reject Men

I want to illustrate something of the variety—and shrewdness!—of the rejection strategies used by the women in the U.S.–Canada study discussed in the last chapter. We encountered few, if any, Belindas—women who set impossible standards of courtesy for men to meet—and we encountered *no* women who wanted their men to conquer cities. Instead, we discerned two strategies, the first in some ways much clearer than the second, but both observable in women's behavior.

Avoid Proceptivity and Reject Signals

The first strategy was described by approximately one-half the U.S. and Canadian essayists. I will illustrate it first with the U.S. author of Essay F1 quoted in the preceding chapter. She starts with a brief comment comparing seduction and rejection and then moves directly to her strategies.

ESSAY F13
_____

The U.S. woman of example F1, with 8 percent of the entire sample more liberal than she.

> This situation I find infinitely more simple to cope with. The easiest way out is to make sure wherever you're going on the date will be a place where sex is practically impossible, e.g., a bar, out to dinner, bowling, etc. However, if I do somehow find myself in a secluded environment I never fret because I always carry a pack of cards in my purse and I find suggesting a good game of GIN-RUMMY will get the message across or at least tone down the romance for the time being. This "no sex mood" can be easily reinforced by sticking to topics of conversation like current political problems, household disasters like the toilet overflowing this morning, or going to the extreme of talking about current disastrous social problems like the increase in teenage pregnancy and V.D.

_____

In essence she is trying to *forestall* a sexual encounter with a tour de force of distractions and diversions designed to deflect his signals, should he send any. Moreover, hers are contingency plans: if going to a bowling alley doesn't work, then maybe GIN-RUMMY will (the uppercase letters are hers). Though her strategies might fail—after all, it is said that the fastest way to a man's heart is through his stomach, and other women describe what they call "seduction dinners"—nonetheless her *intention* is to reject the man clearly and directly from the outset.*

Avoidance of proceptivity is also part of this rejection strategy. Compare the following to the writer's seduction essay (F4):

ESSAY F14

The U.S. woman of example F4, with 79 percent of the sample more liberal than she.

Try to keep your distance as much as possible. No body contact whatsoever. Gear the conversation towards mundane topics, such as the weather, the place you're at, etc. Act really uninterested. The point will come across. No invitations back to your apartment, just a thank-you and a goodbye.

She is explicitly not doing what she *would* do if she were interested. It sounds complicated, and might confuse a man who is unfamiliar with her proceptive repertoire and so cannot compare it to her present behavior. However, her intention is again clear, and so is the principle of this kind of rejection: if interest is expressed proceptively, then lack of interest is expressed non-proceptively.

This we called the *Avoid Proceptivity and Reject Signals* strategy. Though some women embellished one or the other aspect of the strategy, both parts were usually present.

ESSAY F15

20-year-old U.S. woman, seeing one man seriously, a fairly devout Protestant, with 16 percent of the sample more liberal than she.

First of all, I would avoid any opportunity for us to be completely alone and in close physical contact. If I am really turned off by this person, I would be just as unresponsive to his advances as I would be responsive to someone I was turned on by. My favorite line to someone who makes advances toward me to whom I am not "turned on," is "I'm sorry, but I'm not allowed." Most times, it baffles the young man to the point of realizing that he should leave me alone.

With her essay, we encounter a new theme: the man who is *explicitly* said to make the first move. A reader might wish to read such men into essays F13 and F14, but in fact the behavior of those men is not described. However, here she explicitly

---

*As mentioned before, the ethnographic record is weak in descriptions of actual courtship behavior. But here is an exception, concerning a *rejection* strategy said by Kroeber (1925/1976, p. 401) to characterize the mountain Maidu, an Indian tribe of California. He writes that "[t]he suitor merely visited in the evening and remained [with the woman]. If the girl did not want him, she sat up all night, if necessary." I rather suspect that this young woman and essayist F13 might have a good deal to say to each other about how to spend such an evening—and I wonder what the Maidu equivalent of GIN-RUMMY was!

describes what she would do if confronted by that eager man. We are, in brief, moving towards the classical ardent man and reluctant woman.

But unlike the myth of the Reluctant Woman and Ardent Man, the Avoid Proceptivity and Reject Signals strategy is not a flirtatious game designed to keep the man's ardor within limits. These women are saying what they mean: *No.*

ESSAY F16

The woman of example F5, with 43 percent of the sample more liberal than she.

> I'd stay on my side of the car seat. I wouldn't advance my hand or my arm to be held. I'd keep a space between us when walking down the street. I would not ask him to my place after our date. If he got really obnoxious I'd tell him that I'm simply not interested. I don't like to beat around the bush about things I want or don't want.

ESSAY F17

21-year-old U.S. woman, seeing one man primarily, a fairly devout Protestant, with 16 percent of the sample more liberal than she.

> I would avoid being alone with the person first off and be cold to any seductive moves he may make. Keeping my distance is important as well as keeping on clean subjects and not responding to "dirty" comments. If it got to an extreme point where he did not recognize my hints then I would verbalize my actions.

Other women are even more explicit in their rejections of the man.

ESSAY F18

21-year-old U.S. woman, seeing one man seriouly, a fairly devout Lutheran, with 31 percent of the sample more liberal than she.

> If this guy got really physical and was ultimately persistent and I wanted nothing to do with him, I would fight his hands off physically. If that didn't work (you would think he would get the message) I would verbally abuse the man until he felt so degraded that he would be too embarrassed to go any further. If that didn't work (at this point I would not only be turned off but repulsed!) I'd leave wherever we were and either call someone to get me, walk if I were close enough or threaten him to take me home. I feel a man should have enough respect that if a woman says "no," he should abide by her wishes and not continue any further. If they really like the woman, then they blew their chances. If they just want to get down her pants, then they went about it all wrong and really are out of luck. Both ways, they've lost out!

These essayists are not the Reluctant Females of myth, who accede to male sexual power and then play tricksy, flirtsy games with it in order to control its otherwise prepotent powers. Instead, they give to female reluctance very clear form: not moralizing hatred for men, nor timid deference, nor coquettish manipulation. To the contrary. The pyrotechnic rejections of essay F13 are not coynesses arising from feminine passivity or submissiveness. She *means* it. These women are turned off and they know it. They want the man to know it too.

Nor are they one-dimensional people, ruled by simple rules of sexual prudery and who automatically enact the proper-sex rules for rejecting all men. They are nearly all highly proceptive with men who interest them (compare essay F13 with F1; F14 with F4; F16 with F5; each pair of essays was written by the same woman). These women's rejection strategies therefore do *not* represent ironclad rules of propriety imposed from without and reflexively transformed into rejective behavior. Their rejections are far more complex than suggested by the social scientific functionalist analysis with which I began the preceding chapter.

As with proceptivity itself, these rejections express the woman's own emotions autonomously through her behavior. These women see it as their inalienable *right* to say and mean *No*. Accordingly, we can discern the operation of both the smart-sex and proper-sex rules in the Avoid Proceptivity and Reject Signals strategy. Essay F13 is very *shrewd*: it is paradigmatically smart (Freilich, 1980).

Moreover, under the specifics of rejection, the proper-sex rules give these women their sure sense that they have the *right* to reject the man. When Essayist F18 implies that a man should respect the woman's wishes, she tacitly refers to norms of behavior, manners, and courtesy that she feels *should* regulate male-female relations. A man who makes advances against her wishes violates not only her sexual autonomy, but also her profoundly held beliefs about *proper* sexual behavior. Her anger rises as much against his physical advances as against his refusal to obey the rules of proper-sex behavior that give her the right to engage in intercourse—or not. He has offended not only against her, but against the rules she believes in. His is a double sin.

But these women's strategies are not a blur of affect or outrage. Rejection represents an intellectual activity as much as emotional, as the analytical clarity of the essays illustrates. When these women avoid proceptive behavior in order to reject the man, in essence they *integrate* their proceptive and rejective strategies. They have defined rejective behavior as the antithesis of proceptivity. For them, saying *No* and saying *Yes* are not the mutually exclusive categories of the moralist. Instead, underneath proceptivity and rejection reside emotional polarities whose opposition is expressed behaviorally. Thus, to touch and not to touch have become *symbols* of interest and lack of interest.

Symbolic Meaning

Indeed, these women have vested nearly all their actions with such symbolic meanings. Physical distance, topic of conversation, degree and intensity of eye contact, choice of locale have all been assigned an exquisitely developed and coordinated set of proceptive and rejective meanings. These women employ their total environment symbolically: every thing and every act in it consciously expresses how they *feel* about the man.

However, we cannot conclude that women actually succeed in communicating with men through these symbolic meanings. In part, that depends on what *he* thinks the woman's behavior means, and profound chasms of misunderstanding can exist between men and women concerning these meanings (Chapter 7). Nonetheless, for the women, these meanings emerge during the moment-by-moment creation of the courtship sequence and are as palpable as the behavior patterns used to express them. (The skilled objective observer therefore has little trouble understanding the woman's intentions, even if her male partner cannot.)

Incomplete Rejection or Delay

Another dimension of complexity is added by the second rejection strategy employed by the essayists. It contains a snag—or ethnographic short circuit, if you prefer.

ESSAY F19

22-year-old woman, seeing one man seriously, not religious, with 12 percent of the sample more liberal than she.

> When the come on is strong and I'm not interested I usually give a few short resistive signs, like pushing him away or saying it's late. I hate to seem so obvious that I hurt his ego, but I do usually wait until he makes a move before I try to stop him. Why go out on a date if you are just going to be a cold rag? If a guy can't take the hint I'll just say "No, I'm not interested" and get up and go, if I have to. I sure won't go out with him again.
>
> Anyway these aren't the best answers 'cause I'm not so typical. I've been going steady with a guy for a year. He says I was the one who got him hooked, but I think it was very mutual. Other episodes have been either I'm interested and I let them know and we go, or I'm not and just close myself up. I figure if a guy really cares he'll respect your wishes and if all he's after is sex he ain't gonna get me. Usually that means I'll stall for several encounters to see how he reacts, then reward him for the way he has treated me.

In this essay, a new theme appears: if the man respects her wishes, then she might *not* reject him at all. To be sure, she mentions rejecting the man's overtures, but those rejections have been tempered: "Why be a cold rag?" she asks. In fact, it is hard to read her essay as containing any real rejection at all. Likewise, the following essay, written by the *extremely* conservative woman of seduction Essay F6.

ESSAY F20

The U.S. woman of example F6, with 99 percent of the sample more liberal than she.

> Now I'm on a second date with someone who is really turned on by me but I'm not interested in getting involved. I would act resistant when he kissed me and definitely not let him touch me in any way. If he got fresh and tried to, I would pull away real quick and look shocked and level with the guy. I would tell him I didn't want to get involved too quickly or tell him that I think we should get to know each other a little bit better, if I wanted to give this fellow a chance. I mean after only 2 dates you really don't know a person and you may get interested when you do get to know each other.

Her answer ought to eliminate any residual impression that sexual "conservatism," as measured through attitudes, has anything to do with women's strategies for dealing with *real* men. Now, he has kissed her: she is not going to bowling alleys, playing GIN RUMMY, or abusing and degrading the man. The tone has shifted from absolute rejection to something that has genuine interest in it.

ESSAY F21

The U.S. woman of example F8, with 40 percent of the sample more liberal than she.

> This situation can happen in a number of ways. If we were in a public place and I felt that he was really turned on I would make sure to stay near other people and I wouldn't leave until he had calmed down. If, on the other hand, we were in the car or an apartment and if he were pawing me I would say "Please stop, I like you but I don't like that much." Then I would explain my values to him. I don't want to hurt him or embarrass him but I think I would if it were the only way to get my point across. If he still doesn't stop there is always the story of another possessive boyfriend who is 6'4", 240 lbs. and very mean.

Another possessive boyfriend? But the word may be well chosen, for she *does* say that she likes him. (She reported herself as not seeing anyone.) Now she clearly draws the line at rape. But it seems implicit that if he does respect her values, then a romance may have begun.

ESSAY F22

21-year-old U.S. woman, seeing one man primarily, a fairly devout Protestant, with 73 percent of the sample more liberal than she.

> I would say that it was too soon and that we really didn't know each other. I

think that the relationship was moving too fast and I would mention the fact of TIME. That there is plenty of time for us. [Capitals original]

This we called the *Incomplete Rejection* or *Delay* strategy. In it, the woman does *not* reject the man either completely or once and for all. Instead, she sees either the germ of a relationship present, or foresees that one might be possible in the future.

20-year-old U.S. woman, not seeing anyone, a very devout Presbyterian, with 33 percent of the sample more liberal than she.

I don't think that only knowing a person for 3 weeks that I would ever have sex with him. You can't know a person well enough in 3 weeks. I think that I would try to discourage his coming on to me and if that didn't work, I would simply be honest with him and tell him it was against my morals to have sex with him, explaining that I don't know him well enough. If he is really interested in me for being myself he will try to understand my feelings. If not and he never calls me again, then good-bye, I would let him go and conclude that he wasn't worth seeing.

Have we, then, finally encountered the Reluctant Woman of myth, she who holds back through fear of pregnancy, through fear of seeming "loose" or "easy," or through fear of a single, ignoble moment of ruinous surrender? Not really.

20-year-old U.S. woman, seeing one man seriously, not religious, with 12 percent of the sample more liberal than she.

Don't talk seriously if you're not. Keep all comments regarding sexuality and going to bed with this person at a humorous level, but every-so-often seriously indicate that you have no intention of sleeping with this person. If this person is all over you an abrupt push might work and a serious statement about *why* you needn't make love to this person to enjoy their company. You are not just a body, but a mind also.

These women are not saying *No*. They are saying *Maybe, if . . .* And the *if* is everything. It is not the "if" of the coy woman who offers the tantalizing allure of her body in exchange for a wedding ring or cash on the barrelhead. It is far more profound. *If* the man respects her wishes, *if* he does not come on too strong, *if* he wants her for herself and not purely for sexual purposes—in a word, *if* he *responds* to her needs and desires—then these women can foresee sexual involvement of some kind with him.*

Delay: Reluctance Plus Proceptivity

The women who describe the Incomplete Rejection strategy also integrate their proceptive and rejective techniques, but very differently from what occurs in the Avoid Proceptivity strategy. Now rejection does not simply mirror the symbols of proceptivity, as it did before. Instead, there arises a kind of dynamic tension between proceptivity and reluctance: the woman's behavior *simultaneously* symbolizes interest and hesitation. The following pair of essays, both written by the same woman, illustrates the curious duality of meaning that can arise when a proceptive woman adopts the Incomplete Rejection strategy. I quote in full both her seduction and rejection essays, partly because her attempt to signal simultaneous interest and hesitation forms the groundwork of profound problems for some *men*.

ESSAY F25a
___

Seduction essay of a 20-year-old U.S. woman, seeing one man seriously, a fairly devout Episcopalian, with 79 percent of the sample more conservative than she.

Since this is only the second date and I only know the man [for a little while], I am not in love with him. Therefore intercourse will not be incorporated into the evening. Nor would any other advanced stage of intimacy such as oral sex or any kind of stimulation of either partner's genitals with the hands. Even if this were a love relationship I doubt if anything beyond kissing and caressing of the whole body (that is any part except stimulation of genital areas) would occur.

Because I wish to maintain these limitations I would not try to turn on my partner in such a way as to encourage him to desire more advanced stages of intimacy. This is obviously quite difficult and it would be best to communicate these limitations in some terse and mature manner. There must be mutual agreement and acceptance of values in order to prevent any embarrassment and discomfort. In other words without mutual agreement one partner will end up begging for something more intimate while the other is put into the uncomfortable position of saying "no."

To encourage the man (my partner) to engage in kissing in a more intimate manner then the casual kissing of the first date I would initiate a more passionate kiss simply by kissing more passionately, kissing French style,

___

*A caveat is in order here. Although the essays fell into two groups, it does not follow that a given woman will use only one strategy and never the other. Indeed, it seems plausible that she would consider each strategy as quite sensible under appropriate circumstances—for example, the Avoid Proceptivity strategy for someone whom she cannot easily escape, and the Incomplete Rejection strategy for someone who seems a *possible* partner. This presumption underlies the entire discussion in the text.

kissing the neck, kissing for a longer period of time. At the same time I would compliment those parts of his body I find attractive such as shoulders, face, hands. I would not be wise to compliment more intimate parts of the body since this would indicate a more intimate and advanced desire. To encourage a man to touch my breasts I would stroke his and make any advances on his part as easy as possible. For instance should he wish to unbutton my shirt I would not roll onto my stomach but rather onto the side so my front faced him. Since men often have trouble with bra fasteners I would undo the snap for him.

If my partner should make any moves towards my pants or genital area I would swiftly and gently remove his hand and continue to do so on repeated attempts. Should I feel there is any danger of his being overly persuasive or forceful I would offer some other interest to distract him such as a drink or movie—or if I felt too uncomfortable I would offer him his coat.

Her reluctance to proceed past petting does not represent a moral position (something she never mentions), but, instead, symbolizes her emotions. The genitals have been made to carry the full symbolic weight of love. In the symbolic world this woman has created—like the world of many other women—*not* to touch the genitals means *not being* in love, while touching or caressing them (or, of course, intercourse itself) means *being* in love. She thus divides sexual activities into those representing affection, interest, or even arousal, which are non-genital, and into those representing love, which *are* genital. Her overtly proceptive behavior occurs in the first domain, and her overtly reluctant behavior in the second. Hers is then a fundamentally different way of creating sexual symbols than the woman for whom hesitation or reluctance means avoiding all proceptive actions, as in the Avoid Proceptivity strategy. In her rejection essay, which follows, we again see that reluctance does not preclude proceptivity or sexual involvement: it precludes genital sexuality.

ESSAY 25b

The same woman's rejection essay.

Since I am not interested in sex of any kind other than the casual kissing which is usual for dates I would not allow us to be in the more secluded, romantic surroundings. For instance I would not go to a movie, a "lookout" in a car or either apartment. Since I do not want a more intimate sexual encounter I would not respond to his verbal turn-on's such as "I find your body so warm and exciting . . . " or "I really want us to make love" but would rather caution him and communicate my own disinterest (verbally and physically).

Should he try to rest on top of me or bring his whole body close to mine I would politely but firmly change positions. I would not continue kissing if it became overly passionate or involved and should he try to unbutton my shirt or pants or touch me in any of those more intimate areas I would remove his hand. As a last resort I would remove any interest from kissing and caressing and concentrate on something else such as music, dinner or something else or ask to be taken home.

Though her first paragraph says that she will not allow herself to be in an intimate environment, her second paragraph is set in precisely such a setting. After she says that she would not let him unbutton her shirt, her thought is drawn to the symbolic center of the Incomplete Rejection strategy: the genitals themselves. Unlike the essayists of the Avoid Proceptivity strategy: she sees nothing *really* inconsistent between a degree of sexual involvement, kissing, for example, and her refusal to have genital sex. Again, her distinction between non-genital and genital sexuality and their attendant emotions has been symbolized behaviorally: the first is behaviorally proceptive while the second is behaviorally reluctant. In fact, the only difference between the two essays is in the amount of non-genital sexuality she will permit.

Now, we cannot assume that women employing the Incomplete Rejection strategy are accommodating the man in giving in to some of his sexual advances. They are not deferring to him, for if he does go "too far," whatever "too far" is for the woman, these women will angrily and contemptuously reject him. "Such men blew it," they say, "they're out of luck." Such a man has his coat handed to him, not the woman's body—or he has his hand removed, in the no doubt inadvertently violent image of essayist F25.

Once again we encounter the responsive man. If the Incomplete Rejection strategy seems both confusing and cautious, nonetheless its rules are those of proceptivity itself: if the man paces his sexual interest to hers, then he is *responsive to her.* He has proved himself, if not by slaying dragons, then by revealing himself to be a *good* man. He is then an acceptable potential partner and, perhaps, father of her children, for *he lives up to the desired and valued ideal of the responsive, sensitive man who attends sympathetically and empathetically to her needs.* He knows when she *is* interested and when she is *not*, and, no matter how her interest or lack of interest is expressed, will "respect her wishes." He is therefore acceptable under the proper-sex norms themselves: now, his intentions *are* honorable. He wants her for her mind *and* her body, and has proved it.

This scenario is virtually identical to the plot of *Pride and Prejudice*. Elizabeth is cautiously proceptive towards Darcy (she walks to his house, and he notices her "flashing eyes") but she has serious initial doubts about him and refuses his first offer of marriage. Only later, when he reveals himself as a good man who is *responsive* to the needs of her and her family, does she accept him. I rather suspect that Elizabeth would have sympathized with many of the essayists, for they too are not simply acceding to the man's desire for them, either for intercourse or for marriage, but evaluate his character and behavior *before* starting a relationship with him. These essayists believe that they have the inalienable and autonomous right to *choose*: either proceptively and directly with a man who interests them, or to accept or reject a man who expresses interest in them.

So it is not paradoxical at all that a man who is not initially interesting may later become a perfectly acceptable partner—*if* he displays respect, patience, under-standing, sensitivity, interest, in a word, love. His behavior has now fulfilled the requirements laid on him by the traditions that surround proceptivity itself: he is responsive to the woman.

The Tradition of Giving the Man a Chance

We can now see one reason why ardent males and reluctant females echo so far back into Western history. Female reluctance is not a built-in, natural modesty struggling against masculine sexuality in a melodrama of surrender, ruin, and regret. It is not coy, manipulative feminine allure enticing men towards the altar. Rather, the traditional idea of male sexual assertiveness and concomitant female hesitation represents a culturally and personally adaptive response of women who find themselves confronted by an interested male, *in whom they are not certain they are interested, and about whose character and trustworthiness they as yet know little.* This traditional pattern is therefore not a norm for expressing feminine interest in a man: *that* is represented by proceptive behavior and its rules. Rather, the traditional idea of male aggression and female reluctance represents a strategy for gaining essential information about the man and his motives *before* intercourse. It tests the man; it does not defer to him.

We now begin to see some *reasons* women are sexually reluctant. When men—or moralists—say women are "naturally" hesitant, they *deny* that reluctance has an underlying rationality. But it does: women can be reluctant for good economic and biosocial reasons that have long existed in female tradition.

Making a Good Marriage

Yet from a feminist viewpoint, it might seem that female sexual reluctance could not be part of *women's* traditions. First, it permits sexual rights to men that it denies to women. Second, it actively suppresses the woman's sexuality. For example, the Incomplete Rejection strategy seems incompatible with what is sometimes called "recreational sex." This perspective might imply that the idea is thoroughly male, in its repressive power and seeming justification of male sexual prerogatives. Yet—and the point may well be controversial—this interpretation cannot possibly be true.

First, it would be in the man's sexual interest to inculcate in women not sexual *reluctance*, but the idea that women should be sexually *available* to men whenever they want them. As an ideology serving *male* sexual appetites, female sexual reluctance makes no sense. Indeed, Wollstonecraft's (1792/1967) most devastating attack on the sexual ideology of the late 1700s is precisely that men—*if* they have the power—make women their sexual servants, and reinforce sexually obedient or submissive, not reluctant, ideologies in women. [Friedan (1963) makes a similar point about modern male–female relationships.]

Second, norms of female sexual repression are documented in women's history, especially literary history, as an exaltation of virginity, purity, chastity, and modesty (Calder, 1976; Marcus, 1964/1977, Chapter 1; G. M. Young, 1953; de Beauvoir, 1952, pp. 394ff; Brownstein, 1982). Bernard (1981, pp. 463–465) points out that women's lore contains extensive anti-sexual advice and beliefs (e.g., "Men only want one thing," with its implicit tag-line "and they're not going to get it." Compare essay F19). It is therefore extremely unlikely that *men* created the image of the aggressive man and the *reluctant* woman. Instead, the idea seems to represent a female tradition, whose point is to advise caution and restraint about men. The notion of aggressive men and reluctant women seems far less associated with any *male* idea that women should be pure, virginal, or unavailable, than with *feminine* ideals of purity and virginity (a conclusion borne out by those essayists who refuse to have sexual intercourse) and, perhaps, with a rejection of sexual libertinage (W. Young, 1964, especially Chapter 23; Wollstonecraft, 1792/1967).

However, social and economic inequalities between men and women have assuredly shaped the Incomplete Rejection strategy. Whereas in the Avoid Proceptivity strategy the woman has the forthright privilege to reject a man unambiguously, the Incomplete Rejection strategy embodies an asymmetry between male and female sexual prerogatives. In this, it accommodates itself to social realities by providing a *marital* solution to the unequal distribution of wealth between men and women.

The behavior of Elizabeth Bennett in *Pride and Prejudice* is the prototype of this form of courtship, for it is economically, not emotionally, motivated. Her father's land is entailed and cannot be inherited by his wife or daughters. Unless his daughters make good marriages, they will become paupers. So, if Elizabeth lets her courtship with Darcy proceed too casually towards a premarital involvement, not only would her *own* reputation be ruined, but *her family's place in society*. A great deal more than sexual emotion rides on Mrs. Bennett's strategy of having her daughters make "good" marriages: she knows that they must marry wealth or face disaster. (Immune to these pressures, *Mr.* Bennett can defend his daughters' happiness.) Accordingly, such women must *sift* through their suitors, never rejecting any completely, until they can make the best choice possible. Elizabeth is caught in an iron trap of economics that sets impassable, extrinsic limits to her behavior.*

Behind Incomplete Rejection is an ideology that is expected to evolve particularly in societies like Victorian America and England, in which the middle- or upper-class woman's status depended on her marital connections and in which her primary mode of social advance was by making a good marriage. But even before

---

*I am not saying that Elizabeth's love for Darcy is economically motivated, though the great house at Pemberley doesn't hurt. However, the form of their courtship *is* powerfully influenced by economics. The word *love* has other instrumental meanings as well, for example, when one refers to a "love-child" thereby to justify its birth as the product of its parents' "love." Perhaps when Ira Reiss (1981) observed that in the conservative tradition "Love redeems sex," we see a similar usage of "love" to justify sexuality either before or after the fact.

the Victorian era, courtship and love were tied to economics for some women. To quote Wollstonecraft (1792/1967):

> Girls marry merely to *better* themselves, to borrow a significant vulgar phrase, and have such perfect control over their hearts as not to permit themselves to *fall in love* till a man with a superior fortune offers. (p. 124, italics original)

Of course, it takes social skill to induce such a man to make an offer, and, in these accommodations to male power and wealth, the woman's personality, looks, manners, and charm all come to the forefront. Even today there is an immense literature on this subject (Bernard, 1981, pp. 475ff; Walster and Walster, 1978, pp. 139–141). And, as long as women's social place and mode of advance depends even partly on men's wealth or on the possibility of marriage to a rich man, so too will the courtship strategies of some women depend on Incomplete Rejection. One of the most cynical and bitter clichés of the singles scene in large cities, such as New York or Washington, D.C., is said by women about men: *You never know when a better one will come along.* In that world, "better" often is measured economically—by job-titles, credit-card limits, expense accounts, possession of fancy vacation homes—and, for these women, the emotions are entailed as powerfully as were Elizabeth Bennett's.

Dependency and Search Polygamy

Other women are sexually reluctant for emotional reasons, for example, dependency needs that could not possibly be met by *any* real human being. In their popularly written book, Nir and Maslin (1982) give some very accurate and insightful descriptions of dependency needs in modern single women [see Eichenbaum and Ohrbach (1983a, 1983b) and Greenspan (1983) for feminist perspectives]. Though Nir and Maslin seem to believe that dependent women are a type, actually many women pass through stages of great emotional vulnerability. Then romance seems the *only* cure for loneliness and need, especially when it is elaborated into a full-scale fantasy of the perfect man—Prince Charming—who will provide all the love the woman ever wanted.

Prior to oral contraception (1961), one can imagine that such needs only rarely led to intercourse itself. The reason is not fear of intercourse *per se*, for, as I have stressed, that fear had not been general among women, Rather, I would speculate that intercourse symbolized *commitment* for women, and especially for a dependent woman for whom only a man could solve life's problems. If so, then intercourse commits her, and brings her search to a halt. The idea was "When I find the perfect man, then I will sleep with him, because then I will love him. In the meantime, though, I won't sleep with anyone." So she saved her virginity for that man, and used intercourse to symbolize her perfect love for him. Her physical "purity"—virginity—symbolized the purity of her feelings for him.

Yet that equation has assuredly weakened since 1961. One crucial result has been that many women now incorporate intercourse into their search for the perfect (or not so perfect) man, and purely *coital* reluctance has nearly vanished among single people in large cities. For example, before 1961, *looking* meant dating a number of men, being more or less obviously unattached, and going no farther than kissing or necking. In contrast, *having* a man—that is, commitment—was symbolized by genital intercourse either during engagement or after marriage (among other symbols). By 1980, however, those symbols no longer had much power (even Essayist F25 goes much farther sexually than a woman her age in the 1950s).

To replace the weakened *sexual* symbols of commitment, the children of the baby boom—who formed and form the demographic basis for the modern "singles scene"—have developed symbols that stress the emotional relationship *itself*. The cliché "meaningful relationship" is one example, but so are *good vibrations, committed relationship, feeling close, working at a relationship,* and *copacetic.*

In this, a "dependent" woman can easily have intercourse very quickly, for she can just as quickly drop away from the man and continue her search. Far more importantly, however, so can a "normal" woman—that is, a woman who is *not* motivated primarily by fears and anxieties. For such women, intercourse seems more like a reasonable *extension* of the traditional male-female dating pattern than anything symbolically over-special. Now, this process is *not* coital promiscuity. Instead, I will call it "search polygamy." Some women (not all) may go through a series of coital partners, and therefore *seem* promiscuous to a moralist, but they are not. Their ultimate hope is to find a man with whom to form a permanent marital or quasi-marital bond, that is, a mateship.*

Search polygamy has become common among single women in large cities. In fact, one (sociological) function of singles bars is to provide a place where people who are searching can meet each other. However, as soon as they *do* form a couple—an "item" as the cliché went—they drop out of the bar scene. Accordingly, the naive observer may think that singles bars are filled with "losers" and "airheads" who want just sex, and does not see people who enter the bar scene, eventually find someone, and then drop out. The woman interviewed on p. 142 was an example.†

Sexual reluctance has therefore taken on some very new meanings. During search polygamy, a woman may not be sexually reluctant at all. For her, the "wait-and-see" attitude is part of looking for a man. And who knows? Maybe this is him. Simultaneously, she is perfecting her sociosexual skills and refining her criteria for men. When she finds *him*, then search polygamy ceases, and she becomes essentially monogamous with him, and will reject other men. Accordingly,

---

*I obtained a dramatic example from a woman informant who had extensive experience with swinging. She said, "The men join swing clubs looking for sex, and the women join looking for mates. When they find them, they drop out of swinging," She added, "They don't always find their mates among other swingers, but either way they dropped out." Though this pattern might not be universal among such women, it is a striking example of search polygamy.

†Heterosexual personals advertisements represent one way people leave the bar scene. In mass market magazines, these advertisements virtually always seek partners, not sexual playmates.

female rejection strategies not only vary by women, but also within an individual woman's lifetime. Reluctance exists only at those times in her life when it serves emotional and symbolic purposes.

Thus, search polygamy seems peculiar only from the viewpoint of the old belief that intercourse *per se* symbolized a successful search for a man and the woman's involvement with him. However, given that contraception has freed women sexually, search polygamy makes good sense to some women: it still centers on the search for a man and on satisfying genuine emotional and sexual needs.

Biosocial Reluctance

So we must not push too far the model of reluctance that Elizabeth Bennett seems to afford. Women do *not* simply accommodate themselves to a society that denies them wealth, social status, or position except on their husband's accounts. Such accommodations are historically contingent, and not even Elizabeth Bennett *liked* them. We cannot argue that women's sexuality is inherently reactive, or claim that she, and it, are but plastic in the hands of economics or her own "feminine" psychology, to which she submits, meek and willing.

Female sexual reluctance is *not* a matter of guilt, fear, or an upbringing that equated sex and sin. These emotions and beliefs—which are very real—are only ways to express and perhaps experience reluctance. When a sexually active young woman says she "feels guilty" about having sex, I suggest that she is adding a tacit qualification: "with *him*." The feeling of guilt is not global, but specific. It amounts to saying "I don't like what I'm doing to myself, sleeping with that creep."

No generalized fear of sex motivates female reluctance, at least not in this study. The great majority of these women were highly proceptive with men who interested them. Under those circumstances, they *want* the man to respond. These women are not reluctant: they are *selective*.

So, when a woman says that a man is "not her type," or that he isn't "rich enough," or that he "plays around" too much, I suggest that she is, in fact, in the midst of search polygamy, and is autonomously expressing her emotional, economic, and sexual dissatisfaction with the men she has met *so far*. Her complaints only *sound* petty, dependent, or like feminine fickleness. In actuality, they are all ways of saying, "No, not him."*

---

*There is a large, heavily quantitative literature on sexual reluctance in college women, e.g., Mosher and Vonderheide (1985). However, little of it deals directly with women's reproductive feelings and beliefs or with proceptivity. Sexual guilt and reluctance therefore often appear as *global* character-istics of certain women, rather than specific to a given man or to men she has met so far, as I suggest may often be the case. In this, and consistent with the biosocial approach, I feel that sex guilt and other seemingly "characterological" aspects of women's feelings about men may change—and change *very* quickly—when she meets the "right" man, that is, a man who is genuinely interested in her, and is responsive and attentive to her emotionally and sexually.

There is also a largish social scientific literature on "mate selection." However, it does not deal with questions that a biologist would subsume under "mate selection," but, instead, with male–female attraction, characteristics of one's ideal mate, and with the dynamics of how socioeconomic status, ethnic

Underneath the diversity of women's reasons for rejecting men are therefore not only personal, emotional, and social criteria, but also a recognizable biosocial core. In essence, rejection and reluctance *always* involve a reproductive decision. Whether made consciously or not, such decisions have immense reproductive impact on her personally, and, when multiplied by the millions of women who have rejected men, for the population at large. Such rejections say very clearly that she will not let *this* man father her children. For whatever myriad of reasons she had, she as yet doubts his commitment not only to her, but also to her future children (Quinn, 1982; Remoff, 1980, 1984).

Again, however, I stress for the reader caught in the Nature/Nurture dichotomy that a woman's reproductive reluctance is *not* caused by a biologically determined and secret knowledge that the man is somehow not genetically "fit." Instead, whenever a woman says *No*, she *de facto* has made a reproductive decision. It is as simple as that.

Nonetheless, many women are *quite* conscious of making sharp reproductive calculations about men (Remoff, 1980, 1984). And, when totaled over millions of women, we see that women, not men, macroscopically decide the reproductive future.

Reluctance Faded

At least for now she has doubts. Sometimes, the man *does* slowly and gradually prove himself trustworthy. Perhaps she is feeling more and more ready to have children, and, as her feelings change, so do her criteria for men. No longer do they need to wine and dine her, or impress her with expense accounts. Instead, *personal* generosity becomes more important—the fact that he spends time with her, or they eat in a little restaurant that has suddenly become special. "He isn't half-bad," she thinks to herself, "that is, as men go." Not that it *hurts* that he has a half-way decent job, or seems in line for a promotion, but, increasingly, those are *not* the reasons she finds him interesting and, well, *likeable*.

Or perhaps she is fed up with the singles scene, the bar scene especially, or with search polygamy. "No more one-night stands with losers," she says, and enters a period of near-celibacy. She dates a bit, but is no longer obsessed with men. In that mood, she can meet someone with whom simply to have a good time. And things grow—first sex and affection, then something akin to love. She finds herself

background, and other demographic variables limit people's *general* marital choices (reviewed by Winch, 1967; R. S. Cavan, 1969, chapter 14, pp. 317–349; Walster and Walster, 1978; and Francoeur, 1982, pp. 393–398). These are all important questions and approaches. However, my concerns are less with global constructs such as "romantic attraction" in general (e.g., Nevid, 1984) as with the specific *behavioral* bases of mate choice. Given real limitations on who one can marry or live with, male idealizations of feminine beauty are less important than whether or not the woman is interested in the man, even if she is *not* his "ideal mate." The same applies to women evaluating men. Love grows from interest and responsiveness, not from choosing the "best" from a list of eligibles who fit pre-formed criteria, either sociological *or* romantic. In a distinction I develop in the Appendix, my approach here is not neoclassical but realist.

thinking suddenly and unexpectedly about *marriage*. Even the thought of children passes her mind from time to time. She laughs to herself. "Well, I never thought I'd want *kids*!"

And one evening they're in a restaurant together, sitting, talking, looking at each other, their eyes filled only with each other. They see allure, not anatomy, in each other's eyes. She puts her hand on his arm, lightly, because this is how women touch. And he smiles, and their fingers touch. Suddenly, both sit back, laugh, and reach forward for their wine glasses. They lift them, sip, put them down, still looking at each other.

And the observer also smiles. They're *in love*.

Finding a Good Man

If we are to understand how courtship progresses to intercourse and birth, we must stand apart from the economic and psychological instrumentalities that sometimes trap people in marriage. We must also stand apart from the instrumentalities of upward mobility, which find attractive only men who own fancy cars, have big expense accounts, or know all the right people and places to go. The proper sex rules, with their moralities, do *not* fully determine what a woman will do when confronted with a man in the real world. We must, instead, consider the kind of love that occurs between two people for whom the problems of the great and wealthy do not exist, and for whom morality does not have teeth sharpened in a struggle for social place.

What if the woman *cannot* make a marriage that raises her above her social class? What if she is a serving woman in the great house at Pemberley, whose mistress alone has had the good fortune even to be considered by Darcy? For her, the doors of marital upward mobility are closed.

What if, for her, men with gold credit cards and huge expense accounts have no appeal? What if she does not *like* fancy restaurants, glittering parties, or mansions filled with the very best people? What if, like many women, she does not *want* to attract the boss, to snag him away from his wife and revel in his fortune?

What if she has refused to dwell between the class-ridden pinions of property and name and has, through her own free will, remitted herself of the slavery of name, position, and ladyship—in title or in fact—over vast acres of land? Are we to see *all* women as motivated by instrumental greed for power and position they cannot obtain on their own? Does pure rapacity hide as the dark shadow behind every woman's proceptive interest, or behind her willingness to give the man a chance? Do *all* women fall in love only on the promise that the smoking ruins of a pillaged city will provide the backdrop of her nuptial solemnities?

Or what if the woman's femininity was valued not for its crystalline purity and chaste virginity, but primarily for her abilities to weave, to spin, to card? And what if, for *him*, honor is an unattainable property of a class into which he was not born and into which he could never marry? What of the men who have vanished namelessly into history, but who, when alive, were known for their ability to work the fields, to build, to work metal? What of the woman's choices if, for her, that man's "honor" therefore mattered less than his smile, his touches, his gazes?

We cannot subsume all female sexuality, be it proceptive interest or contingent reluctance, under the instrumentalities of upward mobility. For millions of women in history, the possibility of marrying a man like Fitzwilliam Darcy exists only in Jane Austen's magnificent novel.

Thus I cannot believe, as Lawrence Stone seems to (1979, p. 398), that all cultural standards of femininity are based only on the brittle manners of the elite and upwardly mobile. If, by proceptive choice or reluctance faded, the women of history have met men, sometimes to marry them and sometimes not, I will not retreat to the position of the elitist Hobbesian for whom the birth of children to these women represents only the brutish morals of bawdry and rut in a class "too poor" to comprehend honor.

Instead, I want to repeat a distinction made in the previous chapter. If we take the overall sequence, from meeting through courtship, intercourse, and birth, and unromantically delete its vicissitudes, hesitations, and troubles, then we see that custom has placed the division between proper and improper at different places at different times. The timing of ceremonials which publicly mark the couple's intimacy can vary independently of the sequence itself. Thus, there is no place in the sequence when public or social recognition of the couple's intimacy must naturally or inherently occur. Sometimes marriage must intervene between courtship and intercourse if the sequence is to be deemed "proper." At other times, and for people less burdened by the instrumental qualities of marriage for attaining status or position, strictly nuptial ceremonials can vanish totally, to be replaced by the equally public rules of cohabitation (see, e.g., Berlanstein, 1980).

Under these circumstances, love can emerge from the courtship sequence itself, and from the signals sent back and forth between the man and woman. This kind of love—or intimacy, if you prefer—emerges after an evening of full-body synchronization and fully mutual attention. Now the couple *is* prepared behaviorally and, I suspect, physiologically, for intercourse. And, as that intimacy grows to enwrap the lovers in a cradling power that perhaps not even they can explain, what happens if the rules of propriety, and instrumental purposes they serve, do *not* entail the woman's emotions as they did Elizabeth Bennett's? What if the man *has* proved himself to the woman, even if first she was suspicious? What if the woman has surveyed her "field of eligibles"—in the family sociologist's oddly Medieval sounding phrase (see, e.g., Winch, 1967, p. 95)—and has decided that *this* one is the best of the lot? A knight in shining armor he isn't, but then who is? Then the courtship sequence *will* progress to intercourse.

ESSAY F26

21-year-old U.S. woman, seeing one man primarily, a somewhat devout Protestant, with 73 percent of the whole sample more liberal than she.

If we both felt something for each other, then I think that to go as far as intercourse would be all right. If it is a "one-night" stand, I don't think that having intercourse is right (But then again . . . what are "one-night" stands for?)

When there is a feeling between two people—such as the ones in this example, and it was a good positive feeling, then I believe it would be O.K. [ellipsis original]

And because this kind of love is freer of the entailments of economics than is the proper sex search for a good marriage, it can center on finding a good *man*, in whom the emotions and symbols of love are embodied. To be sure, this kind of love *seems* less exalted than the love of the Medieval Court of Venus, with its elaborate rules for codifying the types of love (see, e.g., Andreas Capellanus, ca. 1200/1941) or of the love implicit in Keats' *Endymion* or of the philosopher's codification of love into Eros, Agape, Storge, and so on (J. A. Lee, 1976; Hagstrum, 1980). But I cannot believe that the behavior of men and women in the West has been governed solely by the rules of formal conduct so precious to a landed or upwardly mobile elite. Sometimes, a man's smile can be worth all the "honor" that ever existed.

And, in this, we finally see what a *good man* is. He is not the man who provides a fortune, a name, or who slays armed foemen to wed her amidst the wreckage of cities. He is the man whom she has picked, or finally accepted, and with whom she will now stay. He is the man who responded eagerly to her proceptive hints and cues, or responded patiently and lovingly to her reluctance and hesitation. He is *her* man, and he will remain her man regardless of where morality puts its divisions between proper and improper. He is part of her life, and she part of his: their commitment is to each other.

Envoi

In proceptivity and reluctance echoes a single theme, that of the responsive man for whom the woman is not merely a body, but a mind also. When the essayists and women like them invite men into their proceptive and symbolic worlds, it is not to manipulate them, or coyly to seduce them. Rather, she builds around him her dreams of a responsive man who loves her. Despite the myth of the Reluctant Woman, not even essay F25 finally communicates rejection. In it echoes the voice of the man who will speak the words *she* has written for him: "I find your body so warm and exciting . . . I really want us to make love." If essayist F25 has put those words into the man's mouth, it is not to resist them: she *wants* to hear the love they imply. So, in essay F25, is the reason the essayists so rarely speak of love, and yet so centrally weave it into their tapestries of symbolized behavior and emotion. Only the man—the responsive sensitive man—can speak the words of love that the essayists, liberals and conservatives alike, want so much to hear. When, finally, the man's behavior does embody love, and when he can say he loves her, then proceptivity and reluctance each reach their end: then the essayists will say *Yes*.

For these women and for so many like them in history, men are not objects of terror. These women are not motivated by fear of pregnancy, fear of ignoble ruin of reputation and family, or even fear of intercourse. Nor do they fear what an older woman might understand—that sometimes men are not heros, responsive or otherwise, and that sometimes marriage is not all it is cracked up to be. Despite their reluctances and hesitations, these are not the Reluctant Females of myth, who try to limit the man's ardor. Their purposes are far less "moral" than that.

Above all, the essayists communicate to us their *interest* in men. Hatred, suspicion, guilt, greed, and distrust are *far* too thin to capture the essayists' thought. Rather, they are attempting to determine if *this* is the man whom they want to father their children and to bond with them in what is, potentially, a never-ending sequence of signals sent and received, and of symbols created and re-created. Despite their own words, much of the essayists' impatience and anger with men arises not against male sexual assertiveness, but from disappointment and frustration that he fails to embody their own ideas of love and seduction.

Yet, also, the essayists are not women in their late 30s or 40s, who have had 20 or more years of experience with men, and who have their own 20-year-old daughters. They are *young* women—like Elizabeth Bennett, who was the age of our essayists when she met Darcy. They are not Jane Austens, Simone de Beauvoirs, or Mary Wollstonecrafts, at least not yet. Their essays are filled with contradictions and puzzles, sometimes shrewd, sometimes proper, sometimes idealistic, and—it must be admitted—sometimes naive. We read their thoughts with admiration for their fiercely defended femininity, its powers bright and undefeated; with amusement at their commentaries about maculine weaknesses yet so integrally interwoven with fascination for men; and in sorrow that time and experience may yet shatter their pride and their clarity. Ultimately, one *wants* to believe that each will meet a man who equals her in pride, sensitivity, and autonomy—the man whom Brownstein calls the heroine's hero.

Biology Once Again—and a Transition

It has come time again to draw some biological conclusions. Proceptivity and reluctance both have important biosocial implications for how women select men. On the one hand, in proceptivity, female selectivity is quite direct: it sees and feels the man of her template, and says *Him*. And, if *he* responds, then the romance begins. Now, not all men will respond to a given woman's proceptive overtures. She may have to try several men, sometimes in search polygamy—sometimes in despair—before finding *her* man. But once she finds him, and barring artificial contraception, she *is* likely to become pregnant.

However, if the woman must make a good marriage or if she must submit her sexual behavior to public scrutiny, then her "freedom" is limited. The *respectable* woman cannot marry just anybody, templated or not, and pressures of social place and the realities of economics often check her proceptive overtures. Yet, under the social conditions of U.S., Canadian, and British history, she must *still* be selective, this time for a man who is economically and socially responsive to her needs.

Under both extremes—from complete proceptive freedom to pick a man for his smile and his love, to the completely entailed choice of a rich or upwardly mobile man—the woman tries to make the best choice she can. True, the criteria of choice may differ greatly, from emotional and behavioral responsiveness to the possession of a great fortune. Women's templates for men are not all the same. But below each criterion of choice is the presumption that the man *will* respond to what the woman wants and needs, be it for responsive sexuality or for paying the bills. Below the seeming diversity is the ideal that her chosen man will and should fulfill her needs, *whatever* they may be.

And the needs of her children. The entire system is built on an idealized form of biosocial functionality. In it, the man's primary responsibility is to the woman whose children he has fathered. If it works that way, then all will be perfect, of course; but even if it does not work, the ideal remains. In it, the woman has a *right* to select the best man possible, given her possible choices, her emotional needs and desires, and her social and economic position.

Here, then, is the third layer of how courtship becomes adorned with cultural meanings and symbols. First, the courtship sequence itself, with its powerful abilities to re-shape people emotionally and, presumably, physiologically. Second, the emotional and symbolic meanings that women attach to their proceptive and rejective behavior, e.g., the belief that intercourse *means* love. Third, the twin idealizations that female sexual and marital selectivity is the autonomous privilege of women and that the chosen man will and should fulfill her needs, whatever they may be. The third level also has its symbols, for I have stressed that the community *does* require that intimacy be celebrated publicly, even if the timing and meaning of those ceremonials have varied during history.

It is a complex system, yet it centers on the irreducible fact of sexual reproduction. Even if the couple medically cannot have children; even if they choose not to have children; even if she had her own job or fortune and he does not; even despite these possibilities, the system presupposes that a reproductively functional male–female dyad is at the center. Moreover, even if the world is not perfect, the system *has* functioned after a fashion. Now, the reader must not confuse that conclusion with the ethnobiological statement that this system is foreordained by the Genes or by Nature, or that it is biologically "good," "optimum," or even "necessary." The point instead is that this system is simultaneously fully biological and fully cultural, and represents a particular historical *solution* to the inescapable biological need for sexual reproduction. And even if I suspect that certain parts of this system will prove universal—e.g., the behavioral communication that exists in the courtship sequence, and the existence of proceptivity—nonetheless this system *is* part and parcel of Western history. However, that fact does not mean that this system is *not* biosocially functional, for it has been just that. For millions of people in U.S., Canadian, and British history, this is the *only* system for having children, and its blend of neurophysiologically quite real love, emotional symbolism, and public cermonial *have* functioned biologically to allow children to be born and to grow in some degree of safety and health.

Furthermore, this tripartite system itself has developed still further outward, so to speak, and has become adorned with symbols that are fully sacred. But that is a later chapter, and for now it suffices to say that this system of behavioral communication, symbolic meaning, and social celebration *does* have a center in the biological facts of sexuality. It is *not* built on the ideal that men will marry ferns or that women will marry turtles. This system does not center on an arbitrarily chosen "symbol" that is free to vary as widely as people's imaginations can make it. To be sure, arbitrary sexual symbols *do* exist, such as equating white with virginity. But the central core is not *merely* a symbol: at the core exists the biologically real and biologically functional reproductive dyad, whose behavior *directly* is responsible for making more people.*

And in proceptivity and reluctance, we see how women choose their men. Together, proceptivity and reluctance represent "female choice"—a Darwinian and biological concept—in human beings. It is not a simple matter of women choosing only rich men or wanting only true love, for these are but aspects of a much more complex system. The women in this study have wanted responsive, attentive, and interested men—be that interest to involve financial support or love or both. So women do *not* have "instinctive" or "natural" knowledge of the genetically most fit man: they are not searching among genes but among people. Nor do women have an "instinctive" or "natural" morality which forbids them to be "forward" or mandates their "modesty." Those are the fictions of ethnobiology, be it found among social scientists, sociobiologists, or moralists. Instead, we see that *sometimes* women are reluctant, as many social scientists have said, though not for the reasons of innate morality they so often attribute to women. And sometimes women are proceptive, but again not because they are "naturally" flirtatious. Instead, both strategies represent biosocially functional ways women optimize their selections, at least as well as they can.[†]

---

*I will leave open for now the fascinating question of *how* this biosocially functional system developed and evolved historically. My primary purpose here is to show that this system *exists*. Once that has been accomplished, then we can turn to the question of how it arose in past history.

[†]A biologist colleague objected to my analysis by saying that for proceptivity to evolve (that is, be "functional"), proceptive women would have to have had more offspring than non-proceptive, reluctant women. At the simplest level of analysis, that must be true by definition, at least if reluctance is general. But, more deeply, the objection misses the fundamental point. The comparison is not between proceptive women and reluctant women at all, because one and the same woman can sometimes be proceptive and sometimes be reluctant. The only evolutionary comparison is between women like this, who can *switch* strategies according to who the man is, and women whose strategies are limited to proceptivity or reluctance *but not both*. Then, it is biologically clear that the ability to switch strategies is more adaptive,

And, above all, the conclusion is that the biological and social sciences each have only part of the truth—the social scientists with their ideas of female reluctance, and the biologists with their ideas of female activity—so that we understand much more when we synthesize biology and social science than we do were we to insist that these fields must remain apart. In this, if biologists learn that cultural, social, economic, and emotional processes mediate female choice in human beings, so too social scientists may learn that biosocial principles are directly relevant to understanding how women select their men. The result is that we all have learned more. In brief, everyone benefits.

So far, however, I have focused only on one part of the dyad, the woman. Yet, if people do not reproduce by telepathy, neither do they reproduce parthenogenetically. It is time to turn to *men* and see how sexual culture also grows outward from the simple but biologically inescapable fact that sperm, as well as ova, are needed for reproduction.

because the "reluctant" woman can actively and proceptively search for a man responsive to her needs, and the "proceptive" woman can reject unsuitable mates, e.g., men who would abandon her. It is a good example of how the capacity to respond and to *change* responses can evolve.

Chapter 7

Men: Love, Hatred, and Poetry

Women say men are peculiar. But men's behavior makes sense—if we look at it right.

My first purpose is to show how understanding the courtship sequence, and women's proceptive roles in initiating it, clarify male sexual behavior and strategies. The myth that ''male culture'' promotes a rapist's mentality is only very partly true. In the main, men's sexual strategies are *responses* to women's real or perceived proceptive overtures, and dovetail quite neatly with them.

Second, men talk about women and sex in what I will call *oblique sexual discourse*. It is a language of allusion and metaphor, under which are highly emotional and even sentimental sexual meanings and beliefs only rarely explicitly expressed by men (or understood by women). Third, women's elaborate integration of sexual symbols, meaning, and behavior often eludes and bewilders men.

Together, these facts create some profound male misunderstandings of women. Of particular importance are men's reactions to women's Incomplete Rejection or Delay strategy. Often, men do *not* see it as contingent reluctance with a possible *Yes*, but believe that it is teasing and goading, and represents female hostility toward men.

One consequence is an intense and widespread male hostility to women that verges on sheer, raw hatred. In some men, this hostility produces violent pornography, violence against women, and rape, as forms of anarchic and pathological *revenge* against women and their powers. These problems are rooted in profound differences in what men and women believe about each other, not in a Nature that makes men rapists and killers.

Thus, an intensely emotional and private world of experience can arise from men's templates for women. In that world, women are the central symbols of love, security, and safety. Historically, this world has received its fullest public elaboration in poetry and drama. Though, sometimes, the sequence that begins with a proceptive overture made by a woman who fits the man's template can lead to tragedy (e.g., ''Romeo and Juliet''), it can also lead to a biosocially profoundly functional bonding which holds the man and woman together during pregnancy, childbirth, and after.

175

Partisanship

When one writes about the difference between men and women, willy-nilly one seems to stand on one or the other side of the battle of the sexes. One's words are all too easily taken as cries of encouragement to one or the other side. For many men, women are precious and virtually magical beings. Few men feel that women are automatically sexually available to them, or that the encradling security of love is easy to find. In men's beliefs and experiences, far more women say *No* than *Yes*, and for many men, sexually and emotionally empathetic women are rare indeed. Yet in an embattled world, partisanship is presumed. A man hearing me say that men believe that women are precious might retort, "Aah, you're nuts. Chicks are just crazy." And a woman might say, "Precious? Are you kidding? Men systematically mistreat and exploit women, and they assume we are *always* available!"

Few women know how unsure men feel of their appeal to women. Moreover, many men whose experiences have involved repeated rejections by women might easily argue that women are crazy, self-centered people for whom men are sources of money and good times. Such a man would probably not easily recall a time when, for him too, women were fascinating. We must let the pendulum come to rest where we can find objectivity and quiet in the midst of these hatreds. So let us set aside the angry passions of sexual partisanship to ask some questions about men. What, exactly, is the ideal of femininity that men so exalt and so strongly wish to find embodied in a real woman, rather than, say, in ferns or turtles?

Men Talking and Writing About Seduction

The ruling stereotype about men is that they are avid for sex, and will do just about anything to get it, usually violently, unpleasantly, or with indifferent disregard for the woman's needs and desires (e.g., Cherry, 1983; Zellman and Goodchilds, 1983, p. 55ff; Hatfield, 1983, p. 107). In fact, this image of masculinity is embedded in the English language itself.

Thus, Roget's *Thesaurus* says that *to seduce* means "to allure, mislead, ravish, rape and deflower." The *Oxford English Dictionary* then adds that seduction is "the action of inducing (a woman) to surrender her chastity" (meaning 3b, parentheses original). The words conjure up images of Don Juans plotting to ruin innocent virgins while villainously twirling their mustachios and contemplating the illicit delights to follow from ravishing the maiden. We can even flesh [!] out this villain a bit more. The *Oxford English Dictionary* adds that *to seduce* is "to lead (a person) astray in conduct or belief; to draw *away* from the right or intended course of action *to* or *into* a wrong one; to tempt, entice or beguile *to do* something wrong, or unintended" (meaning 2, parentheses and italics original).

"Unhand me, you brute!" cries the maiden. "Never," replies he, "I will have my way with you!" "I am lost," she sobs.

Given such melodramatically hostile images of men, men's seduction strategies ought to be gems of tactical planning and analytical reasoning, especially if they are shaped by the sexual "bull sessions" that some scholars believe male sexual discourse always normally involves (Korman and Leslie, 1982; Cherry, 1983; Kutner and Brogan, 1974). After all, there is nothing like explicit lust and ardor to refine the strategies of a Don Juan.

Furthermore, it ought to be easy to elicit such strategies— simply ask men and they will tell you all about it. For example, we have asked men, "How would you influence a woman to have sex with you?" or "How do you know if a woman is interested in you?" or "How did you meet your wife/fiancée/girlfriend?" Since women provide detailed answers to such questions, so too our Don Juans—that is, men skilled in the arts of seduction and supposedly made articulate by their endless bull sessions—*ought* to answer equally explicitly.

However, sometimes life does not imitate art or reduce to such simple, familiar formulas. Here are some samples of *men* answering McCormick's how-to-seduce-someone question, from both our U.S.–Canada sample and McCormick's own, West coast, U.S. sample.

ESSAY M1

22-year-old U.S. man, from the U.S.–Canadian sample.

Assuming that I am relatively sure about the response to my attractional behavior as positive, I would more than likely try in some way to seduce this person. Seduction is a vague concept for me including essentially arranging for us to be alone, comfortable, secluded privacy and various additional attractions which can range from a large bed to a mountain peak—beaches are OK. But cars (not vans) are out of it. Sex includes for me all forms of epidermal contact. Music is nice, too.

The ability to touch pleasurably is rare and requires intelligence and sensitivity. Generally I like to search out intellectually how the particular person might be pleased sexually. Then I would regard their relation to sexual contact.

Even the most generous reader must admit that this answer lacks a certain precision. Indeed, sexuality depends on privacy, and it is nice to hear that this man "searches out" his partner's interests, but exactly what is he looking for?

The following answer is even less specific, though no less typical of men's answers.

ESSAY M2

18- to 19-year-old U.S. man, from McCormick's West coast sample.

The idea here is simple. There are steps that one follows which lead up to the actual act. No words are desired or necessary. A positive response to one step allows the next step to be initiated, and this continues until she conveys to me the desire to stop the progression. I find it no problem to *know* when she would like to stop. If we don't stop, we arrive. [Italics original]

To be sure, one might say, but *how*? This answer is oblique to the point of being opaque.

The next essay contains more details, but they focus our attention even more sharply on this odd difference between the data and our expectations that men ought to know all about seduction.

ESSAY **M3**

18- to- 19-year-old U.S. man from McCormick's West coast sample.

Become very quiet—while listening attentively to whatever she continues to talk about—light touching of her hands—arms leading gradually into another "necking" session. Then while kissing caress her breasts and thighs. Suck on her earlobes and blow lightly in her ears.

Though this man is enacting—consciously or not I do not know—a responsive and attentive role, how comes it that she is sufficiently close to him that he can touch her thighs or blow in her ears? The essay has an unmistakable ring of experience to it, but Essayist M3 is not describing seduction, but *foreplay*.

In fact, all three essays are equally vague about the stages of seduction that *precede* foreplay. Details that women so often describe—e.g., about setting, clothing, moving closer—are either simply absent, as in Essay M2, or are mentioned only in passing, as in Essay M1. But, like Essayist M3, many men can describe what happens *next*—for example, the following essay.

ESSAY **M4**

18- to 19-year-old U.S. man from McCormick's West coast sample.

I probably would just try to give her the impression that if she wants to have sex, then it's all right with me. I would give subtle hints like "Do you have a place to stay tonight?" If I liked her very much, I wouldn't try to force anything on her since I knew her only 3 weeks. I would probably turn the lights down, make the situation more comfortable (shoes off, lying on couch, etc.) maybe start necking, rubbing, etc., to see how she reacts to it. One possibility of loosening up everything would be to have something to drink. There are certain things like how she breathes or how forward she is to you that sometimes gives it away. Another way is to jokingly suggest something (like turning off the lights or going into the other room) to her to see what she does.

This essay makes no sense as a seduction strategy—his initial question is about as subtle as a rock in the head. But as a response to the woman's proceptivity, it is lucid (his term is "forward"). He also knows that sometimes women are reluctant, but his strategy is not based on force, even though he uses the word. Rather, he observes her reactions while simultaneously he tries to arouse her physically. The strategy is even clearer in the following essay.

ESSAY M5

18- to 19-year-old U.S. man from McCormick's West coast sample.

I would begin to make sexual passes at the girl such as feeling or rubbing her breasts to start and after that I would gracefully [sic] move my hands underneath any shirt and/or bras and after achieving this state (if not already thrown across the room) I would feel that my date was as willing to perform sexual acts as I was. After relieving [sic] her upper clothing I would proceed to undress the remaining portions of her body. And after some sexual play with hands and hoping she took the hint and undressed me the time would be right.

These essays are typical of a very general class of answers men give when asked how to seduce a woman. Far from being detailed, analytical plans for seduction from start to finish or descriptions of how intimacy develops in the first place, these essays focus on how to arouse the woman sexually. It is like coming into the middle of the movie: all the preliminaries have been left out.

However, before concluding that men's ideas of seduction are recipes for rape, we might wonder what *women* might say. Perhaps *they* would feel that these men "have gotten the hint and taken it from there." For example, if the reader will allow me to play match-maker for a moment—

ESSAY F7

19-year-old U.S. woman, from the U.S.–Canadian sample.

I would influence this person by asking how he viewed the relationship at this point. I would feel out what he says, then I would give little hints like: how would you like to come over to my place or your place for a drink. I then think he would get the hint and act accordingly.

ESSAY M6

18- to 19-year-old man, from McCormick's West coast sample.

I would first ask my date if she would like something to drink. Then I would put on some soft music from which the two of us could get up and dance to real smoothly. Proceeding with our dancing I would begin to influence and get her desires aroused by putting my body tightly against her while rubbing in a circular motion my body (waist down) against her body. At the same moment my hands would be moving about her entire top half of her body. Gradually,

I would begin to move more in a dancing pattern heading toward the end of the living room, again using all my motions in my body to arouse her sexually and intimately.

After about half an hour or so I would lead her into the bedroom by dancing slowly into the hallway near the bedroom, thus suggesting to her that I want to make love with her now. As we approach the bed I would undo her clothing in a graceful [sic] approach while feeling her out with my fingers especially. Then I would press my half-nude body against her and begin to go in an in-and-out movement thus leading to sexual intercourse.

By itself, this man's answer sounds unromantically explicit and even abrupt. But read immediately after hers, their answers dovetail, and suddenly each makes excellent sense. Together, women's and men's essays represent a kind of division of romantic effort: the woman initiates the encounter proceptively, and, in response, he arouses her sexually and overtly.

In these answers, we hear the participants' own view of the role women and men play in courtship and seduction, and each is describing what he or she knows best and, very probably, enjoys most. In exquisite detail, women describe the proceptive preliminaries and stop by saying the man must take over. Men provide equally detailed descriptions of how, next, to arouse the woman. When the couple is matched, the sequence flows smoothly in a repeated pattern of escalation and response, with proceptivity eliciting the man's sexual efforts, until they can have intercourse.

The first implication is that, usually, women are *not* acted on by men eager to rape, ravish, and mislead them. Instead, these men are trying to arouse a woman whose interest has (they hope) *already* been expressed by her proximity to him, by her willingness to join him in his apartment, by her desire to have a drink with him, or by her sexy and alluring dress. Thus, men's strategies cannot be understood if we do not first understand proceptivity, and the romantic division of labor that *women* envision for a proceptively initiated encounter. *She* moves closer and starts kissing, and *he* takes it from there. Men's essays omit the proceptive preliminaries in part because these men presuppose that the couple has *already* reached the degree of intimacy that proceptivity in fact produces.

Secondly, these men are trusting the woman to have said *No* already if she meant not to have intercourse (and, like essayist M2 or M5, men know that women sometimes send very firm *No* signals). In brief, these men *de facto* presuppose the woman will say *No* if she means it. For example,

ESSAY M7

20-year-old Canadian man, from the U.S.–Canada sample.

—Convince the person that you really feel something for them and an act of

love would be an expression of my feelings.
—They should ask me to stop if I'm going too fast/far.

If women see it as their *privilege* to say *No*, then these men—and many others with them—see it as the woman's *responsibility* to do so.

These conclusions do not come only from men's interpretations of women's behavior. They also come from women's descriptions of their *own* intentions when acting proceptively. By definition, the overall process is therefore not rape. No rapist ever spent a half-hour dancing with an interested woman, thereby making intimate, if clothed, genital contact with her (Essayist M6, first paragraph, and a good example of men's oblique sexual discourse), or trying to make the situation more comfortable while watching her responses (Essay M4), or concerning himself so much with her reactions to his "attractional behavior" that he mentions it in the very first sentence of his answer (Essay M1). Below the seeming unromanticism and the nearly (but not quite) explicit physical sexuality of these essays is a profound male desire to have intercourse with *a willing and aroused woman*.

In this, men are primarily *responsive* to women's proceptive behavior even if they do not describe it. Thus, courtship involves more than a romantic division of labor; it also contains a shift or transition from the woman's proceptivity to the man's responding with overtly *sexual* behavior (e.g., the dancing described in essay M6). Physiologically, proceptivity functions to arouse him, and to signal her emotional interest. Now, she is a potential lover and mate. She, in turn, becomes receptive, in the sense that she is physiologically aroused (e.g., lubricating) and has become behaviorally willing to permit intercourse (even if her ideology would not permit her to do so). Thus, the couple has emotionally, physiologically, and behaviorally passed through a transition state which begins proceptively and ends with both people sexually aroused and with him initiating sexual fore-play.

This shift I call the "power transition." The term comes from those women who want the man "to take it from there." Initially, they see themselves as having the unquestioned privilege of signaling interest to the man and, therefore, of arousing him sexually. They then see it as *his* responsibility to arouse them in return—and that is *precisely* what these men are describing. If, in plain English, we ask who is in charge of the interaction, first it is the woman, with her articulate and clearly defined proceptivity. During the initial, proceptive phase of the courtship sequence, it is her privilege and responsibility (or so men say) to guide the interaction as she sees fit, and she has the power to say and mean *No*. In the second, responsive phase, it has become the man's responsibility to arouse her, and, as Ira Reiss (1981, p. 276) puts it, to "stage direct" their interaction towards intercourse. Simultaneously, some men also believe that she no longer has the power to say *No*, a fact that has immense significance in understanding how such interactions can turn into rape.

I want to stress that this description is only an abstract or summary of the essays themselves. If the woman *is* willing to make love, then the entire two-part sequence is not only emotionally powerful, it is also biosocially functional. Barring contraception, it is how babies are conceived.

Public and Private

If, for women, these biosocial events are surrounded by an elaborate set of symbols and meanings, so too men are surrounded by symbols, meanings, and rules. The biosocial process does not stop with foreplay and intercourse. Once again, we must move outward.

The fact that the entire courtship sequence is biphasic has an important implication. It is not merely that women often initiate the sequence proceptively and men later respond by attempting to arouse the woman sexually. Between these phases, and prior to the power transition, there is typically a change in setting. Thus, as our observations demonstrate, for a couple in a bar or restaurant, much proceptive behavior occurs *in public*. In contrast, foreplay and, therefore, the man's contribution to completing the sequence, customarily occurs *in private*.

The point is not to document how couples negotiate this often anxiety-producing transition. Rather, I want to stress that a great deal of sexuality follows a similar pattern. In our society, female sexuality is typically public, while male sexuality is typically private. These associations between female and public, and between male and private, have important consequences for understanding sexual symbols and meanings.

Blank Spots on the Ethnographic Map

The curious opacity of the men's essays quoted above is quite widespread. Over and over, the men I interviewed—even men much older than the male essayists—proved strikingly and reliably inarticulate about women's behavior and their sexual signals. For example, the more common answers to "How do you know if a women you've just met is interested in you?" included one-sentence statements like "She'll talk to me"; "She'll dance with me"; or "She'll give me her phone number." When these answers are added up, together they form a fairly accurate description of *some* aspects of proceptive behavior, but few men could describe more than one or two examples of proceptivity.

The exceptions—between 5 and 10 percent of the men I have interviewed—were themselves very interesting. They could describe both the courtship sequence and proceptivity in as much detail as could women (though they never described synchronization, as is also typically true of women). One such man said that his friends in high school were in awe of his abilities to read women's signals, and would ask his advice— "Hey, Jim, does Sue like me?" Unlike most men, he could answer: Was Sue behaving proceptively, and, if so, how? (As I have said, this procedure works quite well.) However, few men like this seem to exist, and quite often men's "strategies" for determining if a women likes them are simply wrong.

For example, occasionally a woman will give a man a false phone number in order to get rid of him. One woman gleefully said that she would give the man the number of the local morgue. (This is one reason why a man is sometimes reluctant to call an interested woman who gave him her telephone number: men have had some great disappointments with such phone calls.) Or she might dance with him, come off the dance floor, pick up her purse, and head for the ladies' room—and never return. Likewise, conversation: as a number of women said in their rejection essays, talk is sometimes a distraction, not a come-on. So, though there were some exceptions, men proved startlingly unlike women: their answers were typically brief, vague, and, very often, inaccurate. "You know, the chemistry was good," such men say.

Now, this observation is odd: men are capable of *performing* the behavior patterns that courtship involves. They look, turn, touch, smile, reciprocate the woman's lean, synchronize, in brief, enact *all* the patterns that were described in Chapter 4. However, most men could not describe what either they or their partners were doing. My rough guess is that something like 90 percent of men cannot coherently describe the courtship sequence, even though most men can *enact* it with a proceptive woman.

Moreover, men's descriptions seem more clichéd than original. Men often mention eye contact as an important cue about the woman's interest. However, given how frequently books on body language mention eye contact (for example, Fast, 1970, pp. 129–143), one suspects that these men are drawing not on their own experience, but are simply repeating what they have read and heard. One's suspicions grow when men cannot describe what *kind* of eye contact signals interest. (It is described in the Appendix.) It is, again, an ethnographic short circuit. Against expectation, men are usually unable to describe what actually occurs during a male–female interaction.

In *other* situations, however, men are exquisitely attuned to non-verbal behavior and its nuances, for example, in a team sport like basketball or football. Likewise, two men working with each other depend heavily on non-verbal cues to signal their intentions and needs. For example, on a construction job, one man silently reaches out his hand and the other responds, appropriately, by silently handing him a measuring tape. Men talking in a bar can often "read" each other's intentions and emotional states accurately and subtly. Men also communicate non-verbally in business interactions.

Furthermore, men can often describe, in words, what kinds of non-verbal behavior are involved in these interactions, especially between teammates in a team sport. In fact, one part of a coach's job is to teach such abilities. Thus, there is no general deficit among men in deciphering non-verbal behavior. Instead, it is as if there were a blank spot in men's abilities to understand other people that centers specifically on understanding women's proceptive—that is, *public*—sociosexual behavior. [Abbey (1982) has drawn very similar conclusions about men's inabilities to understand women's sexual intentions from their behavior in laboratory experiments; but see Appendix, pp. 271-272.]

By contrast, as the essays suggest, men have little trouble understanding women's *private* reactions to them. Essayist M4 knows that an aroused woman breathes differently from an unaroused woman. When other men are questioned directly, they too are quite able to describe how a sexually excited woman behaves. Thus, men are not insensitive to women's behavior in general; rather, they are inarticulate about those parts of the courtship sequence that women perform in public.*

However, the women's essays, as well as interviews, have their own blank spot. Few women will describe in any detail what happens *after* the "man takes over." (Essay F2 was among the most explicit I have read, for it mentions pelvic thrusting.) Typically, however, overtly sexual details and anatomical comments are absent from descriptions of love and courtship we obtained from women. Thus, corresponding to the romantic division of labor these men and women envision, there is also a division into things that each can and cannot *talk* about, at least easily or comfortably: each talks most openly about what their own sex does.[†]

Thus, men's inability to describe proceptive behavior is not an isolated curiosity. The opacity of men's descriptions of seduction and courtship touches on far deeper aspects of how we in North America assign sexuality its social and cultural meanings, and reveals that some important differences exist in how men and women feel about sexuality and its engagements. Indeed, men's and women's collective systems of belief, behavior, attitude, and ideology about sexuality differ so much that we can speak of a difference in sexual *culture* between them.

Public Sexuality in Men and Women

One difference in sexual culture centers on what is kept private or made public by each sex. For women, sexuality and its emotions are always connected overtly and publicly. However, for men it is very different. With the possible exception of the Gay press, sexuality is rigidly and intensely *privatized* for most men. Such privatization goes far beyond the mere opacity of men's descriptions of seduction, as I want to describe next.

There is an immense popular literature on female sexuality. For every book I own concerning male sexuality and written by a man, I own five or more books concerning female sexuality and written by (or for) women. Entire advertising budgets depend on female sexuality displayed openly and even lasciviously, as in lingerie advertisements. Moreover, a woman's clothing accentuates her sexuality

---

*There is a nicety of scientific inference here. Personally, I am convinced that most, if not all, men really do *not* know much about women's proceptive behavior. However, I can rigorously conclude only that many men do not *describe* such behavior. Even so, however, the blank spot remains: even if men really know all about proceptivity but for some peculiar reason were refusing to tell me about it, *why* don't men speak readily or directly about such knowledge?

[†]I am *not* suggesting that women do not know about male sexuality, in the way men seem not to know about women's proceptive behavior. To the contrary. However, when speaking spontaneously— as opposed to answering direct and pointed questions—women often seem to choose not to talk about what the man does after he "takes over." In other words, and more technically, I am now analyzing what happens at the "formal plane of discourse."

even when she dresses in "proper" business clothes. By its very propriety, such dress reminds the viewer that at *other* times, the same woman may dress in overtly sexual ways. Likewise, when a woman wears an engagement ring, or when she changes her name upon marrying, her social and sexual relationships with a man have simultaneously both been displayed publicly. The color of the bride's wedding gown displays her virginity—or lack of it. Women's magazines contain endless articles about love and sex, about meeting a good man, on what to wear to attract Mr. Right, or about how to have a satisfying marriage emotionally and sexually. Men's magazines, by contrast, lurk half-hidden at the back of the display rack, and even the name "men's magazine" evokes a sense of sleazy impropriety.

Nor is it all recent. Michel Foucault (1978) has argued persuasively that much of Victorian "repression" of sexuality was only a way to speak about sexuality continuously and often, so that Victorian euphemism and prudery in fact focused *acute* attention on sexuality. If so, then in the 19th century advertisements for women's clothing, with their bustles, skirts layered on skirts, and elaborate head-dress, we again see that female sexuality was centered in the public eye even in the last century. (Space does not permit analysis of how dress has changed over history or how those changes relate to other aspects of sexual culture.)

Moreover, throughout these depictions is the idea that female sexuality is *irresistible*. Obviously, no marketing purpose would be served if most readers were repelled by a semi-nude woman in an advertisement. But we will miss an important point if we simply dismiss these parts of sexual culture as "media hype," as "profit-motivated exploitation of women," or as "popular culture." The immense popularity of female sexuality depends on the *cultural* premise that its public expression is legitimate and licit. None of these books or advertisements could be published in a traditional, patriarchal society—for example, present-day Iran under the Ayatollah (Nirumand, 1984; Wood, 1984) or Czarist Russia (Benet, 1970). In North America and in much of Western Europe, female sexuality is proclaimed by accessories, clothing, hair style, jewelry, shoes, makeup. North American women are not veiled, nor kept in purdah or in the *harîm*. Their sexuality is open, public, and legitimate, and occupies a central place in our culture.

Now, these comments do not necessarily deny the feminist critique of Western culture. Indeed, the point may well be that female *sexuality* is licit and public rather than female *personhood*. Yet, that too would prove my point: female sexuality *is* publicly licit.

It is *very* different for men. For example, no book exists called *Liberating Masturbation* written by and for men, as there are guidebooks on masturbation for and by women (Dodson, 1974). Even the seeming exceptions prove the point. Some male sex educators and therapists have written popular-market books about male sexuality, but typically their advice is expressed in austere and even clinical language (e.g., Zilbergeld, 1978, pp. 174–175). Other material on male masturbation exists, but seems likely to appeal primarily to gay men. Heterosexually oriented pornography also proves the point: once sexual processes and activities that interest or arouse men enter the public purview in books, magazines, and film, they are deemed *filth* and can be censored and suppressed legally. Romance, which corresponds to the public aspects of proceptivity and courtship, is publicly licit; overt sexuality, which corresponds to aspects of the man's role in courtship, is not.

Moreover, for every nearly nude female model in advertising, there seems to be at least one man wearing a three-piece suit, all buttoned up, flesh hidden behind layers of fabric. Now, the suit may be beautifully tailored, but still the only visible flesh is the man's face and hands.

A woman reader can sense what it means that men *must* wear such clothes by imagining how she might feel if she were told that she must cover all parts of her body at work—no stockings, high heels, open blouses, or skirts. Her ankles cannot be visible. No makeup, jewelry, or accessories, for such finery is deemed inappropriate. Nor can her hair extend past her collar, no matter what color it is or how attractive it might be if worn longer. Moreover, she can wear only blue, grey, or dark brown, no matter how attractive other colors might be. If a woman reader experiences anger, outrage, or shock at being thus constricted and controlled, then my point is made: men operate in a world in which fleshly sexuality is hidden and private, not public.

Thus, the opacity and vagueness of men's answers to questions about seduction and courtship are part of a much larger phenomenon. Men operate in a world that is for them primarily asexual. In it, symbols, beliefs, meanings, and rules all act together to *keep* male sexuality private. If a *woman* can talk spontaneously and openly to other women (or to a woman interviewer) about love, sexuality, and men, then a *man* can talk openly only to himself, in fantasies or daydreams, and, in our culture, can see his sexual role in courtship depicted openly only in an illicit pornography that exists at the shadowy edges of society and that typically denudes it of its origins in his emotional response to a woman's proceptive interest in him.

Oblique Sexual Discourse

A second example of the privatization of male sexuality concerns language. It is a commonplace cliché that men "talk dirty," and more explicitly and more directly than women. For example, the great linguist Otto Jespersen (1922) wrote that

> . . . women exercise a great and universal influence on linguistic development through their instinctive shrinking from coarse and gross expressions and their preference for refined and (in certain spheres) veiled and indirect expressions. . . . [T]he feminine point of view is unassailable, and there is reason to congratulate those nations, the British among them, in which the social position of women has been high enough to secure greater purity and freedom from coarseness in language than would have been the case if men had been the sole arbiters of speech. (p. 246)

Once again, we hear that women are vessels of instinctive purity, whose presumably "natural" modesty makes them recoil from the crudities and vulgarities of male speech. And even today, by and large women do not use the same expressions as men for sexual and related acts (Jay, 1980; Philips, 1980).

Yet I wish to suggest an iconoclastic hypothesis concerning these differences. It is not, I propose, that women's sexual language is inhibited, repressed, or veiled, and certainly not that it is "instinctively" pure (an idea no modern linguist would accept). Rather, I suggest that *men's* language for sexual body parts and acts is primarily allusive, indirect, and oblique.

For example, Terry (1983) collected synonyms for "sexual intercourse" from 145 female and 93 male college students in the Midwest (total: 238 students). The women contributed 126 synonyms and the men 157 synonyms (for a total of 283 synonyms). Because there were fewer men in the sample, this means that men gave proportionately more synonyms.

Many of these terms were given repeatedly, and all told, the students provided 1,533 answers when all repeats were counted separately (886 from women, 647 from men). Now, of these 1,533 answers, a total of 1,034 (67.4 percent) represented 19 synonyms that were each given ten or more times by different students. These "common terms" ranged from medical and scientific words like *copulation* and *coitus* through expressions like *make love* and *do it* to the usual obscenities. That leaves 264 synonyms, each given less than ten times (499 of the 1,533 answers, or 32.6 percent; the "less common terms"). But the sexes were very different in whether or not they included the less common terms. Of the 886 answers women provided all told, there were only 207 of the less common terms, or 23.4 percent. However, of the 647 answers men provided, there were 292 of the less common terms, or 45.1 percent. Thus, these men's sexual language included nearly twice as many idiosyncratic or unusual terms for intercourse as did the women's.

Some of these idiosyncratic terms were both non-standard *and* vivid: e.g., *wrestle, slide, make fudge, take a road trip, get stink, touch the belly button from the inside, fission, afternoon delight,* [put] *honey on the stinger,* and [put] *mud on the turtle.* Each of these really quite metaphorical phrases appeared only once in the overall list, and all were provided only by men.

In two important categories, which Terry (1983) called "domestic" and "affective," women's idiosyncratic terms exceeded men's. They included *sleep with* (three times), *cohabit* (twice), and once each, *consecrate vows, unite in love, become close,* and *intimacy,* among others.

The prevalence of love and domestic terms among women's answers follows not surprisingly from the equivalencies between love and sex that the seduction and rejection essays also contained, a point long known to linguists. The elaboration of rare and unusual terms for sexual intercourse therefore seems to occur in the direction of people's emotional concerns. But if so, what are *men's* emotional concerns that they so often develop *their* terms?

It is not an easy question, simply because men's idiosyncratic terms represent such a range of metaphorical inventiveness. We can cite a number of possibilities—

discomfort with the proper medical terms or with obscenities; a desire for a highly personal term that developed in a specific relationship and became generalized afterwards; linguistic inventiveness perhaps arising from a locker room conversation among somewhat embarrassed but enthusiastic young males; acquisition of a unique family (and male?) tradition; a private elaboration on common sexual events (e.g., perhaps *take a road trip* arose from going to a motel or a lovers' lane in a car); or a purely local language adopted by boys as a sign of their sexual maturity—but nonetheless we do *not* know why men have such elaborate and personalized vocabularies.*

But the fact is that this highly personalized male vocabulary is highly metaphorical, that is, allusive and indirect. Perhaps the point is that this vocabulary exists because many men feel a *need* to speak indirectly and allusively about intercourse. Perhaps some sociolinguistic rule (or set of rules) exists that *redirects* men's language from primary dependence on standard (if sometimes obscene) terms into dependence on private metaphor.[†] Thus, Essayist M2 may have spoken for many men when he wrote that "No words are desired or necessary."

It is not impossible, since a similar phenomenon seems to occur in the language women use for menstruation. It too is highly metaphorical and allusive (Joffe, 1948; Ernster, 1975). Thus, perhaps metaphor is elicited primarily by those aspects of sexuality that are most anxiety-producing and least shame-free to the speaker. But, *if so*, then, for men, sexuality is not a comfortable topic about which they can speak openly and unashamedly, even—and perhaps especially—with each other. The conclusion is borne out by many hours of participation in male conversations about sex: even men's sexual *boasting* is strikingly vague.

Yet, one part of male sexual language does seem to represent a recognizable class of metaphor. These are the sexual terms and expressions that Terry (1983) called "aggressive" and that Sanders and Robinson (1979) called "power slang." In Terry's sample, "aggressive" terms for sexual intercourse included *bang* (given 21 times by men and 7 by women), *poke* (given 13 times by men and 5 by women), and—given once each by men—*slam, ram, stuff, beat, bump, break, rip, harpoon, shoot,* and *flog* among others. Sanders and Robinson's "power slang" includes terms for the penis such as *rod, unit, tool, pistol,* and *stick.* The common denominator appears to be a sense of suddenness and power, coupled with a visual metaphor for the organ or act (e.g., *harpoon*). By contrast, as stressed above,

*I want to thank Martha Cornog for extensive discussions of the linguistic issues involved with sexual terminology (Cornog, 1981). Her research interests include the study of genital pet names, which are proper names bestowed on the genitals, like Mellors' and Lady Chatterley's name *John Thomas* for Mellors' penis (in *Lady Chatterley's Lover*, Lawrence, 1932/1959). Such names are quite common, and are often developed by a couple jointly. Their existence raises very similar questions to those produced by men's idiosyncratic sexual vocabularies. Furthermore, I stress how important it is for linguists to publish complete list of sexual terms and their actual frequencies. Reinhold Aman's journal *Maledicta*, which published both Terry's and Cornog's work, is a crucial resource for such information.

†Private or only locally known, e.g., by a given group of men like those in a single fraternity or men's group. Such male sexual language has some striking similarites to what Halliday (1976) calls "anti-language," a topic that deserves careful research attention.

women's language contains relatively few such terms and tends to employ standard (if sometimes "obscene") expressions for sexual acts and organs, or metaphorically, to emphasize domesticity and love.

Sanders and Robinson (1979) suggested that such differences exist because female sexual terminology is relatively rigid and "reflects attitudinal constraints of the stereotypic female role" (p. 24). They also concluded that the verbal norm for sexual communication in college women is "silence, or limited expression," while males, they felt, may be "more free" to recognize variation in sexual situations and activities (p. 25). Once again, this view corresponds to the notion that women are sexually reluctant—in this context, linguistically—and seems to echo Jespersen's view that women shrink from coarse and gross expressions (though Sanders and Robinson do *not* accept Jespersen's ethnobiological explanation that "instincts" create female linguistic purity). I sympathize with Sanders and Robinson's effort to place these differences between male and female language into the theoretical framework of scholarly feminism, and thereby perhaps to see men's language as a political act directed against women (Lakoff, 1973; Kutner and Brogan, 1974). Nonetheless, I disagree with their analysis.

When women discuss proceptivity or their role in courtship, they are *far* from silent. As the women's essays show, theirs is *not* a limited degree of expressiveness. Hardly! Rather, those adjectives fit men far more aptly than women. Furthermore, even if women do not spontaneously discuss overtly sexual activities in their essays, nonetheless when they do—e.g., with a woman interviewer—women's language is quite explicit in its use of terms like *intercourse, penis,* or *vagina.* Thus, it is not that women's language is *restricted* to such terms; instead, such terms seem *sufficient* for sexual communication. Women seem to have no general need to employ the range of sexual metaphor that men employ, and, I suggest, need to employ. Unlike men's language, women's sexual language is *precise.*

Thus, the basic phenomenon appears not to be a greater male freedom in language, but a greater redirection of male language into metaphor, allusion, and, sometimes, downright incomprehensibility. Heard out of context, the phrase *to put mud on a turtle* does not even *sound* sexual. Nor is power slang evidently sexual when heard out of context. Thus, I suggest that male sexual language is primarily allusive, indirect, and context-dependent, unlike female sexual language.

Of course, it is not only male college students who speak indirectly about sexual intercourse—or love. Male oblique discourse has also produced one of the great literary synonyms for making love: Swann's "faire catleya" in Marcel Proust's *Swann's Way.* For Swann, the cattleya orchid becomes far more than a flower—and Proust's words can stand as a summary for far more than Swann's feelings for Odette.

> He climbed after her into the carriage which she had kept waiting, and told his own to follow.
>   She held in her hand a bouquet of cattleyas, and Swann saw beneath the veil of lace covering her head that she had orchids in her hair, fastened by a swansdown

plume. Under her cloak she was wearing a flowing gown of black velvet, caught up on one side to uncover in a large triangle the bottom of her silk skirt, and which revealed a yoke, also of white silk, in the decolletage of her bodice, where other cattleya flowers were inserted. She had scarcely recovered from the fright which the sight of Swann had given her, when some obstacle made the horse start to one side. They were thrown forward; she uttered a cry, and fell back quivering and breathless.

"It's nothing," he said to her, "don't be frightened."

And he held her by her shoulders, supporting her body against his own; then he said, " . . . It won't bother you if I put straight the flowers in your bodice? The shock has displaced them. I'm afraid you'll lose them; I want to push them back into place a little more."

She was not used to being treated with so much formality by men, and she smiled as she answered, "No, not at all; it doesn't bother me."

But he, intimidated a little by her answer, perhaps, also, to appear to have been sincere in adopting the stratagem, or even because he was already beginning to believe that he had been, exclaimed: "Oh! No, don't speak. You will be out of breath again. . . . If I just push them down a little further. Seriously, I'm not offending you? And if I just sniff them to see whether they've really lost all their scent? I don't believe I ever smelt any before; may I? Tell the truth."

Still smiling, she shrugged her shoulders ever so slightly, as if to say, "You're mad; you know very well that I like it." . . .

But he was so shy with her, that having finished by possessing her that evening, after beginning by arranging her cattleyas—whether from fear of offending her, or from fear of appearing afterwards to have lied, or from lack of audacity in devising a more urgent demand than that (which could always be used again, as it had not annoyed Odette the first time)—during the following days he used the same pretext. If she had cattleyas in the decolletage of her dress, he would say, "It's unfortunate—tonight the cattleyas don't need to be fixed; they haven't been disarranged like the other night; [yet] it seems to me that this one isn't quite straight. May I see if these have more scent than the others?" Or else, if she had none: "Oh! No cattleyas tonight, no excuse to indulge myself in rearranging them." So that, for some time, there was no change in the order which he had followed the first night, which began with his touching Odette's throat with his fingers and lips, and with which their caresses began each time; and much later, when the arrangement (or the ritual pretense of the arrangement) of her cattleyas had fallen into desuetude, the metaphor "to do a cattleya" [became] transmuted into a simple verb which they used without thinking about it when they wished to refer to the act of physical possession—in which, however, one possesses nothing—[and] survived in their vocabulary to commemorate this forgotten usage.

And perhaps this particular manner of saying "to make love" did not mean exactly the same thing as its synonyms. We can well feel blase about women, consider the possession of the most different of them as always the same, and known in advance; on the other hand, a woman becomes a new pleasure if it is a question of a "difficult" woman—or thought so by us—so that we are obliged to begin with some unforseen episode in our relations with them, as the arrangement of the cattleyas had been for Swann the first time. He had hoped, trembling, that evening (but Odette, he told himself, if she were deceived by his ruse, could not guess it) that it was the possession of this woman which would emerge from between their large mauve petals; and the pleasure which he already felt (and which Odette, perhaps, only tolerated, he thought because she had not yet recognized it) seemed to him, because of it—as it could have appeared to the first man who tasted it among the flowers of the earthly paradise—a pleasure which had not existed until then, and which he was striving to create, a pleasure—as well as the special name which he gave it to preserve its identity—entirely special and new. [Proust, n.d., pp. 335–336 (translated by C. K. S. Montcrieff), and Proust, 1954, pp. 279–280. The translation, by Martha Cornog and Timothy Perper, tries to hold closer to the original than Montcrieff's. The original passage is extremely complex.]

Proust's incredibly dense images return us to many already familiar themes: the man for whom overt sexuality is primary but who cannot foresee how a *woman* might act to elicit his interest, for example, by placing orchids in her decolletage; the man for whom her attraction to him is completely uncertain; the man who must rely on metaphor to speak of an event so special that only flowers can represent its paradise. And if it is a world very different from women's, then that fact was not Proust's literary invention.

A great deal—emotional and symbolic—is hidden by male sexual discourse. In its obliqueness and opacity, male sexual discourse leads us once more to the privatization of male sexuality and its emotions (Goldberg, 1976, 1979; Novak, 1983; Perper, 1980), below which—though it sometimes takes a Proust to see it—exists an intensely emotional and even anxiety-filled, hidden world in which women are *very* special.

Biosocial Functionality, Once Again Briefly

Given the extraordinary power that these processes of privatization have, it is remarkable that men even *retain* their interest in sexuality and in women. But men still *do* look at women and, suddenly or not so suddenly, find them fascinating.

Of course, it is biologically functional that men retain their interest in women, despite pressures to the contrary. If men—en masse—did yield to those forces and became as asexual as they are somehow supposed to be, then quite quickly there would be no more people.

It is therefore easy to guess at what hides under the oblique sexual discourse of a heterosexual man: a genuine interest in women and a genuine interest in having intercourse with a willing and aroused woman. Under the layers of social fabric that hide men's sexuality, that interest is at the functional, biosocial core of men's sexual lives. With her, interest becomes behavior, step-by-step, escalation-by-escalation, touch-by-touch, until they are—in *both* their words—making love.

Yet, just because something is biologically functional does not mean that it will occur. Nothing in biology guarantees that we shall survive or reproduce: no ethnobiological genes guide our fate infallibly toward life and love. Sometimes courtship and the man's role in it goes wrong—*very* wrong.

Rape: A Biosocial Pathology of Courtship

What creates the intense hostility that some men feel for women? How can interest and fascination turn so bitter? That hostility underlies much of the violence expressed by parts of male sexual language, and appears in pornography and in both stranger and acquaintance rape. It poses serious social problems.

I argue that these phenomena are pathologies of courtship and the courtship sequence. They grow in certain men's minds from the complexities of the Incomplete Rejection or Delay strategy and are coupled with a general social *over*-valuation of women as vessels of emotional solace and intimacy. Emphatically, male hostility towards women—as expressed in violent rape, for example—does *not* represent some kind of indwelling "natural" urge towards violence encoded in the "genes" and expressed as an inevitable consequence of "male biology." If, before, I treated such ethnobiological ideas as simply silly, now they become dangerous, for they can serve to *legitimate* rape as "natural," and as a biologically valid, if socially misguided, way for men to "maximize their fitness" by having as many offspring as possible [e.g., Barash, 1979, pp. 53–55; see Bleier (1984) for a sharp critique of these ideas, and Shields and Shields (1983) for an excellent and well-balanced discussion of the evolutionary biology of rape. Allgeier (1984) and Freund et al. (1983) have briefly reviewed the relationship between rape and courtship].

Now, such ethnobiological arguments *might* make sense if rapists stopped at forcible impregnation of a woman. But they do not: rape can lead to murder. Therefore—and by definition—it is not a biosocially functional reproductive strategy, even if some "sociobiologists" think otherwise. The central component of rape is *not* sex: it is violence directed against a woman [e.g., Groth, 1979; see Burgess (1985) for a recent discussion].

A number of feminist writers have made this violence the centerpiece of their analyses of rape. For them, rape, pornography, and violence against women, in fact or fantasy, are parts of an organized system of male belief and are intrinsic to male culture itself (the "patriarchy"). Men seek to exploit women sexually, believing that it is their prerogative, and do not hesitate to use violence to keep women "in their place" (e.g., Brownmiller, 1975; Greenspan, 1983, p. 83; Griffin, 1981; Gager and Schurr, 1976, p. 209). Sometimes the feminist view that male sexual culture promotes and tolerates rape is coupled with the idea that men are "naturally" more violent than women (Holliday, 1978; Arnold, 1979). In this, male sexual coercion and hostility to women have been seen as both naturally and culturally *intrinsic* to masculinity.

Other theories for the origin of male violence against women also exist. For example, Friday (1980) seems to suggest that "pre-Oedipal" rage leads to such violence: The little boy is infuriated and enraged when the mother removes the nipple from him, thus denying him love. Later, he seeks revenge against mother-substitutes in violent ("sadistic") fantasies, or, presumably, in rape.

My own viewpoint is very different, and is influenced as much by my observations as by the work of the psychologist Paul Wachtel (1983). I suggest that rape arises as a pathological reaction to women that takes form from men's *adult* (post-pubescent) relationships with women, rather than from ethnobiological "genes" (that is, from inescapable pre-natal "forces"), or from frustrations in infancy, or from a macho conspiracy that exists in Western society.

Even though social scientists most often stress symbolic communication [e.g., in symbolic interactionism (Stryker, 1977)], people also communicate behaviorally. Thus, men's adult relationships with women are created by a cycle of emotional, symbolic, *and* behavioral communication (the escalation–response sequence in courtship is one example). If a man is lying close to a woman, touching and kissing her and caressing her body, his behavior does not merely have sexual "meaning": it *is* sexual. For him their interaction is mediated not only symbolically, but also behaviorally.

Thus, consider the following scenario. The woman is enacting an Incomplete Rejection or Delay strategy, and hopes that although they will neck or pet, no further *genital* intimacy will develop. The man is "interested" in her—perhaps she fits his template, or perhaps he finds her sexually exciting. If he goes farther than she wants—that is, farther than her Delay stragegy permits *her* to respond—then he suddenly encounters *resistance* to his overtures. What began behaviorally as a sexually arousing and satisfying interaction for him has reached a blockade that seems to him to have no behavioral basis. She is responding behaviorally to his non-genital overtures, yet is rejecting him verbally. Not making her distinction about the "meanings" of different types of sexual activity, he perceives a contradiction between her verbal and non-verbal messages.

Under these circumstances, many men simply feel that women say *No* but "mean" *Yes*. He may then entreat, wheedle, cajole, or otherwise attempt to persuade her to continue. She, *in response*, sees him as an over-eager and "pushy" man who does not "respect her wishes." She escalates her rejections.

For him, however, her behavior is suddenly senseless. The interaction now has a real chance of spiraling outward to a physical confrontation in which—if they are both a little drunk—his superior physical strength can easily tilt the balance towards what *she* calls (date) rape, and about which *he* says "She was asking for it." [Kanin's (1984) study of 71 self-reported date rapists seems to confirm this description in some detail.] It follows that the man's and woman's versions of the interaction will differ completely.

This spiral towards unwelcome and forced intercourse is made even more likely if the man believes that "A real man doesn't take *No* for an answer." Finally, date rape is virtually assured if he *also* believes that after the power transition she no longer has the right to say *No* and that it is now his privilege to use force, or that women like such male aggressiveness.

The crux is that *for the man* the woman has switched modes of communication from behavioral to symbolic. She expects him to understand that sexual intercourse is shaped not only by behavioral communication, but by *symbolic* limits, e.g., the idea that genital intercourse "means" love. However, he lives in a world in which sexuality is only rarely discussed, and then usually only obliquely. To him, women's symbolic meanings are obscure, especially if he is 18 years old and has had very little experience with women. So he continues with his advances.*

A second, far worse consequence of such miscommunication also exists. Now, assume that the man does stop, bewildered and unhappy, but nonetheless he stops. She may believe that he "respected her wishes," and, operating within her own symbolic interpretations, assumes that he *understands* her motives for wanting to stop. However, he may *not* understand her behavior or its symbolic meanings. For him, a pleasant, delightful, intimate, and perhaps even wonderful experience was cut short. If—again—she is close to his template, he may not want to lose her. So he stops only because she asks. But he does not understand that she does not yet trust him or, as *she* would say, "Love him yet." He is left still puzzled, and—I suggest— a little bit angry, *even though he believes he loves her.* In brief, love and anger are getting mixed up.

Next, let us assume that their relationship fails. Sooner or later, each finds a new partner, but let us consider the man. If his next, equally fascinating, partner also enacts a Delay strategy, then slowly but surely he will come to feel that he is *always* the slightly angry sexual supplicant, and that the woman always has all the power in the relationship. He does not see himself as over-eagerly and aggressively pressing himself on the woman (though *she* may think so). Instead, he sees himself as enacting a behavioral sequence that follows from her initial expressions of interest and that is, for him, love and sexuality combined. But he also sees himself as begging the woman for her favors.

To be sure, a psychologically "normal" man may have no great trouble dealing with such frustrations, or such mixtures of anger and love. But nonetheless, the consequence is that many men feel a deep ambivalence about women.†

On the one hand is fascination and attraction to women, as seen, for example, in the essays written by young, virginal men in Nancy Friday's (1980) collection of male fantasies, or in men's descriptions of their first love (often from high school). Powerfully romantic, these responses depict women as wonderful and marvelous beings.

On the other hand, men find their sexuality *devalued* by repeated rejections by women they like, either in sexual rejections, as in the examples just given, or in social rejections, as in the case of a man who dances with a woman who then leaves permanently for the "ladies' room." In the *man's* eyes, his sexual and emotional state, valid and worthwhile to him as a legitimate expression of masculine sexuality, has been reduced and treated as "animalistic," "sexual coercion," or "disrespect." When she disdains him, sneers at him, or pulls back in displeasure from his interest, even a healthy man might find fascination turning sour. Under such a continued schedule of negative reinforcement, and in a pathological case, I suggest that the man's emotions can turn to hatred, loathing, and to an incoherent and

---

*The woman is *not* sending "mixed messages," as is sometimes said. To *her*, her message is perfectly clear. *He* just doesn't understand it.

†Encountering and disentangling this ambivalence was the most difficult part of this study.

anarchic desire for *revenge*: to inflict on women all the pain that he himself has suffered at their hands.

Here, I suggest, originate men's fantasies of violence against women, of the violence seen in certain kinds of pornography, and of violence against women in date rape or in stranger rape at knifepoint. In essence, for men, consensual intercourse with an aroused and willing woman represents the legitimation of his sexuality itself. Furthermore, as Wachtel points out (11 July 1984, personal communication), sexual intercourse allows a man to break out of whatever restrictions and constrictions have limited and dulled his whole life, sexual and non-sexual. The *medium* of that fulfillment is total sexual immersion in a woman. Thus, for men, the symbols and fantasies that surround sexuality are utterly unlike women's. When, in the Delay strategy the woman says *No* to a sexual overture, the man does not hear *Not yet*, with its implicit invitation to build a relationship first (or simultaneously but more slowly). He hears *I do not love you*, and for him, that eliminates the possibility of a relationship. To her, *No* has symbolic meaning; to him, it is taken literally. And some men *hate* women in return.

One way certain men seek revenge is in violent pornography. Its origin, which has deeply disturbed and angered many women (e.g., Women Against Violence and Pornography; see Griffin, 1981; Malamuth and Donnerstein, 1984), is not in any universal, "genetically" determined and culturally legitimated norm among men that women must be raped to keep them in their place. Rather, violent pornography provides bitter, angry men with a vicarious enactment of their yearnings for revenge against women. In the fantasy world of pornography, these men possess what they do not have in reality: the power to possess a woman and to punish her for her resistance.

It is a power that *men do not otherwise have*. In reality, most men do not have the power to "make use" of a woman's body whenever they wish (*contra*, e.g., Greenspan, 1983, p. 166; see Kronhausen and Kronhausen, 1967, p. 162). We would not have violent pornography, nor violent and sadistic male fantasies, if men had such powers in reality. People do not fantasize about power they already have: they simply use it (Wood, 1984). For example, if I own a Rolls-Royce, I am unlikely to fantasize about owning a Rolls-Royce. I merely call for the car, and a liveried servant brings it around. If I am a prince, I do not fantasize about political power. I have it. Only people bereft of such wonderful things fantasize about them and about the solace their possession would bring—or about the revenge they shall enact on people who *deny* them what they want.

In violent pornography and in male sadistic fantasies, the woman has been stripped not nude, but powerless. In fantasy, she has been denuded of her traditional right and privilege to say *No*. Pornography that depicts rape is wish-fulfillment for such men. Even as she begs and pleads not to be violated, she has been confronted, in his fantasy, with a male power that she cannot set aside merely by asking him to stop. *Unlike the real situation*, in his fantasy the man need not obey the woman's wishes. When, next, she yields to him and explodes in the usual pornographic depiction of sexual ecstasy, the fantasy comes back to its starting point: the desire to have intercourse with an aroused woman who, despite her every protestation, *becomes* willing. She is aroused because he is male. In fantasy, now she wants him as much as he wants her.

Stranger rape, I suggest, follows a similar, though far more pathological, avenue from frustration through feeling powerless to fantasized revenge to rape. (Virginia Greendlinger and Donn Byrne are currently gathering data relevant to this idea, a version of which they reached independently; Byrne, 18 September 1984, personal communication.) Contrary to the image of the rapist as an over-sexed man whose essentially normal "instincts" lead him misguidedly to seek sexual outlets in rape, rapists themselves commonly feel socially and sexually powerless, or uncontrollably angry at women (what Groth calls "power" and "anger" rapists, respectively). For such men, rape is *not* a sexual act at all, and is sexually not satisfying (Groth, 1979, pp. 93–96). Furthermore, rapists are startlingly often sexually *dysfunctional* ["impotent" in various ways (Groth, 1979, pp. 84–93)].*

The next step depends on seeing, again, that female sexuality is socially and publicly licit. It is not that the media depict women as "sex objects," thereby to elicit from over-sexed men a desire to rape lasciviously depicted women. That possibility—which appears in much feminist writing about rape—has a missing component: why should men then want to *rape* women rather than *seducing* them according to whatever social norms exist for seduction? The answer, I suggest, is that the media do *not* depict women as sexual objects available to all, but, instead, depict female sexuality *as a licit vehicle for satisfying non-sexual emotional needs, like affection, respect, and happiness.* Now, to be sure, sex is *not* junk food for the soul. Sexuality can offer genuine emotional and behavioral intimacy. But when an advertisement shows a woman in sexy lingerie, or a man with his fancy brand of liquor accompanied by an attractive woman, we see possession confused with process. The advertisement says that by possessing *things*—like cars, certain kinds of liquor or clothing, or a *woman*—a man can leap painlessly over courtship and all its uncertain bumps towards a guaranteed intimacy that will satisfy not merely sexual needs, but also his needs for love, respect, admiration, affection—in short, all the things that are produced only by the courtship process and its emotions.

Like advertising, pornographic fantasy and, especially, rape fantasy depicts a shortcut to the embittered man's most desired goal: sexual and emotional bliss with a woman, painlessly achieved simply because he wants her. Yet, simultaneously, pornography—like advertising—sneers at him. It implies—just as he fears that *women* feel—that there is something wrong with him when he cannot arouse a woman so completely and so against her seeming will. In comparison to the all-powerful pornographic male of fantasy, he is nothing. Yet, pornography reinforces his belief that only a completely yielding woman will cure his loneliness and solace his uncertainties. Like the advertisement, such pornography *over*-values the

---

*These facts, plus rapists's sometimes all too successful attempts to kill or disable their victims, eliminate the possibilities that rape is a "biologically" functional act, or that it is a "reproductive strategy." It is tragic that certain scholars adopting the sociobiological perspective see rape in such ways.

woman by portraying her body as a living vault of emotional and sexual gold while simultaneously displaying her as powerless and his for the taking—*if* he is man enough. Pornography, like advertising, *taunts* the man with what he does not have. It is self-destructive, and it takes only a short step to smashing the store window and looting—or to rape. For certain men violent rape is a revenge both anarchic and pathological that sees in the possessing *and* destroying of a woman a fitting termination for *all* women whose taunting and irresistible sexuality has been and still is forever inaccessible.

Accordingly, rape is a pathology of courtship not once, but twice. First, it arises from pathological reactions some men have towards women's rejection strategies. Steadily, it builds from a quite specific inability of some men to deal with the complexities of women's sexual behavior and symbols. But, secondly, it is also a pathology of the power transition itself. The sexuality of rape—which exists by definition—enacts itself not in a slowly developing sequence of mutual escalation and response that moves from proceptivity towards his overtly sexual efforts to arouse her. Stranger rape occurs without any prior engagement between rapist and victim, and, in essence, moves the relationship directly to the power transition. In rape, the man says that the woman will accept his sexuality *now*, by force if necessary. Thus, rape is pathological not merely because the rapist ignores the woman's proceptive role in establishing the pre-conditions for intercourse. It is pathological because the rapist wants to override that role, and to seize and overpower her in angry, murderous hatred of *all* women who seem so publicly to flaunt what they deny to him privately and personally.

Yet, to many women, rape seems to be an incomprehensibly evil crime. I suggest that, while evil it is, it is not incomprehensible. If my argument is correct, even partly, then rape is rooted quite comprehensibly in men's lack of understanding of women's culture, and especially its sexual symbols, as well as in a general social representation of female sexuality as something overwhelmingly wonderful. The eradication of rape may therefore take much more than male "re-education," as some writers seem to suggest (e.g., Korman and Leslie, 1982). It will also take changes in how we value female sexuality generally. Even if some women assign immense symbolic value to genital intercourse, even if advertisements often do so indirectly, or even if pornography always does so explicitly, it is not the possession of her body and its sexuality that is so important. Instead, proceptivity and response must both come to the center, for process must replace possession (and product). In that, we will no longer de-value men's sexuality to elevate women's, but see that each has a crucial place in the biosocial process of courtship.

Men and Courtship

Despite rhetoric to the contrary, not all men are rapists, although an angry woman may feel raped by male language and behavior. There is more to it than sexual partisanship might see.

Although many men are inarticulate about women and proceptive behavior, men still have their own ideas about courtship. Exaggerating only slightly, you use a good line with her, go out with her, eventually have sex—and here male oblique discourse omits something about falling in love—form a relationship, marry—now male discourse becomes even more oblique—and live happily ever after. The sequence corresponds more or less roughly with women's ideas, but there are some strking differences concerning the formalities of courtship and dating, the relationship between love and sex, and "opening lines" like "Come here often?"

The Rules of Courtship

Formal courtship—the domain of asking someone for a date, escorting her or wining and dining her, and even asking her to marry—is primarily still a male activity (Rothman, 1984), even though as people increasingly often meet through personals advertisements, women are beginning to call men and ask them out. Formal courtship is subject to quite detailed rules of etiquette and much gossip among men (though, of course, *oblique* gossip!). Single men, especially in large cities, know what restaurants and bars are appropriate for what kind of woman (or they *think* they know), what kinds of clothing are suitable and when, what kinds of non-sexual social activity are fitting for the present stage of their relationship with a woman—in a word, men are familiar with a complex *code* of behavior that regulates their interactions with women.

This code—and the word invokes not only a code of etiquette, but a code that requires deciphering—can be extremely detailed, especially in cities with many single people, like New York City. By their own lights, men play the game of formal courtship quite strictly by the rules. Indeed, the closest parallel to such activities might be an immensely complex game of basketball or tennis, played as much for its own sake as in the desire to "win the woman."

Although the game of formal courtship may sound competitive and even hostile, yet it is played genially and gives many men a good deal of pleasure. Many men find it particularly pleasurable if played with a woman who knows the male rules, which are often quite different from women's own strategies and rules for proceptive and reluctant behavior (see Appendix, pp. 282–286, for details). If one wants to speak of "love" for such activities, love based on this kind of mutual and pleasurable appreciation of each other's skills would be called "ludic," that is, playful (Lee, 1976). Sexuality can also enter such play, but it too goes according to formal rules and, as Lee points out, never becomes *too* emotionally strenuous or involving, at least initially.

Men who play the courtship game strictly by the male rules are sometimes disturbed by proceptive women. At least some "recalcitrant males" fall into this category. If they arouse a woman's ire, they can also arouse *men's* scornful amusement, as Gawain probably did for the author and audience of *Sir Gawain and the Green Knight* and as Thurber and White's (1929/1957, pp. 160–174) sardonicism was tickled by men who freeze when a woman's knee "accidentally" touches them. However, in cities with large and sophisticated singles populations, these male reactions are seen for what they are: timidity, not machismo. For many single men, it is a mark of sophistication to know that proceptivity exists, even if they cannot describe it accurately (rather as knowledge of cars is deemed sophisticated even if the man cannot tell a carburetor from a camshaft).

By the time a man is in his 20s, he is familiar with most, if not all, of the formal male rules of courtship in his particular ethnic or socioeconomic subculture. He learns them not only from his own experiences, but also from the media, in particular, magazines like *Playboy*. Despite its seeming stress on overt sexuality, *Playboy* is primarily an etiquette book for male behavior, especially in columns like "The Playboy Advisor" (which gives excellent advice).

He also learns the formal rules from his male acquaintances and friends. Such discussions—the "bull sessions" mentioned by Korman and Leslie (1982)—typically are exchanges of information about places to go and things to do, rather than being overt discussions of women and sex. In fact, they are often masterpieces of oblique male discourse, for almost never do men *explicitly* refer to women's sexuality or to love, and certainly not in the crudely explicit language that women *think* such discussions always entail. To be sure, men may boast or "pass comments" about a woman, but a man who boasts too explicitly or too frequently will be pressured into silence. The tacit assumption of such discussions is how hard it is to find or entertain women. No one wants to hear someone saying how successful he is, especially when (a) he is probably lying and (b) everyone else feels unsuccessful. However, since the topic will typically change if a woman joins the discussion, women may feel that men talk about sex all the time, even when they do not, at least not explicitly. (This fact holds with *special* force for men past college age.) In particular, men do *not* "egg each other on," in the way the media depicted the men doing in the New Bedford rape case. Men do not talk openly about how to seduce women. Indeed, if there is one topic that never arises, it is this.*

In brief, then, formal courtship has its fascinations for men because—if I may generalize perhaps overmuch—men admire people who *play* by the rules and occasionally even *win* by the rules.

Love and Sex

Yet it *is* only occasionally that men "win." In part, it is because few men know about women's proceptive and rejection strategies and the symbols they involve, but it is also because, for men, "winning" a woman is very different than "winning" a man is for a woman. Here again there is immense confusion between the sexes. Women often believe that for men "winning" means *scoring*—that is, entering a non-binding, non-emotional, and purely sexual relationship, e.g., a one-night stand.

---

*A woman reader may doubt these conclusions, especially if she thinks that men in private talk about sex the way women talk in private—that is, openly and quite explicitly. Yet it is not so, and I am summarizing many hundreds of hours listening to men talk.

Yet it is not so. Even if scoring represents one *kind* of win in male thought, the most highly valued outcome of the game of courtship is an emotional relationship with the right woman (Masello, 1983; Novak, 1983).

Confusion arises here because men and women connect love and sex very differently. It is not that men treat sex *unemotionally*, as some women think. Sex is profoundly emotional for men, so much so that it is the deleted center of oblique sexual discourse. It is particularly emotional when the woman matches the man's template, even though it might not necessarily be as *physically* satisfying as with another woman. After all, if men did *not* treat sex with a woman emotionally, why would they want it so much? They *could* masturbate.

Recently, William Novak (1983) pointed out that men enjoy doing things *with each other*, like playing softball, standing around a car speculating about its innermost workings, talking about politics, sports, whatever comes to hand, like someone getting a flat tire on Route 232, and what a killer *that* is. *Why* men feel that doing something with another person is emotionally satisfying I cannot answer, but it is, and profoundly so. [Tiger's (1970) greatly misunderstood *Men in Groups* describes something of this problem; it is *not* displaced homosexuality.]

Furthermore, Novak also commented—most accurately, I believe—that the same is true of sex (and courtship). Because these are done *together* with a woman they create particularly powerful bonds of shared experience. In shared sex, the man wants, and hopes, that the woman will enjoy sex with him for the same reasons he does: it creates their bond, as well as being physically pleasurable. Of course, sex alone is inadequate to maintain that bond, but for many men, it is a very reasonable starting place for a relationship. Even so, women often misunderstood men's sexual emotions: for many women, sex comes *after* love, and symbolizes it, rather than creating it.

Differential Sexual Investment

How comes this difference? After all, North American men and women are raised in the same general culture, and one would think that the forces of socialization would act more or less equally on them to instill in each the belief that love comes after sex. I suggest that we must once again turn to biology, rather than invoking a question-begging difference in male–female "socialization."*

In essence, this difference is biosocially functional. It depends on a theory first proposed by Darwin (1874) and called "sexual selection," and developed much further by Robert Trivers (1972).

The idea is that differences in sexual strategy between males and females represent what Trivers called "differential parental investment." The phrase refers,

---

*It is question-begging because if we ask, say, why rose bushes are different from chrysanthemums, and are told "Because they develop differently," the answer has in fact told us nothing. Obviously, it is important to study *how* male–female differences develop, but we cannot assume that such descriptions explain why those differences exist or what biosocial functions they serve. In biology, this problem is at the root of the science of embryology. It is not trivial.

first, to how much metabolic energy is expended in having a single offspring.* It is biologically obvious that females expend much more energy than males in bearing children. Now, I do *not* mean that women do all the housework! Rather, the theory refers to the *biological* costs of pregnancy and childbirth, such as obtaining more protein during pregnancy and lactation, obtaining more iron and calcium, and similar purely physiological processes. Compared to males, who produce only sperm, fertilization and pregnancy represent much higher physiological demands on females. Furthermore, such biological "costs" are inescapably part of pregnancy for the female, but not for the male (again, biologically; men may pay the bills, but I am speaking of physiology).

Trivers next pointed out—it is the heart of the theory—that in essence both males and females have a fixed metabolic income: only so much food, calories, iron, calcium, vitamins, and so on can be processed in one's reproductive lifetime, even if a person lives in the lap of luxury. It follows that for every offspring a *female* has, she has invested a large part of her fixed metabolic income in the child, whereas the male invests very little of *his* fixed metabolic income. Thus, by having a child, the female invests *more* of her biological income than the male.

Arguing essentially from economic analogy, Trivers now suggested that females would therefore be far more cautious in how they invest their income, for each time they do so they reduce the investment they can make in *future* offspring. Men, in contrast, hardly reduce their metabolic income by simply ejaculating. Accordingly, if all goes reasonably well, males and females will have different *strategies* for sexual interactions. The female should, in all likelihood, be far more reluctant to enter into a potentially very expensive metabolic arrangement, because if she does so "unwisely"—that is, the man disappears, leaving her without friends, family, lover, and relatives—then she has reduced her biological income for *future* children. She must care for the child alone, she is friendless, and so on. Men, by contrast, have no such worries. If follows, then, that women will—in all likelihood—be more cautious than men in entering into a sexual relationship.

In this calculus, which is widely accepted in evolutionary biology, it is strikingly sensible for a woman to have intercourse only if she is "in love"—that is, if her man has passed certain tests of trustworthiness, sensitivity, and responsiveness, as described in the chapter on Reluctance. However, unless a man *knows* about such biologically functional calculations, he is likely to make a very different calculation based not only on his *reduced* investment in sperm but also on his emotional belief that sex is fun and good a way to make friends. He will not understand the woman's belief that it is best to be friends—and often much more!—*before* sex.

This conclusion must be tempered, however, with an additional caveat. It assumes a certain kind of economic relationship between men and women (and now I mean *economic* in the financial sense). In a society such as ours, in which births

---

*Note that I said *metabolic*: the theory starts with biology, and only later involves the economic expenditures involved in having children.

typically occur only in a wedded ("nuclear") family and in which, until recently, women have been excluded from the workplace, Trivers' argument has particular force and power. Moreover, when economic relationships reinforce biological facts, then we should see—as we do—women holding very powerfully to beliefs that associate love and sex, presumably in a bonded and marital relationship (Cassell, 1984). The connection is biosocially functional, for it follows not only from biology, but also from economics and social arrangements that have, until recently, made many women dependent on men economically.

Now, Trivers' calculation represents a so-called "rational" economic argument, in which sexual costs and benefits are measured coolly and objectively. Though matters are changing, under certain circumstances—e.g., the woman's support comes *only* from her husband, rather than from her own kinfolk—such arguments have overwhelming power. However, at other times—e.g., she is self-sufficient or has strong economic (and emotional) ties to her own people—a woman may argue quite differently. She may then easily decide to "invest" her biological income with a man who is responsive, interested, and loving, regardless of how wealthy he is. Under these circumstances, her calculus is far less restricted by purely bioeconomic considerations, and she can afford—literally!—to choose a man *proceptively*, according to her own emotional interest and curiosity in him. If, next, she is close to his template, there forms an intensely powerful and mutual bond which can last for years, and, barring contraception, will produce many children. However, in the middle-class West, with its working husbands and nuclear families isolated from both sets of kin, Trivers' argument reveals how biological and economic facts can profoundly reinforce each other to produce a female sexual calculus utterly unlike the male's in its cautiousness.*

Thus, men and women differ not only in their beliefs about sex, but also in some underlying biology. Though men and women both treat sex as a powerful emotional cement, women's sexual hesitation has been, and in some ways still is, biosocially and bioeconomically functional. In consequence, women do not so easily enter into a sexual relationship simply because it makes friends with people, as men do. The consequence is that men are often puzzled by women. "It's just sex," they say. "It's fun. What's the big deal?"

Well, it *is* a big deal, especially without contraception. But, if these comments help explain something of women to men, likewise I hope they explain something of men to women. For men, sex *is* fun, and it is *not* a big deal in the way that it is for women. Thus, men are not terrible and insensitive people when they want to make love. Their sexual calculus is different, and for understandable biosocial and historical reasons.

*The reader should be warned that my argument is *very* different from the usual sociobiological presentations of "parental investment" theory. Unfortunately, few "sociobiologists" have seen that Trivers' theory centers on *differential* investment, or that economics can powerfully reinforce it. Instead, such writers often enter into mysterious domains of genes that cause promiscuity, and other kinds of ethnobiological thinking. Space does not permit a detailed and radical critique of the "sociobiological" misuses of Trivers' work, but they are great. Finally, like all "macro" level theory, Trivers' ideas apply to the average or mode, a comment that also applies to my own biosocial approach.

Come Here Often?

The last difference between men and women concerns lines—those strange utterances men seem to be fond of when approaching a woman. What do men hope to accomplish with such banalities?

Given female reluctance or delay, and given a generic male ignorance of women's sexual strategies, such lines are a kind of *magic* with which men hope to overcome a woman's distance and hesitation. Of course, men do not take the magic *too* seriously, but still, there is the hope that a "really good line" will cause the woman to become interested.

Such lines are often quite peculiar, especially the infamous "What's your sign?" However, *if* the woman is already interested, then virtually any opening line will begin the conversation, provided that it is reasonably polite. Kleinke (1981) found that effective openings include simply saying *Hi. My name is Ed. What's yours?* (such introductions are indeed the best openings I know of), or, in a bar, asking her opinion of the band (an oldie but goodie), or, in a restaurant, asking her opinion of the food, or, in a supermarket, offering to help carry her bags of groceries.

Each of these "lines" has two characteristics. First, it represents a genuine expression of interest, even if politely phrased. Second, and more importantly, it gives the woman a chance to *answer*, that is, to respond to an escalation. There is quite a difference between saying "Hey, that band stinks," which might evoke a simple "Uh?" in response (or worse, "Oh, yeah? The guitarist's my boyfriend"), and saying "What do you think of the band?" which invites a specific reply, and therefore opens the escalation–response pattern that courtship involves. To be sure, the woman might reject that invitation, but at least he tried.

However, often men use such lines because they cannot interpret the woman's behavior, for example, her moving closer to him in the bar or party. If she does so, then *she* has begun the interaction non-verbally and proceptively and, in her mind, his "opening line" is actually a *response* to her overture. But he may think that *he* began the interaction: as men sometimes say, "Well, she was standing there, and I began to talk to her."

Likewise, if he compliments her appearance—which only some men can do without being offensive—he may think that *he* began the interaction, whereas, in fact, her choice of clothing was carefully calculated to evoke male interest (compare essay F3). For example, if he has enough good taste to recognize that her earrings are really quite elegant, then, when he compliments them, she may think that he is being "charmingly responsive," while *he* thinks that he took the initiative.

There is a quite practical conclusion here. Women often believe that if a man does *not* respond to her physical proximity, say, then he has *rejected* her proceptive overture. In fact, however, he may not have attached much importance to it or perhaps did not even notice it. She could, of course, begin the conversation herself, a procedure that ought to get his attention.

Another class of lines Kleinke (1981) called "cute-flippant" and most women

204 Sex Signals: The Biology of Love

simply call offensive. The best (worst?) example in my own research was a man who claimed that it always worked if, looking her up and down, he said to the woman next to him "Say, are you wearing any underwear?" Most women react very poorly to such lines, to put it mildly, but *many* opening lines fall into this category. Kleinke lists others, such as "I bet I can outdrink you;" or, in a restaurant, "I bet the cherry jubilee isn't as sweet as you are;" or, at a laundromat, "A man shouldn't have to wash his own clothes," assuredly a line that deserves a prize for masculine stupidity and insensitivity.

The existence of these lines poses a curious puzzle. Few men are *deliberately* offensive when dealing with a stranger, but some men feel quite free to use such lines. It is no explanation to say that they are impolite, aggressive boors; that is a fact, at least as such things are assessed, but not an *explanation*.

One explanation concerns the man's fear that no matter what he says, he will probably be rejected ("shot down," as men say, thereby to impute considerable hostility to women). If she turns away from him when he uses one of these lines, he can soothe himself (or try to) by saying that she did not like the *line*, rather than disliking *him*. Second, such lines express resentment against the woman in *advance* of any possible rejection. For a man who simultaneously yearns for a woman and who dislikes her, the line then embodies the same abivalence we saw in pornography and men's violent fantasies about women.

Is it, then, that men employ lines like these because they are trained to use words as weapons against women, as a woman might readily believe? Perhaps not. I suggest that many men feel *powerless* when starting an interaction with a woman. By using such lines, the man attains power over the woman and the situation, a power that he feels he otherwise does not have. Because, in imagination, these lines are supposed to *command* attention, they are the verbal equivalents of love-potions: they change the woman's feelings magically, and *cause* her to become interested, even against her will.*

The point is not that such men are quite wrong about the effects of lines or that men know nothing about behavioral feedback (Chapter 4). Rather, such men consider their interactions with women as *different* from the usual run-of-the-mill conversation, so that, for them, the rules of "common courtesy" are set aside. The domain has shifted from everyday matters to something else, in which he can trust only magic—"good chemistry"—and can hope to manipulate only by using the right words, spells, and incantations to counter her power (and magic) over him.

Now, sometimes these lines work, even the bad ones. In those cases, the objective observer can see that the woman was already interested, and therefore tolerated his breach of courtesy or perhaps even was intrigued by it. But the man does not know that. He therefore does not know *why* his line worked—or seemed to. He can readily believe that the line *did* have magical power—and that magic

---

*Cross-culturally, men tend to use love-magic more than women do (Ford and Beach, 1951, pp. 100–101), suggesting that the powerlessness implicit in men's lines may be widespread. See Carter (1977, pp. 181, 213).

works only sometimes. But, of course, that is like all magic. It depends on demons, and spirits, and God only knows what other kinds of elemental forces, all of which reside, somehow, *in* the woman and from whom they take their power. Underneath these lines, we again see men vesting women with immense and incomprehensible power to evoke and control men's reactions.

Needless to say, women may find these beliefs utterly baffling (though one might make a similar case of women's belief in the magic of clothing). Yet consider the following piece of advice, taken from a book called *A New Look at Love*, by Elaine and G. William Walster (1978), highly respected scholars in the field of human sexuality and marriage. They address some advice to a shy person who wants to start a conversation:

> Try self-disclosure. You'll find that when you make an obviously personal statement, it will elicit a positive sympathetic response.
> Try: "I'm not sure what I'm doing here, I'm really quite shy." (Walster and Walster, 1978, pp. 33–34)

The line sounds fairly reasonable, but if we envision a scenario around it—a man using the line at a party—we shall again see a belief in the magical power of words and lines.

What might the woman say in response? Though the Walsters evidently believe that she will be positive and sympathetic, a real woman might respond negatively:

> —Let me know when you figure it out.
> - I was shy once. Then I took dancing lessons.
> —That's a good line for someone who's shy. (She doesn't believe him.)
> —So am I. (What does he say next?)
> —Boring.

A *real* woman might not respond to the man's overture, and who says she should? Perhaps she is thinking, "What a nerd." Surely, she has the right to ignore him or even rebuff him!

Yet, by assuring the reader that a woman will *not* have such a reaction, the Walsters implicitly attribute to this line the *power* to command a polite, positive and sympathetic response from the woman. Once the man utters the magic words, the world changes in the direction he wants. The line gives him *control*. Indeed, that is the symbolic function of all such lines.

Such magical thinking is surprisingly common in men's beliefs about women and about sexual behavior, especially if they are in love. It represents not only men's metaphysical over-valuation of women's powers, but also a way to understand why men and women are so different. It says that women are magical, and that is *why* they are different.

It also provides a way to speak about women metaphorically, as creatures basically *unlike* men. Thus, if men are rational—that is, *cultural*—beings, then

206 Sex Signals: The Biology of Love

women are the opposite, and, in the logic of this system of male thought, *that* means non-rational and non-cultural, in brief, "natural." Women's magic, then, is the magic of Nature: procreative, powerful, mysterious, and, above all, *different*.

Poetry

Nowhere, perhaps, does this male sense of women as different and powerful emerge more than in men's poetry about women. Because poetry and its close relative, drama, are both public, through them men can express feelings about women that would otherwise disappear under the clouds of oblique discourse.

Poetry about women is ancient. It forms an immense body of feeling and knowledge. Like biology, it cannot be summarized. Nonetheless, even if the reader "does not like" poetry, I invite you to consider the following near-sonnet by William Blake (1783/1925). It is called "To the Evening Star."

> Thou fair-haired angel of the evening,
> Now, whilst the sun rests on the mountains, light
> Thy bright torch of love; thy radiant crown
> Put on, and smile upon our evening bed!
> Smile on our loves, and while thou drawest the
> Blue curtains of the sky, scatter thy silver dew
> On every flower that shuts its sweet eyes
> In timely sleep. Let thy west wind sleep on
> The lake; speak silence with thy glimmering eyes,
> And wash the dusk with silver. Soon, full soon,
> Dost thou withdraw; then the wolf rages wide,
> And the lion glares through the dun forest.
> The fleeces of our flocks are covered with
> Thy sacred dew; protect them with thine influence.

At first reading, it sounds like a prettily worded plea, or prayer, to the Evening Star to shed its protecting light over nature and humankind alike, and to cover both with sacred protection against the beasts of the night. Alternatively—and somewhat more ploddy-footedly—we might read the poem as a prayer to God to shed His grace and light on the "flocks" of the faithful, and thereby to protect them from the raging beasts of sin, symbolized by wolves and lions.*

Frankly, I rather suspect that by now even Blake would have gone to sleep (or gone off to write more poetry, inattentive to such interpretations). The poem is neither a prettily worded plea nor a ploddy-footed and ambiguous prayer, written by a sermonizing preacher eager to make obvious (and trite) parallels between sin and

---

*My copy of the 1925 Watt and Munn anthology of English literature, which contains Blake's poem, has margins filled with little handwritten notes, made, I imagine, by a nameless student recording the Professor's comments. The idea that Blake's poem refers to the "flocks of the faithful" appears in that student's handwriting in the margin next to the poem.

wolves in the night, or between light and God's grace, or to concoct other equally mawkish Freshman poetry devices and clichés. The Evening Star is Venus, the "fair-haired angel of the evening," whose *other* name is Aphrodite the Golden (Friedrich, 1978). Deeply and fundamentally, "To the Evening Star" is a love poem.

It is also a good example as any of men's oblique discourse about love, for the subject of love—a particular women, or even women in general—appears only in allusion. Around her, the poem is anchored in the *visually* sensuous: on light, bright and radiant; on a woman's smile embodied in the evening around which the blue curtains of night are drawn (a magnificent image for evening's darkening blue sky); on the silent speech of glimmering eyes, on silvery dusk and on sleep. And, as sleep surrounds the lovers' bed,

> Now the hungry lion roars,
> And the wolf behowls the moon;
> Whilst the heavy ploughman snores,
> All with weary task foredone.

as Puck put it at the end of *Midsummer-Night's Dream*, when he, Titania, and Oberon bless the beds of the newly united lovers of *that* play. It does not matter much if Blake consciously intended to invoke Shakespeare's imagery, for it is an old image, far older than Blake: around the lovers' bed and intimacy, the evening closes and, far off in distant forests, wild animals rage and howl.

For many men, it is as Blake says. Love itself *does* protect against rage, fury, and hate. Blake is not writing greeting cards, nor is he talking about God's grace and sin (except in a far deeper way than might be thought). His is a poem about the *two most potent emotions men experience: love arising from a woman embodied in exalted physical sensuality, and a rage that howls in the distance.*

Of course, not all men are as explicitly romantic as Blake, and, indeed, some men are virtually inarticulate compared to him. Yet I am arguing that most men experience love and fury as polar opposites between which they are pulled now one way, now another. This opposition exists as the hidden center of all male discourse about women and love. It is a man's emotion, and perhaps few women understand it: for many men, love, timely sleep, and protection exist where one's evening bed is—in the unspoken world of domesticity and home—and not in the external world of raging violence in which wild beasts snarl and threaten life itself. Blake is telling us that it is encradled in intimacy with a woman that men find *safety*.

But could it not be that Blake represents an exception, an unusually sensitive man whose poetic mysticism permitted him to experience and describe a lovely but unique emotion that most men never have? In one sense, Blake was assuredly unusual: few men are great poets. But just because *Blake* was articulate, we cannot conclude that *other* men have no feelings, or that Blake did not touch on something that most men experience but cannot describe particularly well, if at all. Once again, I will not retreat to an elitist Hobbesianism which sees most men as dumb beasts, caught in grey worlds of tedium and of mindless, emotionless rut, or as slovenly, indifferent boors for whom women are but objects of momentary lust. We cannot exalt Blake as an individual genius. We must understand that he speaks for *many* men.

But Blake speaks obliquely—perhaps too obliquely, especially for a pop-psychoanalytic world in which everything is reduced to the child's yearning for its Mother. Thus, we hear in the popular media that men "really don't want to grow up"—the Peter Pan syndrome—and that men's needs are really no more than a whining desire to be a child again. Isn't Blake *really* saying that Mommy makes the nightmares go away, or that a few moments of cuddling will solace the child in the man?

Certainly there is a large folklore to the effect that men are really only overgrown boys at heart. But behind that folklore, and its elevation into the psychoanalytic tradition, rears up again the Nature–Culture dichotomy. In this reading of Blake, or of the male emotions he records, is the idea that men typically operate in the world of Culture, and that they seek—clumsily and blindly, like newts in a cave—for a *return* to the days of Nature. But if the Nature–Culture dichotomy is false, then the psychoanalytic interpretation becomes myth and art, not science.*

There is no doubt that such myths are potent. Yet, curiously, they minimize men's feelings by seeing them as but pale reflections of the earlier emotions of childhood. These ideas find the origin of emotion in Nature, in the time the child was associated with its Mother, and when it was little more than a collection of instincts without mind or ideas, only a vessel of mute Nature. Accordingly, in this reading, we see that women, as Nature, are the source of men's feelings in childhood or adulthood, and not that men *themselves* are the origin and source of their own feelings.

Like pornography, such ideas place to the center the woman's power to evoke emotion while, simultaneously, they degrade the man into a merely reactive robot. If, in pornography, he is merely a sex machine overpowering the woman, then in the psychoanalytic reading, the man is merely a child overpowered by fear and humbly needing the woman to comfort him. In a curious sense, pornography and psychoanalysis are mirror images of each other, in which the figure of the woman is central, either as unwilling victim or willing nurturer.

And, again, the crucial question: what is so important—so *very* important— about women that such myths develop? Why is the *woman* the central icon in such readings of men's emotions? Psychoanalysis does not provide the answer, for it assumes that *of course* the Mother is all important. Even if—which I doubt—Blake's poem is merely a text in a psychoanalysis, then the psychoanalytic reading simply shifts the ground from one woman to another, and our question is not answered. Why women? Why not ferns or turtles?

Something—and it is neurophysiological and biological—keeps men's atten-

---

*This is true for even the most serious psychoanalytic thinkers, such as Jacques Lacan (1982, pp. 74–85).

tion focused on women, rather than letting it drift anywhere and everywhere. Hidden under men's oblique discourse—be it Blake's, or the essayists', or even the elaborate mythology of psychoanalytic discourse—is a center, templated and adorned, which is identifiably an embodied human female.

She is fascinating, this female. Over men's history, she has taken a myriad of kaleidoscopic forms, but always she is there. And when she is not, there is grief.

> Methought I saw my late espousèd saint
> Brought to me like Alcestis from the grave
> Whom Jove's great son to her glad husband gave,
> Rescued from death by force though pale and faint.
> Mine as whom washed from spot of childbed taint,
> Purification in the old law did save,
> And such, as yet once more I trust to have
> Full sight of her in heaven without restraint,
> Came vested all in white, pure as her mind.
> Her face was veiled, yet to my fancied sight,
> Love, sweetness, goodness, in person shined
> So clear, as in no face with more delight.
> But, O, as to embrace me she inclined,
> I waked, she fled, and day brought back my night.
> Milton, On His Deceased Wife.
> ca. 1658/1925, p. 402

But Milton writes too obliquely for a world turned noisy with greeting card sentimentality. He was *blind* when his wife died after childbirth. So, when *Milton* writes that it will be heaven when once again he has full sight of her, we should not presume that it is simple for a man to *see* a woman and love her. Men's visual templates for women are powerful—powerful indeed.

Yet his grief is uncomprehended in a modern world filled with empty yammering and with the slick, media grief of *Love Story*. A blind man's sorrow at the death of his wife—so who *cares*? The voices break in—"We've all got troubles, pal," a man says; "Why do men want so *much* from women?" a woman says. Milton's voice vanishes, too quiet, and becomes private and oblique. Under the pounding voice of television, Romeo becomes a buffoon, and when he says of Juliet that

> I am too bold, 'tis not to me she speaks;
> Two of the fairest stars in all the heaven,
> Having some business, do intreat her eyes
> To twinkle in their spheres till they return.
> What if her eyes were there, they in her head?
> The brightness of her cheek would shame those stars,
> As daylight doth a lamp; her eyes in heaven
> Would through the airy region stream so bright
> That birds would sing and think it were not night.
> See, how she leans her cheek upon her hand!

O, that I were a glove upon that hand,
That I might touch that cheek!

Romeo and Juliet, Act II, Scene II

The foolish student says only that Shakespeare is trying to show the reader that Romeo is in love, or that Milton is trying to express sorrow. And these are the same students who form the inevitable sample for the statistical investigation of attitudes about sex and love! Their voices too are mute, silenced under the pounding of clichés and the terminally cute prose of advertising. Poor Romeo—his momentary pang of very masculine doubt, his sight filled with Juliet, his eyes so much wanting to touch her. Tragedy undeserved waits for him as it has waited for many. But below the voices silenced by a world of indifference, scorn, and menace, Milton's words *still* speak the grief of *every* man who has lost a woman—or woman who has lost a man. Poor Milton—mute, inglorious Milton—and with him, all the men who have vanished namelessly and silently into history, for whom the sight of their woman's eyes was worth all the honor and wealth that ever existed, and for whom her loss was death itself!

Finale

We have come nearly full circle to return to the encradling power of love and the man's vision of something nearly Divine in the woman he loves. In doing so, we learn something of the function of the template, and of men's so intense reactions to women. When he sees *her*, his world is reorganized. Now, thoughts that preoccupied him previously—such as playing football with his buddies, being the young son at home, studying for college examinations, working at establishing himself in school or job—all suddenly vanish. Now, he begins to think of a life with her, and the color and meaning of everything changes. Football is time spent away from her (unless she comes to cheer him on), and he studies less for himself alone than for building a career that includes a family with her. Her appearance in his life has catalyzed a complete reorganization of his thinking and feeling, and he judges himself as *different*. Now, he is becoming a *man*, for he is linked—bonded irretrievably, though he may not know it—to a woman with whom he dreams of spending his life. His world *re-centers*, and everything is different.

Even years later, he may have the same reaction when, after a divorce, say, he again sees the woman of his template. The induced asexuality of men's existence suddenly evaporates, and once again he is entranced by her eyes, her mouth, her voice, her body. And yet it is not sex, for he has had *that* feeling before, and he knows the difference. *This* woman is different, though he can't quite put his finger on *why*. When she smiles at him or talks to him, or dances with him, or even goes out with him, his cynicism changes, providing, or course, he is not *too* far gone down the road to open hatred and violence. If, slowly, he comes to trust her—for example, she finds him just as interesting, even if he isn't perfect, but then who is?—it is because *she* is different, not because such cynicism was never really warranted in the first place. Again, he rebuilds his world, and, once again, it centers on a woman.

Under the mute voices of so many men, this process occurs over and over. It is the true biosocial core of men's reactions to women: an intensely fascinated reaction that triggers a reorganization of his life. And, provided she is willing—through proceptive interest or reluctance faded—then they shall re-center around each other. In this, we—the objective observers—can see them looking, and touching, and leaning, and finally, in full body synchronization. For them, the lovers, it is a time endless and always new, for they will, together and mutually, rebuild their perceptions of the world. The very notion of causation itself changes, and they see their relationship pre-figured in everything that has ever happened to them.

"You know, we wouldn't have met if it hadn't been for . . . " she says, and he agrees.

"I was really interested in you the first time I saw you," he says, and she smiles, remembering how carefully she arranged for them to be alone.

"I really liked you," she says, "and remember when we went to dinner the first time? We had scallops . . . " or whatever, in memory changed, they actually had.

"I had gone through a pretty bad time when I got divorced from Delores," Joe says—for his name is really Everyman, and his myth far more ancient than it seems—"but when I met Sally, well it was just different. She was nice—you know? She left me alone, I guess, but that wasn't it." He stops. "She's just quite a girl," he adds. "I guess that's it."

Under the seemingly inarticulate voices of such men is ultimately a process that makes a great deal of good sense. It is, after all, the way men and women, meet, touch, fall in love, and—in all likelihood—have children with each other. Romeo and Juliet did not fail each other, the world failed them: their tragedy was circumstantial, not biosocial. Biosocially, this process *is* functional, after its own manner, even if *other* people in other places reach the same result in other ways.

Moreover, outward from that biosocial core grows an increasingly complex set of symbols and meanings. For her are the meanings that attach to sexuality itself, and the proceptive and reluctant strategies that arise from them. For him are the doubts and silences that surround his fascination with her and that can express themselves only in private language, or in the oblique discourse men use so often. External to those feelings are other people's reactions and the rules for recognizing when—if at all—a sexual relationship becomes socially legitimate. Now, we are in a world of rules, smart and proper, which regulate the social appearance of male–female relationships, though, as I have stressed, they do not *create* those relationships. And still further outward. . . .

Chapter 8

The Sacred

For the lovers, love has grown from their touches, looks, and synchronization to encounter processes that involve more than a dyad which establishes its own rules of sexual conduct. They have come into direct contact with social principles which they neither created nor over which they alone have much control. These are the smart and proper sex rules, the economic facts that help determine the woman's choice of mate, and the rules that, for men, help create a desexualized world. But now the lovers apprehend that they soon will touch something even more special: they have decided to get married.

With marriage and the wedding, the couple encounters still other rules which, in sociological language, pertain to the "sacred" aspects of sexuality. These beliefs and their associated institutions and rituals will concern me in this and the next chapter.

Once again, my purpose is to place sexual behavior and its customs into a biosocial framework. But when we ask why people *marry*, the level of analysis has widened. We must deal with forms of sexual behavior that represent customs, traditions, and meanings held or enacted by *collectivities* of people. Personal feelings and definitions no longer suffice for understanding what weddings and marriage mean *socially*. In the wedding, we encounter sociology and ethnography, as well as psychology. We also encounter that last challenge to the biosocial approach: can it help us understand social behavior, or is its value limited to individual actions?

In this and the next chapter, I will tie together a number of themes already mentioned, including such apparently diverse phenomena as the belief that love is *very* special, men's belief that lines and gambits are somehow magical, and even questions of morality itself. Like the petals of a flower, these questions all center on asking why marriage exists as a social institution. Then, using Durkheim's concept of the Sacred, I suggest that our beliefs about marriage are woven around a sanctified idealization of the biological life cycle. It begins with love—seen as a mystery, even if it is biologically very real—and leads, via the symbols of the wedding, to the idea that life originates in Sacred, not material, processes. In this belief, *women* are the crucial mediators between us and the Sacred powers. Around the biosocial core of courtship, love, and reproduction has grown virtually every Western belief about men, women, sexuality, Nature, Culture, God, and—finally—biology itself and its position in Judaeo-Christian tradition.

But this system of belief, symbol, and custom has been seriously undermined by changes in economics, technology, birth control, science (especially biology), and feminism (Chapter 9). Yet the biosocial core has remained, and new symbols and beliefs are being re-woven to replace old symbols and beliefs. And I submit that the biosocial approach is required if we are to understand what these new symbols are and how they are being created.

An Ethnographic Short Circuit—and a Caution

Why Marry?

The rules of marriages, weddings, and the family are not established solely by the involved parties. Law-givers and religious leaders have long been concerned with the social regulation of procreation and of sexual intercourse. These rules reach deep into society and culture themselves and, implicit in them, is an immense library of beliefs and rituals that transcend the merely personal lives of the lovers.

When the lovers decide to marry, they cross over from the domain of personal feelings to domains of *community* concern (Chapter 5). Their affection has been noticed by others, and has become the beginning of a *new* process that involves not merely the couple itself, but everyone around them. Ultimately, that process will lead them to become the centerpieces of the wedding itself, a role that they may accept happily or wonder about, but over which *they* have little control. Indeed, the rules have now become unbreakable: the groom *cannot* place the wedding ring on the bride's *right* hand during the ceremony. But some far more serious rules now appear, rules that touch on profound symbolism and arise with immense power. For example, if the woman has a child but is unmarried, only the smart sex (informal) rules require that the father provide for her and the child. But if they are married, social and legal sanctions of great power enforce his support. If he abandons her, in theory legal mechanisms exist to *cause* him to support his wife and child.

These are but examples of how much is distilled into the wedding. In fact, in weddings symbols pile on symbols to form a detailed and complex web of belief that incorporates the most profound mythologies of the West as well as its strongest rules. Why is this? What is so important about the couple's love that it attracts so much attention, ritual, and, finally, sacred significance?

To sharpen the question, we can ask if community and religious beliefs explain why men and women fall in love and want to marry in a public ceremonial. For some people the answer may be partly *Yes*. We are surrounded by community standards that encourage or require marriage. But the question is far subtler: why should the community, or its religious leaders, *care* if two people marry? Why not simply let them form deep, but non-marital relationships based on private and personal attraction? True, given that the "community" cares, people will often yield to community pressure, but why does that pressure exist? In brief, why does the community become involved in love and courtship at all?

These are difficult questions because, as natives of our own culture, we take weddings and marriages for granted. To an individual born in the West, *of course* such institutions exist. *It's just customary*, people say, or they will tell you that *People are raised that way*, or that *It's following the dictates of religion (or society) to marry*, or that *People marry because they want children*. These are not explanations, but simply versions of saying *We do it because we do it (or are told to)*. These answers do not tell us why we think sexuality and love are so important that we have built the ceremonial, cultural, and emotional processes of the wedding around them.

Moreover, if people's behavior did nothing more than enact *social* rules, we have again encountered the problems of infinite regress and endless behavioral variation discussed in Chapter 1. If only social rules operate, they should be free to vary endlessly, as the idiosyncrasies of history twist and turn. Yet, the center of the wedding is not a man marrying a fern, nor a woman marrying a turtle: instead, throughout Western history, the immensely complex symbolic and ceremonial events of the wedding have focused on the couple: a man and a woman. Even though, over millenia, religious beliefs have changed; even though, in past centuries, the timing of the wedding has shifted in relation to the overall courtship sequence; and even though, in modern times, weddings have lost some of their purely liturgical and devotional qualities, nonetheless we all still agree: the crowning event of courtship will be the wedding, an event both public and private which reaches an emotional intensity perhaps never again to be attained by that man and woman.

Something has kept the seemingly purely social processes of marriage and weddings centered on the now-to-be-wed couple. As in Chapter 1, one explanation is again God, who works through His churches and congregations, through canon law, and the ancient and wise words of the inspired, to assure that the couple's love is celebrated and made licit by all. But we need not "believe" in God to attribute such sociological functions to religion. For example, the anthropologist Roy Rappaport (1971) suggested that religions act "homeostatically," by which he meant that they tend to preserve a society in a given path and to prevent it from diverging too far from the path.

Though his argument seems correct as far as it goes, it cannot be the whole story. Why have religions themselves so consistently taught (in the West, at least) that marriages and weddings are so important? It is the paradox of Chapter 1: why haven't religious beliefs wandered this way and that, until, finally, religions say nothing at all about marriage?

Paradoxically, this question is mirrored in the singles scene as a curiously pervasive sense of failure in being single, accompanied by an idealization of the past as *better* than today's world. In this tragic ethos of the singles scene is a yearning for an imagined time when a person could find a committed mate as a matter of course in the equally imaginary American ideal of the small town, the neighborhood, or the community. There is great pain in this yearning for a golden past even though being single seems to offer the nearly ideal combination of independence, sexual freedom, and whirl of fun and pleasure. Being single has become a metaphor for a general social malaise and of a general failure of life to provide a stable, central core around which everything else is built. In the tragic ethos of the singles scene, marriage and family are not auxiliary to social stability and happiness, but are believed integral and necessary to it. Such people believe that a normal and productive life should be a *married* life, and that if marriage is not forthcoming, then something is deeply wrong, not only with the individual but with society itself.

Again, what is so important about marriage that we hear it exalted, if only by the misery of its absence? Sex is not the crucial issue, since one often hears that the problem is too *many* sexual partners: "Sex is everywhere," people say, "but commitment is not." Much more enters these beliefs than a yearning for the mere convenience of a bank account shared between husband and wife.

From this viewpoint comes the often intense dislike single people have for each other. "What's wrong with men," the woman asks. "Are they afraid to grow up? Settle down? Open themselves up emotionally?" Then the question turns inward and asks, in despair, "What's wrong with *me*?" The singles scene becomes self-accusatory, and people yearn even more strongly for the surcease that love—and love *alone*—seems to offer in a world that is otherwise torn by impersonal forces, tensions, and dilemmas.*

Why is "committed love" the central icon of the singles scene? It is no answer to say that people want love and despair of finding it. That is the problem to be explained, not its answer.

Then we hear the conservative voices that speak of sexual morality and ask in genuine distress why sexual habits have changed so very much from the old days. For millions of North Americans, sexual intercourse belongs *only* in marriage, and the singles scene and adolescent sexuality are both inexplicable. But what is so immensely important about marriage that its absence signals—to the conservative— a deep failure of American life?

Although many writers have argued that conservative religious thought seeks to "repress" sexuality (e.g., R. A. Wilson, 1967; Whitehurst, 1971; Ginder, 1975), religious moralities regulate, not repress, when and with whom sexual activities can licitly occur. In particular, conservatism seeks to regulate the *public* display of sexual behavior (e.g., in the anti-pornography movement). But, equally—and it is obvious from the characterization of conservatism in Chapter 5—conservatism sees sexuality as a proper and legitimate part of the *private* behavior of the married couple. But what is so important about sex that people feel that it *should* be

---

*These comments draw not only on my own field work but on published accounts of the singles scene: Cargan and Melko, 1982; Cassell, 1984; Dowling, 1981, Chapter 5; Gordon, 1976, e.g., Chapter 3; Mullan, 1984; Simenauer and Carroll, 1982; Stein, 1981.

regulated? Why don't we assume that it is merely a pleasant activity, and let it happen when and where it happens? Yet, in a profoundly emotional and symbolic public ceremonial, we marry, thereby to restrict ourselves—in ideal, at least—to the private expression of sexuality with one person alone.

These multifaceted questions come to a focus when we ask why weddings are such very special occasions. They are not merely parties, nor do they merely render the children legitimate. Weddings and marriages are not merely contracts, and more is involved than merely a marriage license. For example—

Every now and then we receive a wedding invitation. In formal script and old fashioned language, it announces the forthcoming wedding between two people, and requests the "honour" of our presence. So we decide to go, and get all dressed up, in our best suits and dresses, and participate in the solemnities. "Very lovely," we all agree. "The bride is very beautiful." We also understand that now—though not before—this couple can have licit sexual intercourse, and that if the bride were indeed a virgin before the ceremony, she certainly won't be for long.

In one of the back pews is sitting a Martian, a blue spherical creature, with tentacles and violet eyes, wearing formal Martian attire. As we leave, we ask him how he liked the wedding.

"Very interesting," he replies. "But tell me something, if you will, for I am unfamiliar with your ways of life. Why does the bride's white gown display her virginity, and the ceremonial celebrate the fact that soon she will not be a virgin? I thought you people repressed sexuality. But, here, it lives in a public ceremonial, surrounded by men of God, flowers, and sunshine. *Everyone* now knows that her husband will, this evening, insert his penis into her vagina and ejaculate. Is that not an odd way to repress sexuality? But I am only a Martian, unfamiliar with your ways of life. Can you enlighten me?"

Once again, an ethnographic short circuit. The Martian is right. People usually do not reveal their sexual lives in public, nor display their virginity (or lack of it). Why then do we openly, overtly, and publicly celebrate sexuality at a wedding?

The Martian's question reminds us that other questions have lingered at the edges of our minds throughout the book. Why is sexuality sequestered? Why is pornography deemed so dangerous? Why does male oblique discourse exist? And, then, a crucial question: why do all these rules about sequestering sexuality so strikingly reverse themselves at the wedding itself?

. . . and a Caution

It is not simple to ask why marriage exists, why single people yearn for a golden past, why the sexual revolution has stirred moral fervor, or why weddings reverse the normal rules. But, though these questions have been studied extensively, I suggest that we can understand them better if we take a viewpoint that is more organic, so to speak, in its ability to synthesize than can finely grained studies of marriage itself, the singles scene itself, or even morality itself. By seeing them as part of *one* phenomenon, rather than isolated questions, we can see them as part of a *single* system of beliefs about which some answers may be forthcoming.

There *is* a central coherence to these symbols, beliefs, hopes, traditions, and customs. *Ultimately*, they center on the biosocial functionality of human reproductive arrangements, rather as the petals of a flower surround its reproductive structures. But before I can discuss the biosocial functions of marriages, weddings, and their associated customs and beliefs, I must describe the flower first. However, a serious problem stands in our way.

As with much sex research, the problem concerns partisanship. The connecting link between these customs and biosocial functionality resides, in part, in what Émile Durkheim (1915/1965) called the Sacred. And that word, by itself, is the problem. It seems virtually impossible to argue—as I will—that religious beliefs (more correctly, beliefs about the Sacred) have been profoundly functional in the biological sense without many, and perhaps most, readers erroneously believing that my argument represents polemic in *favor* of those religious beliefs.

Because the problem is so acute, I will illustrate it with an iconoclastic but serious suggestion concerning the relationship of religion and people's desire to marry. Perhaps the causal arrow is reversed when we say that religion causes us to marry. Perhaps we want to marry, and perhaps it has been biologically functional to marry, so that we therefore adopt, create, or believe in precisely those religions that tell us that we *should do so*. Perhaps religion does not act on *us* to tell us what to do and believe, but we create and adopt religious beliefs to represent and glorify what we already want.

Here, however, we come close to the ethnobiological notion that *Nature* causes certain forms of behavior to appear ready within us as instincts the moment we begin to act and think (to quote Bertrand Russell's definition once again; Chapter 2). Even Aquinas believed that marriage was the ''natural'' state for men and women, and saw God's hand in that Nature. In this ethnobiological view, religion, canon law, and ancient wisdon are all manifestations of a ''human Nature'' that causes men and women to be attracted to each other, and, once attracted, to seek to unify themselves in the public and religious ceremonial we call the wedding. In this, if there is anything Sacred in love or in weddings, then the Sacred is literally present as the living hand of the living God.

But, throughout, I have insisted that ethnobiology has no genuine explanatory power. The biosocial approach rejects the claim that Natural instincts are available to us at birth, as it likewise rejects the claim that Culture and its rules determine our behavior. And if the Nature/Culture dichotomy is false, there are not one-way arrows from Nature *to* Culture, or from Culture *to* Nature, but instead there are reciprocal relationships between biological realities and cultural forms that serve those functions.

In this and the next chapter, I argue that the institution of marriage has been functional in the biosocial sense and has simultaneously filled biological and cultural needs (if not always *personal* needs). Equally importantly, I argue that the ethnobiological concept itself of a human Nature that predisposes us to fall in love and marry has had biosocial functions. Regardless of the truth or falsity of ethnobiology, *it has been functional to believe it*. In fact, we must recall (Chapter 3) that biological functions can be met even when the individual does not know that such functions exist. In this sense, the Sacred has had immensely significant biosocial functions, which help explain why people *believe* they should marry.

But that argument is *not* the same as saying that I, the author of this book, "believe in" or espouse religious solutions to problems posed by sexual reproduction. My argument is not partisanship, but exposition: I seek to explain, in part, why people adopt and believe religious solutions to those problems. With that caution, I will turn to the Sacred.

Durkheim and the Concepts of the Sacred and the Profane

The Sacred is a complex concept. It is not a euphemism for various vaguely defined non-denominational aspects of religion nor does it express a vague apperception that some kind of "higher Power" operates in the universe. The concept is descriptive, not theological, and can be defined with empirical precision sociologically and ethnographically (Friedrich, 1978; Mauss, 1902–1903/1975; Leach, 1969; Lévi-Strauss, 1966). Above all, the word refers to what people believe, and not to what is "true."

Durkheim employed the concept to understand how non-Western peoples, like Australian aborigines, may lack the apparatus of formal religion and be without churches, formal worship, creeds, holy books, canon law, and priestly hierarchies, yet still believe that some things, events, and processes have power *transcending* the mere physical laws and appearances of the world. In Durkheim's sense, the Sacred is not associated with organized Western religious beliefs or with forms and ceremonials of worship. Accordingly, when one uses the term, one stands *outside* the belief system of the natives—Australians *or* Westerners—to say that something is "Sacred" when its *believers* attribute to it those transcendent powers and properties.

Thus, the Sacred is in no way a *personal* experience or sense of the Holy. It is not a synonym for the combination of fear, wonder, awe, reverence, and dread that mystics experience when they feel themselves near God. Nor is it a synonym for *holy, blessed*, or *sacramental*, terms that refer to specific parts of Western beliefs about formal, organized religion.

Instead, Durkheim recognized that people create cultural dichotomies for *everything* in their lives. One part, which he called the Profane—and which could be translated roughly as the Ordinary—refers to events and phenomena that are socially deemed commonplace and even banal. Though necessary to life, no vast or cosmic significance is socially attached to activities such as going to work or buying a newspaper. Durkheim saw that, for most people, life usually surrounds them with such things: the normal, run-of-the-mill, regular, predictable, and thoroughly unremarkable events of daily life.

Yet he also recognized that not all experience falls into the Profane. Sometimes, people believe that they are touched by something else, or it touches them, and the world seems transformed. For such things, processes, and events that stand outside the normal, Profane world, Durkheim used the term *Sacred*.

When personified, as in Western religion, the Sacred can become the Deity or Divine force that people sometimes believe acts in transcendence over the rules of the world of the here-and-now with immense and irresistible power. But not everyone who believes in Sacred power personifies it as a Deity nor associates it with religion. A strikingly accurate, if now clichéd, example occurs in George Lucas' *Star Wars*, where the Sacred is "the Force." But the concept involves much more than movie mysticism. Instead, for Durkheim, the Sacred is defined as being believed apart from the commonplace and, by being different from it, as special, rare, very powerful, potentially very dangerous, and, under usual circumstances, prohibited from our access.*

Sexuality and the Sacred

Because the Sacred is not defined by personal experience or by formal religious dogma, but only by what people believe about powers set aside from the Profane, Durkheim's analysis has an astonishing consequence for my argument, as the following quotation from his work illustrates. The Sacred is not the only theme in his words.

> Since the ideal of the sacred is always and everywhere separated from the idea of the profane in the thought of men, and since we picture a sort of logical chasm between the two, the mind irresistibly refuses to allow the two corresponding things [the sacred and the profane] to be confounded, or even to be put in contact with each other; for such a promiscuity or even too direct a contiguity, would contradict too violently the dissociation of these ideas in the mind. The sacred thing is *par excellence* that which the profane should not touch, and cannot touch with impunity. To be sure, this interdiction cannot go so far as to make all communication between the two worlds impossible; for if the profane could in no way enter into relations with the sacred, this latter could be good for nothing. But, in addition to the fact that this establishment of relations is always a delicate operation in itself, demanding great precautions and a more or less complicated initiation, it is quite impossible unless the profane is to lose its specific characteristics and become sacred after a fashion and to a certain degree itself. The two

---

*My definition depends not only on Durkheim, but also on Lévi-Strauss (1966), Mauss (1902–3/1975), Leach (1969), and above all Friedrich (1978). There are many other characterizations of the Sacred in anthropology. For example, Rappaport (1971) defined the Sacred as referring to " . . . the quality of unquestionable truthfulness imputed by the faithful to unverifiable propositions" (p. 29). Although Rappaport focuses on tests of the person's beliefs, whereas ultimately I am stressing how people behave in relation to the Sacred, our arguments nonethless converge to similar conclusions. I see no ultimate incompatibilites between the "structuralist-functionalist" approach of this chapter and the "cultural materialism" of writers like Rappaport or Harris (1968).

classes cannot even approach each other and keep their own nature at the same time. (Durkheim, 1915/1965, p. 55)

In a series of metaphors that range from *promiscuity* to the wonderfully Gallic phrase that the "establishment of relations is always a delicate operation," Durkheim has profoundly illuminated Western beliefs about *sexuality*. One need only read "male" for "profane," and "female" for "sacred," and an immense and complex equation appears: sexual relations between men and women *exactly* parallel the relation between the Sacred and the Profane, in exquisite detail. Indeed, the parallels are so precise that they will occupy the rest of the chapter.

Many—in fact, millions—of people believe that outside the normal, everyday world there is Something Else. In metaphors borrowed from Joseph Conrad's *Heart of Darkness* (1971), which is about precisely these powers, the lovers are led from their tranquil everyday lives to the uttermost ends of the earth, drawn by an immense power, alive with shimmering allure, able to command and create, which, be it hidden or open, they sometimes touch, and thereby are transformed. Or, perhaps *enchanted* or *entranced* is a better word. For them, the world changes under the touch of this immense Sacred power—for that is what they believe it is—and becomes special, and beautiful, for it centers on someone else, so very wonderful . . . and their friends shake their heads. "They're madly in love," they say. "Just crazy about each other."

The mystics express the same when they say that *God is love*, and, in English, words like *passion*, *rapture*, *ecstasy*, *transport*, and even *divine* are used only when speaking of erotic love or religion. These domains are deeply entangled in Western belief. And even if it startles someone who believes that an act is sacred only if devotional and liturgical forms of worship are associated with it, nonetheless sexuality meets the criteria for defining the Sacred. When Symons (1979) rather dryly said that sexual experience is largely adapted to the exceptional (p. 167), he expressed a similar thought: sexuality, religion, and the Sacred are *very* closely related.*

The parallels between sexuality and the Sacred go much deeper in Western belief than exaltation, transcendence, and exceptional emotionality. The conservative deeply believes that these two classes—one male and Profane, the other female and Sacred—cannot approach each other and retain their "natures." When people say that a man needs a "good woman" to set him straight, they believe that communication between these domains alters the participants, even if commonsense experience suggests otherwise. Likewise, it is often believed that "bad" (i.e., male) influences, like pornography, can permanently degrade a woman. Here too her "nature" has changed. And some people believe that when a man in a singles bar approaches a woman, it can only be for "promiscuous" reasons: he "wants only

---

*Since I am taking Durkheim's ideas only as they apply to sexuality, I do not need the full apparatus of Durkheimian thought, e.g., of collective representation. I strongly agree with Wallwork (1984, p. 61) that Durkheimian and Darwinian thought are compatible, and hope that my discussion provides some raw material towards the analysis of that compatibility.

one thing." Is it any wonder, then, that some men use their magical lines and gambits? In their minds, the "establishment of relations" may be a very delicate operation indeed! Throughout, the relationships between men and women are treated as if they were relationships between the Profane and the Sacred, and are surrounded with all the "complicated initiations" that Durkheim mentions.

There are also many who believe that *one cannot touch with impunity*: that sexual promiscuity, adolescent sexual activity, birth control, abortion, pornography, the breakdown in marital stability—what Stone (1979) called the collapse of all standards of honor—are but symptoms of an illicit contact and contiguity between things that must touch only with great care, with necessary and proper respect, and in a state of ritual purity or of exalted transcendence. For such people—and they number in the millions in the United States and Canada—it is no small matter to treat sexuality promiscuously. The Sacred must *remain* special, set apart, and, under usual circumstances, forbidden. The order of the cosmos is at stake:

> A native [Australian] thinker makes the penetrating comment that "All sacred things must have their place" . . . It could even be said that *being in their place is what makes them sacred* for if they were taken out of their place, even in thought, the entire order of the universe would be destroyed. Sacred objects therefore contribute to the maintenance of order in the universe by occupying the places allocated to them. (Lévi-Strauss, 1966, p. 10, reference deleted, italics added)

In this, we hear an echo of a more familiar belief: the woman's *place* is in the home. Westerners believe that something about women *is* Sacred, in precisely Durkheim's sense. It is treated as special, as set apart sexually from the Profane world of business and the men in it, very powerful in the abilities to allure, command, and even compel, and certainly prohibited from casual access.

Nor do the parallels between sexuality and the Sacred arise merely because organized religion has long treated sexuality as sinful. "Sexual sin" establishes a symbolic border between the domains of the Profane and the Sacred, a line of demarcation over which one crosses at vast "spiritual" risk. The theological apparatus of sexual sin marks, stresses, and displays the Sacred qualities of sex as set aside from the commonplace, but the relationship between sexuality and the Sacred is not *explained* by the idea of sin. Sometimes, as Durkheim said, the Sacred and the Profane must communicate, and the barriers of "sin" must be lowered. And, from the wedding ceremony itself, we can draw a far-reaching conclusion about Western sexual beliefs: only *sometimes* is sexuality veiled behind oblique language, sequestered to the privacy of people's intimate lives, or seen as necessarily representing moral decay and contiguity between domains best kept apart. At other times, it openly occupies its "properly allocated" place. Then, Westerners believe, contact with it removes us from the everyday world of the Profane towards an immense power that we feel surrounds and embeds us. Then, in Western beliefs, it becomes the most important channel and conduit to a Sacred domain wherein, in Western belief, exists the power to create life itself.

Transcendence to the Sacred: The Wedding

In the wedding and in the ceremonial union of bride and groom is enacted a vaster symbolic "communication" as Durkheim put it, between two domains that normally remain apart in Western thought. In the celebration of personal love and public ritual at the wedding, sexuality has become the basic metaphor for *how* this communication is achieved.

That night, when the couple has intercourse for the first time as husband and wife, sexuality will appear in its "properly allocated" place and time. Surrounded by ritual purity and ritual celebration, it will fill them with ecstasy, transport, and rapture, at least in belief. And, very possibly, she will become pregnant.

In that, we see the meaning of Durkheim's metaphors: *in belief*, the Sacred has reached down and life is conceived: Their newly licit, fertile sexuality connects them to the Sacred domains from which life comes. *It is that event—a purely biological one—that is deemed Sacred in Western tradition.* Sexuality is a *symbolically* Sacred channel to a Sacred domain.

Thus, the outwardly visible social, religious, and ceremonial aspects of the wedding—the white gown, the music, the flowers, the exchange of rings and vows—all serve, like the petals of a flower, to surround and embed the central core symbol: the act of sexual union which, in belief, *really* creates the marriage.*

Simultaneously, the outwardly visible acts of the wedding serve to render the couple's fertility socially licit and blessed. In the wedding, the couple becomes the central *icon* of a ceremonial process that, in belief, communicates between the Profane world of the here-and-now and the Sacred powers that, in belief, create life. Only through their sexuality do human beings—in belief—make licit contact with those Sacred powers and—in fact—make the mutual biological contact that ensures fertilization. Weddings celebrate that duality, one reason why the change from virginity to non-virginity has been so important. The change is simultaneously symbol and reality for how people reproduce. So *of course* Puck, Titania, and Oberon dance to bless the lovers' beds in *Midsummer-Night's Dream*! That is the function of such magical beings: not biosocially, but symbolically, to accentuate the Sacred time by their presence. In this, the Sacred has become the last layer of symbol and meaning woven outward from the biosocial interaction of the couple itself.†

---

*Thus, even in Catholicism, a wedding is not a marriage until it is consummated. Nor do we believe that couples marry "by stages": that if one has passed this stage—the engagement, say—then one is a "little more married" than before. Instead, we say that the couple is getting *closer* to marriage, a discrete event of all-or-nothing character. Consummated, it is marriage; unconsummated, it is not.

†These Sacred symbols and meanings are far more widespread than creed alone would predict, and occur even in highly secular weddings (Greenblat and Cottle, 1980). Anthropologists stress how marriage creates complex alliances between kin-groups and between the men who make the marital exchanges

On the Threshold

Liminality

Neither the bride nor the groom approaches the wedding casually. From the moment they decide to get married to the end of the honeymoon, they are in a special state of being. They are "in love," and are forgiven a variety of otherwise socially intolerable actions: for example, when they have "eyes only for each other," they are not accused of impoliteness. People smile warmly at them. They are also in a special state socially. Thus, they are no longer "really" single, and if either is dating other people while engaged, friends may well think that they are not at all "serious" about getting married. But even after the wedding, they are not yet "really" married until they settle down socially in their new home and with new relationships to people. For example, they will be expected, in the modern middle class of the United States, to form friendships primarily among similar couples (e.g., "Wedding bells are breaking up that old gang of mine"). Being in such a special social and psychological state marks and displays the new relationship between the couple and the rest of society, between each of them personally, and between them and the Sacred, that is, *external* powers that (in belief) create their fertility.

During the transition between being single and being married, the couple is neither here nor there—not yet fully married, but not really single. As yet, they are only on the threshold of their new life together. And *threshold* is not merely a reference to the tradition that the husband carried his new wife over the threshold: rather it refers to Victor Turner's (1967) term *liminal* (from *limen*, threshold in Latin) which he employed for the analysis of similar rites of passage among the Ndembu of Africa (pp. 93–111). When one is *liminal*, one stands *between* two kinds of life, each very different from the other.

Although the culminating event of the liminal period is the wedding ceremony itself, the Sacred symbolism begins to operate before the wedding. As it does, specific rituals accentuate the transition from the Profane to the Sacred.

Rites of Reversal

As the couple nears the wedding, their everyday world increasingly slips away. These changes are all *reversals* of the usual norms of behavior. For example, the groom's friends may ask, "Hey Jim, getting nervous? Heh, heh." The "heh-heh," or other lasciviously worded comment, begins to reverse the norms of oblique discourse among men. Now the groom's friends can openly tease him about the wedding night, or tell (endless) jokes about impotent, stupid, or over-eager grooms. As Gershon Legman (1968, 1975) argued, such jokes betray considerable male

(Lévi-Strauss, 1967; Bradburd, 1984; Kolenda, 1984). Without disputing the importance of these ideas, I want to point out that marriage and kinship have reproductive symbols and consequences as well (Fox, 1967, 1980).

anxiety about sex (reinforcing a conclusion drawn in Chapter 7), but socially they mark the change to the forthcoming Sacred time.

Like Carnival with its rites of reversals, the period before the wedding becomes a time of *license* for the groom and his friends. Nowhere is such ritual license more obvious than the "bachelor-party" the evening before the wedding. In tradition, though not necessarily in fact, his friends "treat" the groom to an evening of drunkenness, pornography, or even a visit to a prostitute. Now his sexuality is not only overt; in a sense it has become public property. But the groom's buddies, especially if they are young, think that's fine. "What the hell," they say, "you only do it once, right, Jim?"

The reaction of the bride-to-be also illustrates the ritual quality of these reversals. At *other* times, she might well be outraged and feel deeply rejected if friends of "her man" offered to get a prostitute for him (in actuality, or even if "only kidding"). But *now* the meanings have reversed: the bachelor-party symbolizes not fleshly sexuality or lust, but accentuates the immediately forthcoming transition to a *new* kind of life and sexuality. "It's your last chance," the groom's friends say, and he can only grin sheepishly.

In this, virtually all the proper-sex rules are reversed for the groom. Sex is now public, not private; discourse is open, not oblique; behavior is explicitly sexual, not covert; and even his sexual attraction to the bride is subject to teasing. "Can't wait, huh, Jim?" If, as is often true today, they have been more or less openly cohabiting, this comment does not make *literal* sense, but now he is *supposed* to be openly aroused by her.

By contrast, I have never heard a groom teased for *loving* the woman. Indeed, I suspect that *that* might produce immediate violence. In other words, love really *is* Sacred.

The reversals continue into the wedding itself. After the ceremony, other (married) men may tease the new husband: "Feeling henpecked yet?" In mock commiseration, other men extend sympathy: "You're an old married man now—how does it feel?" Or, most dramatically of all, a married man may say to the groom before the ceremony, "You'll survive it—look at us! We all did, didn't we!" And the other married men will laugh.

These reversals of normal male behavior have parallels in the reversals in the *bride's* liminal world. However, for her and her female friends, there is no sudden burst of explicit fleshly sexuality. In the Profane, female sexuality is already quite open (though Pure). Instead, female bridal liminality contains another, and qualitatively very different reversal: by considering her a virgin (real, imaginary, or technical), she is explicitly elevated towards the Sacred. In this, "virginity" has become symbolic, not anatomical: it stresses her Sacred purity, and is further emphasized by the groom's "impurity," that is, by his openly lustful sexuality.

Around her are now gathered the rich array of traditional symbols of feminine purity. They include her gown—no small matter!—flowers, food, gifts, and music, all of which, in a traditional wedding, *her* family will arrange (and pay for). If, on the one hand, the groom's tuxedo is rented (and subjects him to much teasing), then on the other, her gown will be carefully selected and kept for years afterward. She and her friends will look at gowns, finger the lace, select colors, discuss trains, veils, beading, ribbons, hair-styles, and headdress; they will select the bride's and her attendants' bouquets (and pick the men's boutonnières, much to the men's amusement and *pro forma* fidgeting and embarrassment); she and her mother will negotiate with caterers and rental agents for chairs, tables, glassware, and dishes; and, finally, spend endless hours constructing the bride's persona in a pageant that has to be "just right."

It all centers on something that is otherwise kept sequestered: an act of embodied intercourse between two people that is to be given profound *social* meaning. Thus, the wedding represents a great deal more than a public celebration of the couple's *personal* love. In its symbolic reversals piled on reversals, in its admixture of license and purity, and in its suspension of the usual rule that intercourse is symbolically private, the wedding suspends rules which normally prohibit communication between the Profane and the Sacred. The reversals say that a channel is now *open* between the Sacred and the Profane, where, before, it was closed, just as a channel of sexual communication is now licitly open between the man and woman themselves. In this, the personal sexual intercourse of the couple has *itself* become a symbol, this time of the *social* relationship believed to hold between *all* human beings and the Power that creates life. Through that new opening between domains otherwise kept separate, once again, in belief, life will be renewed in the ecstatic core symbol and act of intercourse that represents the center of the liminal period. And *that*, people believe, deserves celebration by all.*

An immense range of symbols, from personal to completely social, is distilled into the wedding. In them, symbol and meaning grow outward from a biologically functional core of reproduction to become fully psychological and fully social.

A Threshold Passed

After the wedding, liminality will slowly fade—as people say, "The honeymoon never lasts." Soon, he and she will return to the prosaic details of marriage and the day-in, day-out banal events of the Profane. Typically, sex also changes. It becomes routine and less frequent (James, 1981). The birth of the first child can briefly reinstate the Sacred, but sexuality is no longer transcendent. Indeed, it is now sequestered both socially *and* psychologically. It is not only private, but it no longer touches emotions as it once did. And since sex in now not "really" very arousing, they may feel that something is wrong. "The romance is gone," she says, and he

---

*The belief that sexuality connects people to Sacred spiritual power has parallels in Tantric and Chinese yoga (Anand, Fabri, and Kramrisch, 1962; Gross and Gross, 1983; Watts and Elisofon, 1971) as well as in ancient Roman art (Johns, 1982). Moreover, "Tantric" sexual beliefs have entered the modern United States as expressions for self-transcendence (Woods, 1981). They also enter the *Playboy* cartoon character Holistic Harry's blundering but rather endearing efforts to seduce women. These efforts to assimilate "Tantrism" to sexuality may arise from a desire to find a "mystical" framework for forms of sexuality that have hitherto lacked rituals except as cults (King, 1971).

replies, "Well, honey, I still love you." But eventually they agree that they've settled down now, and things have changed.*

But regardless of how, or even whether, such changes occur [for some couples they do not (Cuber and Harroff, 1965)], each nonetheless remembers the wedding. She remembers the gown, the flowers, getting the bridesmaids all together, the music, the processional. She occasionally will look at the photograph album, especially with female friends, and identify everyone present. She still has her gown, and when—on some special occasion—she asks girlfriends if they'd like to see it, *of course* they would. And once again its lace, veil, train, or just simple lines become important.

He hasn't forgotten either, even though now he "never remembers the anniversary." He recalls how Cousin John found a fishing pole someplace and tried to catch the angelfish in the aquarium at the reception; or how he and his buddies played touch football in their tuxedos two hours before the ceremony; or how he wore sneakers with his tuxedo—brand new and white, but still they were sneakers— or how one of the ushers wore one white and one black shoe, "One for the bride and one for the groom." (These are all real examples.)

Primarily, both remember their *own* role in the wedding, a Sacred time that still sends its tendrils, in memory, to touch and, ever so slightly, to transform them again. Under the sentiment and nostalgia, there still echoes back to them the *power* of the Something Else that they believed they symbolized the day they married.

Pure and Impure

Western beliefs about the sacredness of sexuality are not exhausted by the liminal exaltations of the wedding. We must not forget Durkheim's word *promiscuity*. The Sacred symbols of licitly fertile sexuality do not stand alone in this tapestry. Instead, they have mirror-image counterparts in a *second* form of sexuality, to which we often attach words like "sinful" or "perverted." To some readers, true marital love and adultery, say, have nothing "really" to do with each other. But symbolically they can exist *only* if they are defined together. Moreover, when we examine the symbols of this second form of sexuality, there soon appear the beliefs about Nature and Culture with which the book began. We shall see that the Nature/Nurture controversy is *not* independent of Western sexual symbolism, but is, instead, integral to those symbols themselves. Ethnobiology *itself* is part of this tapestry of symbols. To reach it, and to explore sexual symbols further for their own sake, I will begin with the lower—and darker—half of the tapestry.

Impure Sexuality

Now, sexuality has become symbolically dangerous and illicit, if no less Sacred, and we encounter acts and deeds that Western tradition considers improper

*The literature on so-called "marital sexual dysfunction" is by now quite large, but it often does not observe that socially it is *expected* that sexual urges and activities decline with marriage—and with age.

and maleficent: Adultery, illegitimacy, prostitution, perversion, sexual coercion. With these, we also encounter the proper-sex rules, but now they are more than rules of behavior. Now they embody an entire world view of how sexuality should be treated.

Durkheim's analysis of the Sacred has great power for illuminating the symbols of impropriety. His subtle metaphor for *illicit* relations between the Sacred and the Profane teaches us that for Westerners "sexual promiscuity" represents *unregulated* contact and contiguity and the Sacred. Now sexuality occurs without the properly ordained rituals, in improper places, or between symbolically inappropriate people. In one of Durkheim's central distinctions, it is not Pure but *Impure* (Durkheim, 1915/1965, pp. 56, 455ff; Douglas, 1966). The difference between them pertains to *how* sexuality connects us to the Sacred, and paradigmatically is represented by the difference between *love* and *lust*.

In this, people have vested Impure, "lustful," sexuality with an immense power to destroy. Thus, its occurrence outside of a marriage—once is enough!—can induce a total reorganization of the couple's relationship to each other, and their children, to the rest of society, and between them and the Sacred. Until recently in the United States (and elsewhere), adultery was the *one* generally acceptable ground for divorce (Wright, 1909, pp. 160–176). An act must be believed powerful indeed if but *one* occurrence can end a marriage legally, socially, emotionally, and theologically!

Accordingly, we see that Impure sexuality is as powerful, and thus as Sacred, as Pure sexuality (and, to reiterate, Sacred does not mean *holy* or *blessed*, but treated as set apart as special, powerful, and dangerous physically and spiritually). For millions of people, it has been deeply felt that the sexual allure of the "other woman" has the power to destroy a marriage.

We cannot explain these beliefs (and laws) by saying that an extramarital liaison means that the husband, say, no longer loves his wife, or that the marriage is in trouble (as, in fact, many people do say: Weis, 1980). This "explanation" leaves unanswered why sexuality is thought so important and so powerful in the first place. But, symbolically, the equation *is* clear: people believe that sexuality has immense power both to create *and* to destroy.

Moreover, no *individual* can set aside these meanings and simply re-define the Sacred out of existence. Though the husband may protest about a "casual" encounter—"Aw, honey, I was *drunk!*"—nonetheless, for her, he has been unfaithful and therefore no longer loves her (or loves her "the way he did"). In the reverse, if *she* has a "casual" encounter, it can be even worse, for men *also* believe that sexuality always has profound meaning. In this, sexuality is no longer a personal experience, its symbols subject to *personal* interpretation. These meanings are neither private nor idiosyncratic, and are quite unlike the symbols psychologists find in people's dreams, or the symbols an artist uses to communicate a personal and individual vision to an audience. Nor are they like the symbols the lovers themselves evolve for expressing their love, such as revisiting the restaurant that was so special. The symbols of Pure and Impure are *cultural*, not the whims and fantasies of an individual. They *cannot* be assigned purely personal meaning. Sometimes, new meanings can be added on —for example, the "liberated" idea that an affair can be "good" for a marriage (Weis, 1981)—but no individual can *replace* the socially derived and socially fixed set of oppositions represented by *love* and *lust*.

So, in this, the last layer of adornment of the courtship sequence, are *cultural* symbols that not only assign meaning to sexuality, but also lock it socially into place (its "properly allocated" place!) by saying not only where it *does* belong, but also where it does *not*. The symbols of the Pure and Impure are both central and powerful because, as Durkheim and Lévi-Strauss imply, they *stabilize* beliefs about sexual behavior around the two, irresistibly distinct poles of the Sacred.

White and Black, Plants and Animals

The symbols of Pure and Impure therefore have importance far beyond sexuality or marriage. Because the symbols of love and lust are mirror opposites, they have become affixed in Western belief to a much wider range of *other* symbolic oppositions.

For example, take *white* as a symbol of purity (as in the white wedding gown). Historically, we could use other colors—e.g., green for fickle sexual love and blue for fidelity, as Chaucer did (Ross, 1972, p. 44)—but in fact today *white* symbolizes purity. White seems connected to ideas of being clean, spotless, stainless, and immaculate, a word used to mean *sinless* in the peak Catholic symbol of sexual purity, the Immaculate Conception.* But white is defined culturally, not physically, as a symbol of purity: it is used *arbitrarily* to represent a licit connection to the Sacred, for example, in the association of *white* lilies with the Virgin Mary in Western art. Thus, as a symbol, white differs subtly from the belief that the couple at the wedding symbolizes a connection to the Sacred. For the first, we could in principle adopt any color whatsoever—or none at all. For the second, the couple as symbol or icon is not free to vary, at least so long as weddings exist to celebrate the licit creation of new life. As a symbol, white is *not* locked into the biosocial realities of reproduction.

But white *can* stand in symbolic opposition to *black*. Then, if white symbolizes purity, black can symbolize its precise opposite, sexual lasciviousness, as in sexy black lingerie. Again we encounter the symbolic opposition of love and lust. If Westerners believe that love is holy, blessed, and, at the wedding, a sacrament, then lust is believed unholy, sinful, and assuredly not sacramental. In belief, lust dwells not in the church or temple, but in brothels, sleazy meatrack pickup bars, or in the "back seat of the car." If love is seen as a spiritual, uplifting, transcendent, and exalting *emotion*, lust is not an emotion at all, but the fleshly and carnal satisfaction of physical *desire*. If love grows from the soul, heart, and mind, then lust grows

---

*In Latin, *macula* means *spot*, so that *immaculate* means "not spotted," or free of stain and, by symbolic extension, sinless. The same metaphor occurs when we speak of "dirty" words or of "filth" for pornography.

from the body and the genitals. It leads to "casual sex," or "mere physical coupling," rather than "true intimacy." The phrase "one-night stand" nicely captures the belief that lust is transient and is easily satisfied, utterly the opposite of the love that can create a life together in lifelong commitment.

This series of oppositions also includes contrasts concerning sexual motivation. Here too emerge mirror image opposites. In belief, Pure sexuality exists for the *highest* of reasons: love, passion, devotion, respect, admiration, deep affection. But, in belief, lust pulls on us through the *lowest* motives: lechery, the animal instincts, selfishness, and a desire for bodily pleasure. The woman asks "But will you *respect* me?" when the man urges her towards intercourse.

When a man and woman "fall in love," the phrase records the belief that love "just happens," that the "chemistry was good," or the "vibrations were right." It is "love at first sight" and, as I have been stressing throughout, is considered a *magical* experience.

But seductions are believed Impure. People speak of "putting the moves" on someone, of using lines and gambits, and, at the extreme, widely believe that the rapist *plans* to overpower his victim for his sexual purposes. Now, none of these oppositions need be true to reality or even precisely expressed in people's ideas. Yet it is still understood that the Pure and Impure pull in opposite directions.

Thus, like *right* and *left*, *hot* and *cold*, *up* and *down*, the Pure and Impure are defined not by any absolute properties that inhere in them, but *solely by their opposition to each other*. So, the beliefs I have been discussing are not merely clichés, assembled at random and transmitted higgledy-piggledy generation after generation. Rather, behind them is a profoundly important *logical* process: that of opposition, of *A* and not-*A*. In fact, this process of logical and symbolic opposition is the mechanism, so to speak, whereby these symbols grow. The point is not whether individuals believe in these dichotomies. Rather, the crux is that they *represent social oppositions which orbit the two poles of the Sacred*.

This principle, which comes from symbolic and structuralist anthropology (e.g., Lévi-Strauss, 1966), is not always obvious. Thus, one might naively think that *right* and *left* exist in themselves as well as being opposites. Yet they do not. If human beings had only one hand and arm, it would be neither right *nor* left, except in comparison to an existing standard of oppositeness. So it is with sexual symbols. For example, *leers* and *ogles* belong to the Impure, but in the Pure, looking becomes *gazing lovingly*. In the Pure, the pregnant woman is "expecting" (or, more strongly, "expecting the blessed event"), but, in the Impure, she is "knocked up."

Thus, not only does virtually every aspect of sexuality have symbolic meaning, but these symbols all come in pairs in Western beliefs. For every Pure symbol, there is a mirror image symbol in the Impure. Moreover, every emotional valency reverses symbolic tone and meaning when we move back and forth between the Pure and Impure. In brief, the symbol system is *dual*: it has a top and a bottom, mirroring each other while simultaneously reversing every emotional and symbolic meaning.

And nowhere are these reversals more important than when they pertain to the crucial opposition between Male and Female. In this system of belief, Male and

Female are not defined biologically or even socioculturally, but, instead, solely by their opposition to each other. Now, themes that have appeared previously suddenly coalesce into a single family of symbolic oppositions. Male sexuality represents the Impure in its aggressive, fleshly, overeager lust. The *reality* of men's lives is now no longer an issue: the myth of the aggressive male is part of this system of belief, and, even if we know *factually* that men do not fit this image, in belief, men are the symbolic opposites of women.

For example, we recall the myth of feminine passivity, reluctance, and hesitation. Unlike male sexuality, female sexuality is Pure. When she struggles against his lust, he seeks to drag her down to "his level"—to the gutter, in degradation, shame, ruination, guilt, and despair. But it is *not* merely melodrama. Hardly! When Mead spoke of the girl playing a game she can always lose, we see not real men and women, but the *symbols* of this system enacting a symbolic struggle between High and Low, Good and Bad, Spiritual and Carnal. In brief, the backdrop for the social scientific functionalist interpretations of male and female sexuality (Chapter 5) is Western belief in Pure and Impure sexuality, in which ineluctable war exists between men and women as *representatives* of Impurity and Purity.*

And yet in this system even the Pure can be corrupted. The woman falls; she is no longer the vessel of Purity she once was. In her now open sexuality, she has power to equal men, and more, for now she is seen as the sultry temptress in whose hands men become putty, and who traps them with her wiles. To parallel this reversal, her colors are no longer white. Now they are black and scarlet, as in a "scarlet woman" or the "scarlet letter" of adultery.

In the Pure, the woman is treated as the guardian of morality who teaches virtue in the sanctity of the home. But in the Impure, it is the opposite. Now, she is the vamp who destroys marriages rather than creating intimacy. She is the witch, who copulates with Satan. From her come not blessings, but disease and damnation: syphilis, and the shame of having a "social disease."[†]

And, at least for some people, she lives today. In his fashionable and depressing book *The Culture of Narcissism*, Christopher Lasch (1979) expresses great concern over how men and women relate. For Lasch, the source of sexual troubles is not hard to find:

> Women today ask for two things in their relations with men: sexual satisfaction and tenderness. Whether separately or in combination, both demands seem to convey to many males the same message: that women are voracious, insatiable.

---

*In *Religion as a Cultural System*, Geertz (1966/1973) describes a similar symbolic war between the Balinese mythical beings Barong and Rangda. They too are male and female and between them too is ineluctable war (pp. 114–119).

[†]These beliefs form a major problem for organizations that offer VD counselling, testing, and treatment. They *must* offer anonymity, for otherwise people do *not* readily present themselves for treatment. But few people are happy to admit that their sexuality is "impure," and the shame induced by this belief system prevents them from seeking help.

Why should men respond in this fashion to demands that reason tells have obvious legitimacy? Rational arguments notoriously falter in the face of unconscious anxieties: women's sexual demands terrify men because they reverberate at such deep layers of the masculine mind, calling up early fantasies of a possessive, suffocating, devouring and castrating mother. The persistence of such fantasies in later life intensifies and brings into the open the secret terror that has always been an important part of the male image of womanhood. The strength of these pre-Oedipal fantasies, in the narcissistic type of personality, makes it likely that men will approach women with hopelessly divided feelings, dependent and demanding in their fixation on the breast but terrified of the vagina which threatens to eat them alive; of the legs which popular imagination endows the American heroine, legs which can presumably strangle or scissor victims to death; of the dangerous, phallic breast itself, encased in unyielding armor, which in unconscious terror more nearly resembles an implement of destruction than a source of nourishment. The sexually voracious female . . . has emerged into the daylight of literary respectability. Similarly, the cruel, destructive, domineering woman, *la belle dame sans merci*, has moved from the periphery of literature and the other arts to a position close to the center. Formerly a source of delicious titillation, of sadomasochistic gratification tinged with terrifying fascination, she now inspires unambiguous loathing and dread. Heartless, domineering, burning . . . she unmans every man who falls under her spell. . . . Child or woman, wife or mother, this female cuts men to ribbons and swallows them whole. She travels accompanied by eunuchs, by damaged men suffering from nameless wounds. . . . (Lasch, 1979, pp. 344–345)

Even if, like me, the reader does not share Lasch's vision of woman as devoid of humanity, all-devouring, and mercilessly evil, we nonetheless sense the power underlying his description. Arising from whatever sources it has in Lasch's beliefs or experiences, or from neo-Freudian theory, in these images of horror, the woman is *no longer in her place.* She has crept upwards from the deepest strata of men's fears into reality, from fantasy to daylight. The symbolic barriers that separate the two parts of the tapestry have been breached and, from the lower, darker side, *things* are creeping upward to devour men, castrate them, suffocate them. Below a thin veneer of Freudianism, Lasch has expressed male hatred for women in the images of the myth of the Impure.

It is an old hatred. In the late Middle Ages, medieval Churchmen expressed very similar views of women: woman is " . . . the confusion of man, an insatiable beast, a continuous anxiety, an incessant warfare, a daily ruin, a house of tempest" (Tuchman, 1978, p. 211). From whatever *immediate* sources it has, in rejection, bitterness, disappointment, frustration, this misogynist's view of women wends its way back in history, its rhetoric nearly unchanged, to a medieval indictment of women and their sexuality: their "lascivious and carnal provocation" (Tuchman, 1978, p. 211; Michelet, 1939). In these symbols, psychosis seems to lurk near the surface—and they are the same psychoses that can lead to rape and, perhaps, witchcraft trials (see Sabbah, 1984, for a brilliant feminist analysis of similar, deeply misogynist mythologies in Muslim belief).

So, as we near the Sacred center of the Impure, mere melodrama fades. In its place now stands a female who touches on domains of *immense* power. We see her in the commanding figure of the Queen of the Night in Mozart's *The Magic Flute*. In Conrad's *Heart of Darkness* (1971), she is the woman who shrieks in despair when her lover Kurtz is taken from her as he is dying, and about whom, in part, Kurtz utters his last words: "The horror, the horror" (p. 71). Soon, she is no longer Aphrodite the Golden, but is Kali, the Goddess of Death, who wears men's bloody, severed heads on her girdle (Mookerjee and Khanna, 1977, pp. 75–78; plate III, p. 83; Adams, 1980).

It is perhaps the most profound reversal of all. In the Pure, the woman's sexuality is treated as bringing new life, conceived in licit and sacramental connection to the Sacred. But in the Impure, the woman has herself *become* Death.

And soon we see that symbols of Nature also adorn this tapestry of belief. The Pure woman lives in a symbolic world of flowers and plants. In the cliché, a shy woman is a *wallflower*, but floral symbols for feminine purity are quite extensive. In her girlhood, a woman's sexuality *blooms*, *buds*, or *ripens*, phrases never used for a boy's adolescence. When the bride has flowers in her train and carries a bouquet, the groom's boutonnière has nothing of the magical importance of her symbols: when she tosses her bouquet, people say that the woman who catches it will be the next to marry. We can even say that "God plants the seed" when she becomes pregnant. In English and American tradition, women, not men, have flower names like Rose, Iris, Violet, or Lily.* And, again, we recall that the lily belongs to Mary, the Virgin Mother of God.

But *men's* sexual nature is never treated as Pure. Therefore, men's symbols are the opposite of the peaceful world of flowers. Men are *animals*, *beasts*, or even *brutes* (as in the wonderful phrase of melodrama, "Unhand me, you brute!"). Male sexuality is "animalistic" (and never "floral," so that it is an insult to call a man by a flower name, e.g., *pansy*). The sexually active man is a *wolf*, a *bull in a china shop*, or an *old goat*. The horned, animalistic visage of the Devil appears before us.

And we believe that when the man nears the Sacred, he too changes after a fashion: sometimes his "true nature" is revealed—and it is Impure. He has become the precise opposite of the innocent woman he seeks to ravish or rape. Again, the hostile images of "animalistic masculinity" arise.

Yet I stress that these symbols of Pure and Impure are defined *only* because they are opposites of each other, and not because male and female sexuality are *actually* "animal" or "floral." An elegant example of these reversals occurs when a woman enters the domain of the Impure. Then she no longer has flower symbols, but, instead, *also* becomes an animal. She is *foxy*, or a *vixen*, a sex-*kitten*, a *bitch*, or even a *pig* or a *dog*. Words like *chick* also assimilate female sexuality to animal— that is, Impure—symbols when it seems overly accessible. (There is an implication for rape trials: if the woman victim can be made to appear Impure—e.g., that she did not resist—then she was not "raped." Such defense maneuverings have no basis in truth, but *do* have their roots in this set of symbols.)

*My mother's tradition was German Lutheran; her name was Hazel.

Now she is "hot" or like an "animal in heat," or has "the morals of an alley cat." Her genitals are "pussy," in symbolic, if often unprintable, correspondence to his "cock." Symbolically, the Impure woman is like a *man*, and has taken on his symbols as well as attributes (thus, she is *forward* or *wanton*, like men in this myth).

Two practical conclusions now follow within the logic of this symbol system. One is that women who are "like" men in non-sexual ways—e.g., they are "working girls" or "career women" rather than "staying home with the children"—are deemed similar to men in *sexual* ways. For example, some men consider them as sexually available, or potentially so, even when they are not.

Secondly, pornography is deemed dangerous to society and morality not merely because it "panders" openly to "male lust," but also because it depicts female sexuality as symbolically similar to men's: open, lustful, and animalistic. Pornography therefore *degrades* women from their status as Pure (see Penrod and Linz, 1984), perhaps one reason why anti-pornography feminists can ally themselves with ultra-conservative proponents of censorship of pornography (Duggan, 1984; Drakeford and Hamm, 1973).

In these symbols, we see Nature in a different light. In this myth, women are Naturally or instinctively Pure, like the "natural" purity of their symbol, the flower. but they can be degraded from their Natural Purity, and then they take on the symbols of an equally "natural" or "instinctive" male Impurity. They become animals. But, by contrast, men's sexual Natures (or "instincts") are never Pure. They want "only one thing," and to elevate them towards purity, connubial fidelity, or even holiness requires that they either forswear sexuality completely or be reformed by a woman's "good offices" and "moral nurture." In brief, women Naturally have a Culture that is elevating and uplifting, while equally Naturally, men's Culture is oriented to the lower bodily pleasures.

So, "naturally" enough, women's sexuality, when Pure, is procreative and untainted by "bodily lust." Likewise, men's sexuality is "naturally" animalistic and requires restraint by women lest it break loose in rape, ruination, and rampage. And when women become contaminated by men—e.g., when they enter the spheres of male economic power—then in this symbol system they too become Impure. Now, in images worthy of Hieronymos Bosch, the woman becomes deadly, for she—*She*—is evil, utterly dangerous, and, of course, *irresistible*.

. . . Nature and Culture . . .

It all reminds one of something else. It is an astonishingly small step to the social scientist's ethnobiological theories of sex. Thus, a woman is instinctively averse to the crudities of male language (Jespersen, 1922). Her normal mode of sexual discourse is "silence" (Sanders and Robinson, 1979). She is attuned to the "cautions of her body" and therefore resists sex (Mead, 1949). She is reluctant, and fears intercourse and pregnancy. In these social scientific writings, woman is Pure, so that from her feminine Nature flows all that is moral and good in Culture—as Georg Simmel said in 1911 (1984).

But in the Impure, Nature is masculine. So of course men want, equally instinctively, to have intercourse and impregnate as many women as possible (Bell, 1966, Barash, 1979). Open sexual discourse is the man's domain (Sanders and Robinson, 1979; Lakoff, 1973; Kutner and Brogan, 1974), even if the opposite is true *in fact*. In bull sessions, men's sexual natures act to socialize one another towards aggressive sexuality (Korman and Leslie, 1982), and in their patriarchies, men seek to control and use female sexuality as they wish (Greenspan, 1983). In brief, from Impure natural masculinity flows all that is immoral and bad in our Culture.

And if the reader now asks if *I* believe this system, the answer is *No, but many scholars certainly seem to*, for this is the Nature/Culture dichotomy with which Chapter 1 began. We have come full circle. But now we see that dichotomy in its own, proper place: not as a statement about the relative importance of social and biological processes in shaping human sexual behavior, nor as reasonably true descriptions of men and women, but as part of Western *mythology* about the Sacred and about the Pure and Impure.

"Nature is irresistible"—*if* it acts, and most social scientists want to deny that it does. In that Nature, the Genes watch and whisper, and men become rapists and murderers. It is no longer Russell's gently philosophical image of a Nature that gives us ways to perceive a world of Pure ideas. Instead, it is the Nature with which the ethologists sought to explain evil in men, and which, paradoxically, social scientists still fear to find below the thin surface of Culture. When those social scientists deny that there exists a universalizing, uniform Nature, we see in their denial the same dread and terror that appeared in Lasch's bitter images: the "nature" that the social scientists deny is not biology, but an old myth of natural and innate evil.

Social scientific models of sexual development follow the same mythology. Before birth, the baby dwells under the Pure influences of its Mother, and is therefore asexual (Table 2.1 in Chilman, 1983, taken from Gagnon and Simon, 1973). Then it is born, and slowly acquires the scripts and beliefs that will make it a member of its Culture. But below Culture, these social scientists fear that ever-watchful, ever-selfish Genes *do* urge the male to desire women for their flesh. Against him, and under the exalted emotions of the Pure, the female learns to resist, as *her* Natural cautions urge.

Torn to the core, these beings grow, struggle with their instincts and Genes, and acquire a "veneer" of civilization, as Freud put it. Then, incomplete and distorted, they seek each other, to heal the violences that created them [as described by Shoham (1983) and by Dinnerstein (1976)]. The only force that Westerners believe can connect them is "Love," in whose hands this polarity is neutralized as, once more, the two people merge and a channel appears to the immense Sacred powers from which life itself comes—or so the West has believed for centuries.

Is it any wonder that single people seek "love"? Or that for the conservative, the breakdown of "sexual morality" signals a profound falling out of place of things that should not—*must not*—touch and mingle promiscuously? It is any wonder that abortion is called "murder"? Or that marriage is deemed so vitally important? Given this system of beliefs, the answers are *No, it is no wonder at all.*

And, given this ancient system, is it any wonder that *biology*—which, in this mythology, represents the source of profound danger—must be kept away from the social sciences? Is it any wonder that social scientists deny that biology has any "place" for studying human affairs? Is it even *possible* in this mythology that the biologist's vision of Nature as a magnificent web of evolved and evolving life be called anything except "biological determinism" and "reductionism"?

Of course not. In this mythology, communication between the domains of Nature and Culture is "promiscuity" and, unless sanctioned by the Sacred itself, will lead only to the creeping upward of *things* that are utterly evil and utterly irresistible. And so, in seemingly endless and eternal cycles of mythical belief, the story repeats again and again over history, ever orbiting the two poles of the Sacred. There we see Nature and Culture, Purity and Impurity, the symbolic opposites which, even today, still form the basis of our scientific beliefs about sexuality.

. . . and the Instincts

With this, we return to the instincts. In this belief system, they exist to carry forward the Divine and Sacred plan whereby reproduction is ensured. But they are also *much* more. In belief, the woman's "instincts" regulate access to the *Sacred* by regulating man's access to her *body* (explaining why Mead spoke of the "natural" cautions of the woman's body). But this vision of instinct is not Freud's or Lasch's dark picture of anti-social sexual forces lurking below: the "female instincts" are socially Pure.

In belief, the woman "instinctively" seeks to prevent the misuse of the sexual channels to the Sacred, but her "instincts" are not innately anti-sexual or simply sexually reluctant. Sometimes those channels must be open, as we learn from an essay written by Charles Lamb ("Elia," 1775–1834). He is talking of the father's reluctance to see his daughter leave home and marry. But *mothers* are less reluctant:

Mothers, besides, have a trembling foresight, which paints the inconveniences (impossible to be conceived in the same degree by the other parent) of a life of forlorn celibacy, which the refusal of a tolerable match may entail upon their child. Mothers' instinct is a surer guide here than the cold reasonings of a father on such a topic. To this instinct may be imputed, and by it alone may be excused, the unbeseeming artifices by which some wives push on the matrimonial projects of their daughters, which the husband, however approving, shall entertain with comparative indifference. A little shamelessness on this head is pardonable. With this explanation, forwardness becomes a grace, and maternal importunity receives the name of a virtue. ("The Wedding," p. 210; Lamb, 1935)

This passage reveals a crucial logical link in the argument. The smart-sex rules—to use the modern term for what Lamb is discussing—have been believed both virtuous *and* instinctive in women.

Independent of the truth of that belief, it contains a profound reversal. When the mother's "instinct" to push forward the matrimonial projects of her daughter triumphs over the "cold reasonings" of the father, feminine and Pure Nature—that is, the Sacred—triumphs over the male Profane in the marriage ceremonial. Symbolically, the smart sex rules are the vehicle of this triumphant reversal. At the wedding and in all it symbolizes in this tapestry of beliefs, Female has become greater and more powerful than Male. [It may be one reason why men are said to be so reluctant to marry: perhaps some men sense these powers and resist them as they also resist other female powers (Chapter 7).]

It is the precise opposite of Muslim myth, which denies the fatherhood of God, thereby to see women as intrinsically Impure (Sabbah, 1984). But, for the Christian West, in the birth of the child Who is the Child is the final metaphor for every theme discussed so far: the elevation of *women*, not men, into the instinctive source of Purity. Pure, the woman is the source of morality and, in the myth of the Virgin Birth, the source of God's grace and redemption. As at the wedding itself, which recapitulates the entire myth system, the bride in Pure white shines forth, as she does in this tapestry of myth and belief: *God's* Love is embodied in the birth of the Saviour from a woman one starry night in Bethlehem long ago. Impure, she is a being of Hell, the source of evil and the cause of the Fall. She is the mother of *sinful* men. In this, sexuality and its biological consequences have become elevated into symbols fully Sacred in all senses Durkheimian and theological.

And neither anti-clericism nor, in my case, a non-Christian and strongly feminist upbringing should blind us to the immense power that this myth has had in Western history. It is, today, the source of much anti-sexual feeling and is, I strongly suggest, the root of some, if not all, conservative antipathy to sexual equality, sexual liberalism, and, in biology, to evolution. And yet, once again, a caution is needed. Even to characterize this mythology brings the risk that some readers may believe that *I* espouse this system in its repressive and newly threatening forms. I do not. But I insist that we must *understand* this system, for it has placed the woman's reproductive generativity to the center. In Western belief, especially devout religious belief, *everything* else comes after that.

The Rhythm of Life

The Sacred Fades

No one can live his or her whole life so close to the Sacred power of these symbols. Indeed, even in the life of the lovers, the Profane soon reappears, in a pattern that is as widely believed standard and normal as the lovers' exaltations are believed inevitable.

As the years pass and as love loses its power, people find themselves "working" at their marriage or relationship. The word tells us as clearly as could be that now marriage is thought to belong to the same Profane world in which dwell salesmen negotiating the price of aluminum with a client or stockbrokers working out a contract with lawyers and stock-exchange officials. Lust too passes, both as memories of premarital single life fade and as marital sexuality changes. Physical needs seem easily gratified. As the years pass, the lovers feel "tied down" or even "trapped" in a marriage. Nothing in the Profane has the power of the Sacred.

Now they have become sober, hard-working people, clad in drab business tones, gray, blue, brown. At home, they "share the chores," and it becomes routine, monotonous, boring—*Was it all worth it?* they wonder. Even the children, who once were anticipated with great excitement and love, have become a bit of a nuisance: "It's a real bother trying to keep up with them all the time." They're in school now, and the parents wonder if they'll be able to send them to college easily, or if they are going to come out all right in their jobs.

Perhaps they have a clandestine affair, even though, as is appropriate for illicit dealings with the Sacred, they keep these matters secret. But usually the Profane hardly ever touches sexuality. It is avoided, and now *they* are the people who avert their eyes when they see the lovers. They speak obliquely and sequester sexuality from open display. Now the woman is described by what she does—a housewife, a career woman, a writer. He becomes a job title more than a person—"Oh, Jim is manager now."

They see themselves passing the stages through which adults pass: anticipation of success, some advancements and promotions, then stability and perhaps even a dead-end in their careers. With more than a little anxiety, she wonders what it will be like when the children are gone—"The empty nest syndrome, they call it," she says to her friends. They nod; they've been thinking about it too.

Or perhaps she too has her job and career, which she went back to after her children were able to take care of themselves. It's been a long time, though, and she's not so sure of herself. In fact, they both worry about money; it's not so much fun anymore to be poor, like they were when they were younger.

They see the children beginning to grow up and realize that they themselves are getting older. The boy isn't so little anymore, and he's becoming interested in girls. The girl is also growing, and soon she'll have boyfriends. And then the kids will be in college or starting out on their first jobs.

By now, love and familiarity, and a shared life together have all moved the parents very far from the early days of their sexual enthusiasm and what *they* thought was excess. "That stuff is for the younger kids," they say, oddly happy that they no longer feel so sexually aroused by each other, and perhaps even by anyone.

In these changes, we see how this system functions *symbolically*. The sequence from the exalted liminality of the wedding through a return to the Profane represents a social norm for life, a cultural idealization of the biological life cycle against which people judge their normality and success (Levinson et al., 1978; Cuber and Harroff, 1965; Blumstein and Schwartz, 1983). The Profane maps the course of life from youthful love and courtship to marriage, parenthood, career, and finally old age, with only a brief interlude of contact with the Sacred.

In this system, the Sacred and Profane are *balanced*, one never overwhelming the other for too long. Sexuality, with its perceived powers to reorganize life, has been governed, not repressed. Indeed, it cannot be repressed, because without it, we die off (as has happened to Utopian communities: Nordhoff, 1875/1966). Yet, if sexuality has its "place" in marriage, ultimately it is seen as only one form of communication in what is called a "good marriage." Originally, if sexuality represented love, then, as control shifts back to the Profane, companionship, respect, responsiblity, and appreciation become equally, or more, important. Even if people believe that they fall in love for reasons ranging from utterly fascinated romance through convenience and accommodation to economic reality, yet many also believe that *mature* love finally should be a compound of sexuality and friendliness, of the Sacred and the Profane.

And when a marriage does not "work," we still use this idealized sequence and description to explain why it failed. An affair, especially if discovered, represents not only an improper return of lust, but also an *imbalance* which we believe spells trouble, either by creating it or as a symptom of it (Weis, 1980). "Something is wrong in that marriage," people say, "where there's smoke there's fire." These beliefs are much more than moralities: they contain the Western belief that sexuality is centrally important, that its governance is essential, and that *out* of place it is dangerous.

In the distinction between the Sacred and the Profane, and between Pure and Impure, the Westerner believes that the social universe is kept in order, its emotional and behavioral parts in their proper and allocated places. Throughout, Nature and Culture are balanced against each other. In the Pure, feminine Nature is balanced against masculine Culture, in the one-to-one relationship we call marriage. The feminine Pure is balanced against the masculine Impure: as she resists him sexually, her Nature struggles against his, and as she tries to reform him, her Culture struggles against his. As she succeeds with time, his becomes the world of the Profane and hers the Sacred. Between them is a barrier, not so much of miscommunication but much higher and much stronger. Their worlds are now literally different, and the places they occupy in the tapestry of what once was love are no longer together at the center, but at the periphery where they stand, static and balanced in symmetry, each upholding what this system says men and women should uphold.

In this system, life and birth continue, provided that *women* carry the burden of the Sacred. As long as they transmit the Pure to their daughters, then, in belief, all is well. But if the woman falters, falls, changes, the system falls with her. Then the balances of symbolic meanings shift, and once again evil incarnate can creep upwards. *Everything* focuses on the woman: at no matter what cost to her personally, this system requires that she—and all women—shelter men not only from the *biological* realities, but also from the *symbolic* dangers of sexual menace and impurity. *She* is the central icon, and in her white gown, the bride stands forth not as a person but as a *symbol*.

With her the process continues. When, one day, one of the children decides to marry, once again the everyday world of the Profane will vanish, slowly to be replaced by the rituals and ceremonials of the wedding which, like all ritual, functions sociologically to assure that everything is kept in its proper and Sacred place. Then the children, being part of this tapestry of belief also, experience the immense shimmering allure of the Sacred. They know, in their ever new intimacy, that the other is special, and rare, and wonderful, and that they can't live without each other. In these feelings, the lovers replicate and repeat what their parents and parent's parents felt, at least in ideal. Then, in one biological act, they too will reproduce, and this system will once again adorn their embodied sexual intercourse with the meanings the myth of the Sacred provides. And people will say that once again life has been *created*, as it has been in the past and will be in the future. As long as the dance of the Sacred and Profane continues, then life too will continue, or so people will assure each other. Then, everything will be in its place—its properly allocated place. The tapestry is safe.

Or is it?

Chapter 9

Unraveling

Some years ago, a new phenomenon entered Western history. *Its* name is science. In the name of that science, we have slowly pulverized this ancient and sometimes very beautiful mythology of the Sacred. Despite the adherence of individual scientists to that mythology, from science has nonetheless come the theory of evolution, in which the interplay of necessity with its iron laws of existence and chance produce new forms of life, not Divine creative will; endocrinological and embryological understanding of fertilization and conception as the union of gametes produced under hormonal control, not the mystery and sacrament of conception and birth; endocrinological and behavioral understanding of the estrous and menstrual cycles in female mammals and of the role of hormones and neurophysiology in establishing sexual anatomy and behavior, not the potent and generative Sacred force called *love*; sure and unobtrusive methods of birth control, which depend on biology and chemistry, not faith; effective, inexpensive, fast, and safe methods of abortion; an understanding of human sexuality, both male and female, that overthrows the idea of female passivity; and immense technologies that have irreversibly brought women by the millions out of the once Sacred home into the outside world.

We have, at every point and place, disconnected this myth of the Sacred, disarticulated its elements, and by subjecting them to the kind of scrutiny called *objective*, contradicted them. Our effect has been immense. Without malice, but irresistibly, we have reached the heart of Western belief—the connection that we have long believed holds between the creation and procreation of life and the Sacred—and have said *No, it is not that way.*

In this, the sexual revolution is only an epiphenomenon growing on the rubble of an old mythology. It represents the collision of an old, stable culture with a newer philosophy that has grown from science and from its unrivaled power to explain, predict, and control natural events. Far deeper than the singles scene, which came to epitomize the sexual revolution, are changes in what we believe about the place of humanity in the universe. Science has taught the West, and soon the world, that sometimes believing a myth does *not* make it so. If conception is a matter of germ cell fusion, not Divine creative will; if embryonic development occurs according to the rules of biochemistry and genetics, not by the infusion of mystical essences that shape us irresistibly, universally, and without exception; if genes are not secretly whispering embodiments of Divine or Natural will, but are merely sequences of nucleotides in DNA that encode protein structure; if we are all descendants of organisms that once dwelt in the ancient oceans, rather than being created in fixed permanence; if all these, then we have said, over and again, what Galileo also said: *E pur se muove—it still moves.* Regardless of symbol, myth, and belief, nature moves according to laws we can understand and, by understanding, control.

Like the Copernican revolution, which long ago deprived us of the glory of being the center of the universe and set the sun in our place, the biological revolution deprived us of being the center of God's creation, around which all other living things circle in lesser splendor. What Darwin taught was not merely that species change according to the conditions of their existence. His message was deeper, and, in a way, simpler. From Darwinian thought, we understand that *all* living organisms are connected to each other, not by invisible threads of Divine Thought set forth in fixed exemplar of Divine Plan, but by chemically real connections: the self-reproducing biochemical engines that we call *cells,* in which the storage and transmission mechanism is, with equal reality, composed of nucleic acids, like *deoxyribonucleic acid,* DNA itself. In this, biology replaced species fixity, and the vision of life as eternally ordained and unchanging *state,* with a new idea: that life is *process,* in constant flux over years that slowly become millenia and reach back, in unbroken line of genetic continuity, to the beginning itself. Biology is teaching the world that life is *not* built, in virtually architectural solidity, on a plan that rises from Low to High, from microorganisms through mere animals to culmination in something born from Biology, but above it, Culture. Biology has said that we *too* are living organisms, special only unto ourselves, but not subject to transcendent and immaterial laws.

For two and more centuries of cool, objective, and ever-renewed interest, biology has looked also at the origins of life in embryonic development. It has taught the world that development is *not* the unfolding of a fixed plan that takes the embryo from formlessness to Mind, through stages that recapitulate, in microcosm, the Divinely ordained scale of life from low to high. Biology has said that development is *not* a set of fixed states, each entering when called, leaving when its time is done, to be replaced by new, higher states, each in their turn. Instead, development too is *process,* in which the universal capacity of living cells to adapt, change, and alter themselves is everything. When the brain develops, it develops from the same fertilized egg that also produces kidney cells, muscle cells, bone cells: development is *differentiation,* not fixity produced by an unalterable Natural will.

And, in cool, objective analysis, biology found ways to prevent conception. In that step, it severed the ancient link so deeply believed to hold between life and the Sacred. Biology has said to the world that life does not arise only when, with the full power of Its Omniscience, a Sacred and Divine Will ordains. Instead, it gave to millions of women a power that equals that Divine omniscience: the power to control *when and if life is created.*

The Biosocial Function of the Sacred

And some—they also number in the millions—hate us for creating that power. They hate us for depriving them of their seat of imagined glory at the peak and pinnacle of God's creation. They hate us for intruding into the Sacred places, and for destroying a world that is, for them, the *only* world.

For them, and for millions before them, this system *has* been functional, in its own fashion. It has made reproduction a Divine, not merely earthly, blessing. By affixing reproduction to the Sacred and by making the woman's reproductive potential its central icon, this system *protected* reproductive relationships from reformers, tinkerers, and the simply idiosyncratic individuals who would alter them, perhaps to the reproductive worse. This system has removed women from *non*-reproductive labor, for example, the back-breaking work of farming or, later, of factory work. It is said that in ideal such is *not* the woman's place. She is too Sacred for such things, and her role as mother is too important to waste her on work that mere *men* could perform.

To be sure, this system of belief did not free all women from all work. Economically, that would simply have been impossible. Few women and girls on farms or, later, in working families, could sit idly by and let the produce rot, the fabric decay, the wool grow moth-eaten and useless. But in this division of labor is also a reproductive fact: women have been historically physically close enough to the offspring they have borne to feed them, wash them, clothe them—in a phrase, to keep an eye on them. In this system, the woman's place *has* been the home, a place protected by an immense system of symbolic meaning that *has* served biosocial functions.

It has also given women immense power in the Profane: the power and privilege of making food, raising the young, caring for the ill. If the kitchen is the woman's domain, then in it have developed some purely female traditions of recipes that *in fact* contain vitamin C, the needed amino acids, the trace minerals, the substances without which—and without knowing why—we simply die.

To be sure, some readers will hear in these comments my *own* exaltation of a traditional system that has deeply oppressed women. But I am not exalting this system in its symbols or its division of labor. I am simply saying that it *worked:* that it functioned biosocially to bring children into the world, to keep them alive, to feed and clothe them (and everyone else), and at least to minimize the effects of disease. And if this system is not ideal by modern *liberated* standards, the explanation is simple: this system did not grow from such standards, but, instead, in the English-speaking tradition, developed fully somewhere around the time of the Puritans (Karlen, 1971; Stone, 1979). It is based primarily on hand-labor, and on pre-industrial science and technology.

In it, there were no steam-driven machines to weave or to forge metal. There was no immense power grid to distribute electricity to run refrigerators, lights, washing machines. It had no chemical industry to mass-produce baby bottles, first of glass and then of plastic, or to manufacture rubber nipples by the millions (Bullough, 1980). It contained no baby formulas bought powdered and added to the purified water of a modern city. For millions of men and women alike, there were no schools that offered careers alternative to farming, light manufacture, and a life at home. Vitamin C was not available at the corner drugstore, for there was not only no corner drugstore, but no chemical industry to manufacture vitamin C by the ton. In *those* days, vitamin C came from fruits and other plants, and one ate them or died.

It was not Utopia, but, instead, a time of hard, backbreaking work that was necessary for life to continue. In those days, it was not simply *belief* to say that sex was dangerous, or that silly mythologies "repressed" sexuality. Without antibiotics, childbirth infections could be fatal, and a "difficult" birth was not resolved by life-saving devices of a modern hospital. For women, the biological and medical costs and risks of sexuality have been very high. Yet the continuation of life itself depended on women becoming pregnant, as it does today.

And from this inescapable intertwining of great risk with absolute need there arose, I suggest, the beliefs that I am calling the mythology of the Sacred: a belief that through conception human beings touch an immense Divine force that acts to give life and to take it away as It, not we, ordains. If people have surrounded their lives with that protective incantation and therefore hope, then *that* was the original biosocial function of the Sacred, and, in its time, it contributed to survival and reproduction both. I will *not* look back, from a time grown fat with industrial miracles, and call them fools, or custodians of oppressive beliefs, or poor illiterate peasants. Even if they—men and women both—have vanished namelessly into history, nonetheless they integrated their economic, cultural, and biological lives into a single system, and protected and sanctioned it by what they believed—and millions of people still believe—is Sacred power (Rappaport, 1971; Tiger, 1979, pp. 39–80; Leaf, 1974).

Yet those days are irretrievably gone, swept away by winds of change that have altered everything on the face of the earth. And to those who yearn for the old days of what they believe was a higher morality, I say that birth control, abortion, and new forms of sexual behavior are irreversibly part of *our* life. To destroy them it would be necessary to destroy the libraries themselves, in which the words of science are recorded for all to read, in a new burning of the Alexandrian library that would leave the world dead in radioactive chaos. We cannot *ever* return to the old days, because, *for us,* the terrors and powers of nature have been reduced steadily by a biological science that has simultaneously pulverized the mythologies that accompanied the old ways of birth, life, and death, while creating their new solutions.

And, yet, millions hate us for unraveling the old mythologies. They see in science some benefits, but far more they see menace: the danger that if left uncontrolled, science will continue to unravel old ways of life, to leave nothing in their place but disorder, disruption, dissolution—in a word, all that comes from trafficking with the Impure.

Biosocial Reality

In the midst of the collapse of the mythology of the Sacred, and in the virtually complete alteration of its technological, economic, and biological bases, we have a chance to test a theory—the idea that human behavior is purely, totally, and completely a matter of social and cultural process, and that biology is irrelevant. It is a curious test, for it uses beliefs about Culture and Nature, as they exist in the social sciences, to predict what happens when Culture collapses, de-structured by the immense changes wrought over two centuries of history.

There is no question of what that prediction must be: without Culture—the guiding principles of human behavior itself—there can only be chaos. In this view, nothing else anchors our existence. Without Culture, we are condemned to drift aimlessly in a world of higgledy piggledy. It is, of course, the Apocalyptic vision, but this time it comes from the logic of the social scientist's claim that humans depend totally and absolutely on Culture for *everything*.

And I submit that the changes history has produced in the myth of Sacred sexuality qualify it for this test: these changes have been profound. Should we not, then, see men falling in love with turtles and women marrying ferns? Should we not see rape admixed with love, and violence and vandalism in the wedding service? As things heretofore kept apart by cultural rules have entered into promiscuous and unregulated contact, should we not expect chaos as the myths, symbols, beliefs, institutions, customs, traditions, and norms all vanish?

Now, the moralist sees precisely these changes in the world. Yet I submit that the moralist is wrong and that this prediction is false.

It is the heart of the matter. Despite this unraveling, people are still meeting, touching, looking, falling in love, eventually to marry or not, and to have children. Even if social scientists see myth, belief, culture, learning, and socialization as central to our behavior, and as causing it, in the unraveling of the myth of the Sacred, the old cultural tapestry simply no longer shapes and informs our beliefs and behavior as it once did. And, to the millions of North Americans for whom the sexual revolution is only destruction, no new beliefs have replaced the old ways.

Yet people still meet, look, touch, synchronize, fall in love. Something has *not* changed under the unraveling: the biosocial core has remained relatively immune to drastic shifts in our sexual habits, and immune to beliefs that see those shifts as chaos. To be sure, the unraveling has not been complete, as it was for people who systematically have been victimized by forces they could not resist [such as the Ik of Africa (Turnbull, 1972)]. Parts of the old system remain. But they remain as disconnected fragments of a once integrated system.

These historical changes have affected us all, and no one escapes them. Indeed, they are central to the litany of tragic loss and failure one hears in the singles scene. In them, the moralist's prediction of death, doom, and destruction seems well met. But, still, it is not so.

Despite these changes in how people meet and court, the fragments of old beliefs are being re-woven. Now, however, as is appropriate to a new time in history, the tapestry contains new elements: contraception is *integral* to sexuality today, and so is abortion, even if it touches an immense sadness and fury. Changes in women's economic status are integrally part of the newer technologies, for the office, and therefore our economy, cannot operate without the women who run the word-processing machines, the copiers, the computer terminals (the importance of this change cannot be overestimated: it involves not hundreds of women in top-level executive jobs, but *millions* of women who work). It is economically impossible to reverse these changes and send women by their millions back to their "places" at home.

And, as women enter the job market in numbers unprecedented even in the late 1950s, they bring with them new ideologies of autonomy, freedom, and sexual choice. These women have rejected the old beliefs that made their sexuality so Sacred that it had to remain sequestered behind the curtains of their homes, or tied to modes of house care that depended primarily on physical labor. But they have not become promiscuous, as the moralist fears must be the consequence of setting into unregulated contiguity things that must remain apart.

In search polygamy, we do *not* have random sexual coupling whose only aim and purpose is the "transient gratification of lust." Instead, it represents a search for love that is translated into *personal* behavior, and—when appropriate under the smart sex rules—into open proceptive interest in men. In this, old traditions—perhaps Medieval in origin, or even Roman—have been rediscovered and reinvented by millions of women. And proceptivity *still* functions biosocially to create sexual and emotional intimacy, just as it did between Belissant and Amile in the Old French poem, or between Valeria and Sulla.

It is not the destruction of marriage that we see in the increase in premarital intercourse. As has happened at other times in Western history, once again there has been a shift in *when* it is deemed right and proper for the community to celebrate intimacy. Increasingly, as that time shifts, premarital intercourse has become *licit*. Search polygamy has not obliterated intimacy: it *serves* that search. And in that intimacy, couples still bond and create new life.

These historical changes began over two centuries ago, as science slowly began to erode the myth of the Sacred. Yet it has not *destroyed* the symbols, to leave nothing in their stead. As the biosocial bases of courtship and love have shifted, and, particularly, as contraception severed the biologically once inescapable connection between intercourse and pregnancy, the symbols are *also* shifting. If the old ways have gone, it is because the biological and economic bases of those ways no longer exist. They are being replaced by new biological and economic relationships between men and women, and, with that, new symbols.

The Social Sciences as Mythology

Even if my "test" of the prediction of chaos is rhetorically overstated, nonetheless the point is made: something has anchored these changes from drifting *too* far from their reproductively functional center. In the old days, that something became a Something, a personal God who reached down and gently corrected the wandering path of human life. But now, as the myth of the Sacred weakens, we are less prone to see the hand of a personally Beneficient God in everything that happens. Yet something remains: still people meet, look, touch, feel close, and eventually make love, for that is how life is created—not through contact with a marvelous and immense Sacred power, but *biologically.*

And if we no longer see the Sacred in such things, then we must turn towards science. It is the fork in the road with which I began, and, once again, not everyone will want to follow it, for it represents a crisis for the social sciences.

When the social scientific critic of biology denies that processes of "biological origin" influence or shape human sexual behavior, he or she stands firmly *in* this tapestry to affirm that what is *really* important about sexuality—its emotions, exaltations, and capacities to bond people into families and marriages—derive from the Pure, not from Impure fleshly urges that upwell from below. Social scientific rejection of biology is not based on an historical analysis of *ethno*biology and the myth of the Sacred, or of how sexuality left socially unregulated can sometimes reorganize people's personal and social affiliations, or how the mythology of the Sacred served to minimize the perceived threat of such disruption.

When certain social scientists deny biology a "place" in explaining human behavior, they are not saying that *ethno*biology is false. *I* am saying that, not the social scientists whose intention is to *rid* the study of human behavior of biology altogether. For them, biology is Impure, and therefore always dangerous. In this, social science still accepts the belief that human behavior and life orbit the same two poles of the Sacred that we, in our traditions, believe are universal. Nor have the social sciences criticized and rejected the existence of impulses or urges per se; such concepts tacitly enter theories of motivation, intentionality, attribution, and causation, though in more scientific form. Theirs has been no examination of how biology creates and regulates behavioral and physiological variation. Nor is it that *some* social scientists have merely incorporated parts of the myth of the Sacred into their theories, as anachronistic and ultimately unimportant decoration. The myth of the Pure and Impure is central to social scientific thought, for the social sciences have accepted the *dichotomy* that underlies that mythology. In the social sciences, sexuality therefore still appears as a conflict between High and Low, Soul and Body, in a phrase, Culture and Nature.

For example, when Simon and Gagnon relegate nature to mute oblivion, they not only are expressing the mythology of the Sacred, but also the hope that sexuality shall remain Pure, untainted by biology, the flesh, or the crude materiality of this world. They *want* sexuality to be only words and sociosexual drama. When Jessie

Bernard dismisses behavioral communication as protocommunication of the kind existing between a dog and his master, she *wants* sexual communication to transcend fleshly signals and meanings (Bernard, 1972b, pp. 97–110). When Mead spoke of the young woman heeding the cautions of her body, she hoped that the Pure Nature of women equips them to resist Impure male sexuality.

Proudly embedded in the mythology they wish to study, all too many social scientists cannot see how deeply *they* believe in a division of things into Sacred and Profane, Pure and Impure. And it then follows, by the logic of this mythology itself, that they *must* deny a place to biology in shaping or influencing human behavior. To be sure, there is a cliché in the social sciences that "Biology and culture are both important," but like the Medieval scholars who believed that God and Satan were both "important," they too ignore the side which, for them, symbolizes Evil.

So it only sounds paradoxical that social science rejects biology as universalist and accepts the mythology that makes it so. The intent is to purify human behavior of what is believed universally powerful: the Impure. To attempt anything else is to violate our own symbol system and, as Durkheim expressed it, to put into promiscuous contact things that must remain apart. In brief, the Sacred is that which the Profane should not touch, and cannot touch with impunity. Human behavior is still Sacred and Pure in the social sciences, and there is—literally—no place for biology, just as love and lust have no place together.

And yet I argue that social scientists must ultimately reject this mythology as providing neither a sure theoretical nor empirical guide to understanding. At the end, there *is* reason to believe that biology is centrally important.

The Social and Biological Sciences in Crisis

Throughout the behavior of the lovers, we have been able to track the operation of profoundly biological processes. In the presumptive neurophysiology of male and female templates; in the fascinations of the courtship sequence with its looks, touches, and synchronization; in the careful decisions women make about men's attentiveness and responsiveness, and in their caution about too quick intercourse; in men's emotionally charged, if sometimes too private, reactions to women; in the myths of the Sacred, that make the newly fertile couple the central symbol of an immense web of belief; in all these, we see behavior ultimately rooted in ideas and customs that are *not* free to vary infinitely this way or that, but are anchored in the inescapable biological fact that human beings reproduce sexually. The fact is *not* trivial in its implications, as I hope I have shown. It touches us directly and indirectly in far more ways than we would believe if one assumes, with the social sciences, that biology is far away from our daily dramas and problems.

In fact, the contrary is true. No living being can "escape" biology to live totally in a world of Pure ideas: even philosophers must eat and, if there are to be more philosophers, reproduce. Throughout, and for many reasons, the social sciences have de-valued the activities that maintain life, to see idea and belief as *intrinsically* more important and real than our daily bread or the problems of raising children. For the social scientist, the *center* of humanity is not in these things themselves but, as Simon and Gagnon imply, in *talk* about them. But for only the social scientist is "talk about sex" more important than its immensely real consequences and effects on our lives.

In this, the social sciences run a profound risk. By alienating themselves from the "conditions of life" (the phrase is Darwin's) they can drift, as did Greek and Medieval philosophy, to irrelevance and mere scholasticism. They can argue about angels dancing on pinheads and—conveniently—forget that pins are made and used by people for real purposes in a real world. Matters of immense practical importance can dwindle to mere metaphor as social scientists leisurely debate their hypotheses about this, that, or the other "psychosexual drama."

These problems focus in metaphors that make human behavior the mere mechanical enactment of "programs" (or "scripts") that are installed from outside, as if the red and white beads we met in Chapter 1 were nothing but little computers designed by the forces of Nature solely for the purpose of enacting Cultural programs. And I object to these metaphors because I do not believe that they are true. To return once more to Denis Diderot, writing in 1782, matter—and, in particular, *living* matter—is self-moving, self-generating, self-developing. Diderot knew, and all modern biology confirms it, that living organisms are alive not because something *external* to them breathed life into them, but because they are alive all by themselves. They have the felts, hammers, strings of life, and their structure *itself* confers life. As such, they crawl about that way and this, like our amoebas, until finally they became human: aware of themselves but still able to react, respond, and shape themselves and their environments in complexities that far transcend the simple image of a bored programmer feeding cards into an otherwise dead computer.

It is the point that the social sciences have missed in their search for the disembodied Purity of ideas. By virtue of *being* alive, humans have characteristics which they share with *all* living beings and which have been the subject matter of the biological sciences. Even if I dislike the too ant-like accumulation of data which sometimes characterizes biology, we cannot deny that collectively the biological sciences have totally changed our perceptions of the world—and the realities which have, for millenia, been seen as immutable and inevitable.

The question is solely whether or not the social sciences will abandon their search for the Pure—in metaphor, abandon their position in the tapestry of belief I have been discussing—and understand that human beings are *part* of life, with all the attributes attached thereto.

But biologists themselves, including sociobiologists, have not always helped. First, the density of biological writing—both in its prose and in its sheer volume—can pose impenetrable thickets to outsiders, so that one must work very hard to extract the fruits of biological labor. Second, biological theory is subtle—there is nothing *really* simple about the Darwinian idea of function. Third, sociobiology is itself a new field, and is still deeply entangled in myths that seem self-evident (or

Natural) to its practitioners. Familiar with how genes encode the amino acid structure of proteins, the sociobiologist can leap to saying that genes "encode" behavior, thereby failing to understand how complex the sequence is between genes and *human* behavior. With that, the sociobiologist abandons biology to enter the mythical domains of ethnobiology, with no very good consequences for either the clarity of the argument or its applicability to human affairs. Unduly complex in its theories, sociobiology runs the risk of becoming just another form of genetic determinism, locked into a mythology that is all the more difficult to detect for its involved jargon, seeming genetic sophistication, and authoritative tone. Yet, beneath these bristles of a scientific appearance, sociobiologists have not rid themselves of an unquestioning acceptance of ethnobiological myth as biological truth. Given that social scientists are *already* suspicious of biology, no good purpose is served when sociobiologists seem to say (and sometimes actually *do* say) that biology and genetics produce the deathmask of fixity social scientists so fear about biology.

But the fourth problem is perhaps the most serious. For all that biology as a discipline has immense power and capacity for synthesis, it is also increasingly prey to the opposite tendency. It is easy for modern biologists to see living organisms as collections of organic wheels, cogs, gears, and levers, and to see the purpose of the biological sciences as describing those wheels and gears in endless detail. In part, this tendency is technological in origin, and represents the technical power of devices like electron microscopes and ultracentrifuges, which permit the biologist to visualize extremely minute details of cells. This tendency has been called "reductionist," but I suggest that the term is inappropriate. Rather, this tendency is *mechanicalizing,* not because biologists use machinery (like electron microscopes) but because they think that organisms *are* machines, nothing more.

The problem is that the metaphor grows beyond its proper limits. Once again, the idea of fixity lurks in the background. To be sure, the wheels and cogs move (that is, they change positions with time), but their movements occur in pre-fixed ways, like an electric clock that displays the changing minutes and seconds. For example, when we hear the phrase "behavioral repertoire," we might imagine a list of all the actions the organism performs and the conditions which elicit them, and believe that the list is sufficient to understand behavior. Throw in a function or two, and the story seems complete.

But I submit that it is not—and again we reach the biosocial approach. When the biologist applies these methods and modes of understanding to *human* behavior—as the sociobiologists often do—the results are often too *thin.* The well-intentioned biologist tries to assign human behavior to categories like "altruism," but the *meaning* of altruism vanishes. For example, religious altruism seems to defy any *simple* explanation in the mechanicalizing principles I just mentioned. Indeed, the simple genetic calculus with which *biologists* are familiar is inadequate to deal with much human behavior, be it religious altruism or love. To the biologist, the fact— or my assertion of it as fact—may suggest only that such behavior patterns are *not* biological at all (here, they would agree with the social scientists). But I suggest, instead, that animal, plant, and microbial biology must be supplemented by *human* biology if we are to understand such things. And, above all, human biology is a biology that creates *meaning*. This is no time for mysticism, but, instead, I want to raise a challenge to biology akin to the challenge to the social sciences above: what material, concrete, and real biological processes operate in human social symbolic behavior?

The biologist will not find the question easy, just as understanding the biology of multicellular organisms—jellyfish, for example—cannot easily be derived from knowing only how single cell organisms live. If new principles of biology arose when life passed from one- to multi-celled organisms, still newer biological principles arose when certain primates evolved the capacities to talk, make tools, hunt and gather in groups, and to *make love* rather than merely *copulate*. And the challenge to the biologists is this: can they abandon the mechanicalizing desire to see all life as wheels and cogs, and understand the biosocial bases of how meaning is created and changed in the course of our lives (Dobzhansky, 1967)?

And, O Biologists, do not sneeringly and condescendingly say you are not interested in the "meaning of life" and similar questions! The challenge to your science is not in such problems. It is in explaining how an organism can evolve the ability to ask such questions *in the first place*.

Then, together with a social science grown less antipathetic to biology, we might begin to understand the human condition. Am I being too optimistic? Perhaps so. But I still hope that a genuinely biological social science can develop before those who *hate* us for unraveling their world decide to bring it down in radioactive chaos.

And, to the social sciences, the importance of biology is that it does not produce fixity or stasis, but is itself the source of variation, change, and diversity. To ignore this fact will be the end of the social sciences, for if they continue to believe that biology is fixity and permanence—which are only metaphors for Death—then they will not see that people do not stand, fixedly and stupidly, when their lives change.

Reweaving

The changes wrought by contraception, abortion, evolutionary theory, feminism, and worldwide technologies have been immense. But no *living* organism stands still, fixedly and stupidly. Instead, people change and, in so doing, create *new* beliefs, customs, and ways of behaving.

In the last analysis, the tapestry of love *is* being re-woven. But it is not because a kindly Someone has reached down, gently to return us to the appointed path. That is simply a child's hope that its parents will fix everything. Instead, we—human beings by the millions—are re-weaving our *own* cultures, beliefs, and symbols. And when we do so, it is because we are biological beings, and because that is how biology works: to cause living beings to respond, to adapt, and, sometimes, to re-weave. It is not through the infusion of mystical essences that we do so, nor because mysterious life-forces animate otherwise inanimate matter. We do so because that is how living beings are constructed anatomically, physiologically, and, in human beings, neurophysiologically.

What biology teaches is that the capacity to be human derives from our neurophysiology, our anatomy, our development, and from the genes—simply regions of nucleotides in DNA, nothing more!—that regulate development. These living systems *cause* change. That the social sciences must understand, for these are the processes that make our behavior biologically functional, rather than being random, pointless squirmings or the eyes of death staring at us from dead pickled organisms in jars. Thus—'' . . . and immediately, as soon as we saw each other, we took a step towards each other. We just knew . . . '' In a man's template for a woman, a physically real and embodied process creates his immediate fascination. His reaction exists *within* his neurophysiology and biology. But human beings are not rats: also embodied in our neurophysiology is the capacity to conjoin the biology of the template to the cultural meanings given to it.

Thus, he *himself* connects template and love, rather than love arising from Outside to enter him in a moment that, once, could only be understood as Sacred. The template and symbols *coexist* in a man's mind, and the cultural symbols of love are *not* disembodied beliefs that float free in a world of Pure Ideas. Likewise, when she meets the man who embodies her own ideas of how a man should look, act, and respond to her, *her* behavioral communication with him also coexists with the meanings she believes such communication should have. Again, *she* connects behavior and love in neurophysiological processes that conjoin proceptivity and symbol, rather than love arising from Outside.

From the inescapable fact that people must meet, court in one way or another, become sexually intimate, and have children, have grown symbols and traditions which function biosocially to provide *meanings* for the templated and proceptive behavior of men and women. In turn such behavior grows from our highly evolved neurophysiological capacities to interact mutually and, in synchronization with each other, to alter our behavior in response to our partner's.

But the loop closes. As we respond to each other, immediately the symbols appear. Immediately, for millions of Westerners, the word *love* comes to mind. And from it, the symbols and traditions of a life together appear. These symbols do not arise from Outside, but from within, as, today as in history, the quite real and thoroughly embodied biology of thought creates behavior and, seizing upon it, once again builds symbols to surround the reproductive union of men and women.

And, for humans, symbols are essential. Human biology and culture are not different, ranked one below the other, as in the myth of the Sacred *or* in the ethnobiology of the social sciences. Biologically, we have no choice but to create meaning for our actions, and to decorate and adorn them with metaphors, ceremonials, rituals, and even institutions. So the symbols of sexuality cannot vanish, not totally. And they have not: the tapestry *is* being re-woven.

The changes in the last two centuries have not been chaos, but *bricolage:* the *reconstruction* of culture from fragments of old beliefs, new experiences, and still newer philosophies. And reconstruction means not only rebuilding, but also *re-construing*. New definitions appear to replace old ones, new relationships between behavior and belief emerge, new forms of behavior are woven into old traditional institutions, like the wedding.

From feminist writers, especially poets, are coming a new poetry and mythology of women. In them, pride and autonomy are central, as woman's "place" and "nature" are redefined. In place of the Virgin, whose virginity was passive and whose womb only the vessel and receptacle in which the Word of God took form as His Son, are autonomous women whose spirituality *transcends* the old definitions of gender (Ochs, 1977).

From the once most classic and austere of the sciences, physics, has come a new scientific romanticism. From the indeterminism of sub-atomic particles arises a world of mircroscopic uncertainty. New particles proliferate with names whose very romanticism testifies to the human desire to create symbols: quarks, taken from James Joyce; properties of quarks called *charm, beauty, color;* and, at the very smallest, a quantum world of worm-holes through space, supergravity, neutrinos that can tunnel out of black holes, and virtual particles whose reality is so unobservable that they are called ghosts. It matters not one bit if such things are "real." The romantic spirit is in full swing in physics: Creation according to Genesis has been re-interpreted as the Big Bang with which the universe—according to the physicists—began many billions of years ago.

These newer mythologies do not *solely* come from the data of science, if they come from them at all. At least as much their source is imagination, newly unbounded and unfettered from the austere equations of the older physics and theologies. It is as if the ugly determinism of macroscopic physics—in the reality of atomic weapons, for example—is being replaced by a colorful, charming, beautiful world of entities that can be uncertain, unsure, and, therefore, free. Their domain of existence is very much in the world of exact and delightful *truth* that Russell found at the end of logic's way.

The human capacity for metaphor is endless, and so too is our ability to give human names and therefore human meaning to Nature itself. The myths *are* being rewoven, even the most intimate of them.

If, once, the white wedding gown symbolized sexual purity and virginity, now it can symbolize the woman's love itself, regardless of *when* their relationship was consummated. If, once, her flowers stood in symbolic relationship to religion, now they can symbolize fruition and loveliness, and sensuous pleasure in their blooms, their fragrances, their colors. If, for some people, singles bars are sleazy meatracks, still, for many men and women, they are warm, familiar places to meet friends and even potential mates, and have come to replace, in part, the now-vanishing older forms of community. If, in the past, proceptivity has seldom been recognized by men (or by social scientists), today it is a visible and accepted part of courtship. If, once, premarital intercourse was restricted to one's future spouse, now it increasingly is part of people's search for a spouse. And, if, in the old days, cohabitation was *living in sin,* now it is a final stage of courtship itself and publicly signals two people's experimental test of the intensity and strength of their bond.

In these changes a new tapestry of beliefs in being woven. Yet, it still centers on a biological core: the conceptive union of two people and their capacity for reproduction. The biosocial core, experienced as love and enacted in courtship, has remained.

So, if the story of our lovers is an old and ever romantic tale, it is not because the traditions of romance have always been the same. They have not. Instead, the tale of our lovers is a *true* story. And if, today, their story is quite visible and quite real to the objective observer, so too it was equally real thoughout history, simply because its truth is not *merely* symbolic.

At the core is biology: the biology of reproduction, of thought, *and* of symbol. It is a unity, not a war between Pure and Impure. In this, biology and culture are the *same*: they, like love itself, are but aspects of the living human organism, which, be it here now or elsewhere in time, place, or history, has always *constructed* culture moment-by-moment in the living neurophysiology of the brain. As it does, behavior, meaning, *and* symbol are constructed simultaneously. Then, in one other person, these processes focus. It is said that the eyes of love see differently, and so they do: not magically, but biologically, in processes of immense but ultimately understandable complexity. And, as long as they do, these processes—and human life—shall continue.

Appendix

The Art and Science of People Watching: Observations in the Neoclassical and Realist Modes

Science begins with observation, and with questions of how to draw inferences from observations. It is a highly visual skill, and takes time and patience to learn, especially given people's strong feelings about love, courtship, and even bars. The following comments elaborate on observational distinctions and problems that would hardly trouble the layperson, who usually focuses on emotions, and that *never* trouble the "amateur expert," those people who think (often wrongly) that they "know all about" male–female interactions. Such people believe that they already know how to see and understand behavior.

Yet, at times, we are like the man who drives along, worried about his job, say, ignoring the faint pocketa-queep noises the car is making. Then, when the engine stops with particularly emphatic grinding sounds in the middle of traffic, he says, "Oh, I didn't think that was so important." We often miss crucial details. Since people's needs for intimacy are *at least* as important as surviving in traffic, I will explain how and what we observe when watching men and women interact.

Above all, I argue that science and aesthetics have deep connections, and that, know it or not, when one chooses how to observe, one selects among several recognizable *types* of aesthetic. Now, to many people, scientists included, science deals with "truth" and "evidence," while aesthetics deals with "art" and "pretty things," categories that seem mutually irrelevant. Yet, aesthetic choices control not only how one sees behavior, but also how one interprets and gives meaning to the events in the world around us.

Visions in the Expert Mode

To observe is an active process. It only seems as if we passively receive sense impressions through the eyes or ears like a videocamera or tape recorder. But a long history of aesthetics—the study of graphic art, theater, and other fine arts—teaches us that observation is always active. To see is simultaneously and actively to *create* meaning (Nelson, 1977).

The Amateur Vision

Initially, sense perceptions are quite similar from person to person. The image of a woman, say, formed by the lens of the eye on the retina will be similar for most people who look in her direction. It is what happens *next* that differs from person to person: the raw retinal image is processed by the brain in very different ways. One man sees her as simply there. Another man sees her as fascinating, and suddenly she stands out dramatically (i.e., she fits his internal template of a woman). A third man sees her only as having a certain hair color, but not as overwhelmingly attractive.

In turn, each of these men will describe her differently, for each stresses these second-order perceptions as "real." They might even argue genially about "who is right." For these men, determining what is "true" is a matter of "opinion." "It all depends on your viewpoint," they will say, and have another beer. "Beauty is in the eye of the beholder." And, for them, it is.

This way of seeing and reacting is a kind of perceptual democracy in which no one is more "right" than anyone else. Truth is deemed to reside in *collective* opinion, for these men see no contradiction between one man's "truth" that she is beautiful and another man's "truth" that she is "just all right." The purpose of this process of social and collective negotiation of what is real is *not* to determine the "truth," however defined, but to validate each person's opinion in the others' eyes.

Thus, the layperson *sees* courtship, in the sense that its events have impinged physically on the retina of the eye. But, next, each person creates an *individual* version of what "really" happened. And, again, by a principle of perceptual democracy that allows them to accept contradictory descriptions, they say, "It all depends on your viewpoint."

The Expert Vision

Nonetheless, the expert knows that truth is not opinion, even collectively and democratically legitimated. The expert also understands that this process has two faces. One is the perception-reaction-construal process itself. In it, the participants—the men I have been describing or even the lovers themselves—perceive and then reconcile contradictory perceptions. They actively construe the world, and therefore construct their own realities (see George Kelly's essay on tragedy, "Hostility," 1969).*

However, independently of such construals, a second process resides in what

*I thank Dr. A. R. Allgeier for bringing Kelly's ideas to my attention.

is happening "objectively" during courtship. This process *is* accessible to video-camera or tape-recorder. Imagine a videotape of two cars, one in the left-hand lane, and another coming up quickly on the right. Watching that tape, the expert observer may well see that the right-hand car is swerving too quickly and may therefore foretell danger, even if the *driver* in the left lane does not. To the expert, the perception-reaction-construal process *as it occurs in the driver of the left-hand car* is not the whole truth at all, no matter how strongly that driver is convinced that the accident "came out of the blue."

Thus, the expert understands that the accident occurred not only because the driver on the right swerved, forcing the left-hand car off the road. The accident *also* occurred because the driver of the left-hand car construed the visual events in his or her world—in specific, the image of the other car coming up in the rear-view mirror—as *not* signaling future danger. In this, the expert sees *differently* than the participant. The expert's *own* perception-reaction-construal process focuses on different parts of the reality and interprets ("construes") them differently than does the lay participant.

While observing courtship, the expert also sees differently. Events ignored by the lovers or by laypeople watching them take on considerable importance. And these events are important even if the lovers (or other people) ignore them, and even if the layperson thinks "It's all a matter of opinion" how important a touch is, or argues that his *own* opinion is "as good as" the expert's.

So, it follows that to observe expertly requires a different *kind* of visual perception and attention than that of the layperson. Yet even experts and scientists have very different opinions about the best way to observe behavior patterns like courtship. Nonetheless, in science, some methods work better than others. It depends on what one brings to the act of observing in the first place, and on what one wants to achieve. Of these, the *a priori* beliefs of the scientist are most important. If scientists, like laypeople, think in advance that they "know all about" courtship, beliefs will shape and control not only *how* the scientist sees, but also *what* is seen.

A Multiplicity of Visions

When I say the scientist's "*a priori*" beliefs, I do not mean an individual's *theoretical* preconceptions, for example, that one person is a Freudian and another is a sociological functionalist. I am discussing what amount to *visual* preconceptions. They concern *how* to see, and always form the backdrop for even expert interpretation of intimacy and courtship. Since these visual preconceptions differ among different people, they create different paths for understanding intimacy.

Broadly, there are two such paths. One is indirect, and starts with *personal* beliefs and experience which—perhaps unknown to the scientist—focus one's vision. For example, Shakespeare knew that men can doubt a woman's interest, but still look, fall in love, and want to touch her (as in Romeo's speech in Chapter 7).

From this romantic and theatrical way of seeing love, *some* scientists can begin with art and wisdom to build *scientific* models of love and intimacy.

In the hands of a master, the procedure works elegantly. In it, the perceptive scientist builds from knowledge and belief that already exist in our culture to statements of great power and sometimes truth. In particular, this way of seeing leads to what I later call the social scientific *theatrical metaphor*.

The second, more direct, path begins with observation itself and, for a while, sets aside the desire to interpret and explain. In metaphors borrowed from John Locke's *An Essay Concerning Human Understanding* (1700/1928), the mind is cleared of preconceptions, and when it is thus temporarily a blank slate, the data can shape one's thought far more strongly than if they were filtered through belief first. This method allows one to experience surprises, like the ethnographic short circuits between what one firmly *believes* to be true and what the data actually say.

In practice, these two ways of seeing are very different. The first method typically arises when one speaks of "hypothesis testing." It asserts that science necessarily involves testing explicit, well-developed, and well-formulated hypotheses that derive from theory. Because these hypotheses often represent cultural wisdom, common sense, or personal experience, the scientist working in this mode *converts or translates* wisdom into ideas suitable for scientific test.

The second approach arises in field studies and is characteristic of anthropology and many parts of biology. Field workers claim for their methods the advantage of first-hand experience with so-called "grounded" facts that may escape the more theory-bound hypothesis-testing scientist.

Though each method has powers and disadvantages, each has a serious problem that even its most devoted practitioners may not recognize. No matter which method one adopts, one's preconceptions can always tag along and shape the process of observing and construing.

The fact has overwhelming importance when observing and interpreting courtship or love. For example, take observing in a singles bar. For many people, bars have little to do with the *real* emotions of love or intimacy, or even with normal behavior. To be sure, I supplemented my observations in bars with field work in other places—train stations, parties, and, in fact, anywhere men and women meet. Nonetheless, for many people, bars *preclude* intimacy, and they will not understand how one can *see* intimacy in a bar.

Yet, the century-old anthropological perspective teaches us that we must study the common, everyday life of people in *their* real world. From a *scientific* viewpoint, it is therefore easy to justify observing in bars (Cavan, 1966; Roebuck and Spray, 1967; Sommer, 1969; Spradley and Mann, 1975; Byrne, 1978; see also Dubin, 1983; Bulmer, 1983; Cressey, 1983; Thomas, 1983). Indeed, bars have a genuine advantage over the laboratory.

In a bar, the entire courtship sequence is sharply condensed in time, for what may take weeks outside occurs in a few hours, or less, in a bar. Moreover, the bar powerfully facilitates sociosexual interactions by compounding liquor, music, lights, dancing, other people's behavior, and subtler forms of ambience into an overwhelmingly erotic, and even ecstatic, atmosphere.*

Nonetheless, there is a frequent objection to such choices. For some readers, the phrases "real world" and "common everyday life" are intensely irritating. "Whose real world?" they will ask. "What is common?" [For example, Karl E. Weick (1969) lambastes writers who use such terms in his review of Willems and Raush's *Naturalistic Viewpoints in Psychological Research* (1969) and Barker's *Ecological Psychology* (1968).] Though these are perhaps philosophically important questions, and though different people have different ideas of what is "real," still a real world exists. If a man touches a woman in a bar, and she gets up and walks away, her rejection is quite real. He cannot argue with her, and, if he does, bars often have bouncers to make sure that people like him do not pester the other customers. He cannot back away and say, smiling, "Sorry, it was just an experiment." In a bar, we are not seeing the behavior of someone trying to please the laboratory scientist, and to satisfy what Orne (1962) called the "demand characteristics" or "experimenter demand" of the laboratory setting. Men and women in a bar are *really* trying to meet each other, become friendly, and perhaps even more. Their behavior, and its mistakes, have immediate and real consequences, and no individual can set them aside simply by denying them or wishing them away. So, when we observe human behavior in a bar, we are observing it in a rule-obeying social world in which the rules are not set by the scientist him- or her*self*, but by the people we are observing (Fox, 1975).

In brief, then, my *techniques* are ethological and ethnographic: the objective observation of behavior in its natural setting. But, even if these comments make sense theoretically and technically, they do not answer a *methodological* problem: the existence of powerful preconceptions about bars. Granting that we enter a bar with some hope of observing courtship, *what in fact are we really seeing*? So, next, I invite the reader to join me in an experiment. In imagination, we are about to enter a bar and encounter first hand the problems of seeing and construing.

Visions in a Confused Mode

It's just a singles bar on a crowded Friday night. We have walked in hoping to see men and women flirt, court, and become intimate. And, immediately, our

---

*We observed in approximately 80 bars: 25 in New York City (Manhattan); 20 within a 20-mile radius of New Brunswick, New Jersey; 25 in Philadelphia; and 5 each in Detroit and Windsor, Ontario, Canada. Slightly more than 400 visits were made to these bars: 45 percent in New Jersey, 35 percent in Philadelphia, 10 percent in New York City, and the remainder in Detroit and Windsor. Ten bars were visited 10 or more times (five were in New Jersey and five were in Philadelphia). The maximum was one motor hotel bar in New Jersey, visited some 40 times (10 percent of total visits, which was exhausting). Each visit lasted between 1 and 3 hours, and, all told, there were about 900 observation hours between 1978 and 1984, including focal subject and scanning observation evenings, plus formal and informal (participant observation) evenings.

troubles begin. To a neophyte observer, the bar seems like a madhouse. Everywhere there is noise and movement—a blur.

Visions and Revisions

People are talking, crowding together, leaning on potted plants or barstools, looking for somewhere to put a glass, sitting on window sills. They take money out of purses or wallets—"Here, let me pay for that, you can buy me one next time"— they crane their necks to see if friends are there, or look hopefully at the door. Waitresses, trays lifted over their heads, try to weave through the crowd. We catch snatches of conversation—"Those are pretty earrings. Where did you get them?" "Why don't you guess?"—but the voices mingle with the band as it starts its first set. Then, to the untrained eye, the place becomes even more of a madhouse. People begin to dance, jumping up and down more or less in rhythm with the music, or are simply swaying back and forth. The men standing around the dance floor watch the dancers, holding their drinks and standing silently.—"I give up." "I made them. How did you know I was an artist?"—At the tables, groups of young women are talking to each other, drinking, laughing, looking around, and being watched by men standing in groups at the bar drinking.—"You have beautiful taste. I love turquoise and gold. It really looks nice with blue eyes."—The crowding, the noise, the band, the voices, the dancing, the lights, they all blur.

Soon, one's attention begins to wander and one starts to people-watch. You speculate about what this person does for a living, about what that person sees in someone else, and what still someone else might be like sexually. Your mind drifts as if you were floating in a boat, lazily watching clouds and imagining that they look like rhinoceroses or birds . . . Except they're not clouds, they're people.

And sometimes not very *nice* people. It is easy to *re-vision* in a bar, and then quite unpleasant images can creep out of one's mind to replace the real people. A superb example occurs in *Fear and Loathing in Las Vegas,* where Hunter S. Thompson (1971, pp. 23–24, 47–48) describes a Las Vegas bar in which all sorts of insane animals and beasts from Hieronymos Bosch suddenly fill the place. (Ralph Steadman's illustration on pages 30–31 strikingly captures this re-vision.)

Visions of the Impure

And—if we started out believing such things—might not we think that in this bar we are seeing a play driven by lust and a drama of seduction and promiscuity? Might not there creep into our re-visioning, and therefore into our explanations of what happens in the bar, the firm conviction that bars are nasty, sleazy meatracks, in which the Impure reigns supreme?

It is a widespread image of bars. Here is a description of such a place, supposedly in Paris:

. . . we went on to the Rue de Lappe. It is a dingy, narrow street and even as you enter it you get the impression of sordid lust. We went into a cafe. . . . A lot of people were dancing, sailors with the red pompom on their hats, men mostly with their caps on and handkerchiefs round their necks, women of mature age and young girls, painted to the eyes, bareheaded, in short skirts and coloured blouses. Men danced with podgy boys with made-up eyes; gaunt, hard-featured women danced with fat women with dyed hair; men danced with women. There was a froust* of smoke and liquor and sweating bodies. The music went on interminably and that unsavory mob proceeded around the room, the sweat shining on their faces, with a solemn intensity in which there was something horrible.

Though I have sometimes wanted to visit this place, I cannot: it existed only in the imagination of W. Somerset Maugham (*The Razor's Edge,* 1944, p. 206). In this passage, we read not a description of a "real" place, but Maugham's intense emotional and visual *reaction* to it. For Maugham, this cafe was disgusting.

But Maugham's powerful, striking imagery is not original with him. Instead, he selected his images so he could depict Hell. In this descent to Hell, *of course* we see *turkeys* and *losers*! And the men—ah, the men!

> . . . they act funny! If you're [a woman] in a bar alone or with another girl, they figure that you're a little bit lonely . . . and possibly an itsy witsy bit frantic or else why would you be there? Therefore you must be distress merchandise which can be had more cheaply than regular goods. . . . If that's such a great way to meet men, how come these same girls are back the next night forming new friendships? (H. G. Brown, n.d., p. 54–55)

Terrible, sleazy places, the women nothing but distress merchandise, drunken slatterns and harridans to be bought cheap, the men nothing but cynically laughing boors. Though Maugham's prose is far more elegant than Brown's—he says of the end of the evening that "[t]he sad creatures who make a business of love had gone to their sordid dwellings" (p. 295)—still, such people are animals, creatures who make a business of love, horrors swarming upwards from Hell itself.

Belief and Vision

The point is not that Maugham or Brown is "right" or "wrong," or that bars are not "really" like that. Rather, the point is that through their prose we *see* the bar in certain ways. We see—and seeing, construe—bars as worlds of cheap sluts, painted women, ill-formed and ill-behaved men, and sordid sex for money. Thus, in Maugham's and Brown's descriptions, we have a way of *observing and interpreting visual images that form on the retina of the eye as the observer looks at the world of the bar.*

But these retinal images do not *themselves* inherently contain harridans,

*Which is not in the *Oxford English Dictionary,* but does appear in Farmer and Henley's *Dictionary of Slang* (1903/1966) under *bingy:* "frowsty" refers to the peculiar tainted taste of milk when it first begins to turn sour.

horribly painted women, sweating sailors, or distress merchandise. These interpretations are selected from a much larger range of possible descriptions in order to construct, for the reader, what a bar *looks like* to the author. But, in turn, neither Maugham nor Brown is free to select their visual meanings. Their way of seeing in a bar is predetermined, not by observational "truth," but by how the myths of the Sacred deal with, and therefore reshape, a person's visual "reality" in a bar into concrete images of sexual impurity.

So it is not that Maugham and Brown both simply *believe* that bars are sleazy meatracks or sordid places. Rather, my point is far stronger: they also *see* bars as such places. Their observational choices have been controlled by what they already believe. To reverse the cliché, *Believing is seeing.*

However, amateur experts do not understand that they "see" only what they already believe is there. They will notice the young woman wearing high heels, black stockings, and silver hot pants who is approached by a man ("I know *her* type!") but will not see that another young woman in the bar, who is wearing a conservative, blue business suit was *also* approached by a man (both examples are from New York City). To the amateur, the first is interpretable according to the myths of the Impure: she is a sleazy chick, and it was typical pickup. But the second is not interpretable according to those myths, and the amateur observer will simply not see her or how she interacts with men.

Believing is seeing. For the scientist studying courtship, nothing is more misleading than believing that one "knows" what one is seeing. If you do, you will see only what our culture *already* believes, in the myth of the Impure, about lust and *its* settings and symbols. For example, sociologists Allon and Fishel (1981) wrote:

> There is much pressure and tension connected with finding . . . companionship in the singles' bar. Alienation and sociability operate hand in hand. The greater the show of sociability, the greater may be the sociopsychological distance of people from each other.
>
> The atmosphere is strained and forced. Because people are trying very hard to meet people, they seem to smile all the time so that no one will think they're bored or uninterested, and they try to create the impression that they always know the correct thing to do. There is a lot of competition in a singles' bar.
>
> Everyone seems defensive and on guard, not at all natural. . . . (p. 119)

Pressure, tension, alienation, distance, strain, competition, defense, guardedness. Yet are we so sure that these bars are as horrible as Allon and Fishel say in their authoritative tones? Or is it possible that they *too* have succumbed to the myth of the Sacred and believe—and therefore *see*—such places as *unnatural*, as did Maugham?

It is quite easy to walk into a bar, thinking one knows all about it. And the images of the Impure swirl up—sordid, dingy, irregular, unsavory, alienated, distressed, forced, unnatural. The crowding, the noise, they all blur. Soon, your mind drifts idly, imagining that *people* look like birds with evil claws, rhinoceroses, beasts . . . fear and loathing. One runs out.

"You know, they're right—bars *are* terrible places!"

But, of course, they're not. It was all in the mind.

Visions in the Neoclassical Mode

If one's vision is drawn in certain directions under the influence of "common-sense" truths, then beliefs about the proper way to see intimacy also creep into one's conclusions. As other viewpoints and forms of experience elude us, it is a foregone conclusion that bars and intimacy are mutually irrelevant. And given all this visual clamor, can one even *be* "scientific" or "objective"? Isn't it ultimately all a matter of viewpoint, just as the amateur observer always believed?

One answer is to demand that all *genuine* social scientific knowledge derive from hypothesis-testing. One tests hypotheses drawn, by reason, from theory. But where does one obtain these theories?

For one school of social science, "theory" represents a complex elaboration on already existing beliefs. I do not object to this procedure *per se;* instead, I object when these *a priori* beliefs enter as assumptions not to be questioned (e.g., the idea that the "tension" in a singles bar *of course* represents alienation and competition, rather than, say, generalized sexual arousal or a reaction to music, talk, and alcohol combined. See also Schwartz and Lever, 1976). When such *unanalyzed* assumptions enter one's "hypotheses" or "theory," then the exercise finds only what we already believe is there. *That* is not science. Now, of course, most social scientists analyze their theoretical assumptions quite carefully. Yet, even in the finest hypothesis testing work, there still remains an unanalyzed core of assumption which, I suggest, pertains to *aesthetics.*

Aesthetic Visions

By definition, aesthetics concerns how we perceive and therefore choose to *depict and record* reality (e.g., Nelson, 1977). It has profound implications for scientific methods of observation and inference, because several *kinds* of aesthetic exist.

Of course, to some social and biological scientists, to talk of aesthetics is to imply that science is "art." Then, in tones of annihilating disdain, these scientists will say condescendingly "Well, if you *want* to talk about aesthetics, I suppose your approach requires it. Of course we *scientists* don't have to concern ourselves with subjective issues like that!" But of course they *do.* In this, the scientist is like M. Jourdain in *Le Bourgeois Gentilhomme,* who discovered to his amazement that he had been speaking prose all his life. If the observer is *unaware* that he or she makes aesthetic choices when selecting a method, then that selection is made blindly even if the scientist can cite authority and precedent for the method. One should know what one is doing when one chooses how to depict and record reality, for each aesthetic involves a set of assumptions about the world and about people. And, since believing is seeing even if one does not know what one believes, I turn next to these ways of seeing.

Theater or Life?

Imagine a theater. The houselights are dimming, and the audience is becoming quiet. Before us, the curtain separating us from the stage is closed. Soon it will rise, and, lit dimly or brightly, the stage and its scenery will become visible. Then the play will begin—a romance, or perhaps a tragedy, which involves love and intimacy, and the problems of human communication.

From the theater comes one of the great social scientific metaphors. In terms like *gender role, script theory, social setting, performance anxiety, cognitive rehearsal,* and even *actor,* we hear concepts that arose in the theater and have been transferred to the social sciences to describe how and why people behave as they do.

Because the theatrical metaphor is graphic, vivid, and familiar, it has great power over the visual imagination. It invites us to believe that when we see a "social performance," we—like the audience of a play—observe but do not participate. The metaphor seems to promise objectivity and sufficient self-distancing for observing courtship as a drama or text to be interpreted according to a sort of dramatic or literary criticism.

From our imagined seats of objectivity, we then believe that we can discern the principles of composition that are "enacted" during courtship. Furthermore, the theatrical metaphor tempts us to conclude that in social life (as in the play onstage), these principles of composition are unknown to the *characters*—the lovers—even though these principles can be seen by the observer in the *audience.* The observer then believes that he or she knows *more* about the lovers' behavior and emotions than they do themselves.

It is an equally powerful convention that members of the audience do not participate in the stage action (at least in classical Western theater). We sympathize, perhaps we are moved, but our experience is vicarious. However, if we observe in a bar according to this theatrical convention, we may believe that someone feeling horror and revulsion is exhibiting a stage emotion that has little real importance to *our* lives. In this, the observer *feels* objective, and does not understand that very similar emotions may swamp his or her own interpretations of the bar.

It is now only a short step to postulating that in real life actor and character are as unlike as they are on stage. For example, the man who reacts jealously when he sees his wife flirting with another man: in the theatrical metaphor, it is easy to say that he is enacting a *script*, that his anger towards his wife is a *performance*, or that he is *playing the role* of the jealous Husband in a domestic comedy (or tragedy, as it may be). Then, driven by the virtually coercive power of this metaphor, we are irresistibly tempted to imagine that underneath this enactment of the male "role" is a man who stands to social performance as actor does to stage character: as the person behind the mask, or, in classical theatrical terms, *persona*. Then we might say that behind the man's jealousy are totally different emotions, motivations, and character: his true nature, we say, is hidden behind a mask.

The Play as Culture, the Actors as Nature

In this, the theatrical metaphor leads to another version of the ethnobiological belief that biology lies "behind" culture. Culture is, so to speak, the play, while biology—that is, Nature—provides the actor who is capable of learning as wide a variety of roles as imagination can produce. Culture thus *clothes* the actor and actress, and gives them their lines to speak. And what is below those external appearances is formless: not a real man or woman but only entities that can *take on,* as players do roles, whatever Culture—the playwright—dictates.

But the theatrical metaphor allows another interpretation as well. We know, by theatrical convention, that sometimes the character's "real" motivations are not what they seem. The villain, say, lies about his intentions to the heroine; the hero is uncertain of his own intentions. Watching social life in this mode, but compelled again by the theatrical metaphor, we may now begin to guess—that is, generate "hypotheses"—about the man's "real" emotions and motivations. For example, perhaps the jealous man is "really" enacting a scene of jealousy repeated from childhood, or is "really" displaying anxieties and insecurities under his apparent anger.

In the psychoanalytical tradition, this interpretation is expressed as the difference between *manifest* and *latent,* but the metaphor remains theatrical, for it embodies the Western theatrical convention that the actor playing the role and the role *itself* are different. On the one hand, we may see an all-powerful Culture enscripting itself on otherwise formless Nature. On the other, we may see surface and subsurface both as real, but *different*—for example, by saying that a woman enacts a socially learned gender role, but that below it are needs and emotions that are incompatible with social tradition. Then, in turn—and still true to the power of this metaphor—we might seek to "get in touch" with our "real" feelings, or even seek psychotherapy to help us reconcile a conflict between role and actor, between outside appearance and internal emotion.

In an essay on non-verbal communication called "Plays and Players," Miller (1972) commented that " . . . the central ingredient of a play consists of a series of utterances which express, as Wittgenstein points out, *the way things are*" (p. 359, italics original). But Wittgenstein was wrong. The play is *not* life. Instead, theater—and the search for the "script" that some social scientists believe underlies social "performances"—represents *a way things should be understood.* As Mangham and Overington (1983) also argue, the theatrical metaphor provides a *way* to see and, by seeing, to construe, understand, and then depict human life.

The Play as Behavior, the Actors as Numbers

However, in the theatrical metaphor of some modern social science, less personal entities hide behind the mask. Thus, a quantitative sociologist might seek not a frightened man behind the mask of jealousy, but a disembodied apparatus of statistical determinants: socioeconomic status, educational level, religiosity, authoritarianism, sex guilt, or the person's numerical score on batteries of quantitative scales for measuring sexual beliefs and attitudes. Then, behind the mask of jealousy or love enacted in the social performance, there appears an *apparatus:* purely numerical and statistical procedures, like regression and pathway analysis, create a set of machine-like linkages—the gears, levers, and drive chains of quantitative social scientific interpretation—that *replace* the old-fashioned "psychological man" with abstract and numerical determinants of behavior. Under the mask is not a hidden person, but a statistical cyborg.

The elevation of this statistical cyborg in the place of human feeling corresponds to phenomena in both modern theater and the graphic arts, as when portraiture and theatrical realism, for example, are replaced by abstract expressionism, Dadaism, and the theater of the Absurd. Human life has then become a disconnected series of planes, lines, words, and deeds performed mechanically in a world in which the *norm* is a machine-like slickness of interchangeable people performing interchangeable social functions and roles.

Once Again, Theater

I am not attacking statistics *per se* (especially since I have, at times, done statistical consulting). Rather, my point is that the theatrical metaphor represents a way of seeing and therefore understanding human behavior. In this way of seeing, courtship has become *dual*. One part consists of the stage details—the actors' touches, movements, looks, intonations, timing, and so on. The second consists of the plot or plot sketch, which lays out how the action shall unfold from meeting to denouement.

Of these, the theatrical metaphor sees the second as far more important than the first. Miller again put it well: " . . . along with many of the other contributors to this volume [*Non-Verbal Communication,* edited by R. A. Hinde], I assume that *verbal* communication takes precedence in human discourse and that *non-verbal* behaviour achieves most of its communicative significance in the context of syntactically organized utterances," that is, speech (Miller, 1972, p. 359, italics added). And indeed, for anyone adopting the theatrical metaphor, in the beginning was the Word (John 1:i). In this view, life *is* drama, and, as script takes precedence over action, the actor and actress *must* each become only an apparatus or machine for enacting the script (as is implicit in the quote from Simon and Gagnon in Chapter 2).

Thus, the theatrical metaphor simultaneously involves us in decisions about priority of observation and interpretation: script, not detail, should come first in the observer's attention. In this view, my description of courtship, with all its details, is less interesting than determining how those details are organized to form an enacted and scripted unity. In this view, when the organizing script has been identified, the details lose significance except as visible markers of progress through the scripted action.

So, although the theatrical metaphor seems to represent an *interpretation* of behavior, it nonetheless also creates a way to *observe* courtship. If one watches courtship as if it were theater, one brings to the act of observing a set of presuppositions about what one will see and about what one should look for. Drawing on a (probably) unanalyzed body of prior experience watching movies or plays, the observer will predetermine the shape of the observations and, by seeking the story that is being enacted by the lovers–actors, see it as if it had already been written out and were merely being *illustrated* by the actor's bodily movements.

Neoclassicism and Social Science

I submit that this procedure involves a specifiable *aesthetic* of observation as much as it involves scientific method or a theory of courtship. Perhaps without knowing it, when social scientists adopt the theatrical metaphor—in one form or another, it predominates in the social sciences—they place themselves squarely into an aesthetic tradition called *neoclassicism*.

The neoclassical aesthetic in social science can be summarized epigrammatically. In it, one seeks truth that can " . . . be defined only by theory and understood only by reason." For many social scientists, the phrase no doubt epitomizes the scientific endeavor, or at least the ideal *form* of scientific endeavor.

Yet I have been unfair: I omitted the subject of the original sentence. It is not "truth," but "beauty," and the sentence is taken from art historian John Canaday's description of neoclassicism as it appeared in Western graphic *art* at the beginning of the 1800s (1959, pp. 30–31).

I do not apologize for this verbal device. It teaches us that social scientific interpretation has profound affiliations with a particular *kind* of art, in which choices about how to see and what to depict are aesthetically inevitable. And the problem is not that the social sciences *have* an aesthetic: it is that the neoclassical aesthetic in the social sciences is often not *recognized* as having specifiable qualities and properties, and therefore certain strengths and limits. As a set of (usually) unanalyzed assumptions, neoclassicism shapes the social sciences, rather than social scientists choosing and therefore controlling their own aesthetic decisions.

The Neoclassical Crystalline Core of Truth

Take, for example, the philosopher's view that science must begin with explicit hypotheses based on reasoned theory. This vision of science arises less from understanding how scientists actually work than from a Western tradition about how *art* should be constructed. Indeed, the philosopher's ideal of science is *precisely* the neoclassical aesthetic. However, neoclassicism does far more than merely seek to apprehend truth by reason. It *also* says that reason itself requires that we see certain aspects of reality as more central, important, and true than other aspects.

In theater and graphic arts both, neoclassicism seeks the central core of truth hidden below what otherwise seems to be chaotic experience. It abstracts and generalizes from a variety of experiences to seek what is common to them. In this, truth does not reside in the "welter of surface details" of life, for those are accidental, variable, and merely encrust over truth. Only by rational and systematic examination of phenomena can we discern what is typical, general, or in this aesthetic, "true."

But, appearances to the contrary, this description is not taken from a philosopher of *science*. Instead, it is paraphrased from Oscar Brockett's *History of the Theatre* (1982, pp. 158–160) and from his discussion of how the neoclassical ideal arose in the theater of the late 1500s and came to dominate European theater until the late 1700s. Yet it summarizes excellently the *aesthetic* hope that underlies most social science.

In the theater, the neoclassical ideal is represented by stage action which is controlled by a plot that embodies these principles of generalizable truth. This concept is virtually identical to the idea of a "script" in the social scientific theatrical metaphor (e.g., Gagnon and Simon, 1973): the script exists as the core of the performance, and represents what is hidden below the welter of surface details of touches and movements that I have throughout been calling the "courtship sequence." And, when one seeks that hidden core script below the surface details, and, when one next affirms that it is the task of science to describe that script, then one is an aesthetic neoclassicist.

In the graphic arts, neoclassicism sought to capture a fixed *moment* of core truth in a single image. Graphic neoclassicism is represented best, perhaps, by Jacques Louis David (1748–1825). In "The Oath of the Horatii" (Canaday, 1959, pp. 10–11), David has captured the intensely dramatic moment when the Horatii, their faces and swords uplifted, are swearing to their father their lives in defense of honor, family, and country. Into this depiction of a moment in time is distilled the truth, as neoclassicism sees it: stripped away are irrelevant details, confusing and ambiguous complexity, and accidental happenings. What remains is an *ideal*: a depiction of the permanent and central core of truth otherwise hidden below the surface.

In this neoclassical ideal of truth, one hears the voice of the sociologist Max Weber (1947) writing about method:

> . . . in analyzing a political or military campaign it is convenient to determine in the first place what would have been a rational course, given the ends of the participants and adequate knowledge of all the circumstances. Only in this way is it possible to assess the causal significance of irrational factors as accounting for the deviations from this type. The construction of a purely rational course of action in such cases serves the sociologist as a type ("ideal type") which has the merit of clear understandability and lack of ambiguity. (pp. 92–93)

The "ideal type" is that clear, unambiguous center which represents Reason, from which all things deviate only through irrationality. To find the ideal type is to find truth as neoclassicism has always defined it: not in surface detail, but in distillation from it.

The neoclassical mode also exists in anthropology. It was brilliantly summarized by Malinowski (1935/1978):

> The main achievement in field-work consists, not in a passive registering of facts, but in the *constructive drafting* of what might be called the charters of native institutions. The observer should not function as a mere automaton; a sort of combined camera and phonographic or shorthand recorder of native statements. While making his observations the field-worker must constantly construct: he must place isolated data in relation to one another and study the manner in which they integrate. To put it paradoxically one could say that "facts" do not exist in sociological any more than in physical reality; that is, they do not dwell in the spatial and temporal continuum open to the untutored eye. The principles of social organisation, of legal constitution, of economics and religion *have to be constructed by the observer* out of a multitude of manifestation of varying significance and relevance. It is these invisible realities, only to be discovered by inductive computation, by selection and construction, which are scientifically important in the study of culture. (p. 317, italics added)

When Malinowski says that fieldwork " . . . is the vision of the clear, firm outline of native institutions which brings order into the chaos of trifling happenings and details of varying relevance" (p. 321), it is no paradox: in the neoclassical aesthetic, truth is always constructed thus.*

The Limitations of Neoclassicism

I am not "against" neoclassicism. It has been responsible for some great advances in social science. For example, the linguistic (scientific) notions of grammar and syntax are neoclassical, as is the idea that there exists a "formal plane" of language—*la langue*—that can be distinguished from the myriads of speech acts and utterances that people perform in their everyday lives—*la parole* (de Saussure, 1915/1959).

Indeed, I employ neoclassical descriptions several times, most notably, perhaps, in Chapter 8, "The Sacred." Durkheim's concept proves very useful for understanding a welter of otherwise *disconnected* details, and it rather startled me how easily such details fit into the Durkheimian notion. Nonetheless, I know that no *individual* life follows exactly the ideal pattern provided by the myth of the

---

*See also Simmel (1919/1984, pp. 79–80). The same hope motivates regression analysis in statistics. In it, a swarm of separate points is reduced to a single "best-fitting" line, from which individual points deviate through "error" or "chance." Thus, know it or not, regression analysis commits one to neoclassicism. Historically, Gaussian least-squares regression predates Weber; presumably he was working within a well-defined tradition when he wrote this passage.

Sacred, even if each of us lives *parts* of it (and not always willingly). I also recognize that other neoclassical schemes may well fit the same pattern of details, and hope that others will attempt to link the Durkheimian conclusions I have drawn to other theoretical frameworks. Indeed, I tentatively suggest that it is a major task of the social sciences to show how their neoclassical ideas *do* articulate across psychology, sociology, anthropology, history, and, ultimately, biology.

But I also tentatively suggest that at present the social sciences are far from such an integration, and that neoclassicism has therefore had some less beneficial effects in the social sciences. Neoclassicism stresses *form* and can lead the observer to an "integration"—that is, a theory—that itself becomes more important than "trifling" or "irrational" happenings that may be dismissed as irrelevant. Phenomena that do not fit a neoclassical theory can easily be suppressed, not through malice or deliberate falsehood, but by a genuine belief that certain forms of behavior are unimportant. In the hands of a master, neoclassicism has few such risks. But in the hands of lesser folk, it can become a sterile exercise in theoretical formalism. Such dangers are greatest when the social scientist is an *a priori* advocate of a given theoretical framework.

The potential for sterile formalism is not the only risk in neoclassicism. The second, and greater, risk arises because neoclassicism defines what science is and is *not*. For example, in the theatrical metaphor, neoclassicism asserts that science should see, and therefore depict, social life as if it were governed by clear and unambiguous principles of construction that exist less in the "spatial and temporal continuum" of life than in the mind of the observer. Since science then necessarily depends on such principles for generating "testable hypotheses," in neoclassicism observations have meaning *only* in relation to hypotheses developed by reason from theory. This aesthetic defines the *purposes* of science.

And, to encapsulate, the problem is the origin of those principles in the first place. If they are genuinely induced from life, as Malinowski's method requires, than all may be well. But sometimes those principles and hypotheses represent *a priori* ideas of what principles govern life—for example, courtship, love, and intimacy. Then all may *not* be well, for we have predetermined what intimacy is *before* observing it systematically. We may believe that we know how the story should *end* if "true intimacy" is achieved. Anything else can be ignored, very possibly at high risk.

The Neoclassical Ideal of Love

My critique may sound over-bold. But social scientific neoclassicism has powerfully influenced how we see intimacy and its development, particularly in the now classic description of intimacy given by the anthropologist Edward Hall (1963, 1968).

For Hall, intimacy was characterized by a set of bodily positions that two people adopt when they feel intimate with each other. They are physically close to each other, are facing each other fully, and can touch each other easily. Though, in

1963, Hall did not say so explicitly, they are also gazing at each other directly, as later writers added.

If we compare this description with the final stages of intimacy described in Chapter 4, there are some similarities and some striking differences. The postures Hall describes will, in fact, be attained after the two people have gradually turned completely to face each other, are looking at each other more or less continuously, and are touching. But there is a large difference: Hall's description is *static*.

Thus, Hall's description epitomizes intimacy the way a graphic artist would— as a picture, painting, or photograph which freezes the couple's intimacy into a single, fixed image. It captures a *moment* of intimacy, which then comes to represent the entire *process* of becoming and feeling intimate. Around the image a halo of meaning appears in the viewer's mind: love, affection, caring, closeness, warmth—in a word, everything that the process of courtship produces—now center on Hall's single, fixed visual metaphor for intimacy. True to the neoclassical tradition, Hall has stripped away all extraneous substance and process, to leave an ideal—a neoclassical *ideal*—of love.

Hall's neoclassical vision has had immense influence. After him, and sharing his vision, other social scientific students of intimacy focused on touch, gaze, and proximity, the so-called "modalities" of non-verbal communication (Duncan, 1969). They sought to isolate these modalities from each other, to subject them to individual investigation, and to assign each a meaning, or set of meanings, of its own (Weitz, 1979, pp. 87–106).

A particularly important paper in the neoclassical genre was Argyle and Dean's (1965) "Eye-Contact, Distance and Affiliation." For them too intimacy is state, but it is produced by a dynamic equilibrium of opposing forces. Some lead to intimacy; others lead away. In this view, intimacy has components, and is achieved or produced through eye-contact, proximity, and touching. Thus, increased gazing *means* increased intimacy, and if I look at you continuously, it is because I want to be or become intimate. In this, we assign *meaning and intention* to a given behavior pattern, in a neoclassical effort to extract the central core of meaning for behavior. Then, intimacy is achieved as these separate *vectors* of intimacy balance against each other, and come to rest in virtually architectural fixity.

However, if we could read the lovers' minds, would we find such interpretations, meanings, and intentions in their thoughts? To be sure, the image of intimacy as architecture is striking, and calls to mind—for me, at least—images of Medieval cathedrals, their buttresses lifting into the air to support the massive pillars and walls of the church. The image is fitting, but does it exist in the *lovers'* minds as they court? Or would we have to turn to the observer and *only* to the observer, to find these images of love and courtship?

Nonetheless, in neoclassicism, it does not matter what is "in the minds" of the lovers themselves. What *really* matters is how the observer sees and interprets their behavior, for it is the purpose of science itself to construct such meanings for people's actions.

The social scientific laboratory experiment represents an elegant example of this neoclassical process of construing and constructing meaning for people's behavior. Turning again to Argyle and Dean's own belief that intimacy achieved through eye-contact can be counterbalanced by intimacy achieved through proximity, their experiment involved two students who sat at various distances from each other and talked. The stooge sat at a pre-selected distance from the subject (2, 6, or 10 feet away), and gazed at the subject continuously for 3 minutes. From behind a one-way mirror, Argyle and Dean then recorded the amount of time the subject gazed at and away from the stooge.

The results were clearcut. The closer the stooge, the less the other person looked at him or her.

For Argyle and Dean, the results also had clearcut meaning. Continual gazing for 3 minutes produces a high level of intimacy (note that they have *assigned* this meaning to gazing). When the stooge sits closer, intimacy achieved through proximity also increases. The subject then attempts to *reduce* intimacy by gazing less at the stooge, so that intimacy re-equilibrates at a level acceptable to the subject.

Yet, Argyle and Dean have constructed this interpretation less from the actual behavior of the two students than from the (neoclassical) belief that ideally intimacy should be a balance of forces, such as privacy and reserve on the one hand, and involvement with the partner on the other.

So we must pause. Are we so very sure that eye-contact and proximity "mean" intimacy? If "common sense" and "everyday experience" assure us that these meanings are reasonable, then we have brought with us *fore*knowledge that the interpretation is true. It then follows that Argyle and Dean are not describing an experiment at all, but a *demonstration*—in their minds—of what we already think we know. Because it depicts or exhibits their beliefs, it is a kind of *tableau vivant*.

But, in fact *do* we know such things? Could it not be that the subject felt that the stooge's gaze was not intimate, but *hostile,* and instead of returning it with an equally hostile stare, chose to gaze away politely? After all, social rules do militate against staring at a stranger. In that case, gazing away represents the subject's effort to be *friendly* in the face of seeming hostility. In this, the meaning of gazing *away* is exactly the opposite of what Argyle and Dean attributed to it. One can multiply such possibilities endlessly, implying that Argyle and Dean's explanation does not *follow* from the data, but *preexists* them.

On the basis of an experimental methodological critique of the Argyle and Dean study, Knight, Langmeyer, and Lundgren (1973) reached a similar conclusion. They found that observers will record that eye contact decreases between two people as they sit closer even when one "subject" is a confederate whose gaze does *not* change with distance. The result arises partly because it can be very difficult for an observer to detect eye contact between subjects, but I agree with their conclusion that "cultural expectations" influence the observers' recordings. My point is that cultural expectations also influence the experimenters' *interpretations*.

An excellent example is Antonia Abbey's (1982) very striking experimental demonstration that men often misunderstand women's behavior and attribute sexual meaning to it even when the woman intends none. Abbey's paper is important not only for its content but also because it shows *how* an experience-based "hypothesis" is used to explain experimental results. Again, my purpose is not an *ad hominem* attack, but to use the published details of a social scientific laboratory experiment to show that such hypotheses *do* preexist the data.

Beginning with an unpleasant episode in a bar between herself, some female friends, and two over-eager men (described briefly on p. 830), Abbey suggests that men impute sexual interest to women even when it is absent (a conclusion with which I agree, at least for some men, in some bars, and at some times). She then designed a laboratory experiment in which male and female subjects first observed a man and woman talking for 5 minutes and, second, selected (on scales of 1 to 7) various words describing the male and female members of the couple. On the average, male observers (college students) thought that the actress was somewhat more promiscuous and seductive than the *female* observers thought she was (Table 1, p. 834).

It is not a surprising result given my conclusion in Chapter 7 about men's inabilities to decode women's nonverbal behavior. However, the words *promiscuous* and *seductive* themselves were not spontaneously employed by the subjects, but were provided by Abbey to her subjects in a questionnaire. In essence, the procedure puts words into the subjects' mouths—and powerful words at that. Given that the male observers were rather attracted to the actress (more so than the female observers were attracted to the actor; p. 834), their choice of how to describe the actress was *forced* by the experimenter in ways that quite possibly do not correspond to the men's own feelings. (As discussed later, interviews are needed to eliminate this problem.)

However, the forced choice procedure allowed Abbey to conclude, quite globally, that the experimental results indicate that "men mistakenly interpret women's friendliness as an indication of sexual interest" (p. 836, column 1) and that "men are more likely [than women] to perceive the world in sexual terms and to make sexual judgements than women are" (p. 836, column 2). These conclusions amount to saying that men's sexuality is Impure, unlike women's. Nonetheless, *in fact* the experiment suggests only that young men may like young women more than young women may like young men, at least initially. It is *much* too large a jump from forced-choice imputations to a couple observed for just 5 minutes to such unqualified assertions about men.

And yet, many women feel, as Abbey does, that sometimes men are obnoxious and pushy (Chapter 6). Her conclusions thus reflect her beliefs and experiences— and their truth to many women—rather than following from the data themselves through the force of logic. As in the Argyle and Dean experiment, the meaning of the results has been *pre*-determined by the experimenter.

Because experiments like these vivify preexisting ideas and beliefs about intimacy, they do not *test* any hypotheses at all. The hypothesis is a *priori* presumed true, and is used *a posteriori* to explain the results. Such "experimental" research then seems motivated less by a desire to *induce or infer* the truth, than by a desire to *exhibit or display* what is already believed true.

Science as Art

An unkind reader might ask "Why do the experiment at all?" The answer is that such "experimentation" is an aesthetic endeavor, and that social scientists perform such experiments for much the same reason artists draw portraits even when they already "know what the person looks like." The purpose is to produce an aesthetically satisfying representation of the scientist's or artist's vision. And when this representation is designed—as was Argyle and Dean's, or Abbey's—to vivify preexisting ideas about the true core of intimacy, then the aesthetic is neoclassical, and we are in the presence of art in the strictest of all senses: an effort to depict what reality is in the *artist's* eyes.

However, neoclassicism is not the only aesthetic that has moved Western art. There are many others—like romanticism, expressionism, and the most important of all, realism.

Visions in a Realist Mode

One evening early in the study of bar behavior, we were observing two women and a man at the table next to us. The man was sitting next to one woman and facing the other, his feet and legs fully extended under the table, head and shoulders leaned back in the chair, his arm resting on the table halfway reaching between him and the woman next to him. He had come into the bar a few minutes before, approached the two women, and had sat down. As they talked, he remained in his position for the next half-hour or so, moving very little. The woman next to him sat upright, and she and the man both looked at each other continually as they talked. The other woman said very little. Then he finished his drink, got up, and left.

It was totally bewildering. If one applies Hall's criteria for intimacy, none of it made sense, for each "modality" of intimacy contradicted the other. Extensive looking but leaning away; an arm extended halfway towards her but no touching; a seemingly abrupt exit.

Now, *one* way to understand these events is to insist that science constructs meanings for peoples' actions. So, we could have created a (reasonably) satisfactory construction for what these events and contradictions "mean." Intimacy—obviously—was incomplete, and the two people were using different modalities to send signals that *opposed* each other. We see *tension*, as alienation and sociability confront each other. The postures do not represent Hall's ideal of intimacy because the man and woman were not genuinely intimate. And, these ideas firmly in mind, we can now look back at this man and woman and see—literally *see*—these forces enacted and embodied in their postures.

But there is *another* way to understand these events. We got up, went over, and

introduced ourselves as researchers. Did they mind answering a few questions—
e.g., what had been going on?

The woman was quite friendly. She wasn't surprised that we were bewildered, she indicated; she and this man had been having an affair for a year and often met in this bar.

One cannot simply look at people's behavior and think to understand it simply by *construing*. Even if neoclassicism has produced great art and elegant social science, sometimes the neoclassical approach does not work in the *real* world. Sometimes meaning does not exist in the eye of the beholder, but outside.

Testing Hypothesis-Testing

In one sense, this clash between beliefs and the data is a kind of ethnographic short circuit. But here the clash involves not only interpretation of observation but also *how* we study human behavior. If one believes that science construes data on *a priori* grounds, then one develops a hypothesis, sees these three people, construes, and *stops*. One "confirms" one's hypothesis by seeing that people behave in "conformity" with one's predictions. One is then presumably pleased with this verification of not only the prediction, but, by extension, with this demonstration that "hypothesis-testing" itself is a useful method.

But in fact there *was* no verification. The *real* relationship between this man woman was far more complex than this glib procedure understands.

The problem here concerns the properties of "hypothesis" itself. The behavior of this couple did *not* verify the hypothesis that male–female interactions involve some kind of balance of forces. Instead, the more effective scientific procedure is to look at the couple and say to oneself that their behavior *seems* to fit the commonsense notion that bar behavior is alienation admixed with attraction. *Now* one has a "hypothesis" to test: it says that this man and woman, in this bar on this evening, are relating to each other ambivalently. Next, one tests that hypothesis, not by construing but by asking her about their relationship. One then finds that the hypothesis is really quite oversimplified.

The diagram in Figure A1 compares these two modes of observation. The wriggly line represents the on-going sequence of the couple's behavior. In procedure (A), which I have described above as typically neoclassical, the observer begins with a hypothesis, "tests" it by "observing," and concludes *in his or her mind* that it has been verified. The process is exactly like sitting in the audience of a play, watching the action, and saying, "I know this play; she's attracted but unsure of her attraction." The couple's behavior then serves as a kind of moving Thematic Apperception Test which allows the observer to construe as he or she wishes, subject only to one's preformed beliefs.

But in (B), the observer is not watching a play. Instead, he or she simply (!) observes and soon recognizes the seeming *applicability or relevance* of one or

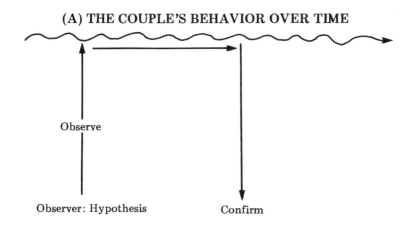

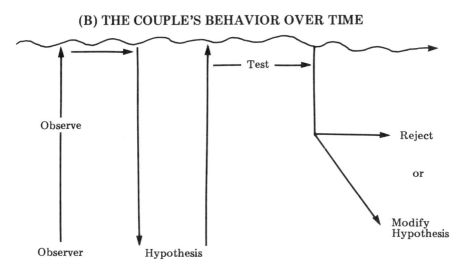

Figure A1   The types of hypothesis testing.

another hypothesis to the behavior. Then, one says, "If so . . . " and the procedure ceases to be theatrical. Now one tests just how relevant the hypothesis *really* is, and discovers its severe limitations.

Like the amateur expert, neophyte observers prefer procedure (A), for it seems to promise easy access to the "truth." However, procedure (B) is generally needed for understanding human behavior *scientifically*. It has several steps. The simplest concerns observational technique, discussed next, after which I return to interpretation.

Observing in a Bar: Starting Out

The basic technique is to locate a flirting or courting couple, or an individual who is likely to interact with someone of the other sex, and observe them systematically and steadily. A typical evening begins by going into the bar, selecting a table which commands a good view (not all bars have them), choosing a woman to observe, and then recording her interactions with men. We begin with a woman because most men in a bar will never interact with women, but will talk to each other, watch the band, or stand around the bar watching television. In contrast, many women in such bars will ultimately interact with a man, and that is what we want to see.

For observation itself, I borrowed two techniques from ethology and animal behavior. They are called *focal subject observation* and *scanning*.

Focal Subject Observation

Focal subject observation involves watching either a woman or a couple steadily for 2 or 3 hours (Figure A2). One then sees how their courtship interactions start, progress, and succeed or fail. The procedure is repeated over and over, couple after couple, evening after evening, until the sequence is clear. (I have spent several hundred hours doing focal subject observations.)

Depending on events, one or two focal subject observations can be made during a 3 or so hour evening. Couple 1, for example (see Figure A2), would occupy one's attention for nearly 3 hours. In contrast, if one had chosen Couple 3, their interaction ceases after about an hour (i.e., when they move away from each other). One could then switch over to Couple 5.

Focal subject observations are stopped if the two people separate permanently (like 3), leave the bar, or are joined by other people. Later in the study, focal subject observations were stopped once the couple had reached stable movement synchronization.

The technique generates data far too rich to record completely. Videotaping may sound ideal, but offers serious technical problems (e.g., lighting) and can be dangerous. Legally, releases should be obtained from one's subjects, and not everyone will sign (as I have found while working with several camera teams associated with television shows). Instead, abbreviated notes are made about the couple's actions.

Focal subject observations take a long time, but are unambiguous. The interaction develops before your very eyes.

Scanning

A second procedure, called *scanning*, was also very useful. One watches several couples, say three or four, and one's attention moves systematically among them during the evening (Figure A2). In scanning, one sees different couples at

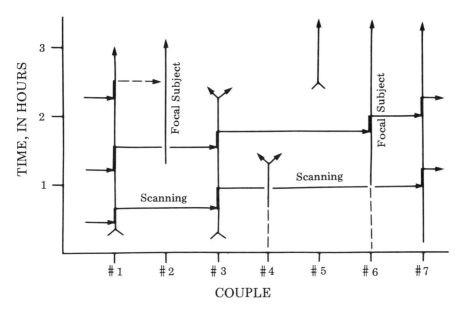

Figure A2   Focal subject and scanning observations. Upright arrows represent the course of focal subject observations made with one couple. The observer would select *one* of the seven couples and observe them steadily until they ceased interacting (e.g., couple 3 or 4) or for at least 2 to 3 hours (e.g., couple 1 or 7). Horizontal arrows represent scanning across three and then four couples every few minutes (the heavy regions on the arrows indicate the period during which the couple is observed).

different points in the courtship sequence, though in less individual detail than in focal subject observation.

There is no hard and fast rule for how long to observe each couple while scanning; observational experience is needed. (I have spent several hundred hours doing scanning observations.)

Focal subject and scanning observations are widely used ethological techniques, and represent "event recording" in Altmann's (1974) sense. The same principles hold for observing in restaurants, train stations, supermarkets, parties, or anywhere else men and women interact. Details of technique require change, but the basics are the same.

Subject Choice

Scanning does not raise problems of whom to observe. One rarely has more than four couples within the observation distance of 15 to 20 feet. One simply watches them.

Focal subject observation does raise questions of bias, especially if one wants to see something "interesting." One then ignores quieter people to watch couples who are flamboyant or who seem to embody one's own ideas of what courting couples *should* do. When I began the bar study itself, I would select a woman to observe as randomly as possible, for example, the next woman to enter the bar. Later, it became obvious that it made little difference whom one observed. Often, in a crowded place, one has no choice: one selects the nearest and most easily observed couple.

If the courtship sequence is similar in all or most couples, then focal subject and scanning observations should give identical descriptions in the long run. Accordingly, bias in choosing focal subjects will be recognizable if subjects seen with scanning behave very differently than focal subjects. However, descriptions obtained with the two techniques proved fully consistent with each other, indicating that focal subject observation had not been yielding artifactual results, at least not systematically.

Reality Is Observable

Now, just because one does all this, it is not guaranteed that one will see accurately. One must choose *what* to observe. In making such choices, we encounter *realism.*

The observability of reality is an unpopular position in physics and philosophy (Gribben, 1984; Aronson, 1984). But I do not have exalted philosophical ideas in mind when I speak of reality. Rather, realism involves observing and interpreting details of behavior as they occur *in the real world as they are performed by real people.* The great French realist painter Gustave Courbet (1819–1877) was once twitted for not painting angels. "Show me an angel and I will paint one," he said (Canaday, 1959, p. 103; Callen, 1980). I will paraphrase him: show me a couple enacting the neoclassical ideal of love and I will observe them. Until then, I maintain that we are forced to observe real people, whose behavior never fits the ideals of social scientific neoclassicism.*

Nor does realism mean that we observe and record details without point or purpose. That is not science, but sterile compilation. Realism is not "anti-theoretical"—for example, Courbet theorized extensively about his realist art (Callen, 1980). Thus, it is a theoretical statement to say that our personal and cultural experiences and beliefs about courtship are often inadequate for formulating "hypotheses" about it, and that therefore fieldwork is needed *before* hypotheses are generated. But, if realism does not seek the "ideal core" of truth under the surface

---

*In the United States, aesthetic realism is sometimes specialized to mean a concern with life's "ugly" side, as in the phrase "the ashcan school" for certain painters of the urban scene (Canaday, 1959, pp. 320–324). I do not mean "realism" in this restricted sense.

details, then what *are* we seeking in our observations and theories? The answer concerns what behavior does and does not *mean*.

Scenario Writing

The problem with focusing on observable behavior is that it only sounds simple. In ways lethal to objectivity, certain observers tend to create scenarios for what they are seeing. "Oh, they're having an affair, I can just tell." These romantic fantasies are closely related to the neoclassical approach in which the observer has a "hypothesis" to test. For example, one might "hypothesize" that men and women often use bars as places of assignation—that is, as private and secluded environments in which they can enact the preliminaries to an evening of sexual intercourse. If one enters the bar with this idea, then one observes as does the person in procedure (A) of Figure A1, and one will, of course, "see" people having affairs.

But it is also possible for such an idea to cross one's mind *while* one is observing a couple. Now we have a subtler problem. Where did the idea come from? One possibility is that, unbeknownst to the observer, he or she has been re-visioning the couple, and *projecting* onto them a scenario written for them out of one's own ideas and feelings. *No one* is immune to such re-visioning, not even the expert. However, because the expert observer knows that it happens, he or she can safeguard against it. The best protection is to work in pairs—one male and one female observer, as I have done throughout the entire study. Then, when one observer starts to re-vision, the other can point it out. Not only does one protect oneself against re-visioning, but one also gets a male and female point of view, especially important for the male observer.

But there is *another* possibility. Assume that one thinks that the couple is having an affair and decides to ask. "Oh, yes," they say. "How did you know?"

And here we have the difference between the amateur and the expert. All the amateur knows is that he or she "guessed right." The expert asks *What did I see that led me to make that guess?*

I cannot stress this question enough. It can be answered only by repeated observation, *until one is able to describe, in detail, not by re-visioning or by scenario writing, what one is actually seeing.*

As one observes, one starts to notice that there are regularities in these readings. And, with many hours of repeated observation, I was able to list at least *some* of those regularities: they are the escalation points described in Chapter 4.

Thus, while doing a focal subject observation, one sees that she leans forward and smiles. He sits still. She continues to lean, looks down, and then up. He sits still. She sits back and glances away. They have reached an escalation point (which she began proceptively), and he failed to respond. In this *realist* description, we no longer have intuition, guesswork, scenario writing, or self-fulfilling hypothesis testing. Instead, the observer discerns *how* details themselves form a pattern, rather than being a jumble of meaningless, trivial, irrelevant happenings that must be stripped away to reveal the neoclassical "truth" under them.

Realism and Lexicality

These comments have some implications for hypothesis testing and generation, for further validation, and finally for understanding how the *non*-expert—the lover, for example—observes and construes behavior. The central issue concerns *meaning* and hypotheses about meaning. Neoclassical social scientific concern with touch, gaze, proximity, and so on is general or global, and its hypotheses likewise are global, rather than pertaining to what two *real* people are doing right *now*. Thus, in the ideal flow and type of love, neoclassicism sees people touching and gazing, and elevates touching and gazing into aesthetic symbols for *all* lovers' touches and gazes. These two forms of behavior then come to *mean* love and intimacy (or, in quantitative versions of neoclassicism, to "measure" them). Such "meanings" can be called *lexical,* to imply that non-verbal behavior has meanings in the same way words have meanings that could be looked up in a dictionary (a "lexicon"). Indeed neoclassicism *seeks* these meanings, as representing the "true" core of behavior.*

Yet, when one observes real people (as opposed to theoretical or neoclassical people), one soon sees that non-verbal behavior has incredibly more elaborate "meanings" than understood by most neoclassicists. For example, consider "eye contact."

First, the woman who tilts her head downward and sideways exposing the neck, and looks slightly upwards at the man while smiling slightly (Morris, 1977, p. 71). Does this behavior pattern imply the same kind or degree of "intimacy"—that is, "mean" the same—as a face-forward gaze made without tilting the head? Should we equate either form of gaze with the "gaze" that occurs when the man looks slowly down the woman's body, and then flicks his eyes directly up and meets *her* eyes? Is this "gaze" the same as when the man looks downwards and *sidewise* and then raises his eyes to hers?

It is *technically* convenient to lump all four kinds of eye-contact into a single category with one, primary meaning—"intimacy." Morever, such a technique has the stamp of neoclassical approval: we have not concerned ourselves with the welter of surface details, or the annoying existence of trifling variations on a core theme of looking in another person's eyes.

But, in *fact,* these forms of "gaze" have profoundly different "meanings." The first—the "coy" gesture—occurs in children (Marvin and Mossler, 1976), between flirting men and women (Morris, 1977), and among men as an expression of pleased embarrassment ("Aw, gee, fellas"). It is friendly, and, empirically,

---

*This comment applies to most research on non-verbal behavior, from Darwin's *The Expression of the Emotions in Man and Animals* (1872/1965) to quite current work. For example, Heslin and Alper (1983) begin an essay on touching by saying that "[t]ouching implies interpersonal involvement. . . " (p. 47), and end by repeating that ". . . touch implies a bond between the toucher and recipient" (p.71). In between, they explicitly seek the "meanings" of touch which, for them, distill down to the notion of a *bond* between two people. Sometimes, the search for these neoclassical meanings can become quite complex (e.g., Morris 1971; Montagu, 1978), but the central theme is always that touch "connects" two people. Of course, sometimes it does not, as in touches made accidentally (e.g., on a crowded train) or when the touch is refused.

tends to elicit friendly responses. The second eye movement—the face forward gaze—is employed by some women, who typically gloss it as representing "interest" in what the other person is saying, male *or* female. Sometimes the interest is sexual, but it "means" attentiveness, not lust. The third form of eye contact—the man's slow eye drop, followed by a flick back up—is sometimes called "mentally undressing the woman." It is overtly sexual, and many women find it an unpleasant and objectionable invasion of their privacy, though *sometimes* the woman will return the man's final look with a faint smile. The fourth example is quite different. In it, the man is avoiding looking at her body. It is, in fact, a rejection.*

What, precisely, does it then mean to "hypothesize" that gaze "measures" or "means" intimacy? What *kind* of gaze?

Yet, to say that gaze "measures" or "means" intimacy is not strictly to oversimplify. Rather, it is to idealize a much richer complexity of detail, and, in a kind of neoclassical synecdoche to select one detail—the lover's glance—with which to represent the whole. In the lover's glance, we see the lovers looking at each other deeply, passionately, tenderly, with fascination. Thus, to hypothesize that gaze "measures" intimacy is to locate this specific symbolic meaning in the global and neoclassical framework of a fixed moment of idealized love, rather than understanding that a welter of surface detail *actually* exists when people look in each other's eyes—and not always for reasons of "loving intimacy."

Of course, the "lover's gaze" exists. It involves relaxing the muscles around the eyes, so that they open slightly more than usual; widening the pupils (a fact cosmeticians know when they recommend eye shadow for women); a movement of the glance around the other person's face; and a *failure* to break eye contact and turn the head away from the listener at the ends of sentences [as happens in casual conversations at the end of speech turns (Duncan, 1983)]. But this description is not neoclassical. It is realist, for it centers on details that, together, form an observable constellation.

Nonetheless, the neoclassicist will say "Surely, if *touch* is part of intimacy, then as intimacy increases, so will touch." Yet it need not be so, either theoretically or observationally. For some women, a single touch may be *extremely* intimate (recall the woman in Chapter 1, p. 17, who said she fell in love with a man who placed his hand on her back as they crossed the street). For such a woman, a man's *repeated* touching may be the opposite of intimate, and may become "over-eager" or even a reason to reject him. Other women, in contrast, may want the man to touch them more and more often as intimacy develops, for example, to hold hands warmly and continuously. These kinds of very real variation and diversity virtually preclude the use of "touch" for measuring "intimacy," or the use of *changes* in touch frequencies to measure the growth or decline of intimacy.

---

*These interpretations all come from a number of woman informants, collectively. They do *not* derive from any neoclassical predisposition of mine to "hypothesize" such meanings. And before the neoclassical scientist decides to "test" these "grounded hypotheses," I should stress that there are many *more* types of gaze as well.

At this level of realist detail, neoclassical hypotheses about "gaze," "touch," "proximity," and so on simply do not apply, and lose their relevance to the real world. These behavior patterns have "meaning"—that is, have specific effects on the recipient—only as part of the *total* behavioral interaction that links the two people into the escalation–response sequence I discuss in the main text. In fact, *no* neoclassical hypothesis about the "meaning" of behavior pertains to the observations I have described, both immediately above and in Chapter 4.

Verification

To the neoclassical social scientist, that fact represents *failure* of my methods. Neoclassicism defines the purposes of science only to develop and test hypotheses. And if we cannot produce confirmable general hypotheses concerning love and intimacy, then, to the neoclassicist, it is not science, but—just as the amateur expert always believed—only a matter of opinion about particular events.

Moreover, in neoclassicism, one validates a scientific statement only by testing its "hypothesized" implications. If so, how can one validate realist investigation if it has no hypotheses? How can we be sure that the pattern formed by observed details is real, rather than being forced on the data?

Ultimately, the *only* answer is replication of the observations themselves. If others can see the courtship sequence approximately as described in Chapter 4, then it presumably has an "objective" reality, even if we cannot yet "hypothesize" about its temporal form or deepest causes. In fact, several television cameramen could videotape interactions proceeding as described, so we have one kind of verification, but others must repeat these observations. Replication is especially needed to study how common the sequence is cross-culturally.

A second form of verification concerns how people describe their own behavior. As discussed in the text, we found that women, far more than men, could describe the details we had observed (as well as assign "meaning" to them, as described below). Indeed, the parallels between observations, which were made first, and commentaries in interviews and essays, which came later, were striking.

Laypeople only rarely describe synchronization. However, it has long been known, and I did not invent it (Scheflen, 1965; Scheflen and Scheflen, 1972; Givens, 1983, pp. 40–43).

Disverifications?

While seeking such verifications, I also encountered what seemed to be *dis*verification. Men, in particular, often believe that courtship behavior is quite different from what I have described. Is it that I have inappropriately overstressed aspects of courtship that women describe? I do not believe so. On closer examination, these male opinions try to see courtship as having global and general properties that it does not have. I want next to discuss four neoclassical, scholarly models of courtship, all from men. In a real sense, each idealizes courtship, by seeing it as *a* *set of fixed phases* through which the lover passes—and those stages closely resemble the male descriptions in Chapter 7.

The first, proposed by Freund, Scher, and Hucker (1983), "conceptualizes" the sexual interaction as developing in four phases: "(1) location of a potential partner; (2) pretactile interaction (looking, smiling, posturing, and talking to a prospective partner); (3) tactile interaction; and (4) effecting genital union" (p. 369). Without doubt, a courting couple sequentially meets, talks, touches, and (perhaps) has intercourse. It is a commonsense description that corresponds to experience—at least to *male* experience. The problem is converting this common-sense description into a series of phases, each of which must, by definition, have its own, unique characteristics.

First, a couple having intercourse will also be looking, touching, and perhaps talking. By itself, "looking" does *not* characterize a "second" phase of courtship because looking occurs *throughout* courtship. Nor does "looking" occur for the first time in "phase (2)," because men and women look at each other from the very outset. Moreover, given that a successful courtship necessarily takes the couple from non-tactile communication to full-body contact, there must, in equal necessity, be a first touch. But why should we divide courtship into pre- and post-tactile phases? If "common sense" tells us that such touches are important, then we might not see that Freund, Scher, and Hucker have not de-scribed what *kinds* of touch divide courtship into pre- and post-tactile phases. Once again, the reader assigns his or her *own* meanings to the description, just as we do when visualizing Hall's description of intimacy. These phases, which ini-tially *sound* objective and well-defined, soon blur and become *symbols* for the passage to love. The emphasis is not on behavior, but on emotion, and on the ideal of loving intimacy symbolized externally by behavior. Again we encounter neoclassicism.

Secondly, in reality, if the couple is in "phase (2)" there is no guarantee that they will pass on to "phase (3)," let alone "phase (4)." Thus, these phases are actually reconstructed *backwards*—from the final result, intercourse, to the initial events of courtship. The description says how the couple gets to intercourse, given that they are so intimately involved, and not how a couple moves *towards* intercourse from a start as relative strangers. There is, of course, an immense dif-ference between these two viewpoints, and to confuse them, even in the name of neoclassicism, is to falsify the complexities of escalation and response.

But the description is also quite characteristic of how *men* describe the courtship sequence. There is none of the loving and lingering attention to the *details* of "pretactile interaction"—they are all lumped together into a single step. Like-wise, in Morris' twelve stages to sexual intimacy (1971, pp. 73–78), the first two involve looking and the last nine involve intimate body contact. The third in sequence, called "voice to voice," includes everything else. We recall the male essayists of Chapter 7 who *also* describe courtship as foreplay. In marked contrast to women's descriptions, these male descriptions slur over details in order to reach the endpoint—genital intercourse—quickly and explicitly. No welter of surface details or trifling happenings here! [In contrast, Money's brief description of courtship (1980, pp. 73–76) is far more balanced.]

If the Freund, Scher, and Hucker model is therefore neoclassical (as well as masculine), so too is the far more detailed phasic description of courtship provided by David Givens (1978, 1983). For Givens, an ethologically oriented anthropologist, the phases of courtship combine behavioral and emotional elements. The crucial phases are (1) attention, (2) recognition, (3) interaction, (4) sexual arousal, and, again, (5) sexual intercourse and its aftermaths. Throughout, Givens stresses the partners' uncertainty and desire to seem friendly, as do other men describing courtship, e.g., the male essayists or Bernard Goldstein (1976, pp. 117–118).

For Givens, the "essence" of the attention phase is "ambivalence—tentative and hesitant approach" (1978, p. 349). Tendencies to draw near and to avoid compete with each other, in an echo of Argyle and Dean's architectural balance of forces. Each person performs "displacement-like" activities, which "function" to "console" the performer, such as hair-preening. In this, Givens first sees courtship as representing a conflict between opposing emotions (which men in fact feel when approaching a woman for the first time) and then interprets behavior in accordance with his vision. Now, to be sure, people sometimes nervously finger their hair. But sometimes such behavior patterns occur without their meanings being at all obvious. For example, some—not all—women twirl their hair through their fingers while talking to a man and looking in his eyes. Whereas one observer might want to say that her behavior "means" nervousness, another might say that it "means" soft, romantic interest. In this, believing is seeing.

In describing the "recognition" phase, Givens retains his interpretation that courtship involves conflict, but this time it is between the two people. "Evident submissiveness appears to be the key message during the recognition phase," he writes (1978, p. 350), although, again, it is not clear that *women* feel submissive when they proceptively initiate the courtship sequence. In fact, the folk-term for such behavior is "bold." But *men* often feel that they must be "polite," that is, "submissive," if they want to avoid appearing pushy.

Throughout his description of "recognition," Givens stresses how various behavior patterns—head-tilting (the "coy" gesture), pouting the lips, joining the hands—all "mean" submissiveness. He parallels these behavior patterns to those of a nursery-age child "shyly" interacting with a "potentially threatening adult" (1978, p. 351). In brief, the man is nervously squirming a bit while he tries to appear friendly, although Givens seems to think that women feel the same way.

As the couple moves on into the "interaction" phase, Givens continues to stress conflict and vulnerability; for example, when one person speaks, he or she "'exposes' the self and assumes a socially vulnerable position" (1978, p. 352). Now behavior represents "anxiety" and "jeopardy," and still the mood is distinctively "submissive" (1978, p. 352).

Givens now moves quite quickly—far more quickly than does the couple, I suspect—to discussing sexual intimacy itself. Now the "barriers" have begun to "relax," and they caress, stroke, nuzzle, groom, and embrace each other (1978, pp.

352–353) and then move on to intercourse. In contrast to the previous mood of tension and apprehension, the couple is warmly and tenderly intimate. The story has a happy ending. [Additional details of the story are found in *Love Signals* (Givens, 1983).]

These attributions of meaning to courtship behavior are not merely neoclassical in their effort to define an ideal core for the development of intimacy. Givens is also a man, and has provided a perceptive and accurate description of how *many* men feel during the courtship sequence. In contrast to the tone of confidence and sureness that women use when discussing the sequence, men, as Givens describes, are *typically* unsure of themselves and, as male essayist M1 put it (Chapter 7), of the woman's response to their "attractional behavior."

But a deeper issue is raised by Givens' description. It contains an immediacy of feeling that is achieved by his vivid translation of behavior into emotion. In this, Givens is a *romantic*: in his words we see a *Sturm und Drang* of feeling enacted by each member of the couple (Canaday, 1959, pp. 30–55).

My purpose in these comments is *not* an attack on Givens. Romanticism is one of the great aesthetics, and my own fondness for it should be obvious from my quotations from Keats and Blake. In fact, Givens may see the man's emotions so clearly *because* he is a romantic. But, nonetheless, my point is that romantic neoclassicism is an aesthetic just as surely as Hall's vision represents an aesthetic. Though Givens' eye observes precisely, yet, in its romanticism, it too sees what it believes.

Of course, Givens is in good company in his neoclassical romanticism. In an essay called "Flirtation," Georg Simmel (1919/1984) wrote that

> [t]he essence of flirtation, expressed with paradoxical brevity, is this: Where love is present, having and not-having are also present, whether in its fundament or in its external aspect. And thus where having and not-having are present—even if not in reality but only in play—love, or something that fills its place, is also present.
>
> I shall apply this interpretation of flirtation first to some observations of experience. A sidelong glance with the head half-turned is characteristic of flirtation in its most banal guise. [From the context, Simmel appears to be envisioning a woman performing this "coy" gesture.] A hint of aversion lies in this gesture; but at the same time it connotes fleeting submission, a momentary focusing of attention on the other person, who in the same moment is symbolically rebuffed by the inclination of the body and the head. . . . It has the charm of secrecy and furtiveness that cannot persist, and for this reason consent and refusal are inseparably combined in it. (pp. 134–135).

In Simmel's words we encounter the same themes: uncertainty, submission combined with refusal, and consent mingled with aversion. In elegant, evocative phrases, Simmel provides the core vision of courtship as the *romantic* sees it. And, as in neoclassicism itself, we also understand that the task of romanticism, even in the sciences, is to elucidate those core meanings of behavior.

These examples of "disverification" all center on what behavior means—that is, on its lexicality according to either a pure neoclassical or romantic neoclassical lexicon of meaning. But another point should also be clear, I hope: *men* are often the romantics who seek profound meaning in the slightest and subtlest movement of a woman's body. (Does this search occur because men are not particularly careful observers? Perhaps so.) In this, like Swann in Proust's *Swann in Love,* men create symbolic meanings for behavior that often differ *very* much from the meanings women attribute to behavior.

And how can realism then understand what behavior "means"? In realist *theater,* the answer was Stanislavsky's: reality is imitated on stage when the actor and actress genuinely *feel* what they are doing (Gorchakov, 1954). It is the first rule of dialogue: *"limitless attention to your partner"* (Gorchakov, p. 318, italics original). In the midst of a two-page comment on how to observe a couple, Stanislavsky spoke thus to the actors of the Moscow Art Theatre:

> . . . The man looks straight into the girl's face, never taking his eyes away from her eyes. . . . And the girl meets his eyes, then looks away to one side, then lowers her head and looks at her muff, and finally she throws a glance up at him somehow from the side and then concentrates her look away from him at something in the distance. (Gorchakov, 1954, p. 315)

It is not the details that make this description realism; it is their accuracy. The young woman performs the "coy" gesture, but are we *certain* that it embodies consent mingled with aversion, as Simmel, the neoclassicist, says?

Hardly. Once again, life is not theater. But can realist *science* answer the question of what behavior means? To begin, I will turn next to lexicality itself, and then, by extension of Stanislavsky's dictum, explain how one can pay, if not limitless, then very careful, attention to one's subjects.

Popular Lexicality

When men and women court, each makes literally hundreds of different movements: shifting one's weight, touching one's hair, smiling, leaning, lifting a glass, looking at the other person's eyes, moving towards the other person, kissing, and many more. They include all the nonverbal behavior patterns sometimes called "body language," even though there is no language here, at least not in the way linguists use the term. Moreover, behavior is constantly changing from moment to moment. It is incredibly rich.

Nonetheless, people want to attribute meaning to their behavior, and to the behavior of others. "She looked away from me," the man says. "What did that *mean*?"

What seems like an infinite number of popular books tell us how to decipher behavior. The classic is Julius Fast's *Body Lanugage* (1970), but there are many others. One book tells you how to read faces (Bellak and Baker, 1981), another how to read hands (Lee and Charlton, 1980), another how to read postures (Kurtz and

Prestera, 1976), *another* on how to read faces (Whiteside, 1974). But these books all share one premise: that behavior patterns have meanings the same way words have meanings. Thus, one man's facial expression conveys placidity, smugness, and thoughtfulness (Bellak and Baker, 1981, p. 65); another man's widespread arms convey power (Lee and Charlton, 1980, pp. 146–155, especially p. 148); we read that a man's chest position may convey a "basic lack of emotional vitality" (Kurtz and Prestera, 1976, p. 83); or that the way a woman rearranges her clothing indicates that she is interested in a man and wants to be liked (Fast, 1970, p. 97); or that an upturned lip indicates an optimistic bent (Whiteside, 1974, p. 148); or—even—that a Roman ("hawk") nose indicates a person who is naturally administrative, likes to talk business, and is commercially minded (Whiteside, 1974, tenth unnumbered page of a "Rapid Reference Glossary of Trait Indicators" following page 120).

The last one gives the whole thing away. Why not simply say that Jews have big noses and are greedy? All of this is folklore and, in my opinion, sometimes very peculiar folklore. It is the " . . . art called physiognomy, that is, the recognition of the characters of men and women, whether they be good or bad. This is done merely by looking at the man or woman." And it is an *old* art, for that quotation comes from Marco Polo (1298–1299?/1958, p. 267)! Despite an occasional insight, this "art"—ancient *or* modern—is little more than an exercise in scenario writing.

Though without their excesses, neoclassical scholarship about non-verbal behavior shares two premises with these books: not only that behavior has lexical meanings, but that *finding* them is part of the scientist's task. However, in the realist aesthetic and method, the objective observer cannot enter the subject's mind and determine what a movement or body position was intended to convey, nor enter the *partner's* mind to find what actually was conveyed, nor even determine if any meaning was intended or conveyed. To do so is to see life as theater, and to believe that people's actions represent the conventionalized stage movements of actors trained to communicate meanings to an audience.

For example, Mark L. Knapp (1978, p. 169) writes that we expect that during a face to face interaction between intimates they will nod, lean forward, and maintain "open arms and open body positions, direct body orientation to the other person, and postural congruence." We also expect, he adds, "positive facial expressions (smiling, happiness, interest, joy, amusement) to predominate over negative expressions."

These expectations involve much more than the neoclassical hope of finding a few core behavior patterns that in themselves will carry the full weight of emotional communication. Knapp has, first, selected these behavior patterns because, to him, they "mean" intimacy. Then, second, he has written a scenario in which the actor and actress will convey intimacy—if they intend to do so—through movements that have the lexical meanings Knapp has given to them.

However, the description is factually wrong. Indeed, intimate couples will sometimes nod, smile, and lean towards each other, but so will two men discussing a business deal or talking "heartily" at a cocktail party. The *actual*, i.e., observable, ways in which men and women express intimacy involve the quite different behavior patterns of the courtship sequence itself, such as touching, gazing at the other's face, and, above all, movement synchronization. Perhaps I should again point out that many men do not notice those behavior patterns, and describe them only very vaguely. Perhaps Knapp is among them, for many such men will mix behavioral descriptions (''smiling'') with emotional descriptions (''happiness''), as Knapp has done in this passage.

But, in realism, we do not look for what behavior ''means'' in these neoclassical and theatrical senses. *In reality, when a man and woman court, they behave for each other and for themselves, for reasons not even they may understand, and not for the benefit of a scientific audience.* To observe *as if* life were theater is to falsify the reality of this man and woman's own world, and, sometimes, even to deny that it exists. Therefore, in the aesthetic of scientific realism I am discussing, one abandons the search for lexical meaning. What does one find in its stead?

Action and Reaction

The moment one puts aside both the folkloric search for meaning and the neoclassical ideas that life is theater and courtship represents a script enacted by performers, one begins to observe objectively. Then one can observe how people *react* to each other. For example, during a focal subject observation, the man turns from the woman to look at the door of the bar, and she moves slightly away from him. If this pattern of action and reaction is regular, as it can be under certain circumstances, then we infer that she responded or reacted to his action.

Throughout the study, I sought these commonly occurring sequences of action and reaction. How does the partner react when the other person leans towards them, or touches them, or swivels slightly to face them? Next, we identified as specifically as possible the behavior patterns that *regularly* elicited responses from the partner. That goal reached, we then determined, again observationally, how these small units form longer and longer sequences of behavior, until, finally, the entire courtship sequence emerged from the data.

Though Chapter 4 described the sequence, an additional example will illustrate how this method differs from the neoclassical effort to assign ''meaning'' to behavior. If a man touches a woman, his touch does not ''mean'' intimacy. It depends on when the touch occurs and on whether or not it was a response to the woman's interest. Thus, a man who touches a woman's hair 2 or 3 minutes after they have started talking will nearly assuredly elicit a negative response from her: she shakes her head slightly, brushing his hand away; she turns away or leaves him. But if the courtship is an hour and a half old, she may react very differently: by leaning towards him, smiling, looking. In interviews, women informants indicate that his touch is understood as a response to *her* interest in *him* (that is, he is a ''responsive'' man).

Thus, by itself, a ''touch'' means nothing, folklore and neoclassical research notwithstanding. Instead, it is the partner's *response* to the touch, the lean, the gaze that tells the observer if intimacy is developing, and it is *an empirical, not theoretical, question to determine the effect any behavior pattern has on courtship.*

This sharp realist emphasis on observing sequences of action and reaction comes directly from biology, and not the psychologist's notion of "stimulus and response." The process of escalation and response—action and reaction—represents one example of the biological universal that organisms respond to changes in their environment. In such organism–environment interactions, the organism brings to its response not a robotic input–output capacity [as Bernard seems to believe this approach implies (1972b, pp. 95–132)], but a complex indwelling capacity to select responses and change them as the situation changes (Chapter 4). To reiterate, "indwelling" does not mean "natural" or "genetically determined," as in ethnobiology, but built into the anatomy and neurophysiology of the organism. Though observational realism is not restricted to biology, nonetheless in the courtship sequence the biologist sees living *organisms,* not statistical cyborgs, robots linked into S-R loops, or disembodied minds communicating through pure idea.

Behavioral Descriptions

For these purposes, one must therefore describe behavior objectively, rather than by its presumed or attributed meanings. Many such systems exist, ranging from kinesiological descriptions of individual muscle movements (Ekman and Friesen, 1976), through frame-by-frame analyses of films of long, multiperson interactions (Kendon, 1970; Condon, 1976), to the use of dance notation (M. Davis, 1979). None of these techniques is suitable for a crowded bar, which demands rapid notetaking.* Nor are checklists appropriate, for they limit one to an *a priori* list of behavior patterns and are difficult to use when recording sequences. After initial experimentation, the following system proved useful and flexible.

- What part of the body is moved? Eyes, head, shoulders, arms, legs?
- What is the direction of the movement? Towards oneself, towards the other person, or away from both?
- How expansive is the behavior? The question refers to the volume of space swept out when the person moves: some people make large gestures, moving their arms widely around them, while others move in a smaller volume. People differ considerably in expansiveness.

*I do not have space to discuss the observational aesthetics of Ray Birdwhistell, Adam Kendon, Albert Scheflen, or William Condon. In their frame-by-frame analyses of films of social interaction, they are aesthetically close to treating non-verbal communication as a form of *dance,* and the concept of movement synchronization is in fact quite valuable for studying dance as an artistic endeavor (Hanna, 1979). In their exquisite attention to detail, these researchers are aesthetic realists, but sometimes one senses an over-interest in detail for its own sake. I suggest—tentatively—that the romantic ideal also motivated their work, but will leave it to others to explore the possibility further.

Two additional categories exist, but are less important.

- Tempo: how quickly is the movement made?
- Intensity, which refers to the speed and force of a movement, and, ultimately, to muscle tension. The English language provides many terms that differentiate according to intensity (e.g., a *pat* vs. a *slap*).

Generally, courtship movements are made in the middle range of tempo and intensity, so that little explicit reference usually need be made to them.

These categories permit one to define other movements without imputing meanings or intentions to them. Thus, a "reach" is an extension of the arm and hand directly away from the body in the direction of some external object. The categories also permit the researcher to compare observational descriptions with descriptions provided by informants. By speaking of a "smile" or a "reach," rather than by dissecting behavior into smaller kinesiological units, one can communicate with an informant in ways that are otherwise impossible. However, the observer must beware of attributing his or her own "meanings" to such named behavior patterns, and, instead, allow the informant to provide them, if they wish.

Whenever possible, notes were taken in a 3×5 memorandum pad, though several students used college notebooks while observing in a college pub. No notes were ever taken on the first visit to any bar. At no point in the study were we ever approached by someone demanding to know what we were taking notes about.

Reliability

Neophyte observers and non-field researchers sometimes raise the issue of "inter-observer reliability" about such observations. Are the two observers "seeing the same thing" when they watch? The question has its greatest importance when recording behavioral frequencies (which we did not), but, in my experience, the problem is often less important than it sounds. The major sources of inter-observer *dis*agreement arise when one observer is scenario-writing or simply not watching attentively. Some "observers" will actively avoid looking at a couple and seem to know exactly when *not* to look. Once, with a young man and a woman, I was observing a man and woman at the nearby bar. The woman at the bar leaned over to her companion and put her hand on his chest. The woman observer and I continued to watch, our attention focused on her movement. Simultaneously, the male observer turned to me and asked what he should watch. The magnificent ill-timing of his question suggested that he did not want to see what was happening. Field "data" obtained by such observers may be valueless, and certainly has no relevance to inter-observer reliability.

Inter-observer reliability also drops if the observational categories require assigning *meaning or intention* to the behavior. Thus, one observer "sees" a touch as "intimacy" and records it as such, while another observer "sees" it as casual. The categories above explicitly avoid this problem.

Finally, inter-observer reliability increases as both observers become familiar with the range and variety of courtship behavior. Trustworthy data probably cannot be obtained by a neophyte without many hours of preliminary observation, and even then some observers still want to write scenarios, *especially* when they dislike bars.

We made no attempt to count how often various behavior patterns occurred, though it is qualitatively unmistakable that frequencies vary considerably. Nonetheless, no purpose of the study is served by knowing that touches occur in 87 percent of all courtship interactions (the number is invented). Even if such numbers existed, were highly reliable, and were adjusted for personal differences in behavior and touch preferences, I am not sure what question these numbers would answer. In the absence of specific questions, numerical data are simply empty of meaning.

Given the non-quantitative purposes of the work, and the complexities of measuring inter-observer reliability in field situations, I have made no effort to calculate *numerical* estimates of "reliability." However, when one works with an observational partner, it becomes *qualitatively* very obvious whether or not the observers both agree, especially if they comment to each other about the observations (a practice which is highly recommended). From many such observations, spent with a number of different women observers, I have concluded that observational reliability in the study was excellent. Indeed, some observers have great talent for watching and will track behavior continuously for hours. (It follows that the observer *must* be interested in what happens between men and women!)

Moreover, I made a serious effort to find exceptions to the core sequence and to the role of escalation as described in Chapter 4. First, with the help of several authoritative informants, who will remain anonymous, we made some observations in what was said to be a high-priced "hooker bar" in New York City, as well as observing prostitutes elsewhere. The behavior of these women was very different from what is given in Chapter 4, suggesting that there was little chance of confusing courtship with a prostitute's solicitations. For example, one prostitute placed her knee directly between the man's legs as she stood slightly behind him and caressed the inside of his thighs with her leg. She had just approached him, so it was clear that they did not know each other. At other times, a prostitute will ignore a man's inattentiveness. For example, she will lean against him and caress his shoulder with her breasts if he turns away from her. Nor is prostitute *de*-escalation at all similar to what happens between other couples: the prostitute will simply walk away and pay no further attention to the man, unlike a flirting or courting couple.

Observation of married couples (both wearing matching wedding rings, for example) indicated that well-established couples also behave very differently than does a courting couple.

Realism, Once Again

Equipped with these observations, the layperson's beliefs became easier to understand. When a man *says* that men "always" make the first move, his comment does not represent truth as the observer sees and records it. Instead, we are struck by the *difference* between the observations and how this man interprets and gives meaning to courtship. Likewise, if he says that it does not "mean" anything if a woman touches a man, while women say that such touches have great meaning, the *difference* in their statements comes to the fore. These differences are discussed at length in the main text, but methodologically they cannot be identified unless the scientist first knows the difference between what "actually" happens and what the participant "thinks" is happening, and, second, can recognize that the "truth" consists not in one version over another, but in the simultaneous existence of objectively observable behavior *and* the participant's own beliefs about it.

Again, this procedure is realism, not neoclassicism of the kind that Malinowski, for example, described. In Malinowski's neoclassical method, the *observer* extracts and construes meanings for the native's thoughts and behavior, thereby to raise the much vexed question of what relationship, if any, exists between the ethnographer's version of the truth and the native's version. In this, the difference between observer and native (or lover) rises to preoccupy our thoughts. But in the realist method I am discussing, another difference attracts our attention just as strongly, or more so. It concerns the relationship the *lover* experiences between different versions of his or her own world, for example, between the man's *belief* that women are hesitant sexually and the *fact* that sometimes they are not (e.g., in Cabell's passage, quoted in Chapter 5). Only sometimes is this difference experienced as cognitive dissonance, that is, as an open clash between contradictory meanings. At other times, these differences are resolved symbolically, for example, in the belief that there are two "types" of women. In that resolution, the man then *expects* to see these types of women behaving differently, and, when different women *in fact* behave differently, he has a ready explanation for the observation.

Though the man's reasoning is circular, he nonetheless sees the world in a self-consistent way, and we—the objective *realist* observers—see that he sees it thus. "No problem," the man says, "women are funny like that." However, at other times, the man may experience acute contradiction between his beliefs about women and the *observable* facts. For example, he thinks that women go to bars to be "picked up," or that they "want only one thing" (like prostitutes), and then he *discovers* that his belief is false. Now that contradiction exists not merely psychologically, e.g., as cognitive dissonance or as conflict between personal construals of meaning, but also as a contradiction between his expectations or beliefs and *fact*.

Thus, by focusing on behavior and describing it as such (rather than by seeking its "meanings"), the realist observer can understand something that the neoclassicist might not: that this man is confused *with good reason*. It is *not* "all in the head" or a symptom of "irrational thinking." There is a genuine—that is, objectively *real*—basis for his unhappiness: *he no longer understands the world, and he knows it*. Yet, if we were true to the neoclassical goal of describing the ideal forms of love and courtship, we might not understand that he does not have a self-consistent way to perceive the world *or* to relate to women. In this, realism sees the world as a less pretty place than does neoclassicism.

Yet, how does the observer *know* that a man or woman experiences contradictions between beliefs and reality? The answer is simple: one *asks*.

Interviewing in the Realist Mode

If the "meaning" of behavior cannot be constructed by the observer, it can nonetheless be inferred from what men and women say about behavior. Indeed, in the realist method I am discussing, such "meanings" take precedence over *all* meanings that the observer him- or herself wants to attribute to behavior.

By "interview," I do *not* mean the formal or semi-formal structured interview often used by takers of opinion polls. Instead, our interviews were designed to elicit, in the person's own words, what they believe, think, and feel about themselves and the other sex. Several questions were particularly valuable:

- How do you tell if someone you've just met is interested in you?
- How do you let someone know that you're interested in them?
- Where and how did you first meet your wife/husband/boyfriend/girlfriend?
- What do you find attractive in a man/woman?

The interviews had several purposes. One was to determine how accurately people can describe a male–female interaction. Do they describe the same observable behavior patterns as discussed before (as women often do) or do they speak in generalities (as men often do)? What details are emphasized and omitted? What language (clinical, formal, colloquial) is used when talking about sex? A second purpose was to define what people believe behavior means. Spontaneous comments are especially valuable—"I knew she was interested because she kept touching me." However, another level of "meaning" also exists, represented by comments about the singles scene generally, or about men and women generally. These comments often reveal a great deal of worry, concern, or even anxiety which coexist with seeming self-confidence.

Such interviews contain a major methodological pitfall. The interviewer and informant belong to the same culture and share meanings with each other. Thus, a man says that a woman is "sexy," and the male interviewer may believe that he knows what is "meant." But in all likelihood, he does not, and has provided his *own* meanings for the informant's words, in a kind of scenario writing. The danger is particularly great if the interviewer believes that he or she *already* knows what other people think and feel, for example, if the interviewer is seeking to "verify" a neoclassical hypothesis about intimacy. Then the interviewer listens selectively for ideas that confirm the preexisting belief, and ignores the rest.

The problem is particularly great when asking about who starts or escalates courtship. The belief in "male aggression" is so strong that it can lead interviewer and informant both to believe that women are passive. An example is the woman who says that she never "makes the first move." The neoclassicist, bent on confirming hypotheses about masculine aggression, may then never hear her describe how she *in fact* typically does initiate courtship proceptively.

In this, hearing is like seeing: one hears people say what one already believes. For example, the man at the bar says that men in bars are really there to meet women. If one is already predisposed to believe that bars are sordid, lust-filled places, one might never notice that for the past hour, this man has been talking to a male interviewer and has been *ignoring* the two women next to him.

As a technical point, bar interviews were never tape-recorded. If the bar has a band, they will usually assume that you are tape-recording them, and difficulties can arise very quickly. One can jot down notes or transcribe the interview later. Other interviews were done in people's homes and were tape-recorded. They ranged from 1½ to 3 hours, and followed the usual procedures for such interviews (Ives, 1974).

The Real World in Focus

Together, observation and interviews produce very rich data. *No* one could claim to summarize these data adequately. Accordingly, it is easy to fall into neoclassicism and seek the ideal core of these complexities. Yet I suggest that one should not: reality is *very* complex, and there comes a point when neoclassicism falsifies it by creating pretty pictures, simplified hypotheses, and a surface glibness that glosses over details that do not fit. But even if the realist methods I am describing are sometimes more difficult to apply, they are also more fascinating— at least to me. Ultimately, that is the final criterion for choosing a method, for both neoclassicism and realism genuinely seek, and value, "truth." As in Western art itself, each aesthetic has its place, and its products can be judged only by its own standards. I submit only that one should choose between them consciously, and not believe that science *necessarily* is defined by its neoclassical proponents. In that, science too is at least as rich and complex as the behavior of people in bars.

So, once again, we look around. This time the bar is no longer a madhouse, a blur of noise and chaos. In having learned how to observe, now we see in focus: behavior, dress, decor, voices, *people . . .*

> M: I'm sorry, but I was staring at you. You're a beautiful woman.
> F: Thank you. I like being appreciated.
> M: Those are pretty earrings. Where did you get them?
> F: Why don't you guess?

A flirtation has begun, and, perhaps, a courtship. Over the next 2 or 3 hours we shall observe this man and woman, and record their looks, reaches, smiles, touches, and finally, synchronization. We shall see what she does and how he responds, and what he does and how she responds. Slowly, there will build before us a gradually deepening intimacy between these two people. It will not be in our minds or our construals, but in their behavior itself. We observe them not as ideals nor as the perfect embodiments of love, but as people—real people, in the here-and-now of this bar, this evening. If the neoclassicist is disappointed that their behavior does not represent the purified and idealized core of love, then we are not. In their behavior, and the behavior of many others like them, we shall find the biological and cultural basis of intimacy. And it will not be located in the Pure realm of disembodied Neoclassical ideas, but in the welter of surface details that form *this* physically real world—the only world we have, and the world that both science *and* art must seek to understand.

References

Abbey, Antonia. 1982. Sex differences in attributions for friendly behavior: Do males misperceive females' friendliness? *Journal of Personality and Social Psychology* 42:830–838.

Adams, Richard. 1980. *The girl in a swing.* New York: Knopf.

Agar, Michael H. 1982. Toward an ethnographic language. *American Anthropologist* 84:779–795.

Alexander, Richard D. 1974. The evolution of social behavior. *Annual Review of Ecology and Systematics* 5:325–383.

Alexander, Richard D. 1979. *Darwinism and human affairs.* Seattle: University of Washington Press.

Alexander, Richard D., and Gerald Borgia. 1978. Group selection, altruism, and the levels of organization of life. *Annual Review of Ecology and Systematics* 9:449–474.

Alland, Alexander, Jr. 1972. *The human imperative.* New York: Columbia University Press.

Allgeier, Elizabeth Rice. 1984. Courtship disorders and sexual health. *SIECUS Report* 13(2):10–12, November.

Allon, Natalie, and Diane Fishel. 1981. Singles' bars as examples of urban courting patterns. In: Peter J. Stein (ed.), *Single life: Unmarried adults in social context* (pp. 115–128). New York: St. Martin's Press.

Altmann, Jeanne. 1974. Observational study of behavior: Sampling methods. *Behaviour* 49:227–267.

Anand, Mulk Raj, Charles Fabri, and Stella Kramrisch. 1962. *Homage to Khajuraho* (2nd ed.). Bombay: Marg Publications.

Andersson, Malte. 1984. The evolution of eusociality. *Annual Review of Ecology and Systematics* 15:165–189.

Andreas Capellanus. 1941. *The art of courtly love.* New York: Norton. (Originally written ca. 1200.)

Aquinas, St. Thomas. 1960. *The pocket Aquinas: Selections from the writings of St. Thomas* (ed. by Vernon J. Bourke). New York: Washington Square Press. (Originally written ca. 1260.)

Ardrey, Robert. 1961. *African genesis.* New York: Dell.

Argyle, Michael. 1969. *Social interaction.* London: Tavistock.

Argyle, Michael, and Janet Dean. 1965. Eye-contact, distance and affiliation. *Sociometry* 28:289–304.

Arnold, June. 1979. The violent sex. [Review of *Male psychobiology and the evolution of consciousness,* by Laurel Holliday.] *Motheroot Journal* 1(3):4, Summer.

Aronson, Jerrold L. 1984. *A realist philosophy of science.* New York: St. Martin's Press.

Atkinson, Clarissa W. 1983. "Precious balsam in a fragile glass": The ideology of virginity in the later Middle Ages. *Journal of Family History* 8:131–143.

Austen, Jane. 1945. *Pride and prejudice.* Garden City, NY: International Collectors Library. (Originally published 1813.)

Barash, David P. 1977. *Sociobiology and behavior.* New York: Elsevier.

Barash, David. 1979. *The whisperings within.* New York: Harper & Row.

Barker, Roger G. 1968. *Ecological psychology.* Stanford, CA: Stanford University Press.

Barthes, Roland. 1978. *A lover's discourse.* New York: Hill and Wang.

Bateson, Patrick (ed.). 1983a. *Mate choice.* New York: Cambridge University Press.

Bateson, Patrick. 1983b. Optimal outbreeding. In: Patrick Bateson (ed.), *Mate choice* (pp. 257–277). New York: Cambridge University Press.

Baum, M. J. 1983. Hormonal modulation of sexuality in female primates. *BioScience* 33:578–582.

Beach, Frank A. 1976. Sexual attractivity, proceptivity, and receptivity in female mammals. *Hormones and Behavior* 7:105–138.

Belden, Jack. 1949. *China shakes the world.* New York: Harper.

Bell, Eric Temple. 1956. The prince of mathematicians. In: James R. Newman (ed.), *The world of mathematics* (vol. 1, pp. 295–339). New York: Simon and Schuster.

Bell, Robert R. 1966. *Premarital sex in a changing society.* Englewood Cliffs, NJ: Prentice-Hall.

Bell, Robert R., and Kathleen Coughey. 1980. Premarital sexual experience among college females, 1958, 1968, and 1978. *Family Relations* 29:353–357.

Bellak, Leopold, and Samm Sinclair Baker. 1981. *Reading faces.* New York: Holt, Rinehart and Winston.

Benet, Sula. 1970. Some changes in family structure and personality among the peasants of Great Russia. *Transactions of the New York Academy of Sciences, Series II* 32.51–65.

Benson, Larry D. 1965. *Art and tradition in Sir Gawain and the Green Knight.* New Brunswick, NJ: Rutgers University Press.

Berlanstein, Lenard R. 1980. Illegitimacy, concubinage, and proletarianization in a French town, 1760–1914. *Journal of Family History* 5:360–374.

Bernard, Jessie. 1972a. *The future of marriage.* New York: Bantam.

Bernard, Jessie. 1972b. *The sex game.* New York: Atheneum.

Bernard, Jessie. 1981. *The female world.* New York: Free Press.

Bidney, David. 1967. *Theoretical anthropology* (2nd, augmented ed.). New York: Schocken.

Blake, William. 1925. To the evening star. In: Homer A. Watt and James B. Munn, *Ideas and forms in English and American literature* (p. 432). Chicago: Scott, Foresman. (Originally published 1783.)

Bleier, Ruth. 1984. *Science and gender: A critique of biology and its theories on women.* Elmsford, NY: Pergamon.

Blumstein, Philip, and Pepper Schwartz. 1983. *American couples: Money, work, sex.* New York: Morrow.

Bock, Kenneth. 1980. *Human nature and history: A response to sociobiology.* New York: Columbia University Press.

Bodmer, W. F., and L. L. Cavalli-Sforza. 1976. *Genetics, evolution, and man.* San Francisco: W. H. Freeman.

Bolton, Ralph. 1977. The Qollo marriage process. In: Ralph Bolton and Enrique Mayer (eds.), *Andean kinship and marriage*. Washington, DC: American Anthropological Association.

Bowlby, John. 1980. By ethology out of psycho-analysis: An experiment in interbreeding. *Animal Behaviour* 28:649–656.

Bradburd, Daniel. 1984. The rules and the game: The practice of marriage among the Komachi. *American Ethnologist* 11:738–753.

Breasted, James Harvey, and Charles A. Robinson. 1914. *Outlines of European history. Part I*. Boston: Ginn.

Brockett, Oscar G. 1982. *History of the theatre* (4th ed.). Boston: Allyn and Bacon.

Brown, Helen Gurley. n.d. *Sex and the new single girl*. New York: Geis.

Brown, Irene Q. 1982. Domesticity, feminism, and friendship: Female aristocratic culture and marriage in England, 1660–1760. *Journal of Family History* 7:406–424, Winter.

Brown, Rita Mae. 1984. One feminist's personal view of feminity [book review of *Femininity*, by Susan Brownmiller]. *Philadelphia Inquirer*, 29 January 1984, Section P, pp. 1, 8.

Brownmiller, Susan. 1975. *Against our will: Men, women and rape*. New York: Bantam.

Brownstein, Rachel M. 1982. *Becoming a heroine: Reading about women in novels*. New York: Viking.

Bullough, Vern L. 1980. Technology and female sexuality and physiology: Some implications. *The Journal of Sex Research* 16:59–71.

Bulmer, Martin. 1983. The methodology of *The taxi-dance hall:* An early account of Chicago ethnography from the 1920s. *Urban Life* 12:95–120.

Burgess, Ann Wolbert (ed.). 1985. *Rape and sexual assault: A research handbook*. New York: Garland.

Burton-Opitz, Russell. 1928. *An elementary manual of physiology for colleges, schools of nursing, of physical education, and of the practical arts* (3rd ed., rev.). Philadelphia: Saunders.

Byrne, Noel. 1978. Sociotemporal considerations of everyday life suggested by an empirical study of the bar milieu. *Urban Life* 6:417–438.

Cabell, James Branch. n.d. *Beyond life: Dizain des demiurges*. New York: Modern Library.

Cabell, [James] Branch. 1932. *These restless heads: A trilogy of romantics*. New York: Literary Guild.

Calder, Jenni. 1976. *Women and marriage in Victorian fiction*. New York: Oxford University Press.

Calin, William. 1966. *The epic quest: Studies in four Old French chansons de geste*. Baltimore: Johns Hopkins.

Callen, Anthea. 1980. *Courbet*. London: Jupiter Books.

Campbell, Bernard (ed.). 1972. *Sexual selection and The descent of man 1871–1971*. Chicago: Aldine.

Canaday, John. 1959. *Mainstreams of modern art*. New York: Simon and Schuster.

Caplan, Arthur L. (ed.). 1978. *The sociobiology debate: Readings on ethical and scientific issues*. New York: Harper & Row.

Cargan, Leonard, and Matthew Melko. 1982. *Singles: Myths and realities*. Beverly Hills: Sage.

Carroll, Lewis. 1960. *The annotated Alice: Alice's adventures in Wonderland & Through the looking glass* (introduction and notes by Martin Gardner). Cleveland: World.

Carter, W. E. 1977. Trial marriage in the Andes? In: Ralph Bolton and Enrique Mayer (eds.),

Andean kinship and marriage (pp. 177–216). Washington, DC: American Anthropological Association.

Cassell, Carol. 1984. *Swept away: Why women fear their own sexuality.* New York: Simon and Schuster.

Catullus, Gaius Valerius. 1966. Poem 70. In: *The poems of Catullus* (p. 182). Baltimore: Penguin. (Originally written ca. 50 B.C.)

Cavan, Ruth Shonle. 1969. *The American family* (4th ed.). New York: Crowell.

Cavan, Sherri. 1966. *Liquor license: An ethnography of bar behavior.* Chicago: Aldine.

Chaucer, Geoffrey. 1957. The merchant's tale. In: *The works of Geoffrey Chaucer* (2nd ed., pp. 115–127, edited by F. N. Robinson). Boston: Houghton Mifflin. (Originally published ca. 1400.)

Cherry, Frances. 1983. Gender roles and sexual violence. In: Elizabeth Rice Allgeier and Naomi B. McCormick (eds.), *Changing boundaries: Gender roles and sexual behavior* (pp. 245–260). Palo Alto, CA: Mayfield.

Chilman, Catharine S. 1983. *Adolescent sexuality in a changing American society.* New York: Wiley.

Chisholm, James S. 1983. *Navajo infancy: An ethological study of child development.* Hawthorne, NY: Aldine.

Chomsky, Noam. 1965. Aspects of the theory of syntax. Cambridge, MA: M.I.T. Press.

Clayton, Richard R., and Janet L. Bokemeier. 1980. Premarital sex in the seventies. *Journal of Marriage and the Family* 42:759–775.

Condon, William S. 1976. An analysis of behavioral organization. *Sign Language Studies* 13:285–318.

Conrad, Joseph. 1971. *Heart of darkness* (rev. ed., edited by Robert Kimbrough). New York: Norton.

Cook, Mark. 1977. Gaze and mutual gaze in social encounters. *American Scientist* 65:328–333.

Cornog, Martha. 1981. Tom, Dick and Hairy: Notes on genital pet names. *Maledicta* 5:31–40.

Cressey, Paul Goalby. 1983. A comparison of the roles of the ''sociological stranger'' and the ''anonymous stranger'' in field research. *Urban Life* 12:102–120.

Cuber, John F., and Peggy B. Harroff. 1965. *Sex and the significant Americans: A study of sexual behavior among the affluent.* Baltimore: Penguin.

Cuzzort, R. P. 1969. *Humanity and modern sociological thought.* New York: Holt, Rinehart and Winston.

Daly, Martin, and Margo Wilson. 1984. A sociobiological analysis of human infanticide. In: Glenn Hausfater and Sarah Blaffer Hrdy (eds.), *Infanticide: Comparative and evolutionary perspectives* (pp. 487–502). New York: Aldine.

Darwin, Charles. [1859]. *The origin of species by means of natural selection, Or the preservation of favored races in the struggle for life.* New York: Modern Library.

Darwin, Charles. 1874. *The descent of man and selection in relation to sex* (revised ed.). Chicago: Rand, McNally.

Darwin, Charles. 1965. *The expression of the emotions in man and animals.* Chicago: University of Chicago Press. (Originally published 1872.)

Davis, Clive M. 1980. Researching sex related attitudes—The importance of conceptual distinctions. Presented at the conference of the Eastern Region of the Society for the Scientific Study of Sex, 25–27 April 1980.

Davis, Martha. 1979. Laban analysis of nonverbal communication. In: Shirley Weitz (ed.),

Nonverbal communication (2nd ed., pp. 182–206). New York: Oxford University Press.

Davis, Nanette J., and Jone M. Keith. 1984. *Women and deviance: Issues in social conflict and change; An annotated bibliography.* New York: Garland.

Dawkins, Richard. 1978. *The selfish gene.* London: Granada.

Dawkins, Richard. 1982. *The extended phenotype: The gene as the unit of selection.* San Francisco: W. H. Freeman.

de Beauvoir, Simone. 1952. *The second sex.* New York: Vintage Books.

De Leeuw, Hendrik. 1979. *Cities of sin.* New York: Garland. (Originally published 1933.)

de Saussure, Ferdinand. 1959. *Course in general linguistics.* New York: McGraw-Hill. (Originally published 1915.)

de Witt, Karen. 1980. Study finds increase in teen-age sex. *New York Times,* 17 October 1980, p. A28.

Diderot, [Denis]. 1956. D'Alembert's dream; A conversation between Diderot and d'Alembert. In: *Rameau's nephew and other works* (pp. 95–111). Garden City, NY: Doubleday. (Originally written ca. 1782, published 1830.)

Dinnerstein, Dorothy. 1976. *The mermaid and the minotaur; Sexual arrangements and human malaise.* New York: Harper & Row.

Dobzhansky, Theodosius. 1967. *The biology of ultimate concern.* New York: New American Library.

Dobzhansky, Theodosius. 1970. *Genetics of the evolutionary process.* New York: Columbia University Press.

Dodson, Betty. 1974. *Liberating masturbation: A meditation on self-love.* New York: Bodysex Designs.

Donne, John. 1952. Song. In: *The complete poetry and selected prose of John Donne* (p. 9). New York: Modern Library. (Originally published 1650.)

Douglas, Mary. 1966. *Purity and danger: An analysis of concepts of pollution and taboo.* Baltimore: Penguin.

Dowling, Colette. 1981. *The Cinderella complex: Women's hidden fear of independence.* New York: Pocket Books.

Doyle, Arthur Conan. 1930. The sign of four. In: *The complete Sherlock Holmes* (pp. 89–158). Garden City, NY: Doubleday.

Drakeford, John W., and Jack Hamm. 1973. *Pornography: The sexual mirage.* Nashville, TN: Thomas Nelson.

Dubin, Steven C. 1983. The moral continuum of deviancy research: Chicago sociologists and the dance hall. *Urban Life* 12:75–94.

Duck, Steve, and Dorothy Miell. 1983. Mate choice in humans as an interpersonal process. In: Patrick Bateson (ed.), *Mate choice* (pp. 377–386). New York: Cambridge University Press.

Duggan, Lisa. 1984. Censorship in the name of feminism. *The Village Voice* 29(42):11–12, 16–17, 42, 16 October 1984.

Dunbar, R. I. M. 1983. Life history tactics and alternative strategies of reproduction. In: Patrick Bateson (ed.), *Mate choice* (pp. 423–433). New York: Cambridge University Press.

Duncan, Starkey, Jr. 1969. Nonverbal communication. *Psychological Bulletin* 72:118–137.

Duncan, Starkey, Jr. 1983. Speaking turns; Studies of structure in individual differences. In: John M. Wiemann and Randall P. Harrison (eds.), *Nonverbal interaction* (pp. 149–178). Beverly Hills: Sage.

Durkheim, Émile. 1965. *The elementary forms of religious life* (translated by Joseph Ward Swain). New York: Free Press. (Originally published 1915.)

Eastwell, Harry D. 1982. Voodoo death and the mechanism for dispatch of the dying in East Arnhem, Australia. *American Anthropologist* 84:5–18.

Eberhard, Mary Jane West. 1975. The evolution of social behavior by kin selection. *Quarterly Review of Biology* 50:1–33.

Eichenbaum, Luise, and Susie Orbach. 1983a. *Understanding women: A feminist psychoanalytic approach*. New York: Basic Books.

Eichenbaum, Luise, and Susie Orbach. 1983b. *What do women want: Exploding the myth of dependency*. New York: Coward-McCann.

Eisen, Carol G. 1971. *Nobody said you had to eat off the floor . . . The psychiatrist's wife's guide to housekeeping*. New York: Ballantine.

Ekman, Paul, and Wallace V. Friesen. 1976. Measuring facial movement. *Environmental Psychology and Nonverbal Behavior* 1:56–75.

Ellis, Havelock. 1928. *Studies in the psychology of sex, volume III. Analysis of the sexual impulse; Love and pain; The sexual impulse in women* (2nd ed., revised and enlarged). Philadelphia: F. A. Davis.

Ernster, Virginia L. 1975. American menstrual expressions. *Sex Roles* 1:3–13.

Exline, Ralph V. 1971. Visual interaction: The glances of power and preference. In: J. Cole (ed.), *Nebraska Symposium on Motivation* (pp. 163–206). Lincoln, NB: University of Nebraska Press.

Farmer, John S., and W. E. Henley. 1966. *Dictionary of slang and its analogues; Past and present*. New Hyde Park, NY: University Books. (Originally published 1903, 1909.)

Fast, Julius. 1970. *Body language*. New York: Pocket Books.

Fedigan, Linda Marie. 1982. *Primate paradigms: Sex roles and social bonds*. Montreal: Eden Press.

Finney, Charles G. 1962. *The circus of Dr. Lao*. New York: Viking.

Firestone, Shulamith. 1970. *The dialectic of sex: The case for feminist revolution*. New York: Bantam.

Fisher, Helen E. 1982. *The sex contract: The evolution of human behavior*. New York: Morrow.

Ford, Clellen S., and Frank A. Beach. 1951. *Patterns of sexual behavior*. New York: Harper & Brothers.

Ford, E. B. 1964. *Ecological genetics*. New York: Wiley.

Foucault, Michel. 1978. *The history of sexuality. Volume I: An introduction*. New York: Pantheon.

Fox, Robin. 1967. *Kinship and marriage: An anthropological perspective*. Baltimore: Penguin.

Fox, Robin. 1975. *Encounter with anthropology*. New York: Dell.

Fox, Robin. 1980. *The red lamp of incest*. New York: Dutton.

Francoeur, Robert T. 1982. *Becoming a sexual person*. New York: Wiley.

Freilich, Morris. 1980. Smart-sex and proper-sex: A paradigm found. *Central Issues in Anthropology* 2(2):37–51.

Freud, Sigmund. 1918. *Totem and taboo: Resemblances between the psychic lives of savages and neurotics*. New York: Vintage Books.

Freund, Kurt, Hal Scher, and Stephen Hucker. 1983. The courtship disorders. *Archives of Sexual Behavior* 12:369–379.

Friday, Nancy. 1980. *Men in love: Men's sexual fantasies: The triumph of love over rage.* New York: Delacorte.

Friedan, Betty. 1963. *The feminine mystique.* New York: Dell.

Friedrich, Paul. 1978. *The meaning of Aphrodite.* Chicago: University of Chicago Press.

Fuller, John L., and Edward C. Simmel (eds.). 1983. *Behavior genetics: Principles & applications.* Hillsdale, NJ: Lawrence Erlbaum Associates.

Fuller, John L., and William Robert Thompson. 1978. *Foundations of behavior genetics.* St. Louis, MO: Mosby.

Gager, Nancy, and Cathleen Schurr. 1976. *Sexual assault: Confronting rape in America.* New York: Grosset & Dunlap.

Gagnon, John H., and William Simon. 1973. *Sexual conduct: The social sources of human sexuality.* Chicago: Aldine.

Garcia, John, Brenda K. McGowan, and Kenneth F. Green. 1972. Biological constraints on conditioning. In: Martin E. P. Seligman and J. L. Hager (eds.), *Biological boundaries of learning* (pp. 21–43). New York: Appleton-Century-Crofts.

Garcia, Luis T. 1983. Sexual stereotypes and attributions about sexual arousal. *Journal of Sex Research* 19:366–375.

Geertz, Clifford. 1973. Religion as a cultural system. In: *The interpretation of cultures: Selected essays by Clifford Geertz* (pp. 87–125). New York: Basic Books. (Originally published 1966.)

Geertz, Clifford. 1984. Distinguished lecture: Anti anti-relativism. *American Anthropologist* 86:263–278.

Giese, Arthur C. 1957. *Cell physiology.* Philadelphia: Saunders.

Gilder, George F. 1975. *Sexual suicide.* New York: Bantam.

Ginder, Richard. 1975. *Binding with briars: Sex and sin in the Catholic Church.* Englewood Cliffs, NJ: Prentice-Hall.

Givens, David B. 1978. The nonverbal basis of attraction: Flirtation, courtship, and seduction. *Psychiatry* 41:346–359.

Givens, David B. 1983. *Love signals: How to attract a mate.* New York: Crown.

Goffman, Erving. 1963. *Behavior in public places.* New York: Free Press.

Goffman, Erving. 1971. *Relations in public.* New York: Harper & Row.

Goldberg, Herb. 1976. *The hazards of being male: Surviving the myth of the masculine privilege.* New York: New American Library.

Goldberg, Herb. 1979. *The new male: From self-destruction to self-care.* New York: Morrow.

Goldman, Marion S. 1981. *Gold diggers and silver miners: Prostitution and social life on the Comstock lode.* Ann Arbor: University of Michigan Press.

Goldman, Ronald, and Juliette Goldman. 1982. *Children's sexual thinking; A comparative study of children aged 5 to 15 in Australia, North America, Britain, and Sweden.* London: Routledge & Kegan Paul.

Goldstein, Bernard. 1976. *Human sexuality.* New York: McGraw-Hill.

Goodchilds, Jacqueline D., and Gail L. Zellman. 1984. Sexual signalling and sexual aggression in adolescent relationships. In: Neil M. Malamuth and Edward Donnerstein (eds.), *Pornography and sexual aggression* (p. 233–243). Orlando, FL: Academic Press.

Gorchakov, Nikolai M. 1954. *Stanislavsky directs* (trans. by Miriam Goldina). New York: Funk & Wagnalls.

Gordon, Suzanne. 1976. *Lonely in America.* New York: Simon and Schuster.

Grant, Verne. 1963. *The origin of adaptations.* New York: Columbia University Press.

Gray, J. Patrick, and Linda D. Wolfe. 1982. Sociobiology and creationism: Two ethnosociologies of American culture. *American Anthropologist* 84:580–594.

Gray, J. Patrick, and Linda D. Wolfe. 1983. Reply to Waldorf. *American Anthropologist* 85:905.

Green, Richard, William Simon, and Joseph Harry. 1984. Why the relationship between boyhood femininity and adult homosexuality? Paper presented at the Annual Meeting of the Society for the Scientific Study of Sex and the American Association of Sex Educators, Counselors, and Therapists, Boston, MA, 6–10 June 1984.

Green, Susan K., and Philip Sandos. 1983. Perceptions of male and female initiators of relationships. *Sex Roles* 9:849–852.

Greenblat, Cathy Stein, and Thomas J. Cottle. 1980. *Getting married.* New York: McGraw-Hill.

Greenspan, Miriam. 1983. *A new approach to women & therapy.* New York: McGraw-Hill.

Greer, Germaine. 1971. *The female eunuch.* New York: Bantam.

Gribben, John. 1984. *In search of Schrodinger's cat: Quantum physics and reality.* New York: Bantam Books.

Griffin, Susan. 1981. *Pornography and silence: Culture's revenge against nature.* New York: Harper & Row.

Gross, Alex, and Aileen Gross. 1983. The Chinese medical explanation of sexual attitudes, behaviors, and dysfunctions. Presented at the Annual Meeting of the Society for the Scientific Study of Sex, Chicago, 18–20 November 1983.

Groth, A. Nicholas, with H. Jean Birnbaum. 1979. *Men who rape: The psychology of the offender.* New York: Plenum.

Hadamard, Jacques. 1954. *An essay on the psychology of invention in the mathematical field.* New York: Dover. (Originally published 1949.)

Hagstrum, Jean H. 1980. *Sex and sensibility: Ideal and erotic love from Milton to Mozart.* Chicago: University of Chicago Press.

Hair, P. E. H. 1980. Bridal pregnancy in rural England. In: Vivian C. Fox and Martin H. Quitt (eds.), *Loving, parenting and dying: The family cycle in England and America, past and present* (pp. 193–200). New York: Psychohistory Press.

Hall, Edward T. 1963. A system for the notation of proxemic behavior. *American Anthropologist* 65:1003–1026.

Hall, Edward T. 1968. Proxemics. *Current Anthropology* 9:83–95, 106–108.

Halliday, M. A. K. 1976. Anti-languages. *American Anthropologist* 78:570–584.

Hamilton, W. D. 1964a. The genetical evolution of social behaviour. I. *Journal of Theoretical Biology* 7:1–16.

Hamilton, W. D. 1964b. The genetical evolution of social behaviour. II. *Journal of Theoretical Biology* 7:17–52.

Handler, Richard, and Jocelyn Linnekin. 1984. Tradition, genuine or spurious. *Journal of American Folklore* 97:273–290.

Hanna, Judith Lynne. 1979. *To dance is human: A theory of nonverbal communication.* Austen, TX: University of Texas Press.

Harris, Marvin. 1968. *The rise of anthropological theory: A history of theories of culture.* New York: Crowell.

Harrison, Beverly Wildung. 1983. *Our own right to choose: Toward a new ethic of abortion.* Boston: Beacon.

Hatfield, Elaine. 1983. What do women and men want from love and sex? In: Elizabeth Rice

Allgeier and Naomi B. McCormick (eds.), *Changing boundaries: Gender roles and sexual behavior* (pp. 106–134). Palo Alto, CA: Mayfield.

Henley, Nancy M. 1973. The politics of touch. In: R. Brown (ed.), *Radical psychology* (pp. 421–433). New York: Harper & Row.

Herold, Edward S., and Marilyn Shirley Goodwin. 1981. Adamant virgins, potential nonvirgins and nonvirgins. *The Journal of Sex Research* 17:97–113.

Heslin, Richard, and Tari Alper. 1983. Touch: A bonding gesture. In: John M. Wiemann and Randall P. Harrison (eds.), *Nonverbal interaction* (pp. 47–75). Beverly Hills, CA: Sage.

Heyer, Paul. 1982. *Nature, human nature, and society: Marx, Darwin, biology, and the human sciences.* Westport, CT: Greenwood.

Hite, Shere. 1981. *The Hite report on male sexuality.* New York: Knopf.

Holliday, Laurel. 1978. *Male psychobiology and the evolution of consciousness.* Berkeley, CA: Bluestocking Books.

Holt, Guy. 1923. Introduction. In: James Branch Cabell, *Beyond life: Dizain des demiurges* (pp. ix–xix). New York: Modern Library.

Hrdy, Sarah Blaffer. 1981. *The woman that never evolved.* Cambridge, MA: Harvard University Press.

Ives, Edward D. 1974. *The tape-recorded interview: A manual for field workers in folklore and oral history.* Knoxville, TN: University of Tennessee Press.

James, William H. 1981. The honeymoon effect on marital coitus. *The Journal of Sex Research* 17:114–123.

Jay, Timothy B. 1980. Sex roles and dirty word usage: A review of the literature and a reply to Haas. *Psychological Bulletin* 83(3):614–621.

Jespersen, Otto. 1922. *Language: Its nature, development and origin.* London: Allen & Unwin.

Jesser, Clinton J. 1978. Male responses to direct verbal sexual initiatives of females. *The Journal of Sex Research* 14:118–128.

Joffe, Natalie F. 1948. The vernacular of menstruation. *Word* 4(3):181–186.

Johns, Catharine. 1982. *Sex or symbol; Erotic images of Greece and Rome.* Austin: University of Texas Press.

Jones, Andrew John. 1982. Nonverbal flirtation behavior: An observational study in bar settings. Unpublished masters thesis, State University of New York, Plattsburgh.

Joyce, James. 1977. A painful case. In *Dubliners: Text, criticism, and notes* (pp. 107–117). New York: Penguin. (Originally published 1914.)

Kallen, Horace M. 1934. Sex morals and the unmarried adult. In: Ira S. Wile (ed.), *The sex life of the unmarried adult: An inquiry into and an interpretation of current sex practices* (pp. 233–252). New York: Vanguard.

Kanin, Eugene J. 1984. Date rape: Unofficial criminals and victims. *Victimology* 9:95–108.

Karlen, Arno. 1971. *Sexuality and homosexuality: A new view.* New York: Norton.

Karlen, Arno. 1984. *Napoleon's glands and other ventures in biohistory.* Boston: Little, Brown.

Katz, S. H., and J. Schall. 1979. Fava bean consumption and biocultural evolution. *Medical Anthropology* 3:459–476.

Keats, John. 1962a. Endymion. In: *Keats: Poems and selected letters* (pp. 97–196). New York: Scribners. (Originally published 1818.)

Keats, John. 1962b. The eve of St. Agnes. In: *Keats: Poems and selected letters* (pp. 233–245). New York: Scribners. (Originally published 1820.)

Kelly, George. 1969. Hostility. In: *Clinical psychology and personality: The selected papers of George Kelly* (edited by Brendan Maher, pp. 267–280). New York: Wiley.

Kendon, Adam. 1970. Movement coordination in social interaction: Some examples described. *Acta Psychologica* 32:100–125.

King, Francis. 1971. *Sexuality, magic and perversion*. Secaucus, NJ: Citadel.

Kinsey, Alfred C., Wardell B. Pomeroy, Clyde E. Martin, and Paul H. Gebhard. 1953. *Sexual behavior in the human female*. Philadelphia: Saunders.

Kleinke, Chris. 1981. Opening lines. Presented at the Western Psychological Association, Los Angeles, April 1981.

Knapp, Mark L. 1978. *Social intercourse: From greeting to goodbye*. Boston: Allyn and Bacon.

Knapp, Mark L. 1983. Dyadic relationship development. In: John M. Wiemann and Randall P. Harrison (eds.), *Nonverbal interaction* (pp. 179–207). Beverly Hills: Sage.

Knight, David J., Daniel Langmeyer, and David C. Lundgren. 1973. Eye-contact, distance, and affiliation: The role of observer bias. *Sociometry* 3:390–401.

Kolenda, Pauline. 1984. Woman as tribute, woman as flower: Images of "woman" in weddings in north and south India. *American Ethnologist* 11:98–117.

Korman, Sheila K., and Gerald R. Leslie. 1982. The relationship of feminist ideology and date expense sharing to perceptions of sexual aggression in dating. *The Journal of Sex Research* 18:114–129.

Kornfield, Ruth. 1984. Quoted in "Who's to blame? Adolescent sexual activity." *Sexuality Today* 7(41):1, 3, 30 July 1984.

Krieger, Monica Schoelch, Deborah Orr, and Timothy Perper. 1976. Temporal patterning of sexual behavior in the female rat. *Behavioral Biology* 18:379–386.

Kroeber, A. L. 1976. *Handbook of the Indians of California*. New York: Dover. (Originally published 1925.)

Kronhausen, Eberhard, and Phyllis Kronhausen. 1967. The psychology of pornography. In: Albert Ellis and Albert Abarbanel (eds.), *Encyclopedia of sexual behavior, vol. IV: Heterosexual relationships* (pp. 145–166). New York: Ace.

Kurtz, Ron, and Hector Prestera. 1976. *The body reveals: An illustrated guide to the psychology of the body*. New York: Harper & Row.

Kutner, Nancy G., and Donna Brogan. 1974. An investigation of sex-related slang vocabulary and sex-role orientation among male and female university students. *Journal of Marriage and the Family* 36(3):474–483, August.

Lacan, Jacques, and the école freudienne. 1982. *Feminine sexuality*. New York: Norton.

Lakoff, Robin. 1973. Language and woman's place. *Language in Society* 2:45–80.

Lamb, Charles. 1935. *The complete works and letters of Charles Lamb*. New York: Modern Library.

Landau, Misia. 1984. Human evolution as narrative. *American Scientist* 72:262–268, May–June.

LaPlante, Marcia N., Naomi B. McCormick, and Gary G. Brannigan. 1980. Living the sexual script: College students' views of influence in sexual encounters. *The Journal of Sex Research* 16:338–355.

Lasch, Christopher. 1979. *The culture of Narcissism; American life in an age of diminishing expectations*. New York: Warner.

Laughlin, Charles D., Jr., and Eugene G. d'Aquili. 1974. *Biogenetic structuralism.* New York: Columbia University Press.

Laurendeau, Monique, and Adrien Pinard. 1970. *The development of the concept of space in the child.* New York: International Universities Press.

Lawrence, D. H. 1959. *Lady Chatterley's lover.* New York: New American Library. (Originally published 1932.)

Leach, E. R. 1969. Virgin birth. In: *Genesis as myth, and other essays* (pp. 85–112). London: Cape.

Leaf, Murray J. 1974. Ritual and social organization: Sikh marriage rituals. In: Murray J. Leaf (ed.), *Frontiers of anthropology; An introduction to anthropological thinking* (pp. 123–162). New York: Van Nostrand.

Lee, John Alan. 1976. *The colors of love.* Englewood Cliffs, NJ: Prentice-Hall.

Lee, Linda, and James Charlton. 1980. *The hand book: Interpreting handshakes, gestures, power signals, and sexual signs.* Englewood Cliffs, NJ: Prentice-Hall.

Lee, Richard B., and Irven DeVore (eds.). 1968. *Man the hunter.* Chicago: Aldine.

Legman, G. 1968. *Rationale of the dirty joke: An analysis of sexual humor. First series.* New York: Grove.

Legman, G. 1975. *Rationale of the dirty joke: An analysis of sexual humor. Second series* [cover title: No laughing matter]. New York: Breaking Point.

Lehninger, Albert L. (ed.). 1975. *Biochemistry: The molecular basis of all structure and function* (2nd ed.). New York: Worth.

Lerner, I. Michael. 1970. *Genetic homeostasis.* New York: Dover. (Originally published 1954.)

Levinson, Daniel J., with Charlotte N. Darrow, Edward B. Klein, Maria H. Levinson, and Braxton McKee. 1978. *The seasons of a man's life.* New York: Ballantine.

Lévi-Strauss, Claude. 1966. *The savage mind.* Chicago: University of Chicago Press.

Lévi-Strauss, Claude. 1967. *Les structures élémentaires de la parenté.* Paris: Mouton.

Lévi-Strauss, Claude. 1971. *Mythologiques: L'homme nu.* Paris: Librarie Plon.

Lewis, Robert. 1973. Social reaction and the formation of dyads: An interactionist approach to mate selection. *Sociometry* 36:409–418.

Li, C. C. 1955. *Population genetics.* Chicago: University of Chicago Press.

Lipton, James. 1977. *An exaltation of larks; Or, the venereal game.* New York: Penguin.

Locke, John. 1928. On ideas as the materials of all our knowledge. In: *Locke: Selections* (edited by S. P. Lamprecht, pp. 96–224). New York: Scribner's. (Originally published 1700.)

Lorenz, Konrad. 1967. *On aggression.* New York: Bantam.

Lowe, Marian, and Ruth Hubbard. 1983. *Woman's nature: Rationalizations of inequality.* Elmsford, NY: Pergamon.

Mackie, Marlene. 1983. *Exploring gender relations: A Canadian perspective.* Toronto: Butterworths.

Mahoney, E. R. 1980. Religiosity and sexual behavior among heterosexual college students. *The Journal of Sex Research* 16:97–113.

Malamuth, Neil M., and Edward Donnerstein (eds.). 1984. *Pornography and sexual aggression.* Orlando, FL: Academic Press.

Malinowski, Bronislaw. 1978. *Coral gardens and their magic: A study of the methods of tilling the soil and of agricultural rites in the Trobriand Islands.* New York: Dover. (Originally published 1935.)

Mangham, Iain L., and Michael A. Overington. 1983. Dramatism and the theatrical metaphor. In: Gareth Morgan, *Beyond method: Strategies for social research* (pp. 219–233). Beverly Hills, CA: Sage.

Mann, Thomas. 1938. *Joseph in Egypt, volume 2.* New York: Knopf.

Marcus, Steven. 1977. *The other Victorians: A study of sexuality and pornography in mid-nineteenth-century England.* New York: New American Library. (Originally published 1964.)

Marvin, Robert S., and Daniel G. Mossler. 1976. A methodological paradigm for describing and analyzing complex non-verbal expressions: Coy expressions in preschool children. *Representative Research in Social Psychology* 7:133–139.

Masello, Robert. 1983. *What do men want from women?* New York: Ballantine.

Maugham, W. Somerset. 1944. *The razor's edge.* Garden City, NY: International Collectors Library.

Mauss, Marcel. 1967. *The gift: Forms and functions of exchange in archaic societies.* New York: Norton. (Originally published 1925.)

Mauss, Marcel. 1975. *A general theory of magic.* New York: Norton. (Originally published 1902–1903.)

Mayhew, Henry, and Bracebridge Hemyng. 1968. The prostitute class generally. In: Henry Mayhew, *London labour and the London poor* (vol. 4, pp. 35–272). New York: Dover. (Originally published 1861–1862.)

Mayr, Ernst. 1970. *Populations, species, and evolution: An abridgement of Animal Species and Evolution.* Cambridge, MA: The Belknap Press of Harvard University Press.

McClintock, Martha K. 1983. The behavioral endocrinology of rodents: A functional analysis. *BioScience* 33:573–577.

McCormick, Naomi B. 1979. Come-ons and put-offs: Unmarried students' strategies for having and avoiding sexual intercourse. *Psychology of Women Quarterly* 4(2):194–211, Winter.

McWhirter, David P., and Andrew M. Mattison. 1984. *The male couple: How relationships develop.* Englewood Cliffs, NJ. Prentice-Hall.

Mead, Margaret. 1949. *Male and female: A study of the sexes in a changing world.* New York: Morrow.

Mehrabian, Albert. 1969. Significance of posture and position in the communication of attitude and status relationships. *Psychological Bulletin* 71:359–372.

Michelet, Jules. 1939. *Satanism and witchcraft: A study in Medieval superstition.* New York: Citadel.

Michod, Richard E. 1982. The theory of kin selection. *Annual Review of Ecology and Systematics* 13:23–55.

Miller, Jonathan. 1972. Plays and players. In: R. A. Hinde (ed.), *Non-verbal communication* (pp. 359–372). New York: Cambridge University Press.

Milton, John. 1925. On his deceased wife. In: Homer A. Watt and James B. Munn, *Ideas and forms in English and American literature* (p. 402). Chicago: Scott, Foresman. (Originally written 1658.)

Mitton, J. B., and M. C. Grant. 1984. Associations among protein heterozygosity, growth rate, and developmental homeostasis. *Annual Review of Ecology and Systematics* 15:479–499.

Molière. 1957. The would-be gentleman. In: *Eight plays by Moliere* (translated with an introduction by Morris Bishop, pp. 324–399). New York: Modern Library. (Originally written 1670.)

Money, John. 1980. *Love and love sickness: The science of sex, gender difference, and pair-bonding*. Baltimore: Johns Hopkins University Press.

Montagu, Ashley. 1978. *Touching: The human significance of the skin* (2nd ed.). New York: Harper & Row.

Montgomery, L. M. 1908. *Anne of Green Gables*. New York: Grosset & Dunlap.

Mookerjee, Ajit, and Madhu Khanna. 1977. *The Tantric way: Art, science, ritual*. Boston: New York Graphic Society.

Mordkoff, Arnold M., Kurt Schlesinger, and Robert A. Lavine. 1964. Developmental homeostasis in behavior of mice: Locomotor activity and grooming. *Journal of Heredity* 55:84–88.

Morris, Desmond. 1971. *Intimate behaviour*. New York: Bantam.

Morris, Desmond. 1977. *Manwatching: A field guide to human behavior*. New York: Abrams.

Mosher, Donald L. 1980. Three dimensions of depth of involvement in human sexual response. *The Journal of Sex Research* 16:1–42.

Mosher, Donald L., and Susan G. Vonderheide. 1985. Contributions of sex guilt and masturbation guilt to women's contraceptive attitudes and use. *The Journal of Sex Research* 21:24–39.

Mullan, Bob. 1984. *The mating trade*. London: Routledge & Kegan Paul.

Nagel, Ernest, and James R. Newman. 1956. Goedel's proof. In: James R. Newman (ed.), *The world of mathematics* (vol. 3, pp. 1668–1695). New York: Simon and Schuster.

Nelson, George. 1977. *How to see: Visual adventures in a world God never made*. Boston: Little, Brown.

Nevid, Jeffrey S. 1984. Sex differences in factors of romantic attraction. *Sex Roles* 11:401–411.

Newman, Louise Michele (ed.). 1985. *Men's ideas/women's realities: Popular Science 1870–1915*. New York: Pergamon.

Nir, Yehuda, and Bonnie Maslin. 1982. *Loving men for all the right reasons: Women's patterns of intimacy*. New York: Dell.

Nirumand, Bahman. 1984. Quoted in: "Iranians hatred of women leads to their disfigurement, rape, death." *Sexuality Today* 7(38):3–4, 9 July 1984.

Nordhoff, Charles. 1966. *The Communistic societies of the United States; From personal visit and observation*. New York: Dover. (Originally published 1875.)

Novak, William. 1983. *The great American man shortage and other roadblocks to romance (and what to do about it)*. New York: Rawson Associates.

Ochs, Carol. 1977. *Behind the sex of God: Toward a new consciousness—Transcending matriarchy and patriarchy*. Boston: Beacon.

Orne, Martin T. 1962. On the social psychology of the psychological experiment: With particular reference to demand characteristics and their implications. *American Psychologist* 17:776–783.

Ortner, Sherry, and Harriet Whitehead. (eds.). 1981. *Sexual meanings: The cultural construction of gender and sexuality*. New York: Cambridge University Press.

Ovid. 1949. *The art of love*. New York: Stravon.

Packard, Vance. 1968. *The sexual wilderness*. New York: David McKay.

Peele, Stanton, with Archie Brodsky. 1975. *Love and addiction*. New York: Taplinger.

Penrod, Steven, and Daniel Linz. 1984. Using psychological research on violent pornography to inform legal change. In: Neil M. Malamuth and Edward Donnerstein (eds.), *Pornography and sexual aggression* (pp. 247–275). New York: Academic Press.

Perper, Timothy. 1978. Behavior of male rats copulating with tethered females. *Behavioral Biology* 23:124–129.

Perper, Timothy. 1980. The silent culture of being male. *The American Man* 1(4):16–23, 52–55, Fall.

Perper, Timothy, and Carmel Schrire. 1977. The Nimrod connection: Myth and science in the hunting model. In: Morley R. Kare and Owen Maller (eds.), *The chemical senses and nutrition* (pp. 447–459). New York: Academic Press.

Philips, Susan U. 1980. Sex differences and language. *Annual Review of Anthropology* 9:523–544.

Piaget, Jean. 1963. *The origins of intelligence in children.* New York: Norton. (Originally published 1952.)

Pillard, Richard C., and James D. Weinrich. 1984. Male homosexuality runs in families. Paper presented at the Joint Annual Meeting of the Society for the Scientific Study of Sex and the American Association of Sex Educators, Counselors, and Therapists, Boston, MA, 6–10 June 1984.

Plato. 1956. The symposium. In: *The works of Plato* (pp. 333–393). New York: Modern Library.

Plutarch. n.d. Sylla. In *The lives of the noble Grecians and Romans* (trans. by John Dryden, pp. 545–573). New York: Modern Library. (Written ca. first century A.D.)

Poincaré, Henri. 1956. Mathematical creation. In: James R. Newman (ed.), *The world of mathematics* (vol. 4, pp. 2041–2050). New York: Simon and Schuster.

Polo, Marco. 1958. *The travels of Marco Polo.* New York: Penguin. (Originally written 1298–1299?)

Pomeroy, Sarah B. 1975. *Goddesses, whores, wives, and slaves: Women in classical antiquity.* New York: Schocken.

Poole, Roger. 1975. Objective sign and subjective meaning. In: Jonathan Benthall and Ted Polhemus, *The body as a medium of expression* (pp. 74–104). New York: Dutton.

Pope, Alexander. 1954. The rape of the lock. In: *Major British writers, volume I: Chaucer, Spenser, Shakespeare, Bacon, Donne, Milton, Swift, Pope* (pp. 680–688). New York: Harcourt, Brace. (Originally published 1717.)

Pope, Hallowell. 1967. Unwed mothers and their sex partners. *Journal of Marriage and the Family* 29:555–567.

Price, Sally. 1984. *Co-wives and calabashes.* Ann Arbor: University of Michigan Press.

Prince, Raymond (ed.). 1982. Shamans and endorphins. [Special issue]. *Ethos* 10(4), Winter.

Proust, Marcel. n.d. *Swann's way* (trans. by C. K. Scott Moncrieff). New York: Modern Library.

Proust, Marcel. 1954. *A la recherche du temps perdu. Vol. I: Du côté de chez Swann.* Paris: Gallimard.

Quinn, Naomi. 1982. "Commitment" in American marriage: A cultural analysis. *American Ethnologist* 9:775–798.

Rancour-Laferriere, Daniel. 1980. Semiotics, psychoanalysis, and science: Some selected intersections. *Ars Semeiotica* 3(2):181–240.

Rappaport, Roy A. 1971. The sacred in human evolution. *Annual Review of Ecology and Systematics* 2:23–44.

Reiss, Ira L. 1981. Some observations on ideology and sexuality in America. *Journal of Marriage and the Family* 43:271–283.

Remoff, Heather T. 1980. Female choice: An investigation into human breeding system strategy. Unpublished Doctoral Dissertation, Rutgers University, New Brunswick, NJ.

Remoff, Heather Trexler. 1984. *Sexual choice: A woman's decision.* Boston: Dutton/Lewis.

Rendel, J. M. 1967. *Canalisation and gene control.* London: Logos.

Resnick, Michael. 1984. Quoted in: Teen pregnancy choices: It's cognitive development that counts. *Sexuality Today* 7(32):1, 3, 28 May 1984.

Robinson, James Harvey, and Charles A. Beard. 1921. *History of Europe: Our own times.* Boston: Ginn.

Roebuck, Julian, and S. Lee Spray. 1967. The cocktail lounge: A study of heterosexual relations in a public organization. *American Journal of Sociology* 72:388–395.

Róheim, Géza. 1974. *The riddle of the Sphinx; Or, human origins.* New York: Harper Torchbooks. (Originally published 1934.)

Rosenfeld, Howard M. 1966. Approval-seeking and approval-inducing functions of verbal and nonverbal responses in the dyad. *Journal of Personality and Social Psychology* 4:597–605.

Rosenthal, Robert, Judith A. Hall, Dane Archer, M. Robin DiMatteo, and Peter L. Rogers. 1979. The PONS test: Measuring sensitivity to nonverbal cues. In: Shirley Weitz (ed.), *Nonverbal communication* (2nd ed., pp. 357–370). New York: Oxford University Press.

Ross, Thomas W. 1972. *Chaucer's bawdy.* New York: Dutton.

Rothman, Ellen K. 1984. *Hands and hearts: A history of courtship in America.* New York: Basic Books.

Rozin, Paul, and James W. Kalat. 1971. Specific hungers and poison avoidance as adaptive specializations of learning. *Psychological Review* 78:459–486.

Russell, Bertrand. 1959. *The problems of philosophy.* New York: Oxford University Press. (Originally published 1912.)

Sabbah, Fatna A. (pseud.). 1984. *Woman in the Muslim unconscious.* New York: Pergamon.

Sanders, Janet S., and William L. Robinson. 1979. Talking and not talking about sex: Male and female vocabularies. *Journal of Communication* 29(2):22–30.

Sarwer-Foner, G. J. 1972. On human territoriality; A contribution to instinct theory. *Canadian Psychiatric Association Journal* 17:169–183.

Sayers, Janet. 1982. *Biological politics: Feminist and anti-feminist perspectives.* London: Tavistock.

Schachter, Zalman M., and Edward Hoffman. 1983. *Sparks of light: Counseling in the Hasidic tradition.* Boulder, CO: Shambhala.

Scheflen, Albert E. 1965. Quasi-courtship behavior in psychotherapy. *Psychiatry* 28:245–257.

Scheflen, Albert E., with Alice Scheflen. 1972. *Body language and social order: Communication as behavioral control.* Englewood Cliffs, NJ: Prentice-Hall.

Scheller, Richard H., and Richard Axel. 1984. How genes control innate behavior. *Scientific American* 250(3):54–62, March.

Schwartz, Pepper, and Janet Lever. 1976. Fear and loathing at a college mixer. *Urban Life* 4:413–431.

Searcy, William A. 1982. The evolutionary effects of mate selection. *Annual Review of Ecology and Systematics* 13:57–85.

Selander, Robert K., and Walter E. Johnson. 1973. Genetic variation among vertebrate species. *Annual Review of Ecology and Systematics* 4:75–91.

Seligman, Martin E. P. 1970. On the generality of the laws of learning. *Psychological Review* 77:406–418.

Shah, Farida, and Melvin Zelnik. 1981. Parent and peer influence on sexual behavior, contraceptive use, and pregnancy experience of young women. *Journal of Marriage and the Family* 43:339–348.

Shepherd, Jean. 1966. *In God we trust; All others pay cash.* Garden City, NY: Doubleday.

Shields, William M. 1982. *Philopatry, inbreeding, and the evolution of sex.* Albany: State University of New York Press.

Shields, William M., and Lea M. Shields. 1983. Forcible rape: An evolutionary perspective. *Ethology and Sociobiology* 4:115–136.

Shoham, S. Giora. 1983. *Sex as bait: Eve, Casanova, and Don Juan.* St. Lucia, Queensland, Australia: University of Queensland Press.

Silverthorne, Colin, John Micklewright, Marie O'Donnell, and Richard Gibson. 1976. Attribution of personal characteristics as a function of the degree of touch on initial contact and sex. *Sex Roles* 2:185–193.

Simenauer, Jacqueline, and David Carroll. 1982. *Singles: The new Americans.* New York: Simon and Schuster.

Simmel, Georg. 1984. *Georg Simmel: On women, sexuality, and love.* New Haven: Yale University Press. (Originally published 1911–1919.)

Simon, William, and John H. Gagnon. 1968. Sex talk—Public and private. *Etc.: A Review of General Semantics* 25(2):173–191.

Simon, William, and John H. Gagnon. 1970. Psychosexual development. In: John H. Gagnon and William Simon, *The sexual scene* (pp. 23–41). New York: Aldine.

Slater, Philip. 1977. *Footholds: Understanding the shifting family and sexual tensions in our culture* (edited by Wendy Slater Palmer). Boston: Beacon Press.

Smith, Daniel Scott, and Michael S. Hindus. 1980. Premarital pregnancy in America, 1640–1971. In: Vivian C. Fox and Martin H. Quitt (eds.), *Loving, parenting and dying: The family cycle in England, past and present* (pp. 200–211). New York: Psychohistory Press.

Sommer, Robert. 1969. *Personal space: The behavioral basis of design.* Englewood Cliffs, NJ: Prentice-Hall.

Spradley, James P., and Brenda J. Mann. 1975. *The cocktail waitress: Woman's work in a man's world.* New York: Wiley.

Stein, Peter J. 1981. *Single life: Unmarried adults in social context.* New York: St. Martin's Press.

Stephens, James. 1967. *The crock of gold.* New York: Collier. (Originally published 1912.)

Stern, Curt. 1973. *Principles of human genetics* (3rd ed.). San Francisco: W. H. Freeman.

Stiles, Henry Reed. [n.d.]. *Bundling: Its origins, progress and decline in America.* Mt. Vernon, NY: Peter Pauper Press. (Originally published 1871.)

Stone, Lawrence. 1979. *The family, sex and marriage in England 1500–1800* (abridged ed.). New York: Harper Colophon.

Stryer, Lubert. 1981. *Biochemistry* (2nd ed.). San Francisco: W. H. Freeman.

Stryker, Sheldon. 1977. Developments in "two social psychologies": Toward an appreciation of mutual relevance. *Sociometry* 40:145–160.

Symons, Donald. 1979. *The evolution of human sexuality.* New York: Oxford University Press.

Tennov, Dorothy. 1979. *Love and limerence: The experience of being in love.* New York: Stein and Day.

Terry, Roger L. 1983. A connotative analysis of synonyms for *sexual intercourse. Maledicta* 7:237–253.

Thiessen, D. D. 1965. The wabbler-lethal mouse: A study in development. *Animal Behaviour* 13:87–100.

Thomas, Jim (ed.). 1983. The Chicago School: The tradition and the legacy. [Special issue]. *Urban Life* 11(4), January.

Thompson, Hunter S. 1971. *Fear and loathing in Las Vegas.* New York: Random House.

Thompson, Hunter S. 1979. Presenting: The Richard Nixon doll (overhauled 1968 model). In: *The great shark hunt: Strange tales from a strange time* (pp. 212–220). New York: Fawcett Popular Library. (Originally published 1968.)

Thurber, James. 1960. Midnight at Tim's place. In: *Lanterns & lances* (pp. 9–15). New York: Harper Colophon.

Thurber, James, and E. B. White. 1957. *Is sex necessary? Or why you feel the way you do.* New York: Harper & Row. (Originally published 1929.)

Tiger, Lionel. 1970. *Men in groups.* New York: Vintage Books.

Tiger, Lionel. 1979. *Optimism: The biology of hope.* New York: Simon and Schuster.

Tiger, Lionel, and Robin Fox. 1966. The zoological perspective in social science. *Man* 1(1):75–81.

Tolkien, J. R. R. 1955. *The return of the king; Being the third part of The Lord of the Rings.* London: Allen & Unwin.

Tolkien, J. R. R. (trans.). 1975. Sir Gawain and the Green Knight. In: *Sir Gawain and the Green Knight, Pearl and Sir Orfeo* (pp. 19–97). New York: Ballantine.

Trivers, Robert L. 1971. The evolution of reciprocal altruism. *Quarterly Review of Biology* 46:35–57.

Trivers, Robert L. 1972. Parental investment and sexual selection. In: Bernard Campbell (ed.), *Sexual selection and the descent of man, 1871–1971* (pp. 136–179). Chicago: Aldine.

Trudeau, G. B. 1977. *As the kid goes for broke.* New York: Holt, Rinehart and Winston.

Trudeau, G. B. 1982. *Ask for May, settle for June.* New York: Holt, Rinehart and Winston.

Truslove, Gillian M. 1956. The anatomy and development of the fidget mouse. *Journal of Genetics* 54:64–86.

Tuchman, Barbara. 1978. *A distant mirror; The calamitous 14th century.* New York: Ballantine.

Turnbull, Colin M. 1972. *The mountain people.* New York: Simon and Schuster.

Turner, Victor. 1967. *The forest of symbols: Aspects of Ndembu ritual.* Ithica, NY: Cornell University Press.

Vatsyayana. 1961. *Kama Sutra of Vatsyayana* (complete trans. from the original Sanskrit by S. C. Upadhyaya). Bombay: D. B. Taraporevala.

Vinovskis, Maris A. 1981. An "epidemic" of adolescent pregnancy? Some historical considerations. *Journal of Family History* 6:205–230.

Wachtel, Paul L. 1983. *The poverty of affluence: A psychological portrait of the American way of life.* New York: Free Press.

Waddington, C. H. 1962. *New patterns in genetics and development.* New York: Columbia University Press.

Waldorf, Saral. 1983. Defense mechanisms generated by some anthropologists when suffering from deep anxieties caused by creationism and sociobiology: Comments on Gray and Wolfe's "ethnosociologies." *American Anthropologist* 85:903–904.

Wallwork, Ernest. 1984. Religion and social structure in *The division of labor. American Anthropologist* 86:43–64.

Walster, Elaine, and G. William Walster. 1978. *A new look at love.* Reading, MA: Addison-Wesley.

Walster, Elaine, G. William Walster, Jane Piliavin, and Lynn Schmidt. 1973. "Playing hard to get": Understanding an elusive phenomenon. *Journal of Personality and Social Psychology* 26:113–121.

Waring, Alicia, and Timothy Perper. 1979. Parental behaviour in the Mongolian gerbil (*Meriones unguiculatus*). I. Retrieval. *Animal Behaviour* 27:1091–1097.

Waring, Alicia, and Timothy Perper. 1980. Parental behaviour in Mongolian gerbils (*Meriones unguiculatus*). II. Parental interactions. *Animal Behaviour* 28:331–340.

Watts, Alan, and Eliot Elisofon. 1971. *Erotic spirituality: The vision of Konarak.* New York: Collier.

Weber, Eric. 1984. *How to win the woman of your dreams.* Garden City, NY: Doubleday.

Weber, Max. 1947. *The theory of social and economic organization.* Glencoe, IL: Free Press.

Weick, Karl E. 1969. Human behavior in its natural setting. [Book review of *Naturalistic viewpoints in psychological research,* by Edwin P. Willems and Harold Raush, and *Ecological psychology,* by Roger G. Barker.] *Science* 166:856–858.

Weinrich, James D. 1976. Human reproductive strategy. Doctoral dissertation, Harvard University, 1976. *Dissertation Abstracts International,* 1977, 37:5339B. (University Microfilms Number 77-8, 348.)

Weis, David L. 1980. Sexual scripting as a factor in attitudes toward projected extramarital behavior. Presented at the conference of the Eastern Region of the Society for the Scientific Study of Sex, Philadelphia, 27 April 1980.

Weis, David L. 1981. "Open" marriage and multilateral relationships: The emergence of non-exclusive models of the marital relationship. Presented at the Annual Meeting of the Groves Conference on Marriage and the Family, Mt. Pocono, 28–29 May 1981.

Weitz, Shirley. 1979. Body movement and gesture. In: *Nonverbal communication* (2nd ed., pp. 87–110). New York: Oxford University Press.

Whalen, Richard E. 1966. Sexual motivation. *Psychological Review* 73:151–163.

White, Leslie A. 1956. The locus of mathematical reality: An anthropological footnote. In: James R. Newman (ed.), *The world of mathematics* (vol. 4, pp. 2348–2364). New York: Simon and Schuster. (Originally published 1947.)

Whitehurst, Robert N. 1971. American sexophobia. In: Lester A. Kirkendall and Robert N. Whitehurst (eds.), *The new sexual revolution* (pp. 1–16). New York: Donald W. Brown.

Whitehurst, Robert N. 1977. Youth views marriage: Awareness of present and future potentials in relationships. In: Roger W. Libby and Robert N. Whitehurst (eds.), *Marriage and alternatives: Exploring intimate relationships* (pp. 294–301). Glenview, IL: Scott, Foresman.

Whiteside, Robert L. 1974. *Face language.* New York: Pocket Books.

Wiggins, Jerry S., Nancy Wiggins, and Judith Cohen Conger. 1968. Correlates of heterosexual somatic preference. *Journal of Personality and Social Psychology* 10:82–90.

Willems, Edwin P., and Harold L. Raush. 1969. *Naturalistic viewpoints in psychological research.* New York: Holt, Rinehart and Winston.

Wilson, David Sloan. 1977. How nepotistic is the brain worm? *Behavioral Ecology and Sociobiology* 2:421–425.

Wilson, David Sloan. 1983. The group selection controversy: History and current status. *Annual Review of Ecology and Systematics* 14:159–187.

Wilson, Edmund B. 1925. *The cell in development and heredity* (3rd ed.). New York: Macmillan.

Wilson, Edward O. 1975. *Sociobiology: The new synthesis.* Cambridge, MA: The Belknap Press of Harvard University Press.

Wilson, Edward O. 1978. *On human nature.* Cambridge, MA: Harvard University Press.

Wilson, Robert Anton. 1967. Modern attitudes toward sex. In: Albert Ellis and Albert Abarbanel, *The encyclopedia of sexual behavior, volume I: Modern sex practices* (pp. 21–35). New York: Ace.

Winch, Robert F. 1967. Courtship and mate-selection. In: Albert Ellis and Albert Abarbanel (eds.), *The encyclopedia of sexual behavior, volume III: The nature of sex* (pp. 93–101). New York: Ace.

Wollstonecraft, Mary. 1967. *A vindication of the rights of woman; With strictures on political and moral subjects.* New York: Norton (Originally published 1792.)

Wood, Trevor. 1984. Iran moves to screen off its women. *The Philadelphia Inquirer,* 22 November, p. 13A

Woods, Margo. 1981. *Masturbation, tantra and self love.* San Diego, CA: Omphaloskepsis Press.

Wright, Carroll D. 1909. *Outline of practical sociology* (7th ed., rev.). New York: Longmans, Green.

Young, G. M. 1953. *Victorian England: Portrait of an age* (2nd ed.). London: Oxford University Press.

Young, Wayland. 1964. *Eros denied: Sex in Western society.* New York: Grove.

Zabin, Laurie S., Marilyn B. Hirsch, Edward A. Smith, and Janet B. Hardy. 1984. Quoted in "New study: Adolescents reveal sexual attitudes and behavior inconsistent." *Sexuality Today* 7(46):3–4, 3 September.

Zellman, Gail L., and Jacqueline D. Goodchilds. 1983. Becoming sexual in adolescence. In: Elizabeth Rice Allgeier and Naomi B. McCormick (eds.), *Changing boundaries: Gender roles and sexual behavior* (pp. 49–63). Palo Alto, CA: Mayfield.

Zelnik, Melvin, John F. Kantner, and Kathleen Ford. 1981. *Sex and pregnancy in adolescence.* Beverly Hills: Sage.

Zilbergeld, Bernie. 1978. *Male sexuality: A guide to sexual fulfillment.* New York: Bantam.

Zillmann, Dolf. 1984. *Connections between sex and aggression.* Hillsdale, NJ: Lawrence Erlbaum Associates.

Zinsser, Hans. 1935. *Rats, lice and history.* Boston: Little, Brown.

Index